''I have never kr... ...generous thing abo... ...a treacherous lady, and that's the truth of it. She is treacherous to absolutely everyone.''

—Truman Capote

''They fought a lot because Lee was put off by Rudolf's (Nureyev) homosexuality . . . I think she realized there was no way she was going to change him. She was still in love with him, and maybe the problem was that Rudolf was much more in love with Jackie than he was with her . . . I remember once Lee telling Rudolf that Anthony was afraid of women, and Rudolf said, 'Of course. Look at you.' ''

—A source close to Nureyev

Upon hearing that Lee had called him a social climber, Andy Warhol retorted, ''Well, she's a talent climber.''

To make matters worse, Jackie once told her words to the effect that all Lee had in the world was because of her. That really burned Lee up, since Onassis had been her catch, not Jackie's. ''She probably felt Jackie owed her some of that $26 million she had gotten after his death,'' a friend remarked. ''Lee should have asked for a finder's fee.''

''I am very sensitive to other people's moods, too much so. It's much easier to be happy if you don't feel for them so much . . . There is something extraordinarily appealing to me about people who aren't quite in tune with the world. Everything about them may seem like perfection, including their achievements, but they suffer terribly . . . That quality of being slightly lost, slightly out of step always makes me cry.''

—Lee Radziwill

more . . .

"Lee is not a warm, nice person. She never looked after her children. She bullied them, and she uses people. She's bitchy, frustrated . . . Lee always wanted to be someone, and it made her desperate."

—former lover Taki Theodoracopulos

"She's much more interesting than Jackie, who was marvelous at the funeral and didn't do a damn thing since. When Lee Radziwill walks into a room full of people, why then you know somebody's there, somebody that you're dying to talk to . . . a woman who still looked eminently good at fifty and even sixty—like a woman a man would still want to go to be with."

—Decorator Tony Hail

"Lee did everything you're supposed to do in AA—except stop drinking."

—Her Hamptons neighbor Clifford Klenk

"She was fascinated by just plain money, high living, big names, all the cheap values that are out there, and so was her sister."

—Jay Mellon

"Her reaction every time Jackie spoke was like her mother was about to spank her. It was as if Jackie controlled her. I could feel the tension, the vibes going between them—it was Lee, not Jackie. It was quite obvious that Jackie intimidated her. It's too bad Lee couldn't get away from that sister of hers."

—Ex-fiancé Newton Cope

In Her
SISTER'S
SHADOW

An Intimate Biography of
Lee Radziwill

DIANA DuBOIS

St. Martin's Paperbacks

Published by arrangement with Little, Brown & Company.

IN HER SISTER'S SHADOW

Library of Congress Catalog Card Number: 94-46560

ISBN: 0-312-96237-1

Printed in the United States of America

Little, Brown and Company hardcover edition published in 1995
St. Martin's Paperbacks edition/May 1997

St. Martin's Paperbacks are published by St. Martin's Press, 175 Fifth Avenue, New York, NY 10010.

10 9 8 7 6 5 4 3 2 1

To My Mother

Contents

Prologue

Saint Luke's Episcopal is a traditional stone church adjoining Main Street in the once-quaint seaside village of East Hampton. Like an idealized set for a stage play, an old windmill flanks its left and the "backdrop" shows an old cemetery and village green nearby, complete with a small pond and flagpole. An asphalt driveway winds discreetly around to the back of the church and halts at a modest little meetinghouse. This shingled addition to the original building cannot be seen from the road, so it is the perfect place to discreetly house the local alcoholic recovery program in a town that is the part-time home of many high-profile residents.

Early one evening in the summer of 1981, at that hour when the rays of the setting sun slant across the green, a group of alcoholics, past and present, began gathering there. They were a typically incongruous Hamptons mix of eastern Long Island locals clad mostly in shorts and jeans and beset with the occasional potbelly, and lean, tanned, vacationing Manhattanites dressed in resort chic. Many lingered outside on the porch railing for a while sipping coffee before they filed into the meetinghouse, past the American flag, and took their seats in the neatly placed rows of metal chairs set up on the varnished wood floor. Newcomers stopped first to take literature from the rectory tables that were lined up in front of the fireplace, and to glance at the framed homilies on the fireplace mantel: First Things First and Easy Does It.

Suddenly a murmur shot through the crowd. While certainly no stranger to the famous, they were not prepared for what they saw this time: Jacqueline Kennedy Onassis had just walked into the meetinghouse with her sister, Lee Radziwill. They gaped as Lee took a seat by herself near the back of the room, and all eyes followed Jackie as she left quickly, striding through the open door to her car, which was parked in full view of the group. She did not drive away. Instead, she sat in her car and stared back at the disbelieving audience that watched her: she was waiting to make sure her sister stayed.

The meeting got under way, and Lee listened intently to those who spoke of their ordeals with alcohol. She did not volunteer to speak herself that day. When she finally did at another meeting, she faced the group, and, observing convention, announced, "My name is Lee. I am an alcoholic." In truth, her real addictions, subtler and more invidious, were to beauty and illusion. Renowned as a debutante, fashion personality, and style-setter in her own right, this beautiful younger sister of a living legend had always wanted to be seen from afar as someone bright and shining, someone to be envied and imitated. Over the years she tried carefully to craft her public image to achieve that effect. Now as she joined this self-help group, she had to detonate the image that she had spent a lifetime creating.

From the very beginning, Lee had believed that her life should be something wonderful and exciting. Speaking of her childhood, she said: "I created a realm of fantasy and lived in it. At about six, I had three imaginary friends with the utterly inexplicable names of Shahday, Dahday, and Jamelle. They were girl-spirits who wore ethereal floating dresses— nothing down-to-earth about them—and they lived in the house with me, except when we took trips together. They said, 'Come, Lee. We'll take you away!' I only remember that we flew and danced and everything was beautiful. They took me out of reality."

Lee saw in these imaginary excursions something faraway and nameless, and she set out for it. "I remember when I was seven and we lived in New York," she continued. "I took my dog and started out across Brooklyn Bridge in my mother's high heels. Even then, I had no idea what I was looking for. Only that it was dramatic, mysterious, and very necessary to me. I ran away quite a lot, but not very far."

Ultimately her quest landed her at the Saint Luke's meetinghouse that warm summer evening in East Hampton.

1. *Bouviers and Lees*

She was called "Lee" from the start, but she was born Caroline Lee Bouvier in New York City on March 3, 1933, the Inauguration eve of Franklin Delano Roosevelt's first term, a momentous event in the crisis-torn thirties. The economic paralysis which had gripped the United States since 1930 was in shocking contrast to the golden days of pre-Crash prosperity that had enormously benefited Lee's family of lawyers, stockbrokers, and investors. Roosevelt, the Democratic standard-bearer, enacted sweeping programs to cope with the national emergency.

One of the measures instituted to prevent another crash was the creation of the Securities and Exchange Commission to regulate the sale of stocks and bonds. Lee's father, John Vernou Bouvier III, was a specialist stockbroker on Wall Street who bought and sold large blocks of stocks for other brokerage firms. He was affected by the Commission's reforms, in essence hamstrung, to the degree that he never again attained the annual income he was earning previous to the Crash. A spendthrift and gambler, Jack Bouvier had been unable even then to live off the $75,000 a year he earned—a godly sum at the time—and had resorted to a series of loans to bail himself out.

He became a stockbroker at the onset of World War I, determined to make a lot of money as quickly as possible. The eldest of John Vernou Bouvier, Jr., and Maude Frances Sergeant's five children, he was born in 1891 and grew up in Nutley, New Jersey, until his family moved to New York City and began spending summers in East Hampton. An indifferent student, Jack was expelled from Phillips Exeter Academy for instituting a weekly poker game in the student dining hall. Later, at Yale, he began his long career of seducing and discarding a great many women. After graduating in 1914 near the bottom of his class, family connections got him a job as a stockbroker trainee at Henry Hentz & Co. In 1917, America's entry into World War I interrupted his career plans, and he served out his time in the U.S. Army Signal Corps as a volunteer and second lieutenant, seeing no action in what he termed in a letter to a friend, "a dirty little war." Jack spent three more years at Henry Hentz before borrowing money from his family and a business colleague to buy a seat on the New York Stock Exchange.

During his bachelor years in the twenties, he lived at 375 Park Avenue and became known around New York for the exciting parties he gave pointedly mixing the social classes. In his behavior and attitudes, the swashbuckling and earthy Jack Bouvier was very much part of the revolt against tradition that defined the decade. As with others in the World War I generation, his gaiety masked bitter disillusionment, and his attitude was very much "take it all now." Jack was luxury-loving to excess and gambled recklessly, choosing to live his life on the surface by maintaining a frenetic pace that left no time for reflection. A fastidious dresser, he wore expensive clothes with a continental European cut, rather than his own social set's conservative Yankee tweeds. Dubbed "Black Jack" by his Wall Street colleagues because of his unusually dark complexion and spectacular success with beautiful young women, he had the good looks, flamboyance, and love of the spotlight to have made a perfect film star.

Jack's early life had been filled with his mother's attentions: Maude Bouvier constantly flattered and indulged him. Consequently, when he grew up, he felt validated each time he saw himself reflected back in the eyes of a new, admiring woman. Although Jack toyed with emotional commitment from time to time, he continued to measure his manhood by the number of his sexual conquests.

Early in the spring of 1928 he became engaged to Janet Norton Lee, a friend of his twin sisters, Maude and Michelle. At twenty-one, she was sixteen years younger than he. To the amazement of his family and friends, Jack actually married

Janet on July 7, 1928, at Saint Philomena's Church in East Hampton in a ceremony much noted in the society columns. A reception followed at the Lily Pond Lane estate Janet's father, James Lee, had rented for the summer.

That Jack Bouvier finally tied the knot reflected the tenacity of his bride's character more than any reform on his part. Janet was the determined and socially ambitious daughter of James Thomas Lee, a son of Irish immigrants who brought wealth and success to his family in the second generation. Lee, whose family emigrated to New York in the 1840s to escape the potato famine, put himself through City College and got an M.A. and law degree from Columbia University. He made money in real estate speculation and married Margaret Merritt, herself a daughter of Irish immigrants. They had three daughters, Marion, Janet, and Winifred. He eventually became estranged from his wife, and, to resolve the situation discreetly, the couple arranged to live on different floors in one of the New York apartment buildings Lee owned.

After pursuing a banking career, Lee eventually became president and chairman of the board of New York Central Savings Bank (later the New York Bank for Savings). He did not retire until he was eighty years old, and when he died he left a fortune made in real estate. A brusque and cigar-chewing archconservative, he was looked down on for his lack of social standing by the Bouviers, with the possible exception of Jack, who appreciated his accomplishments as a bank president and shrewd businessman.

Janet, for her part, was impressed above all by her husband's entry in the Social Register. She had attended the socially correct Miss Spence's School in New York City before making her debut, then went on to Sweet Briar and Barnard for two years and otherwise lived an upper class life with the very new money made by her father. The conventionally pretty Janet had her own horses and automobile by the time she turned Jack Bouvier's head.

According to Jack's niece, Edie Beale, Janet had first set her sights on Bud Bouvier, Jack's older, alcoholic, and divorced brother, and that it was only when her parents opposed the match that she settled for Jack.

The summer following Jack and Janet's marriage, their first child, Jacqueline Lee, was born on July 28. When the Crash came a few months later, Jack's financial difficulties greatly increased, and his father-in-law extended him a non-interest-bearing loan to help him out, though the loan came with strings attached: Jack had to scale down his extravagant living and gambling, forfeit his club memberships, control his penchant for high-risk stocks, and submit monthly profit and loss statements to his father-in-law's bookkeepers. Tension between the two men rose in direct proportion to old man Lee's humiliating control over his son-in-law's life.

James Lee also allowed Jack and his family to live rent-free in a lavish duplex in a building he owned at 740 Park Avenue. Jack did not tell his friends and acquaintances of this financial arrangement in order to give the impression of being much wealthier than he was. The apartment had eleven rooms, including a small gym and a nursery. When the Bouviers' second daughter, Caroline Lee, was born, her sister, Jackie, almost three and a half years older, abandoned the nursery for a room of her own. Shielded from the reality of the Depression, the two children shared a playroom filled with handmade toys, dolls, and stuffed animals and were surrounded by servants.

Jack had anticipated the repeal of Prohibition and in the summer of 1933 he made a profit of $2 million from his liquor stocks, which was virtually all lost the following January when he recklessly reinvested every penny of it in a single auto stock. In the intervening months between such a dramatic gain and loss, the Bouviers threw lavish parties at Lasata, the Bouvier family estate in East Hampton. Jack and Janet celebrated their fifth wedding anniversary in grand style, and Lee's christening on Sunday, July 30, at Saint Philomena's prompted a garden party for two hundred guests after the ceremony.

Caroline Lee Bouvier was named after her paternal great-grandmother, Caroline Maslin Ewing, the daughter of Robert Ewing of Philadelphia and Caroline Maslin, who was named for her native Caroline County in Maryland and whose ancestor served under George Washington at the battle of Yorktown. "Her dear father wanted two boys and named Jackie after himself," said a Bouvier cousin of Lee's, Henry C. Scott, Jr., and it was Jack who chose to call his second daughter Lee.

The Bouviers had their own summer cottage rental, Rowdy Hall, on Egypt Lane, but did their entertaining at Lasata, a far grander mansion on Further Lane, the nearest road running parallel to the ocean. The estate had fourteen carefully tended acres, a stable, paddock, and riding ring, a tennis court, a fish pool, and clipped box hedges and formal gardens; it belonged to the family patriarch, the "Major," John Vernou Bouvier, Jr., a successful lawyer and stockbroker who had been the first Bouvier to receive a college education.

The Major's own grandfather, Michel, was the first Bouvier to reach America. Born in Provence, Michel emigrated in 1815 and settled in Philadelphia, which had a large French community. Impoverished and uneducated, a petit bourgeois artisan and apprentice cabinetmaker by trade, he persevered and prospered in the New World through hard work and good luck, eventually amassing a million-dollar fortune.

Michel built a palatial home on Broad Street (the thirty-room mansion is now La Salle College) and became too wealthy for Philadelphia society to ignore. He married twice, and with his second wife, Louise Vernou, raised a large family, some of whom married into Main Line families. Michel bought seats on the New York Stock Exchange for two of his sons, Michel Charles and John Vernou, Lee's great-grandfather. Michel Bouvier died in 1874, his furniture now prized antiques, and by 1888, the Bouviers made it into the first edition of the Social Register.

The Bouviers were respected but peripheral members of society. John Vernou Bouvier, Jr., was anxious to change that and reinvent his family's past by staking out a claim to an aristocratic lineage more commensurate with their success and scale of living. The brash and boastful Major put together and published a fantasy of Bouvier genealogy called *Our Forebears*, published in 1925 and reissued several times throughout his life, in which he claimed descent from a sixteenth-century French aristocrat of the same name as his real ancestor, François Bouvier, who had been, in fact, an ironmonger from Grenoble who was married to a servant.

Jack Bouvier was scornful of his father's pretensions, reacting with boredom or annoyance to the Major's frequent references to the grandeur of the family tree, and father and son had their own version of a generation gap: "Not a family meeting or gathering passed without Senior expounding upon the magnificence of their forebears and Jack responding from the wings with derogatory asides,'' said one family chronicler. Unknown to either of them at the time, the Bouviers had already begun their slow decline.

2. *Jack and Janet*

When Lee was still a toddler, the good years of her parents' marriage were already behind them. As it turned out, the freewheeling Jack could not abide his wife's demands, quick temper, and nouveau riche insecurities. Janet was the dominant personality in the household and Jack made few demands on anyone—he just escaped the household as often as possible.

Jack took refuge from Janet in his womanizing, a bachelor habit so deeply ingrained in him and never relinquished that on his honeymoon he flirted right in front of his bride with another woman, the tobacco heiress, Doris Duke. Perhaps he was so unsuited to matrimony that it would not have mattered who his wife was. Whatever the reason, the restless and insatiable Black Jack would avail himself of every opportunity for seduction, however indiscreet, and spent night after night out on the town, telling his wife he was with his pals or playing poker when Janet was all too aware of her husband's extramarital flings.

Their fierce arguments about his infidelity, about the household budget, and about how the children should be raised were the surface noise of a deeper problem: they had little in common in terms of values or interests, and shared profound and irreconcilable differences of background and temperament. Janet's painfully proper behavior rubbed up against Jack's hedonism and indifference to conventional respectability. Not sharing her obsession with society, he was confident enough to spurn the rules that Janet, as an arriviste, adhered to rigorously. The alternately stiff and assertive Janet was extremely conservative in her tastes and friends, and she was often a dampening influence on Jack's vitality and enthusiasms.

In-law meddling compounded the couple's marital problems. In 1935, Jack's parents moved into a duplex across the street from them. Maude Bouvier called or stopped by almost daily to offer unsolicited advice to Janet on the running of her household, interfering with her independence.

The Bouviers were also under relentless financial pressure. Jack was now earning a fraction of what he had been making before the Depression and his income was tied to an unstable securities market. And while he assumed that his—and the country's—situation would surely improve, his resources were rapidly dwindling.

Jack and Janet's mutual extravagance and need to maintain appearances, exemplified by Jack's purchase of a custom-made town car at the height of the Depression, also put the couple's lifestyle in jeopardy. The Bouviers experienced some relief, though, when Jack's uncle, Michel Charles Bouvier, who had survived the Crash in comfort, willed his nephew his stock-brokerage business. Jack formed a new firm, which did well in its first years.

Jack and Janet were able to save money by giving up Rowdy Hall and using Wildmoor as their summer cottage; the delightful old clapboard structure had been the Major's summer home before he purchased Lasata. Known in the family as "the Apaquogue house," the Major lent it to Jack at no cost. Wildmoor's impressive vistas of lawns and potato fields and the distant Atlantic were best seen from its widow's walk. In the off-season Jack used the cottage's six bedrooms for extramarital mayhem.

The Bouviers' frequent family quarrels were not enough to spoil three-and-a-half-year-old Lee's delight in East Hampton's ritual summer pleasures: going for rides in the rumble seat of grandfather Bouvier's—"Grampy Jack's"—maroon Stutz, competing in the dog-and-pony shows at the annual Village Fair, and hanging over the post-and-rail fence at the horse shows along with the rest of the family as they watched Janet and Jackie taking jumps.

Janet always took her daughters to the train station on Friday evenings to greet their father when he arrived for the weekend from New York on the Cannonball, the Long Island commuter train. Lee loved to rush and put pennies on the railroad track just before the train pulled into view and would listen raptly to its whistle as it came down the track.

Her most fervent squeals of childish delight were saved for the seaside. While her father would sun himself on the deck of the family cabana at the exclusive Maidstone beach club—a ritual after elaborate Sunday lunches at Lasata—little Lee would remain at the water's edge for hours, gamboling in the waves and shrieking with pleasure at the Atlantic surf. She became a water sprite as she grew older and would often remain at the beach when other members of her family moved on to other activities.

Away from the shore on home territory, Lee noted with frustration that Jackie was a much better climber of the fruit trees that shaded Lasata than she was. It wasn't only three and a half years that gave Jackie an athletic edge over her sister; she was more of a tomboy and physically stronger than the dainty and feminine Lee. As a tiny tot, Lee was a constant tagalong and affectionate follower of her older sister, and Jackie took charge when Lee grew old enough to be bossed around. Although Jackie liked being looked up to and was protective of Lee, she would become impatient with her at times, placing Lee in "sibling subjugation." Their mother usually held the elder girl responsible for any wrongdoing, and Jackie often resented this accountability. "I think as a child Lee got away with murder," said Truman Capote, who knew both sisters. "Her mother was much tougher on Jackie."

When the summer of 1936 came to an end, Jack and Janet separated. He had paid no heed to her ultimatums, and she, exhausted from the domestic turbulence, demanded a six-month trial separation. Jack moved to a single room at the Westbury Hotel just a few blocks away and the Bouvier family became much more peaceful, albeit cheerless, without him.

But they were alone together and Jack was by himself, so he suffered more from the separation, and the following spring he persuaded Janet to try a reconciliation. Skeptical but willing to make an effort, she allowed him to move back into the Park Avenue apartment; she too had been unhappy and felt it was in the children's best interest.

Jack rented a cottage on the dunes in East Hampton that summer. Lee went off on her bicycle with an assortment of male cousins and neighbors almost immediately upon her arrival, showing off to them by riding no-handed. Even as a youngster she always had boys around her, while Jackie remained with her horses, alone. A cheerful and friendly child,

Lee was the adored little hellion of the family, sassy and independent, yet at the same time gentle and irresistible to
adults. As she recalled it: "I was the one that everyone liked
to squeeze. The fat, happy child who would marry someone
in the Racquet Club and drive around in the station wagon all
the time to pick up the twelve children and bring them home
to the rose-covered cottage."

Lee was chubby, not fat, and a pretty child with soft brown
eyes and hair and sharp yet delicate features that easily reflected her feelings. She inherited her father's wide-spaced
eyes and broad cheekbones and her mother's heart-shaped face
and figure. Her conventional prettiness bespoke a more ap-
proachable nature than her sister's and reflected the salad of
racial strains in her heritage: she was one-eighth French, three-
eighths English and half Irish. "Little Lee was a lovable little
mouse, not as high-strung or alert as her sister, but strong,
sweet, and affectionate," observed her governess, Bertha Kim-
merle.

Jack and Janet merely went through the motions of their
vacation that summer. They remained strained and irritable
toward one another rather than companionable. The years of
hostility had taken their toll and even affected Janet's relationship with her daughters. She became impatient with Jackie
and Lee and spanked them frequently. Seeking escape from
her household, she often left her children with their governess
or their father while she pursued a social life of her own.

Lee and Jackie were tearful at the end of their East Hampton
stay. When they returned to New York, Jack and Janet went
on to Havana for a ten-day vacation to visit a Wall Street
friend of Jack's, Earl E. T. Smith and his then wife, Consuelo
Vanderbilt. The two couples kept up a hectic social pace which
did little to lessen the tension between Jack and Janet, and
when they got back home they separated permanently.

With her father gone, Lee wept uncontrollably. She was too
young to absorb the full significance of her parents' actions,
but she understood all too well that her beloved father would
no longer be living with her, and she was disconsolate. She
would no longer have him there day by day to balance out the
reserve she always felt for her mother. Normally irrepressible,
Lee entered kindergarten class that fall a subdued child.

3. *Original Sins*

In the following months Lee did not see very much of her mother. Janet pursued her very active social schedule, dating the new men in her life. Left alone with her governess and sister, Lee eagerly looked forward to the weekend visits from her father. Jack Bouvier cared passionately about his daughters and seemed to make the emotional connection with his children that he failed to make with adults. He was able to relate to them at their own level of adventure and discovery and assumed the role of spoiling them, just as his own mother had spoiled him, while Janet had the task of disciplining the girls.

Jack's keen sense of fun heightened the pleasure of his weekend outings with his daughters. But when Jackie and Lee would come home afterward and breathlessly chatter about the day's adventure, Janet reacted jealously to Jack's hold on them, recognizing it as a variation of the same magnetism he exerted over virtually all women. It was all well and good, she reasoned, that the girls' father only had to amuse them on weekends, while she had the difficult task of raising them in their daily life. Janet's indignation sparked intense jockeying between father and mother for their children's loyalty and affection. And while they were encouraged by their father to stand out and be noticed, their mother insisted they conform to her conservative ideas of dress and proper behavior. Janet brought them up austerely, but Jack indulged Jackie and Lee.

What's more, he kept trying to save the marriage. When summertime came around again, he urged Janet to spend the season with him at the same cottage he had rented the year before. She refused and took a place of her own in Bellport, forty miles away. The separation agreement now called for the children to spend August with their father, and Lee and Jackie spent a listless June and July waiting to join their father and cousins, and the horses and dogs at Lasata.

James Lee reclaimed the Park Avenue duplex that September, saying it was unnecessarily large. Janet took a much smaller apartment at One Gracie Square near the Chapin School for girls, where Lee and Jackie were enrolled. Wearing a linen jumper uniform, Lee entered first grade and was walked to school daily by her governess. Her above-average intelligence, good manners, and sparkling personality made her popular with her teachers.

Grampy Lee was a constant dinner guest at Gracie Square in the waning months of 1938 as he and Janet hatched a strategy for the divorce action. Father and daughter focused on how to carve up the marital pie with Jack's cash reserves dangerously low and his stocks substantially reduced. Lee listened uneasily to the constant litany of angry money talk between her grandfather and parents. Although the specifics of her parents' rancor and bitterness meant little to the five-year-old child, Lee knew that her mother accused her father of misconduct and that since her parents had been living apart her mother's behavior had begun to disintegrate.

Janet drank and took sleeping pills, remained in bed until noon, and was perpetually nervous and depressed. Undone by the breakup of her marriage, she spanked her children repeatedly and had shouting matches with Jackie, whose academic record slipped at school. Little Lee suffered from uncontrollable bouts of crying.

Lee dealt with the havoc in her home life by retreating into a world of daydreams and conversations with imaginary friends. She also began to invent stories about her girl-spirits, Shahday, Dahday, and Jamelle, to help her shut out the surrounding dissension.

Yet in spite of the problems in her home life, Lee was developing a character that was quick and shrewd. In later years Janet often smiled as she recounted for friends an incident that took place when Lee was in the first grade, Jackie in the fourth. There was to be a piano recital at Chapin, and although Jackie was taking lessons, piano-playing did not come easily to her; she struggled painstakingly through the "Blue Danube," the piece she was to perform. One afternoon she came home from school crying and very upset because, she said, Lee had put her own name down to play. While puzzled that something that was so obviously not to be taken seriously would upset her so much, her mother comforted her and pointed out that Lee was just a child in first grade, and that of course she was not going to play in the recital. "She doesn't even know how to play," Janet assured Jackie.

The day of the recital, Janet—revealingly—was "unable to attend" the event, and once again Jackie came home sobbing: her worst fear had been realized. She had managed to lumber haltingly through her "Blue Danube," only to hear the teacher announce, "And now we have a special surprise for you: little Lee Bouvier has asked to perform," whereupon the child went to the piano and zipped through—the "Blue Danube"! She had obviously been practicing in private, and, of course, humiliated Jacqueline.

"That incident shows the competitiveness that was already developing between Jackie and Lee, and it gives you some idea of their relationship and what happened to it," said a friend of Janet's to whom she had once told the story. The episode revealed Lee's intellect and abilities in relation to her older sister before her habits of thought and their histories would tangle an everlasting knot in her psyche.

Because Janet was unable to obtain a divorce in New York on grounds of adultery—Jack would counter that she was seeing other men—she moved the proceedings to Nevada, where she was granted a divorce in July 1940 on grounds of mental cruelty. But not before the New York press got wind of Janet's bitter accusations against her husband and ran the story nationally. This was still an era when divorce was dishonorable and adultery more so, and Jackie and Lee suffered as classmates snickered and they became outcasts in the very Catholic and traditional Bouvier family.

Worse yet, in the aftermath of the divorce the youngsters were no longer merely prizes to be fought over by their parents but outright instruments of revenge in a bitter and ongoing feud. The legacy of all this conflict for both children was a lifetime of great insecurity, though Lee, for one, learned to use the rivalry of her parents to play one off against the other, particularly when it came to getting things she wanted. But her emotional deprivation, her failure to obtain the unconditional love of her parents, who were too lost themselves to meet her needs, became the psychic origin of the vast sense of entitlement she would manifest throughout her life. Such expectations were the unconscious acting out of her deprivation to redress the balance.

Jack Bouvier also never fully recovered from the divorce.

When his mother died in the midst of the proceedings, in April 1940, he got hopelessly drunk at her funeral—an ominous sign of events to come—and he would spend the rest of his life in the company of women who posed no threat to him. Only Janet ultimately triumphed, eventually marrying someone far more monied and socially prominent than her previous husband in a union that endured.

4. Jackie's Little Sister

"Lee's going to be a real glamour girl someday. Will you look at those eyes and those sexy lips of hers?" exclaimed her father to his captive audience of relatives at the Lasata dining table. Jack may have wooed his daughter with endless praise, emphasizing her looks and her manners at the expense of her talents, but then again, he bragged excessively about most of his possessions. His pride in them was really an extension of his own narcissism. "The most beautiful daughters a man ever had" could be uttered in the same breath with "the best damn dog in the world," which was how he referred to his pet, King Phar. Still, it was obvious Lee thrived on her father's compliments. She greatly appreciated the transfusions of esteem in a family where it was often a struggle for her to get attention.

Jacqueline had no such problem. Winning blue ribbons by the dozen, she was the star of the local horse shows that her entire family turned out for, even Grampy Bouvier in his Panama straw hat. Thus Lee was coerced into watching Jackie shine time and again without a balancing opportunity of her own.

In the summer of 1940 Jack rented a cottage near the East Hampton Riding Club, which was a great advantage for Jackie. Lee helped her father and sister with the daily workouts of the family horses in the ring at the back of the house, and she joined halfheartedly in some lessons and horse shows until the day a family pony, Dancestep, rolled over with her on his back and nearly crushed her to death. That incident, together with Jackie's aggressively determined attitude to win in the ring,

took the fun out of riding for her, save occasionally for pleasure, and she opted for her bicycle.

Jackie's riding prizes, however, gave her an authoritative
frame of reference in a family with a heavy investment in blue-
ribbon horses. The Major maintained a stable, paddock, and
riding ring for the Bouvier horses at his country home, and the
equestrian world had been the one real interest Jack and Janet
had in common, apart from stepping out into society. Janet
was a superb and renowned rider who had much to do with
encouraging Jackie's interest in horses. Jackie knew the lingo
and shared the obsession, and this placed her squarely at the
center of family events, while Lee, off on her bicycle, unwit-
tingly cut herself off from a main avenue of communication
and an opportunity to be in the spotlight.

"Lee was a pretty, shy girl," said her cousin John Davis.
"She had a complex about Jackie because Jackie won all those
prizes at horse shows and she didn't. It was a pathetic situation
for her, because Jacqueline, even as a teenager, dominated
over Lee. People paid more attention to Jackie than they did
to her. Even her father and grandfather. Her father was in love
with Jackie. It was so patently obvious that there was a strong
bond between those two. She was older and more on his level
intellectually. Lee was always just the little girl, and I believe
she suffered."

Rue Hill Hubert, once a close friend of Lee's who met her
in their school days, agreed with Davis: "Lee has a lot of
quality, but she always felt Jackie got the recognition. Jackie
was much more obvious, and Lee was a more subtle person.
Lee certainly looked up to Jackie for a lot, yet she wasn't
completely in her shadow. They had their own lives as children. But it's what she felt inside. Lee always felt Jackie had
something she didn't have, something that she wanted. It was
true all her life."

Of all Lee's family relationships, her sibling tie was the
most vital in the formation of her identity, the key familial
bonding that shaped her life. Threads of Jackie's personality
were woven into the fabric of who Lee was, and either consciously or unconsciously she fell into role, especially when
playing children's games, where she was often cast as lady-
in-waiting to Jackie's queen.

*   *   *

Janet remained in New York that summer, visiting her parents weekends on the Island. She was still mired in an interminable round of social engagements to find herself a new husband. Her effort paid off when she married Standard Oil heir Hugh Dudley Auchincloss, Jr., in June 1942. Auchincloss was everything Jack Bouvier was not: dependable, dull, self-effacing, and ordinary-looking, and very much at home in baggy, worn-out tweeds. Hughdie (his family nickname) used his fortune to form his own local stockbrokerage firm, Auchincloss, Parker and Redpath. "Auchinclosses don't really dare to be anything too controversial," said Jamie Auchincloss, Lee's half-brother.

Hughdie kept an apartment in New York at 950 Park Avenue and owned two imposing estates, Merrywood, in McLean, Virginia, which he purchased in the thirties, and Hammersmith Farm, a family summer home in Newport, Rhode Island. It was now wartime, and Hughdie had been assigned to the Office of Naval Intelligence's Planning Unit at Kingston, Jamaica, when Janet drove down to Merrywood with her daughters to see him off. They got married on the spur of the moment on the grounds of the estate. Suddenly Lee was part of an instant family of strangers with Yusha, Nina, and Tommy, Hughdie's children from two previous marriages.

Janet's second marriage was a calamity for nine-year-old Lee. She was yanked out of her school and taken away from all that was comforting and familiar: her grandparents, her favorite dancing-school partner, playing in Central Park, East Hampton at Halloween, even a string of birthday parties she had wanted to attend. Most of all, she was separated from her dear father, who would now become primarily a voice on the telephone and a letter in the mail. "Women are all the victors in my generation," Jack said when he heard the news of Janet's marriage.

Because Janet married in June, she and her children went right to the house in Newport. Lee stayed at Hammersmith only a short time before being sent to join her father at East Hampton. In the rush, Janet forgot to pack enough clothes for both Lee and Jackie, and their aunt Edith lent them her daughter Edie's hand-me-downs. "Jackie and Lee were like little orphans, shunted aside because Janet had another family to take care of,'' said Doris Francisco, a friend of Edie's.

Lee arrived in East Hampton to find a wartime romance going on between her father and the wife of a British officer stationed in Washington. Jack brought his mistress to Sunday lunches at Lasata, and she kept house and cooked for the family at Jack's cottage. The atmosphere actually was a reassuring and happy one for Lee, who was still reeling from the profound dislocation of her mother's marriage. Jack kept up the romance until his sweetheart's husband was transferred home the following year and she went with him.

In September 1942 Hughdie was reassigned to a War Department job in Washington, and he and Janet settled into married life at Merrywood. Janet concentrated on the two sizable estates she now had to run, her large new family of five children, and her customary assortment of bridge games, dinner parties, and charitable endeavors. She could now play the role of chatelaine with great authority: Merrywood had a banquet-style kitchen and wine cellar, stables, a badminton court, a four-car garage with automatic car-washing equipment, and an outsized swimming pool with a bathhouse modeled after a Swiss chalet. The ivy-covered house was surrounded by forty-six acres of secluded lawns, woods, and fields overlooking Washington from the hills above the Potomac. Janet and Hughdie occupied bedrooms on the second floor of the house, and Lee and Jacqueline were assigned to bedrooms on the third floor with the Auchincloss children and their nanny.

All the changes that came with their parents' divorce and their mother's new marriage profoundly changed the dynamic of Lee's relationship to her older sister: she and Jackie became a single unit against their new world. They clung together, drawn to each other as allies. In spite of their early rivalry and many vehement childhood spats, the intimacy Lee and Jackie came to share during this period developed into a close bond that lasted until the sixties.

Janet enrolled her daughters at Holton Arms, a private day school in downtown Washington (it has since moved to Maryland); Lee began fifth grade and had the daunting task of making all new friends. Yet the Bouvier sisters were already being noticed. ''*Everybody* at Holton Arms knew who they were,'' said a classmate, Logan Bentley. ''It was unusual at that age to know the names of girls several grades above you.

Jackie and Lee had an air about them. They acted—special.''

Jack Bouvier's early training of his daughters to take center stage was beginning to pay off. His example and his advice about wearing clothes with distinction to create an illusion of difference influenced the mode by which Jackie and Lee were already presenting themselves to the world.

Slowly Lee began to make new friends. "I was pretty much their age and became good friends with Jackie and Lee," recalled Cecilia "Sherry" Parker Geyelin, whose father was the Parker in Auchincloss, Parker and Redpath. "Lee was a fun-loving little butterball back then.''

During the Christmas holidays, Lee visited her father in New York at his new home, a four-room apartment at 125 East Seventy-fourth Street, where he had moved after his divorce. To his dismay, he would not see her or Jackie again until the following Easter. The bitter fact that his children no longer lived near him had the beneficial side effect, at least, of closing the door on the worst of the Bouvier marital war.

Wartime conditions caused a shortage of manpower at Hammersmith Farm in the summer of 1943, and everybody pitched in to help with the household chores, the farmwork, and maintaining the grounds. The very first (and eventually the last) working farm in Newport, Hammersmith was set in rolling country of hayfields and orchards, perfectly manicured lawns and pastures, with acres of outlying farmland. Herefords grazed beyond the old stone walls at the edge of the farmhouse garden. In summer Hughdie kept a decorative herd of Black Angus steers in the front pasture, and gentle breezes blew up from the water at sunset. The farm's rustic beauty and the mansion's picturesque hilltop setting overlooking Newport's ever-changing harbor and sailboat-studded Narragansett Bay nurtured a feeling of tranquility and lent itself to daydreams.

The main house itself, a charming Victorian sprawl crowned with a photogenic roof of gables, cupolas, and chimneys, had the typically chilly formality and large, drafty rooms of its late-nineteenth-century origins. Plants and many-colored flowers gathered from the farm's extensive gardens helped somewhat to relieve the gloom; so, too, did the alluring views from its many windows.

Again, the third floor was for the children. Lee's blue-and-white bedroom overlooked the front pastures with its grazing ponies and the Newport Country Club beyond. "We all adored Hammersmith," she fondly recalled. Indeed, Hughdie would tell Janet time and again he hoped to die there someday. Hammersmith Farm represented a way of life that gradually disappeared after World War II. The family stake in Standard Oil was able to postpone the inevitable for his lifetime—but just barely.

5. *Auchincloss Years*

Lee's abiding reaction to her new life as an Auchincloss was feelings of alienation and betrayal, that somehow her mother let her father down by divorcing him and that afterward, when she became Mrs. Auchincloss, she had neither enough time nor the inclination to be with her. Moreover, as Lee grew older the lack of warmth and intimacy between her and her mother noticeably worsened. "Both Jackie's and Lee's relationship with their mother was rather strange. It seemed so remote," observed a family friend. "Janet was preoccupied with her homes and a large family. Let's face it—there is just so much you can do."

Certainly tending to the enormous staff she assembled to run her estates occupied a good deal of Janet's time. By the late forties Hammersmith Farm alone had more than two dozen servants. There were so many of them to feed at mealtime that Jackie and Lee were lucky to get a sandwich for lunch. Lost in the shuffle, Lee commiserated with her sister and father, who received lengthy letters from her expressing her dissatisfaction and loneliness.

Unfortunately, when Janet did focus on Lee it was usually in the form of a quarrel. "They were always arguing," attested John Davis. Lee continued to chafe against her mother's values and narrow ideas of proper deportment. Nor was Janet's constant carping necessarily the most difficult aspect of her behavior. Her temper was mercurial, and, once they grew too old to be spanked, both her daughters felt the back of her hand more often than not. "I know Lee hated her mother," said Rue Hill Hubert.

"Lee described her mother to me as rather overbearing and imperious," said an old friend of hers, Jay Mellon, "and many times she made the remark, 'No matter what Jackie and I did, it was never good enough.' And she said that with pain. You could feel it. The mother was awfully rough on those girls, extremely critical and very demanding. When they were growing up, they were always expected to be the best and do the best, and yet whatever they did wasn't good enough."

If Lee always felt her mother was too strict and too demanding as a parent, she soon discovered to her disappointment that Hughdie did little to intervene and soften his wife's harsh regimen. "It was the way of my parents' generation," Lee says now. "Quite a lot was expected of one. We were expected to do what we did well and be decent. But we were never decent enough. We never did well enough. Always we weren't working hard enough." Even her father had such expectations of her: "He was—well, vain but sensitive, shy but demanding and critical," she said. "He always wanted us to be number one. He spoiled us but made up for it by his demandingness."

The advantage to Lee of this constant pressure to excel was a drive for excellence she never lost, but she grew up with a lack of self-esteem. "It's funny, isn't it?" she later acknowledged. "All the compliments and nice things in the world can be said to you all the time, but if you didn't hear them as a child—or even *thought* you didn't hear them—then you just never believe it. In a way, it's almost out of a family's control. They can't do what's best for each child all the time. It's like the Beatles' song: 'We gave her everything money could buy. Why is she leaving home?' "

Janet's ability to dominate her family and household had little resistance from her new husband. Some say the good-natured Hughdie was a kind person who cared a great deal about everybody around him. Others remember him differently and say he was "kind of a wimp." Explaining how one could draw such a conclusion, Sherry Geyelin said: "Hughdie was rather overwhelmed by the fact that he had all those children. He was an avuncular creature who stuttered but tried to be a good father and stepfather and I daresay he was successful up to a point, but these were very strong personalities in that household."

Still other detractors thought Hughdie was curiously cold, remote, and reserved as a family man, even to Janet. Certainly Lee thought so. She was never close to him, and, with the exception of Yusha, of whom she was very fond, she never drew close to any of her Auchincloss siblings either, especially not to Nina, who considered Jackie and Lee intruders when they first arrived in the family. "If anybody showed any signs of rivalry or jealousy, it was Nina Auchincloss for the Bouvier sisters," said Geyelin, who described her as very high-strung and "quite brilliant in her own way. It was just known in our crowd, particularly as they got older."

Having an older stepbrother like Yusha provided Lee and Jackie with a ready-made supply of male companions. Chauncey Parker, a friend of Yusha's (and the son of Hughdie's partner), would join him for weekends at Merrywood now and then for a game of badminton. During these visits, Parker struck up a friendship with Lee. "I met her when she was eleven," Parker said. "She had a *douceur* about her, and I've wondered since whether underneath it all she may not still have it. *Douceur* is a French word that implies more than gentleness, yet is stronger than sweetness. She seemed to have a softness about her, a sense of wonderment. Lee had a rather appealing way of looking at you. She would lower her head and raise her eyes, and her eyes were very warm. She had an almost self-deprecating look and a lilt in her voice and a wonderful smile. She was somebody you really just wanted to take in your arms and hug. She had a delicious aura about her. Yet, much as someone might use a sense of humor to keep people from getting too close, Lee used her gentleness to signal, 'Don't dig any deeper,' as if she were being hurt by something."

In the fall of 1944 Lee began junior high at the Potomac School, a downtown Washington institution (since moved to Virginia) similar in caliber and mission to Holton Arms. The following year brought her a new half-sister, Janet Jennings Auchincloss. (Her half-brother, Jamie, was born in 1947, completing the family.) To celebrate the occasion, Jackie and Lee created a scrapbook called "The Red Shoes of Janet Jennings." Janet always encouraged her children's creativity by insisting on handmade, noncommercial gifts for family events and holidays, and her daughters made a number of such scrap-books when they were growing up.

Always a creature of whims and sudden enthusiasms, with the onset of puberty religion became Lee's latest fad. "I went through a period of being enormously, conventionally religious when I was twelve or thirteen," she admitted. "I built a little altar in my room in the house in Virginia. I even spent every penny of my pocket money on religious statues." But this obsession eventually passed without a trace: by the time she was sixteen, the family maid who would coax her on Sundays with "Come on, Miss Lee, let's go to church," would be met with the reply "Maybe next week."

By now Lee had made a comfortable adjustment to her life in McLean and Newport. Sailing in Narragansett Bay in the summertime with her stepfather or with her favorite friend, Howard Cushing, Jr., became another of her adolescent enthusiasms. Actually she and Cushing had a crush on each other for about two years. "We went around Newport on our bicycles and had picnics on the pier of the Auchincloss house," he reminisced. "We also went around to the great houses and Bailey's Beach in a crowd.* Our relationship was chaste. Jackie tagged it 'puppy love.' "

Puppy love or not, Lee, like so many of her generation, was in a hurry to grow up. Fun-loving and sometimes a bit wild, she and Howard Cushing, Jr., once raced across a field to a huge tent where a debut she was not invited to was taking place. She crawled under the canvas and crashed the party. "I spent my whole life lying about my age, trying to make myself five years older," Lee confessed later, "but then it became a little tricky because it was a known fact that I was a little bit younger than Jackie."

During the summer of 1947, when Jackie was making her debut into society, in yet another bid to appear more grown-up than she was, Lee stole her sister's well-modulated thunder at one of her dance parties, and the incident, no doubt, felt to Jackie like a remake of that piano recital at the Chapin School: By her own description, Lee showed up in a "cheap strapless

*Bailey's Beach Club was the only private beach in town and had been Newport society's daytime gathering place since the early days of the resort's prominence.

number," a slinky, shimmering, rhinestone-studded, pink satin gown, something she says she pulled out of her closet. She made a grand entrance, stole the spotlight, and captured the stag line.

"Lee liked to give the impression that she was fast," said a bachelor from her crowd, Robin Corbin, "and some people did think she was. What may have lent credence to her fast reputation was that she wasn't a girl's girl. She and her sister didn't have any real girlfriends. They fulfilled that need in each other. And while Lee was very pretty, she was still in her chubby stage. She got a lot prettier later on when she leaned down."

Having an older sister also helped Lee to grow up faster. She was more interested in older people than her peers were. She was curious about what one might call the politics of a summer community: what the parents of her friends talked about at their parties, and why some of them were friends and others not.

"I always thought Lee was much more sophisticated than the rest of us, and rather aloof, but that might have been shyness," recalled summer colonist Daphne Sellar Thornton. "Jackie was the same way. We were three generations all living together during the summer in Newport, and our lives evolved around Bailey's Beach and the Ida Lewis Yacht Club. There were twenty or thirty of us about Lee's age that all grew up together. Usually, after we played some tennis, we would picnic in the evenings, then go on to each others' houses and play music, drink soda, and munch on cookies. Lee was never part of the pack I knew at the beach. She would drift in and out. I would see her if there was some dance at the country club or run into her at parties. She was rather quiet, always standing straight and tall and looking stately. I don't know who her close friends were, and I have lived in Newport in the summertime since I was born.

"The whole Auchincloss family lived as though they were in a castle, with their own family functions and friends. Hammersmith was a world unto itself over there. Servants would polish the shoes they left outside their rooms at night. During the day the children rode ponies, swam off their own dock, went sailing with their father, and played golf with each other. There were so many of them, and people were coming and going all the time. If there was a big dinner, the children could have their own tables and friends.''

As much as she enjoyed Hammersmith Farm, Lee never really grew to like Newport itself very much. She thought its town center was far less charming than that of her beloved East Hampton, its beaches less inviting, the weather foggier, and its social customs much too formal and of another time.

The pros and cons of Newport notwithstanding, many in the summer colony remember Lee then as fresh-faced and full of life, very warm, unaffected, and delightful, though Greg Strauss, another summer colonist from Lee's generation, expressed a succinct and dissenting view of her as an adolescent. ''Lee was a real bubblehead and a snippy little bitch,'' he said.

6. *School Days*

With three years at the Potomac School behind her, Lee entered her sophomore year at Miss Porter's School in Farmington, Connecticut. The elite girl's boarding school of approximately 150 students was founded by a minister's daughter, Sarah Porter, in 1843 as a finishing school, and Farmington, as initiates call it, retained a certain high-minded severity when it evolved into a college preparatory institution only a few years before Lee arrived.

Most of the school's dormitories were housed in typically small-town New England clapboard buildings that had been converted from once-gracious private homes. The girls' rooms themselves had a sameness to them, with banners and stuffed animals passed on from graduating classmates. It was customary to have photographs of family members about, and Lee had one of her father on prominent display. Her assigned first-year roommate was a horsy type with whom she had little rapport, classmates say. She subsequently roomed with Linell Nash, the daughter of the poet Ogden Nash.

Farmington students in Lee's day wore a de facto uniform of polo coats, skirts, sweaters, and brown shoes with flaps on the front called Abercrombies. ''Lee was always much better put together than the rest of us,'' said one of her classmates, "and she loved to dress up when she could and looked smashing."

As a teenager Lee resolved to shed her schoolgirl chubbiness once and for all, even though a boarding school in the forties was a difficult place to stay on a diet. "All we did up there was eat," fellow student Alice Gordon Abbett explained. "No sooner would we finish breakfast than we'd file in for the big Sunday meal, then a little after that we'd go out for ice cream and cake, and then we'd come back and have a light snack before supper. We all wore baggy sweaters over our skirts and were twenty pounds overweight."

Lee developed a mania for staying thin. She went on a crash diet and lost so much weight that the school infirmary insisted that she be weighed on a regular basis. She made frequent visits to the infirmary for other reasons as well—Lee was often beset with physical ailments. When she first arrived at boarding school in September of her sophomore year, for example, she returned to Merrywood almost immediately for a couple of weeks in order to nurse a case of boils. Her disposition to sickliness would be a lifelong problem.

Lee's desire not to be compared to her sister was hopeless at Farmington. Jackie had been an exceptional student there and a real star. While Lee did well in subjects that interested her, overall she was just an average student, and her teachers never let her forget it. Typical of their attitude was the comment made by her Latin teacher, Flora Lutz, who said: "I remember sitting across from Lee at the dinner table watching her sulk. Part of her problem was that her older sister had made quite an impression on the school, and this was something that Lee either didn't feel she could live up to or didn't want to."

Yet teachers who had Lee in classes that were of interest to her thought she was bright and imaginative. Her English teacher Grace Comans also worked with her on the school newspaper and drama program, subjects which greatly appealed to Lee, and she had "nothing but fine memories of her." Then again, Lee's modern European history teacher, Katherine Smedley Yellig, was given a very different impression: "My greatest memory of her is disappearing to the infirmary frequently from class, so that she was noted more for her absence than her presence."

The development of Lee's artistic and intellectual interests were especially nurtured by the subject of art history. Sarah McLennan, her teacher, made the subject come so alive, and she took such a personal interest in her, that as Lee herself remembers it, "I believe I survived three years at Miss Porter's School only because of the inspiration of Miss McLennan. . . . She enriched my life forever."

For all Lee's material advantages growing up, she had seldom, if ever, been taken to art museums, the theater, or even concerts. The study of art history confirmed her aesthetic inclinations—Lee was someone so visual by nature that she even fretted over the appearance of her handwriting.

Farmington was an environment where there were a lot of "cliques within cliques," as a classmate of hers put it. Lee soon found her niche of friends and stayed within it. "She was part of our group," said Jane Vaughn Love. "She had a drawing card. She was a loyal friend and had a marvelous sense of humor. But she was never going to come running up to one of us with a personal confidence. Lee was a very controlled, subdued individual. She never acted freely. I'm not sure she had much confidence at that stage in life. Lee had much more love to give than she allowed, much more caring to give than she let herself show. And she was far from unflappable. She never went off the wall or did lots of screaming and yelling, but she was churning within herself."

"Lee was young for her class, very bright, quiet, and thoughtful," recalled another classmate, Carlin Whitney Scherer, "but I work with family systems today as a counselor, and I can see now that Lee was what we call 'the lost child.' I remember a discussion at school with her and a couple of other students. We were sitting around in a circle, and we all kept expressing our sympathy to her, because her teachers were always saying, 'Why can't you be like your sister? Why can't you have the same grades?' "

Jill Fuller Fox, who was a year ahead of Lee (and would eventually become her stepsister-in-law), made a similar observation: "The thing that all of us at school were aware of then was her extreme envy of Jackie, her feeling of being so much the paler of the two. There was some feeling that Jackie and her father were very close and that Lee really didn't have anybody. But the problem of being Jackie's kid sister ema-

nated from within Lee. I remember one time she said to me,
'How would you like to have a sister like *that!*' It was something she and I empathized about because I have an older sister
who was also a great belle [Sage Fuller Cowles], but it was
more painful for Lee because she and Jackie were so very
close.''

"I remember Jackie would come occasionally to school
from Vassar to visit Lee, and there was such light flashing out
from her. She was so dazzling,'' recollected yet another classmate, Lisa Artamonoff Ritchie. "Of course, Jackie could wear
lipstick and we couldn't, but even aside from that, next to her,
Lee looked so washed out, and somehow at fifteen she seemed
as if she were thirty. There was no sense of youngness or
freshness about her. She'd been going to debutante parties for
years before anyone else, so there was a fatigue about her that
was not so much jadedness as a kind of apathy. Lee was
lovely, gracious, intelligent, and she was not dull, but she was
just in a veil. She didn't have any verve.''

Jill Fuller Fox also remembers how "listless and apathetic"
Lee was at Farmington. "She was very sad and anorexic-
looking. Very gray. Her hair was lank. Lee's beauty, I swear
to God, must have come later. I never remember seeing her
happy there or laughing. She hated Farmington, she just
loathed it, and that was another reason why she appeared so
listless. It may have been, a lot of it, just that. When she left
Farmington she cheered up some.''

"No one was happy at boarding school in those days,'' said
Howard Cushing, Jr., who exchanged letters with Lee while
she was there. Students at Miss Porter's were required to take
Friday afternoon tea with the teachers and to attend Sunday
night lectures by visiting scholars in the school chapel. The
curriculum was very demanding, especially for someone not
consistently keen on academics. The social mores and school
traditions meant little to Lee, and she had no interest in ath-
letics beyond the obligatory. She disliked the headmaster,
Ward L. Johnson. She thought him a humorless prig. Most of
all, she intensely disliked the long, snowy Connecticut winters.
Her entry in her class yearbook reflected her disaffection: Lee
put down New England as her "aversion.''

Girls who came to Miss Porter's from other parts of the
country noticed right away how their counterparts from the

East acted snobbish and were so much more sophisticated than they were. Lee in particular had that worldly-wise demeanor beyond her years. When members of her senior class were asked to name a favorite song for the yearbook, their invariable choices were down-home American favorites like "Ain't Misbehavin" or "Anything Goes." Lee chose "Quand J'Étais Petite." "That was so typical of her," sneered one classmate outside her clique.

Most of the girls at boarding school in Lee's era didn't talk about themselves a great deal. Their conversation dealt primarily with school, the faculty, and boys. Mail was a highlight of the day, the girls hoping to get letters from boys. By junior year Lee was no longer corresponding with Howard Cushing, Jr. She set him aside in favor of older boys. "Although chaste, it was poignant for me when it was over," Cushing said.

On Saturdays the older girls at Farmington were permitted male visitors, who were usually students from the Ivy League colleges, but they were not allowed to enter the dorms. Nor were the girls permitted to leave the school grounds without special permission. When Lee did go out, it was usually in a small group or with boys who had a family connection. One exception was Michael Canfield, a Saturday afternoon visitor who made the long drive down from Cambridge to see her a couple of times during her years at Farmington. The couple had met on the debutante dance-and-party circuit in New York. Michael brought his Harvard roommate, Joe Fox, with him and introduced Fox to his stepsister, Jill Fuller, whom Joe would eventually marry. Lee and Michael strolled together along "The Loop," the periphery of the campus lined with old houses and ancient oak trees.

Michael Canfield was a sophomore in the spring of 1948 when he made his first visit, but he had been in World War II before he began college. At fifteen years of age to Michael's twenty-two, Lee was young for him, much less formed and much more impressionable. However, Michael found Lee quite glamorous and sexy, even then. He was seduced by her looks and sophistication, as were many of her other beaus, and he liked her sense of humor and the sound of her laugh.

At the same time Lee was strolling with Michael Canfield, she had another admirer at Harvard who moved a little faster. On one of her coveted weekends away from Farmington during her junior year, she went to Cambridge and paid a visit to Reuben Richards, a clubby, affable, good-looking Harvard freshman. One of Richards's fellow students in Wigglesworth Hall walked into his room unannounced that weekend and to his surprise "there was Lee Bouvier in her bathrobe together with Reuben in his bunk bed."

7. Coming Out

As soon as Lee got away from Farmington for summer vacations, her vitality and buoyancy returned. In the summer of 1949 she began spending less time with her family at Hammersmith and more time hanging out with the older boys she now preferred. The vivacious Lee had become very popular with the opposite sex, and when she visited her family cabana at Bailey's Beach or went there in a crowd, eager young men invited her for a sail, a swim, or a game of tennis. Lee also became an erstwhile member of the "Six O'Clock Club"— the name her gang of teenagers had for the young crowd that stayed on to have fun at Bailey's Beach after the older generation had left.

Tennis Week was another summer colony tradition. During early August, tennis fans flocked to the Newport Casino from all over the eastern seaboard to watch the matches, just as they had been doing since Newport's gilded era. Newport matrons still remember the impression Lee Bouvier would make when she would arrive in the Auchincloss reserved box to watch the games. They said she was just extraordinarily attractive and dressed accordingly. In those days women wore hats and gloves to the matches, and Lee complimented hers with vivid high-fashion garments. Shorter than her sister but more curvaceous, with a classically attractive heart-shaped face and delicate features, Lee, in fact, never left the house unless dressed to the hilt. If she and Jackie went out together, Lee was the one who was stared at, since in her youth Jackie tended to dress in unimaginative, Peck & Peck–style clothes.

Jackie's relative indifference to fashion did not stop them from fighting over clothes anyway. At this point in their lives they were not getting along well, and it took very little to set them off. As teenagers the rivalry between the two of them was silent and unacknowledged most of the time, but when it did surface the quarrels were, as often as not, over money, particularly who got how much from which relative.

"Money has always been a big thing with Lee and Jackie," said Rue Hill Hubert. "It was more what it could buy and what you could do with it than the power of it, and they were both very clever in how they got it and how they spent it." Now that her grandfather Bouvier had died, Lee did what she could to shake down "Grampy Lee," with varying degrees of success. Growing up on the fringes of great wealth while not having much money of their very own gave both Jackie and Lee an insatiable appetite for it. Their mother reinforced those insecurities with the values she imparted and the example she set.

Jackie and Lee spent some of that feuding summer in Cody, Wyoming. Jack Bouvier was acquainted with Larry Larom, who owned the Valley Ranch there. According to his widow, Irma Dewey Larom, Jack had said that he was going to send both his daughters out to stay at the ranch that summer but that since they were not getting along, to please make sure they had separate quarters. When the girls arrived at the dude ranch they parted. Lee made short daily outings—horses were still not her thing—while Jackie went on an extended pack trip through Yellowstone Park.

By the twenty-second of August she and Jackie were back in Newport and again on good terms. Accompanied by escorts, they attended a fancy costume dance at Bailey's Beach and won first prize for their impersonations. Donald Sterling and Lee appeared as the Aga Khan and his begum, and Jackie went as Rita Hayworth, with her escort, Peter Vought, as Ali Khan. (Actually, with the long mane of hair Jackie wore at the time, people said that she looked more like the actress Jane Russell—"that is, from the neck up," quipped one Newport wag.)

When Lee returned to Miss Porter's for her final year, she worked on the school newspaper, *Salmagundy,* and performed in various school plays and reviews. She had tried out for the drama club that year and was accepted. Of all her tasks and accomplishments at Miss Porter's School, her participation in the drama program meant the most to her. Acting gave Lee a chance to literally grab the spotlight away from her older sister and to move center stage, as her father hoped that she would. Lee's tremendous enjoyment of her drama projects would have significant ramifications for her in the future.

"I don't think Lee's plans for the future were much different from any of ours—just come out, and get married," said Edie McBride Bass, one of Lee's closest school friends. "When we graduated Farmington in June we looked forward to going to Lee's coming-out party a few weeks later. Hers was the first of the season and our introduction to debutante excitement."

Lee's debut, traditionally a party which introduced a daughter to one's friends, and hence to society, took place at a dance on June 16, 1950, at Merrywood. Many dinners preceded the party, which was scheduled for 11:00 P.M., and she was the guest of honor at one given by Mrs. Dwight F. Davis for her and her granddaughter Shella Smith at the F Street Club in Washington.

At Merrywood Lee was radiant in white tulle and lace as she stood with Janet and Hughdie in the receiving line to greet her more than two hundred guests. Janet donned yellow chiffon for the occasion, and the flowers in the rooms of the mansion echoed their colors: white daisies and peonies and yellow irises. Outdoors, a dance floor protected by a marquee was set up on the lawn, where guests twirled until a buffet supper was served at one o'clock on the terrace, with dance music by Meyer Davis and his band resuming afterward.

"Merrywood was one of the prettiest houses in McLean, and Lee's debut was very much talked about. It was particularly beautiful," recollected one of the bachelors present.

The scene then shifted to Newport, where, apart from Tennis Week and the boating races, festivities were planned around coming-out parties and weddings. As one of the debs being honored that season, Lee was as busy as a bride-to-be, being feted throughout the colony with nonstop parties and dances. In mid-August Hughdie and Janet gave a black-tie party for the Newport belle and her young friends, with Hammersmith Farm festooned with hundreds of flowers from the estate's gardens for the occasion.

Lee did not give much thought that summer to her father. Jack had once more rented a cottage in East Hampton, but now it was filled for him with painful memories of Lasata and times past. He expected a visit from Lee, particularly since Jackie was in France as part of her college junior-year-abroad program, but Lee did not come. It was not just that with the passing years her allegiance had shifted to the Auchinclosses, or even that she was coming of age now with a life of her own, but rather that the magnetism her father had exerted on her as a child had vanished, and a growing wariness and anxiety had taken its place.

Rue Hill Hubert stayed with Lee at Jack's apartment from time to time, and in her words, "Black Jack had his own problems. He was hardly a great father, and Lee did not have the same adoration for their father as Jackie had."

With no stabilizing influence to help rein him in during the intervening years since his divorce, Jack increasingly turned to the bottle to escape his situation. "He could be very unpleasant when he was drinking," said Lee's Newport friend, Robin Corbin, "and my impression was that it was an embarrassment to her, but she never discussed the problem." In fact, Lee would rarely discuss her parents with anyone outside her family. She would only say, "Oh, you know Daddy. Oh, you know Mummy."

"I had the sensation Lee was a little afraid of her father and didn't like him," Corbin went on, "because I remember something that happened when Lee was in New York at the end of term her sophomore year at Farmington. We were walking down Park Avenue in the late afternoon when suddenly she said, 'Oh my God! I was supposed to have been home!' and she leaped into a taxicab and went off. She was really scared that she was so late, afraid of what her father might say or do. He wanted her back home, and she seemed to feel that she better be there or else. Lee didn't have that reaction to her mother or stepfather or anyone else."

By this time Jack was just shy of sixty and was increasingly reclusive. His relationship to his daughters had become virtually his only meaningful human connection. This need, when combined with his alcoholic behavior, placed a special burden on his children, and oftentimes Lee just wanted to avoid it.

8. *Deb of the Year*

Sarah Lawrence College, in Bronxville, New York, has a pleasant campus of Tudor architecture and several "greens," which calls to mind an English village. Founded as a progressive women's college (now coed) with less constraints academically than sister institutions, it was one of the first colleges in the United States to include performing and creative arts within a liberal arts curriculum. In 1950, reflecting the tenor of the times, Sarah Lawrence was in transition from being a finishing school for the daughters of the rich to a politically charged institution with a left-wing faculty and philosophy.

In choosing Sarah Lawrence for herself, Lee paid no mind to its politics. She liked being close to New York City, and her interest in the creative arts was already clear: drama, art, and design in its many facets, including fashion, engaged her, although none with a strong enough draw to give her a focus. Surprisingly, one of her favorite subjects freshman year was psychology. "Lee worked hard at Sarah Lawrence. She definitely applied herself while she was there," attested her roommate, Rue Hill Hubert, who, like Lee, went on from Farmington to Bronxville.

But as always, her primary interest seemed to be her social life. Lee took continual advantage of the easy commute to New York, and some of her off-campus time in the city during her first autumn of college was spent decorating Yusha Auchincloss's new bachelor digs, to his great satisfaction. He found the results of her work to be "magnificent." (Janet once observed that when Lee was growing up, she was always moving furniture around and redecorating people's rooms. "You'd think they would be furious, but she always improved things," she said.)

More typically on weekends, Lee traveled to Harvard, Yale, or Princeton to see a transitory assortment of male prospects; other times she journeyed home to Merrywood, especially if Jackie was going to be there. Staying sometimes with her father and sometimes with friends, she also volunteered her time in New York for the debutante committees of charity balls and went to subscription dances at the Plaza Hotel or the St. Regis.

When the holiday season rolled around, she made her formal bow at the Junior Assembly in New York and at the Tuxedo Ball in Tuxedo Park; then she traveled down to Baltimore one weekend with Hughdie and Janet to be presented at the Bachelors Cotillion. Other weekends, she made her way to deb parties at country clubs on Long Island and in Greenwich, Connecticut. When her semester break from college freed up her time, her calendar was crammed full every night with the remaining dinners, dances, parties, and balls, and the very late hours, of her coming-out season.

"The invitations came and one went to these thoroughly delightful and extraordinary parties," said Dick Blodget, one of the bachelors on the circuit. "I remember Lee as an extremely attractive young woman, and she impressed me as very vivacious and charming, quite without the mannerisms she was to acquire later."

Another gentleman who did not fail to notice this indefatigable debutante out on the town and to admire Lee's beauty, polish, and poise was Igor Cassini, the nationally syndicated Hearst newspapers gossip columnist known as Cholly Knickerbocker. In his flagship column in the *New York Journal-American,* he proclaimed Lee Debutante of the Year, as he had Jackie three years earlier.

Lee beat out two other noteworthy debutantes that season: the very ambitious Peggy Bedford, who was at Miss Porter's with her but had dropped out in dogged pursuit of her social career (she eventually became Princess d'Arenberg and later Duchess d'Uzes); and the very grand Sunny Crawford (later the comatose Mrs. Claus von Bülow). In this regard, a friend on the scene from Farmington, Alice Gordon Abbett, remembered how Lee "never called special attention to herself, and I would have thought if anyone was the Deb of the Year that year it was Peggy, because she worked at it, or Sunny, who gave the most fabulous party of anybody that season."

"My brother was a very acute observer of the social scene," said Oleg Cassini by way of explanation. "It was he who discovered the Bouvier sisters. Nature so favored Lee with gifts that she had more good fortune than others, a combination of genetics, luck, and manners, and my brother saw that early. That doesn't mean that because she had such gifts she knew how to be happy, because a lot of people don't know what to do with their gifts.''

In the hoopla that ensued over her winning Igor Cassini's accolade, *Life* magazine published a full-page photograph of Lee, who looked stunning in a cream-colored lace gown, and claimed that ''By general consensus of New York's society arbiters and editors, she is the city's leading debutante.''

In the fifties, the title Debutante of the Year meant instant stardom for its recipient. It was still a time when the influence of prewar society on the culture as a whole remained intact, before its standards were to be eclipsed by those of the radical sixties. As a result of all the publicity she received, Lee was flooded with fan mail. She read the proposals of marriage and the love letters avidly, and then she reread them. She was so enthralled with the public attention that she has reputedly saved every piece of correspondence, even the crank mail.

In true Bouvier style, she posted her most treasured letters in a scrapbook, along with the newspaper and magazine clippings of her debut and the press coverage of Cassini's proclamation. Positioned on the very first page of this scrapbook, obviously in a place of honor, she put a letter from Boris Kaplan, the head of Paramount Pictures' talent department, explaining that he had seen her photograph in *Life* and was anxious to talk to her about a screen test. The letter asked Lee to call the studio's New York office "collect." As if to emphasize how anxious Paramount was to talk to her, Lee underscored the word "collect" in blazing red crayon when pasting it in her scrapbook.

She was absolutely thrilled and considered the idea of taking a screen test, but she had not given serious thought to a career, and the culture of Hollywood was, to say the least, alien to her own, so she let the offer pass. She was already involved in college life anyway, and her parents would never approve.

Being besieged with requests for pictures and interviews and mentions in the gossip columns only whetted Lee's appetite for more. Once "her year" was over and the title had passed to someone new, she longed to remain in the public eye—and on the public tongue. She began to covet a starring role in cafe society, and she began to see herself as the heroine of a novel, deserving a heroine's special fate. Lee could not possibly have foreseen, that early on, the long, long coattails of Camelot, but as events played themselves out, destiny gave her answered prayers.

Not surprisingly, Lee's status as America's Number-One Glamour Girl gained her a considerable male following, and she dated on the college circuit even more than before. One frontline admirer was Michael Canfield. Six foot three and blond, with great good looks and all the right social talents, the dashing Harvard senior made a perfect escort for the highlights of Lee's social swirl—and she was now of suitable age to have him accompany her. But seeing each other still did not mean very much to either of them, and such were the scores of admirers eager to date a star that even Michael's stepbrother, Blair Fuller, got into the act and took Lee out a few times.

On semester break that winter, Lee spent a vacation with her family at Hobe Sound, the Old Guard resort up the coast from Palm Beach. She and Jackie used the family get-together as an opportunity to intensify their lobbying efforts with Janet and Hughdie to obtain permission to go abroad that summer, with Lee's trip a belated high-school graduation present. Janet was very anxious about the idea and she required a lot of persuading. "On June 7, 1951, after pleading and pestering and praying for a year, we finally left the country," said Lee.

Hughdie and Janet not only gave the girls their European trip but all the letters of introduction to go with it. They sailed on a Cunard ship bound for England and sent a reassuring stream of daily cables to the other side of the Atlantic throughout their journey.

In England, Lee got a chance to attend a party at Cliveden, the stately home of the Astor family, and there she made social contacts that would be useful to her in the future. She and Jackie bought a Hillman Minx to tool around in, and after their London visit and tour of the English countryside, the sisters had a lighthearted romp through the de rigueur tourist destinations of Europe: Paris, Rome, Florence, Venice—and Madrid.

Like most first-time tourists, Lee's Grand Tour was an od-

yssey of museums, ancient buildings, mellow scenery, border
guards, and shopping, peppered with the standard—and also
not so standard —assortment of eager European males that
pretty young American girls always seem to attract.

She and Jackie got to meet the great art historian Bernard
Berenson, a hero of Lee's whom she discovered in Sarah
McLennan's art history class. As he emerged from a wood by
his villa, I Tatti, outside Florence, he proceeded to sit sagelike
among them dispensing wisdom. "Of course, it was slightly
disillusioning in the way that meeting famous people sometimes is," Lee later recalled. "He was older, and I had grown
up enough to look for faults, but the great mind was still there.
I remember his hands were so beautiful."

Before embarking on the Le Havre boat-train for the trip
home, they sold their car in Paris to a young missionary who,
when haggling over the price, told them that every five dollars
he did not spend on himself would keep an African child alive
for a month. "We were for slaughtering the whole tribe,"
wrote Lee in a journal, "but his conscience would only let
him starve 206 of them."

To show how much the trip had meant to them, Jackie and
Lee presented Janet and Hughdie with a thank-you memento,
a scrapbook of their adventure entitled *One Special Summer*.
It was an aren't-we-funny collection of contrasting words and
pictures which, interestingly enough, except for the visit with
Berenson, focused its attention on them, not on the grand
sights and history lessons. The journal contained a mix of
Jackie's verses and clever cartoonlike pen and ink drawings
and watercolor sketches, with superimposed snapshots and
snatches mostly of Lee's diary-style, exclamatory prose. Their
charming reminiscence captured glimpses of an unspoiled,
fun-loving innocence and of the special sense of time the
young possess. It was a confection to make Mummy smile.

9. Royalty?

Michael Canfield had graduated Harvard and was living in New York when Lee returned to college in the fall. Although they both continued to see other people, they began to spend more time together and their relationship picked up speed. Often as a trio with Blair Fuller, they went to dinner, attended parties and shows, and occasionally spent weekends at Crowfields, the Canfield country home in Bedford Village, New York.

Besides the obvious pull of similar backgrounds and mutual friends, Lee and Michael shared an uncommon glamour and flair, and a love of all things beautiful. Michael Canfield was an endearing man who had much appeal in his quiet manner, and the rare capacity to charm his many friends. "Michael was really very winning," said Blair Fuller. "He had this sentimental quality that made people feel very close to him." Certainly Lee felt easy and comfortable with him, and his highly original and distinctive style made him stand apart from the pack of young men she knew.

For Michael was a raving Anglophile in looks, manner, and speech, a trait both learned and innate. When still a very young boy, he was interested in wearing only the best British tweeds, and when his father finally told him that he was an adopted child whose real parents had been English, he immediately acquired an English accent. This affectation was not discouraged at Saint Bernard's, the very British boys' school he went to in New York City, and he soon perfected it.

Michael also had a mannequin's success with clothes and always wore items of extraordinarily fine quality, right down to his shoes. "One almost joked about Michael Canfield, he was such a paragon of good taste," recalled the author George Plimpton, who first met him at Saint Bernard's. "His clothes were different from ours—the consistency of the material, I mean. He was probably the most elegant figure I've ever seen."

Michael Canfield was verbally elegant too. "He spoke of *le mot juste,* a phrase that he fancied," said Blair Fuller. "He wrote very good letters and was always seeking the exact word for things, and it gave his speech, which was sometimes complicated by a stammer, a great deal of distinction. Michael didn't sound like anyone else.''

But the most intriguing thing about Michael Canfield was the unsolved mystery of his birth. Michael was the adopted son of the book publisher Cass Canfield and his wife, ''Katsy,'' the former Katherine Emmet. In 1924, when Cass was a young man and just starting at the Harper publishing firm, he went to England for a three-year sojourn to manage Harper's London office and to winnow out British books with an American appeal. Cass brought his wife with him and their infant son, Cass Junior.

It was no secret among the Canfields' intimates that after their son was born, Katsy was told she could not have another child. So in 1926 when baby Michael appeared quite suddenly in their London household, it was understandable, if still surprising. For the infant had no adoption papers of any kind, and no birth certificate has ever appeared. The adoption papers that were eventually produced were prepared in New York, two years after the fact, and named ''Violet and I. R. G. Karslake'' as the parents and ''Antony Karslake'' as the offspring. The Canfields officially renamed the boy Michael Temple Canfield.

Granted it was common in those days to disguise the real identity of birth parents—''Karslake'' was clearly fictitious— and for adoptions to be done in such a casual and friendly fashion. Nor would Michael's adoption be of any great interest if it were not for the fact that available evidence suggests that he was the firstborn male of the House of Windsor, the bastard son of the late Duke of Kent and an American, Kiki Preston, who was a friend of Katsy's with other ties to the Canfields. The Duke of Kent was Prince George until his marriage in 1934 to Princess Marina of Greece, the youngest son of George V and Queen Mary. Kiki Preston was born Alice Gwynne around the turn of the century, the niece and namesake of Mrs. Cornelius Vanderbilt II, once known as the chatelaine of all the Vanderbilts.

Prince George had a romantic appeal to his subjects that has never been equaled by anyone in the Royal Family. Born in 1902, he was exposed to ordinary life in the Navy and longed for a meaningful connection to the outside world. He became the first—and only—son of a reigning monarch to hold a conventional job and work alongside ordinary members of the public, first in the Foreign Office and then as a Home Office factory inspector in the thirties. A handsome, charming man of nocturnal habits and a rakish lifestyle, George was sharply different in temperament and outlook from his older brothers: his family considered him to be a "bohemian." He was very close to his eldest brother, the Prince of Wales, whom he adored and who introduced him to the world of show business and the theater.

In addition to the aristocratic girls with fast reputations he usually ran around with, the Prince had many amorous adventures with women outside his own circle. A former equerry to Edward when he was both the Prince of Wales and King has been quoted as saying that George was a "scamp" and always in trouble with girls, and that Scotland Yard chased so many of them out of the country that the Palace stopped counting.

Kiki Preston, in turn, was a rich and charismatic beauty who seduced even the anti-American snob Evelyn Waugh with her charm when he met her on his travels in Africa. Kiki met Prince George in London after the First World War, a time when the old barriers were breaking down and both the aristocracy and the Royal Family opened their ranks to newcomers who could add a scrap to their entertainment.

Kiki's scandalous behavior was beyond anything Prince George had ever experienced. It was typical of that generation's driving push for freedom from convention at whatever the personal cost. An eventual suicide, Kiki had many, many lovers, including Valentino, and was often high on drink and drugs. She would shoot up using a sterling-silver syringe and was considered the epitome of chic by her smart-set friends. She eventually snared even the hapless Prince George himself into a cocaine addiction by becoming his supplier; her behavior earned her a place on the list of the Prince's women exiled by royal edict. Prince George fell madly in love with Kiki, and rumor among their friends has always had it that Kiki became pregnant by him. The story goes that Kiki disappeared from London, most likely to Switzerland, in a cloud of secrecy to have the baby. Presumably, Kiki's husband, Jerome Preston, a friend of Cass Canfield's, did not want a living reminder of her indiscretion.

The Prestons and the Canfields, according to this theory, apparently came to some arrangement about the baby. "The Canfields were quite snobbish and would have been excited as anything to be asked to look after a royal indiscretion," said an intimate of their London circle. Their adopted child would do his part to corroborate that he was indeed Prince George's son by growing up to look exactly like a Windsor, thereby provoking the unending speculation.*

While the theory that Prince George and Kiki Preston were Michael Canfield's natural parents is a plausible one, there is yet another theory to consider: it may be that Michael was the son of Lord Acton, the third baron and thirteenth baronet (and the grandson of the eminent Cambridge historian, the first Baron Acton†), by a servant girl in his household. These two were identified by Cass Canfield late in his life when he was under duress from his family to provide them once and for all with names. Michael's natural parents were almost certainly one controversial pair or the other.

Not a shred of evidence exists to link the Canfields in any way with John Acton, who would have been eighteen and attending Cambridge at the time of Michael's conception, nor is anything known about the servant girl who may have been Michael's mother. Acton's friends and family hotly deny Cass Canfield's claim that Acton was Michael's birth father (unlike Preston family members, who believe Kiki was his mother).

"Cass told me that yes, he had met the parents," said his stepson, Blair Fuller.** "When I asked him if Michael was

---

*One person who needed no persuasion that Michael Canfield was indeed the Duke of Kent's son was Edward VIII. Years later in Paris, when he was the Duke of Windsor, after being told of the rumor by his good friend the third Earl of Dudley, he said to Michael's second wife, Laura Charteris Dudley, in Michael's presence: "Yes, what Eric has told me I am sure to be true. I am certain your husband is my brother's son. Of course, it must have been when brother George was but a boy." See Laura (Canfield) Marlborough's memoir, *Laughter From a Cloud*, p. 157.

†Acton is often quoted for his insight: "Power tends to corrupt, and absolute power corrupts absolutely."

**Cass and Katsy Canfield divorced in 1937. Cass went on to marry Jane White Fuller, who had three children from a previous marriage, Jill, Sage, related to the Royal Family, he said with a little too much vehemence perhaps, 'I met the parents when we were adopting Michael, and they were not royal!' Cass was very discreet, and if he had given his word that he would never say anything about it, then he never would. But then too, he could have been meeting people who were standing in, just saying they were the parents. Who knows?''

Who knows indeed? What we do know for certain is that Michael's adoption was the definitive experience of his life. He remained permanently baffled and unsettled by the mystery of his origins, telling his family at one point in the sixties that he thought he'd seen his ''father,'' Lord Acton, at White's club in London, then, a few years later, showing a photograph to his friends of a woman holding a baby, saying it was a picture of him and his ''mother,'' Kiki Preston. Regardless of which set of parents were actually his, Michael paid a steep price for his distinguished lineage. His genetic dictates gave him the gestures, tastes, and inclinations of the British nobility, which left him perpetually straddled between the life he actually lived while he was growing up in America and the one he was more suited to in the English countryside.

Michael grew up in the Canfield household feeling very much like an outsider, an alienation exacerbated by the fact that by the time he arrived, the Canfields' marriage was disintegrating. He developed learning disabilities and a facial tic, and his parents sought psychiatric counseling for him. After attending the Brooks School in North Andover, Massachusetts, an offshoot of Groton, Michael lied about his age and joined the Marines. (The officer who processed him saw his cockeyed, ersatz birth certificate which gave ''England or Switzerland'' as his place of birth. ''What the fuck is this?'' he growled—''that's what Michael had to put up with,'' said Blair Fuller, who related the incident.)

Essentially a quiet, passive man, Michael was tagged with the nickname ''Toast,'' short for milquetoast, by his Marine buddies because he was terrified of his sergeant. Yet he was ''never as happy as when he was in the Marine Corps,'' his

---

and Blair Fuller. The Canfield and Fuller children had always known each other, so when the two sets of children came together in Cass's remarriage, they made a seamless whole. (Katsy remarried an architect, John Churchill.)

stepsister Jill Fox remembers. "It wasn't the fighting he loved—just the spit and polish of it. He was only a private, but he was shined up like anything. Michael was happiest in his life when things were prescribed and on a routine."

Michael served in the Pacific theater during World War II and sustained a shrapnel injury in the Iwo Jima landing. After the war, he attended Harvard. By now he had heard the various rumors of his Windsor origins, but he could never be sure. "Michael always gave the impression he was a little different from us, the English thing. There was this aura about him, that maybe he was Lord Somebody," said his friend John Marquand, Jr., the novelist's son. Most in his circle—who never wanted to believe anything else—thought he was the Duke of Windsor's son because their profiles were so strikingly similar. "Certainly Michael himself was wound up in the belief that he was part royalty," observed his classmate Chauncey Parker. "I remember well his telling us how proud he was of his long upper lip, claiming it was so Windsorian."

At Harvard, Michael could often be found buried in an issue of *The New Yorker*. His sensibilities were literate, and he could write well himself in a limited way. When his roommates opted to go out, he would often decline. A homebody, he was content to sit happily polishing his shoes, as he had done in the Marines, listening to Billie Holiday and Noël Coward on his record player, and getting quietly drunk. "Michael held his liquor then. He was always a little bit tipsy in a charming way," remembers a roommate.

Another favorite pastime was going up on the roof of his dormitory to brood. Michael's personality had a sad, loopy undercurrent to it, a deep pathos, almost an air of doom. The experience of abandonment he felt as an adopted child never left him and was compounded by the rumor of his royal origins. For if he were a Royal, was he not different from all other men? He used to tell his friends, "I hope I'll die young just to get out of this world," and he meant it. Like Lee, he too would have answered prayers.

10. *Diana Vreeland's Magazine*

With happy memories of her European trip lingering in her mind, Lee was eager to go abroad again. The opportunity presented itself much sooner than expected: over her semester break sophomore year from Sarah Lawrence she and her mother made a trip to Rome. Lee stayed on in Rome for several months "to take some singing lessons," and didn't return to college as expected for her final semester that year. Her family had always thought she had a nice singing voice and urged her to develop it. Jackie, for one, was always prodding her: "Sing, Lee, sing."

Lee once said in an interview that she left Sarah Lawrence in the middle of her sophomore year because she had a chance to go with "a friend and her family" to Rome. "My mother thought I sang well and encouraged me," she explained, "though she was a little disillusioned when she found out my teacher was from Mississippi! Anyway, I studied singing and was rather serious about it. I took textile design courses in Rome, too, just because I loved to draw and paint."

Mary deLimur Weinmann, the friend she spoke of, remembers the event differently. She said she went to Rome with her parents and there encountered Lee Bouvier, who had not been as attentive about her lessons as she might have been, and Janet was furious. "Lee wasn't serious about singing—she just wanted to be in Rome," Weinmann said.

By June, Lee had moved on to England, and a friend, George Plimpton, invited her to a ball at Cambridge. "She was breathtakingly beautiful," Plimpton recalled. "People stared at her. She had a very different beauty than Jackie's. She didn't smile as much as Jackie did. She wasn't as radiant. Lee exuded a slight air of mystery.

"There was this man at King's called Sir John Shepherd, a very cherubic figure whose hair was supposed to have turned white at the news of Rupert Brooke's death—quite untrue, but that was the legend about him. He was a very effusive, very strange type. He was entranced by Lee. He saw her beauty and grabbed hold of her and said, 'My dear girl!' We talked about her for days.''

Lee also paid a visit to Michael Canfield during her London stay. He had gone there on a brief stint as a reader for Hamish Hamilton, a small, quality publishing house financially underwritten by Harper & Row (today HarperCollins), where Cass Canfield was now chairman of the board. Like his brother, Cass Junior, Michael decided to follow his father and pursue a publishing career. Lee had found herself missing Michael's company while studying in Rome, but after anticipating their reunion for weeks, when she finally got together with him, something between them was seriously amiss.

''Michael and I were stepbrothers obviously, but we had been very close since we were boys,'' said Blair Fuller. ''We were roommates all through Harvard too. When Lee came to see Michael he was impotent. I know this because he told me about it. However, Lee was very patient about this, and she did not give up on him. After a while this was no longer the case.''

Michael had been very lonely in England. He wrote a letter to Jill Fuller Fox, who was also very close to him, mentioning the number of gin bottles lined up on his mantelpiece. ''Lee had been rather pursuing him, and they still didn't know each other that well,'' she said. ''Michael was revolted by her totally and repulsed by her physically. He wrote this to Blair. I remember seeing the letter. I don't think she meant anything to him for quite a while.''

Lee had no idea Michael felt this way. For her part, something clicked inside her at this moment. She fell in love with Michael and set her sights on him.

After doing a little more traveling on the Continent and meeting up with Rue Hill in Paris, Lee headed for home, and once back in New York, dropped out of college. ''Sarah Lawrence wouldn't let me take up the year at the same point at which I left,'' she acknowledged, ''so I never went back.''

In the wake of her abrupt departure from college, Lee decided she wanted to learn the fashion business. A mutual contact at the Saks Fifth Avenue department store mentioned Lee's interest to Muriel Johnstone of the fashion advertising agency bearing her name. Johnstone was a pioneer, the first woman advertising-agency owner, a dynamic woman of good family who built her whole business herself, acquiring such important fashion accounts as David Crystal and I. Magnin. She had Lee in to see her at her Rockefeller Plaza office and offered her a position as her assistant with the opportunity to learn the business.

Lee accepted eagerly, and once on the job, made herself useful scheduling appointments with artists and models and attending shoots at the studio and on location, solving problems as they arose. "I didn't write copy—I knew what they wanted, and I didn't want to be responsible for that kind of prose," she remarked ungratefully afterward, "but I kept a schedule and finished the assignments I was given."

Later on, when Lee became a celebrity, she reinvented her résumé. She once told a reporter that her first job had been "as a copywriter in an advertising agency. But that was when I was very young. I was rather appalled. I always thought I had a good imagination—and the language! But it was my first job, so it was quite exciting."

No one would know from those remarks that she only worked there a matter of weeks, not to say days. She left in September 1952 when the opportunity arose to work as special assistant to Diana Vreeland, who was then the head of the fashion department at *Harper's Bazaar* magazine.

Vreeland had a number of fashion editors reporting to her at *Harper's Bazaar* and two employees who worked for her personally: a secretary who did the routine secretarial work, and her special assistant, usually a socially prominent young woman, who helped her on the fashion end. Vreeland loved having very attractive people around her, and if she heard that some pretty girl like Lee Bouvier was looking for a job, she'd get her in there right away.

Her use of both a secretary and a socialite for support reflected the overall policy of *Harper's Bazaar,* which, like the other fashion glossies, had two tiers of employees: the careerist editors who made up the substance of the publication, and the showpiece society ladies, whose glamour helped to sell the clothes and the lifestyle featured in the magazine to their largely middle class audience. Diana Vreeland was shrewd enough to lure some of these socialites into working for nothing, but Lee needed the money and got a paycheck, tiny though it was, for her efforts.

To be Diana Vreeland's assistant was a coup for Lee that landed her right at the heart of the fashion world. She was thrilled to be working for such a talented fashion editor and found her presence, like the atmosphere at the magazine itself, very stimulating. *Harper's Bazaar* was in its heyday in the fifties and celebrated for its creativity and daring. "It was tops. There was real appreciation of the magazine as a visual and literary experience," said D. D. Ryan, one of Vreeland's volunteers. "God! We had Cartier-Bresson, Brassaï, Capa, Truman Capote. It was so alive!" A former editor at the competition, Polly Mellen of *Vogue*, made a similar observation: "*Vogue* was just a fashion magazine then. The *Bazaar* was daring, original, far-out, an extraordinary group of people. Diana Vreeland was totally imaginative, totally futuristic, totally *in toto*."

"Anyone who had any contact with Diana Vreeland caught something special," attested one of her fashion editors, Laura Pyzel Clark. "In the morning she would sweep off the elevator and the whole floor would change. Diana gave off an electric charge. There was a mood you would catch. It wasn't anything that happened to just one person. It happened to all of us, Lee included. She would sweep into the office looking absolutely fantastic. She smelled wonderful—the scent that she wore trailed after her—and then she would go and sit in this marvelous office of hers with its wonderful photographs of, say, some socialite or model wearing a fabulous necklace, and then she would start calling us in, one at a time, and we all got such a charge out of this. Diana was a confidante. She loved to hear news from us after we had been out on the town or dancing all night. She wanted to hear about what we saw, who we saw, and what they were wearing."

As her special assistant, Lee might telephone Diana excitedly to convey gossip she had just heard about someone they knew, or she might bring things to Diana's home for inspection. Sometimes she would accompany her mentor downtown to visit Seventh Avenue designers, or else Diana would send her on her own to choose a hat, say, to wear with a certain coat they were going to photograph, or maybe she might run over to Maximiliam to see what furs they had lying around, because the magazine needed to borrow some for a sitting the next day. At the photo shoots, Lee would help with setting them up. She never knew what she might be asked to do next, which gave her job the quality of an adventure.

Lee was outgoing, eager, and well liked by her co-workers. She had some rather odd assignments from time to time, but she never questioned them, she just went out and did them. Once Diana was hooked on a shade of orange that she wanted to put across at an editorial meeting, and she asked Lee to go out and buy some fresh carrots. "Diana Vreeland was a very visual woman," observed Barbara Slifka, who was then secretary to the executive editor. "I remember once her whole thing was blue, and she couldn't get it across to her staff, and then she glanced at a Kleenex box and said, 'That's the color!'

"Diana was fun, but at the same time she kept a tight rein on her assistants. She liked them standing there when she was in the office, and I mean there with the pencils sharpened and the water poured."

Lee did not mind the discipline, and although her time at the magazine was to be brief, she made a lasting impression on some of her co-workers before her departure. As Laura Pyzel Clark saw her: "Lee was a little bit, not fey, but a fantasy girl. Her fantasy life wasn't evident in anything she said. It was just her air, the way she moved, the way she dressed. She had a little extra something from the other girls, what the French call cachet. She was very smart, very pretty — her skin looked as though it still had dew on it, and she had all kinds of lovely ideas about life and how it should be. Quality was very important to her. Lee loved quality things— handmade shoes, beautiful fabrics. If she could only have one chair in her home, that chair would have to be the best and have the best fabric on it. Lee always looked so adorable too, and she had this little way of speaking out of the side of her mouth. She smiled often and was very dear."

"I remember her a lot on the telephone with private phone calls. I remember a lot of whispering," said Barbara Slifka, who shared the back of a long, skinny office with Lee. "What I remember most about her was her voice; it was so pretty, so sexy, so alluring. Lee's voice was just wonderful."

During Lee's working days at *Harper's Bazaar*, she and her former college roommate, Rue Hill, who had also abandoned campus life that year, lived in an apartment at the Dakota, the castlelike apartment building facing Central Park, long renowned along with its architecture for its extraordinary residential mix of celebrities and swells. The apartment belonged to Rue's parents and adjoined their own living quarters. The girls had their own entrance, living room, bedroom, and kitchen, and all the privacy they needed.

Michael Canfield was back in New York by autumn working at Harper & Row, and Lee began to see a lot of him. Even so, their relationship did not appear serious to those in their circle. They knew Michael still had other romantic interests. But Lee was determined to have Michael for herself, and she began to pressure him to make some kind of commitment. A strain in their relationship developed, which made others take notice. Thomas Guinzburg, a friend of Michael's, remembers having them out to Long Island that fall for a weekend with his family: "It was toward the end of their courtship. They were having a fight, and I was being used to help Lee repair the rift. She was certainly crazy about Michael in those days, but they had been going out together for quite a while by then, and one or the other was getting apprehensive about the fact that it was reaching a stage where it was going to have to be consummated with a wedding or fall apart."

Not long after the Long Island visit, Michael was at Crowfields for the weekend, and he asked Blair Fuller and Jill Fox to go for a walk with him. As Jill remembers it, "He walked us just down through the woods at Crowfields and then told us that Lee had proposed to him. The last we had heard from Michael about Lee was that he found her repulsive and that she was pursuing him, and what was he to do? So we just laughed and said, 'Oh, well.' And then Michael said to us, 'You know, I am going to accept!' Well, Blair and I almost fell sideways on the path. I said to Michael, 'But Michael, you can't do that! You don't love Lee!' And Michael replied, 'Oh, but the dear girl, she loves me so!'

"And that in a way is the story of Michael's life. His pleasures in life were always home, routine, and a few people that he loved, and anybody that stayed around him long enough, he would get very fond of, love in a way, and have regrets for. Lee was very pretty. But I don't think Michael was ever physically attracted to her. I really don't. Michael's acceptance must have thrilled Lee. She really persuaded him to marry her. Lee had the upper hand with him, always.''

11. *Marrying Michael*

Persuading Michael to marry her was one thing, persuading Mummy to let him marry her was another. Lee enlisted the support of friends like John Marquand, Jr., for the task, who came down with Michael to Merrywood one weekend. "We all went horseback riding, and I made a home movie of the girls doing little dramas, little playlets," Marquand recollected. "One of them featured Jackie and Lee waiting on a table that Michael was sitting at. Anyway, Hughdie saw right away that Michael was a nice guy. But Mrs. Auchincloss led me aside to the drawing room and asked, 'What do you really think of Michael?' and I gave a glowing account of what a great guy he was. I suspected that was one of the reasons for my invitation, but I did it anyway."

Janet found Michael charming, as everyone did, but she worried about his lack of a focus and his drinking. He did not appear to be someone who was goal-oriented, or who had a definite agenda for his life and career. He was raised in a publishing family and, through long-term exposure to it, liked it in a leisurely way. But he had no big ambition about it as a profession. Nor did anyone think of him as having any great editorial instinct. Rather, Michael was respected by those he dealt with as having good taste, and he did well, in a limited way, chiefly as a sort of goodwill ambassador for Harper's. His charm made him a great person to entertain writers, but he certainly wasn't out beating the bushes for new authors to sign up. "Michael was awfully good at keeping them though, once they were signed up, which is a talent all to itself," said his friend Thomas Guinzburg, the former publisher of Viking Press.

His drinking was another matter. To a great extent Michael's alcohol problem was camouflaged by the heavy drinking that was prevalent in society in general. Many people drank too much in the fifties. "Michael would start drinking early in the afternoon," acknowledged one of his friends, "but I wouldn't have called him an alcoholic then because he was always in control. Anyway, no one thought in those terms then. Michael was just considered to be a comical character."

At times Lee showed some impatience with Michael's drinking and was beset with nagging doubts and a vague feeling of unease that maybe her mother was right. One Sunday afternoon she went for a drive with Cleveland Amory, the author and animal rights activist. Amory had taken Lee out casually a few times, and they knew a number of people in common. "Do you think I should marry Michael Canfield?" she asked him. "Not if you have to ask," was his reply. Ultimately, Lee chose to brush aside her anxieties and concentrate on his many attractive qualities and advantages.

"For Lee, Michael had elegance," said Blair Fuller. "He was good-looking. He was funny and unusual. He had considerable sophistication and a very clear sense of how things were done. But I was surprised, really, that Michael was the guy for her because he didn't have any force. I thought Lee would choose a man more like Jack Kennedy."

Michael, for his part, had his own reservations about Lee. He made a remark to his stepbrother expressing concern about her reputation for being "fast." "He didn't like what he had heard," said Fuller. "He said something to the effect that she was 'no angel.' He asked if I had slept with Lee on those occasions in the past when I had taken her out. I assured him that I had not. But a lot of things about Lee and the marriage looked awfully good to him—the whole social thing that Hughdie and Janet represented. The money. Michael wanted to live well. And he thought Lee had taste. Her glamour was very important to him. Lee was very glamorous."

To be sure, Michael heard volumes about the Auchinclosses and the Bouviers and very little about the Irish Lees. Janet had reinvented her family's past when she married Hugh Auchincloss, now dropping remarks that they were descended from the aristocratic southern Lees of Virginia and Maryland. Janet's mother was a very ordinary person, actually, and all her life she tried to hide this fact and lived in fear of being discovered. Her anxiety must have been transmitted to her daughters, because they only spoke in public about the Bouvier background. And with Merrywood and Hammersmith Farm as a setting, Lee *looked* rich. Michael had no idea that she was not named in Hugh Auchincloss's will, and that, in fact, aside from the $3,000 her grandfather Bouvier left her, Lee had no real money of her own.

Michael had his publishing salary and the income from a small trust. Janet wanted Lee to marry for financial security, as she had, and was displeased with Michael's monetary prospects. At least her prospective son-in-law's family was socially impeccable and distinguished, she reasoned. One of Cass Canfield's ancestors, Lewis Cass, had been Governor of Michigan Territory and Secretary of War under President Jackson, and later Secretary of State under Buchanan (he also ran unsuccessfully for president as a Democrat against Zachary Taylor). And Michael's adoptive mother, Katsy, descended from the Irish patriot Robert Emmet, who defied British rule early in the nineteenth century and died a hero.

As a couple, Michael and Lee shared very high spirits—after all, she was just nineteen, he twenty-six—which helped draw them close. "They laughed a lot. Michael had a very good sense of humor, and they had a very gay, jolly time," recalled Cass Junior. Jill Fox remembers Lee "sitting on Michael's lap with a button popping on her dress, and we all chuckled about it. She couldn't have cared less, and I thought that being in love with Michael had brought that change in her. Lee was so giggly, so outgoing and rambunctious, so different from the person I had last seen at Farmington that it was breathtaking. That was the only time I got the feeling that she was really in love with Michael."

Their engagement was officially announced in mid-December 1952, and Pat and Jimmy Hill, Rue's parents, gave the couple an engagement party at the Dakota. Michael began instruction in the Roman Catholic faith because it was required if they were to be married in a Catholic ceremony. He and Lee went together for his instruction after work.

"When Michael came by the office to pick up Lee, we got to talking together," said Laura Pyzel Clark. "I don't think Michael was crazy about the idea of taking instruction, but he didn't resist. I have to say I thought Michael Canfield was the most attractive man I ever met in my life. He was absolutely thrilled with Lee. They were such a gorgeous couple. I thought, my goodness, wouldn't it be fun to leave Seventh Avenue and all this stuff behind? I wouldn't stay five minutes if I were getting married to Michael Canfield.''

Just before Christmas, Lee left *Harper's Bazaar* to begin making plans for her April wedding. ''She wasn't there very long,'' said Clark in reference to Lee's four-month employment, ''but it was fun to have her. It was sad when she left.''

Michael's lessons in the Catholic faith set him up for some good-natured ribbing from his Protestant family, who loved to give humorous name tags to people. ''My father used to call him Mackerel T. Canfield,'' said his stepbrother, Jonathan Churchill in reference to the Catholic custom of eating fish on Fridays. Michael labeled Black Jack Bouvier ''The Boiled Ham,'' a reference to the peculiar purplish color of his skin.

But joking aside, Michael got on well with Jack Bouvier. He felt a kinship with him. He saw him as an underdog, like himself, and he felt sorry for him too. Michael enjoyed Janet, who eventually overcame her wariness and resigned herself to Lee's engagement, but he thought she was rather spoiled and always referred to her as ''Mummy'' in a slightly derogatory way. '' 'Mummy' could be a mighty charming woman when she set her cap to it,'' Cass Junior conceded, ''and although we all thought Lee was spoiled, which she was, and wanted to be in the public eye, which she did, she had charm, wit, and coquettishness.''

Jackie, with no prospective husband of her own in sight, was distraught at the news of Lee's impending marriage and suffered acute pangs of sibling rivalry (although she was dating, among others, the young senator from Massachusetts, John F. Kennedy, his attentions seemed scattered, and his pursuit of her was sporadic). In spite of Lee's insecurities where her sister was concerned, it was she who held the trump card when it came to the opposite sex: Lee was considered the beauty who appealed to men in a generation of women whose main chance was sexual salesmanship. She was sexier as well as prettier and laughed more readily than Jackie did. ''Lee and Jackie's rivalry was something that was talked about,'' said a friend in their crowd. ''People were saying that Jackie was really upset that Lee got married first.''

Paradoxically, their rivalry was not a barrier to their closeness, but a mutual part of it. Rivalry was intrinsic to Jackie and Lee's lifelong chiseling of their separate identities, and in a profound way, it was the fuel of their individuality. That is why there was mutual emulation along with the competition and why they still looked to each other for counsel and refuge. They took an intense interest in the minutiae of each other's lives, in their setbacks and triumphs, large or small. What had begun as an isolation from the grownups in the havoc of their parents' divorce ended up as a kind of emotional isolation from all outsiders. It is doubtful their future husbands ever got as close to them as Jackie and Lee were to each other.

Michael, for one, complained. He once rowed the pair of them around a lake, watching them whisper intently to each other in the bow of the boat. He assumed the subject to be one of great importance, perhaps a family crisis involving their infamous father, and he became exasperated when he found out later that they had been discussing gloves. He once grumbled to Blair, "You know, these sisters are always off in a corner talking to each other! I've eavesdropped a number of times now, and what are they talking about? Perfect drivel! They're not saying anything!" "Michael sounded quite annoyed," said Blair, "but, of course, it was very funny."

Yet Lee's insecurities remained where her sister was concerned. She could not so easily put behind her a childhood where her older sister presented such a figure of envy. "Lee was marvelous-looking and extremely feminine. She was terrific—the real McCoy," said her longtime admirer Chauncey Parker. "I always thought she had Jackie's looks beat by a mile but could never convince her of this whenever she would say how ugly she felt in comparison to Jackie, which was often. Yet one of the things that is so fascinating is that having suffered as much as I believe she has in being Jackie's younger sister, she really liked Jackie, and Jackie really liked her. I don't remember Lee ever saying anything derogatory in any way about Jackie. She was just intimidated by her. I felt that then and still do. Jackie was a star, and everything she touched seemed to go so well for her. Lee was swamped by this. I believe that's a major reason she became so introverted as a child, and I have long thought the reason Lee married Mike was that she was absolutely hell-bent-for-leather determined to beat Jackie to the altar, to at least beat her in that."

12. *Sister Brides*

As plans for her wedding continued apace, Lee focused on her trousseau, ordering a number of custom-made items in addition to her bridal clothes—dresses and playtime togs—from a local dressmaker, Mini Rhea, for her Virgin Islands honeymoon in the sun. Her mood remained very gay as her big day neared.

A more ominous note sounded when, a few days before the wedding, Cass Canfield gave an ushers' dinner at his charming, doll-like New York townhouse on East Thirty-eighth Street. As Jonathan Churchill remembers it, "Everybody got a little drunk and Hugh Auchincloss just sat there repeating about Michael: 'He will never be able to afford her. He will never be able to afford her.' I believe he thought that Lee was a little headstrong and that Michael might not be able to provide all the things that she thought she was entitled to."

The ushers' dinner was followed by a wedding dinner for more than one hundred guests at the home of Walter and Wendy Sawyer the evening before the ceremony on April 18. Wendy Burden Sawyer was a stepcousin of Michael's, one of the pack who grew up at Crowfields and who now lived next door to Lee at Merrywood. Many elaborate toasts were made in an effort to be amusing by the throng of attractive young people invited.

An atmosphere of nervousness shadowed the events on Lee's wedding day. There was considerable apprehension in the Auchincloss household about whether Jack Bouvier would be sober enough to escort his daughter down the aisle and do all that was required of the father of the bride. So great was Janet's concern that she insisted Hughdie buy a morning coat and be ready to stand in. She worried, too, that Hughdie would somehow embarrass her at the wedding or make a gaffe in his toast. By this stage of their marital life she had come to look upon her husband as a rather foolish, if well-meaning man. Janet also ran around nervously telling everyone in the wedding party what to do, and as usual, mother and daughter bickered constantly.

The spring of 1953 had been a particularly magnificent one in the Washington area, with dogwood blossoms everywhere, but Lee's luck did not hold out. Her wedding procession made its way to Holy Trinity Cathedral in Georgetown on a gray, drizzly Saturday afternoon. Once she got to the church, though, she finally relaxed, and Jack Bouvier made it to the ceremony and gave his daughter away without a hitch.

The bride wore a floor-length heirloom veil of rosepoint lace arranged in cap fashion that had been worn by her grandmother and mother before her. (Jackie also wore the veil later on at her wedding.) Because it had faintly yellowed from age, Lee chose a bridal gown of ivory Chinese organza to offset it, fashioned with a high neckline, short sleeves, and a bouffant skirt. She carried a bouquet of small yellow and white orchids, and her bridesmaids wore ballerina-length yellow chiffon.

At Merrywood, the hundreds of reception guests enjoyed the music and champagne and the beauty of the superb Georgian mansion. Michael, looking very debonair in his gabardine suit, "got just a little bit tipsy in a nice way" as one of the guests put it, and Lee appeared happy and glowing. Only Jack Bouvier remained quiet, apparently subdued by seeing the lavish house his daughters lived in. "I remember the look of that man," said Blair Fuller, "his Hollywood-leading-man-of-the-twenties look with the patent-leather hair. He didn't seem to speak."

Lee threw her bouquet to Jackie. It was a very deliberate "Here's to you, kid." Then Jackie, at that time the Inquiring Photographer of the *Washington Times-Herald,* went around asking the ushers if she could photograph them for her column after the bride and groom left. When she did, one of the ushers said to her, "But Jackie, what is the question?" And she replied, "I'll make up the question, and I'll make up the answers too!"

One wedding guest, Chauncey Parker, had a disturbing encounter with Janet in the front hall of Merrywood. Other guests were milling about when she buttonholed him, looked him straight in the eye and said: "Has it occurred to you that there but for the grace of God, go you?"

"Janet was a very pretty woman, but she had these ice-cold dark-brown eyes and a tongue like a rapier," observed Parker, who says he remembers the incident as if it happened yesterday. "Obviously she did not mean this kindly. My reaction was that a parent has no right to say that to someone about her own daughter, especially on her wedding day. It was an extraordinarily cruel, appalling thing to say, the kind of remark that an enemy would make." Janet's behavior perplexed Parker all the more because he and Lee were, at bottom, only friends, and he had never entertained the thought of marrying her.

Before the bride and groom had even left for their honeymoon, some of their wedding guests were less than optimistic about their future: "It was a very cool wedding. There wasn't much warmth in the atmosphere," reports Sherry Parker Geyelin, Chauncey's sister. "I just did not feel that Michael and Lee were that much in love. Michael Canfield was a very nice guy. Everybody liked him, and I wondered if he weren't walking into a hornet's nest, because by that time Lee was beginning to manifest her harder qualities. She was no longer the fun-loving butterball that my brother was so crazy about. Her character had set, and she was a very acquisitive, ambitious presence. Her eyes were on the prize, you know, worldly things, and she was going to get it all somehow. Lee was a pretty cool number."

The newlyweds sublet a furnished apartment at 414 East Fifty-second Street, close by the East River, while they waited for a larger place. "Michael told me that there was a fish tank overhead at the foot of their bed, and when they were lying in bed they could watch the fish," said Jonathan Churchill. "And the place was so small that the person on one side of the bed had no floor to get out on—you had to crawl across the other person."

The Canfields' space problems were nicely solved a few months later when they moved into a stylish, sunny, two-bedroom apartment nearby at 14 Sutton Place South, and Janet gave them some money to decorate it. Jill Fox remembers how Michael and Lee had a period of pleasure when they were first married, putting their apartment together: "There was a terrific little honeymoon phase. My husband, Joe, and I would visit and we'd study the chandelier they just bought, and they didn't have a lot of money. They were really searching around for just the right plant stand and the right pictures on the walls.

It was very sweet, and they were having a good time. Michael had a particular ability to make a place cozy and elegant, and he taught Lee a lot.''

The apartment was exceptionally well appointed for a couple their age. Lee even used an interior decorator, which seemed extraordinary to their friends, who shopped for furniture at Macy's or Bloomingdale's. When the Canfields finished decorating their new home, they gave a big housewarming party and several Kennedys came, including old man Joe, for Jackie and Jack Kennedy, as everyone knows, finally did become engaged.

Shortly before their September wedding, Michael went to the south of France to look after Jack Bouvier, who was in a clinic drying out before the wedding. Coincidentally, Jack Kennedy was in the south of France on ''a last bachelor fling,'' and Michael met up with him. He was impressed with the number of women who were throwing themselves at Jack, and he would repeat the stories Jack told him to his own friends. They were all the more funny to Michael because Jack as he related them seemed so amazed himself.

Of course, before Michael married Lee, according to everyone who knew him, he had just as successful a scorecard with women as Jack was enjoying now, but he and other equally attractive members of his family lived by a different set of rules. ''Very few people ever heard much about their conquests, because part of the secret of their success was that one really didn't talk about them,'' said a family friend, John Appleton.

Jackie's wedding to Jack took place on a bright, clear, and windy day in Newport. This time Hughdie did have to stand in for Jack Bouvier, who didn't make it after all, and he gave the bride away. Lee was the matron of honor, Michael an usher. The Canfields kept a low profile and left the spotlight to the bride and groom. Along with every other bridesmaid and usher—twenty in all—they made speeches and toasts to the newlyweds. Lee sat next to JFK at the bridal table and watched intently as he and Jackie opened the scores of congratulatory messages that poured in from all over the country.

Michael and Lee socialized at every opportunity with Jack Kennedy and Jackie, especially when the Senator came to New York. On one occasion, the two couples were joined for lunch at the Pavilion restaurant in New York by a third party, Alastair Forbes, a friend of Jack's who later became a good friend of Michael's. Forbes was meeting both sisters for the first time. "Of course, I had some difficulty in hearing what either of them said," he quipped, in reference to their reputation as "those whispering sisters," a designation given them by Randolph Churchill. "I thought Lee much prettier than Jackie, but then Jack wrote on the corner of his menu for me to see: 'Leave her alone. She's married to the lush opposite.' "

When Lee wasn't socializing with her sister and new brother-in-law, she spent a good deal of time with Michael's closely knit, extended family at Crowfields. The Westchester County estate was not just another weekend country house with a swimming pool and tennis court. In the postwar years, Crowfields served as a summer camp for the scions of American publishing and their friends. It was a playground for all the younger people in that family, along with assorted hangers-on—literary types like George Plimpton, John Marquand, and Peter Matthiessen—a huge milling crowd of people, many who were related or semirelated, who ran together for years. The clique at Crowfields was a golden group, and as a son of Cass Canfield, the head of the oldest publishing house in the country, Michael inherently belonged to this literary circle, and by extension so did his wife.

Once their apartment was decorated, Lee needed another creative outlet, and she tried to use the contacts she made at Crowfields to come up with other projects, but in those early days she was uncentered. Her halting attempts at creativity were but the first stirrings of a vague but powerful yearning, a quest that would come one day to possess her. Even then she was dimly aware that she wanted some centrality of her own, something beyond her home and the glamour others admired her for. But what?

13. *After the Honeymoon*

In the spring of 1954, the Canfields attended another Kennedy wedding, when Pat Kennedy married the actor Peter Lawford. Lee looked smashing and was the center of attention, according to one of the guests. With the same aplomb, she sat in her customary box during Tennis Week the following summer and surveyed the Newport scene with Michael and Jackie. She never tired of the social round as long as she was in her own crowd. But friction occurred when she accompanied Michael to obligatory social gatherings at the homes of authors he knew professionally who lived in places like Greenwich Village and Brooklyn—exotic locales for Lee.

On one of these excursions, a writer friend of Michael's heard her complain: "Oh, Michael, realllly! Do we have to go to those places and walk up narrow flights of stairs to those dreary little parties where the whole place smells of cabbage? Why can't you go into the oil business?" The friend remembers: "Michael just laughed and shrugged."

Lee's complaint was not an isolated incident. Already, only a year into the marriage, the happy spell was broken and the basic disagreement over what each of them expected from life was apparent. "Oh, Michael, realllly!" uttered with obvious impatience, became Lee's constant refrain, even in the company of others. Just as Lee's glamorous quality appealed to Michael the most before they were married, now he was finding that her expectations were too high, her sense of entitlement too daunting—glamour was expensive to maintain.

"Lee liked money, there's no question about it," said Cass Junior. "She wanted money, and she wanted to be in society. Lee cared *desperately* about social position. Yet she was very unsure of herself and very insecure about her place in society. Now Michael rather enjoyed society, but he could take it or leave it." Lee's social insecurities resulted in a two-tiered pattern of behavior: she was very careful with those whom she wanted to make a good impression on, and fairly abrupt and arrogant toward those she thought did not matter.

One person Lee deemed not-very-important was her mother-in-law, Katsy Canfield Churchill, a once beautiful, interesting woman with a caustic wit and a difficult personality who, by the time Lee knew her, had grown fat and slovenly and drank too much. "Lee came to supper at my mother's house one time," recalled Katsy's stepson, Jonathan Churchill, "and she made a terrific impression on her as they chatted about Bernard Berenson and Lee's knowledge of art and her various trips to Europe, and they buttered each other up. But Lee never bothered to do that with Katsy. She never thought Katsy was important enough to try to please. You see, when Katsy married my father, he was an out-of-work architect, and her circumstances were much reduced from what they had been when she was married to Cass. Lee didn't have much use for Katsy and my father. They were not as important to her as the Newport or New York social scene.

"There was one time when Michael and Lee came up to visit my father and Katsy in Cambridge, and Lee succeeded in pissing Katsy off immediately. She walked in and spotted an ornate family mirror on the wall and said, 'Oh, Katsy, I love that mirror. When you die, I want you to leave it to me.' And Katsy, who had no intention of dying any time soon, thought Lee was being very presumptuous.

"Katsy got to dislike Lee quite quickly. In simple terms, she did not think she was a good wife. Lee had no idea about marriage. She thought it was a compact of two people going to parties together. Katsy knew that what Michael wanted was the home she had never really provided for him. So for him to choose somebody like Lee, who was egocentric, after press coverage, after herself really —clearly she was the wrong choice for Michael. And once Lee got outside the favored group, she couldn't do anything right, and that went for Jackie and 'Mummy' too. Katsy made fun of all of them. She disliked their breathlessness and their aggressiveness—Jackie, too, was very aggressive about wanting money, personal attention, and social position."

"The thing that was attractive about Lee was her vitality," reflected Blair Fuller, who saw her differently still. "She had a terrific kind of zest. Lee wanted things, and she was determined to have them, and she was burning with this mischievous energy. It was attractive and amusing up to a point. I kind of liked her for it—for being so willful. But being married to it might have been very difficult, because that was what she was doing all the time—wanting things and trying to get them.

"There was a lack of intimacy in the marriage and Lee's personality was paramount in that lack of intimacy. Her agenda precluded real intimacy with Michael because she was always saying things for a reason. This was something you always felt about Lee, that she had an objective, an agenda, and it was more important than anything else."

"Lee definitely had an agenda," Jill Fox agrees, "but I really don't think it was spelled out in her mind then. She was a little girl, really, when she fell for Michael. She hadn't formulated yet what she wanted. By nature Lee was a hungry, hungry person. She had been hungry all her life, and Michael was supposed to satisfy some of that hunger, which he could not. I wouldn't have thought any man could."

Michael's increasing frustration and unhappiness spurred him to drink more and more, and he lost control of himself. In the words of Cass Junior: "Michael felt that he couldn't provide the kind of life Lee seemed to want. He didn't have that much money, and he didn't know how to cope with her lusting after things. It tormented him terribly, and he began to doubt himself and his capacity to achieve, and he started to drink. He must have been destroyed by the fact that Lee was slipping away from him, and that knowledge only added to the drinking. It was hard on her too. He was probably impotent with Lee at times. This was also part of his frustration."

"About a year into the marriage Lee told me that it wasn't working physically," Jill Fox confided. "Sexually it just completely fizzled. I would imagine that impotence fueled by alcohol was what she was complaining about. I think it was a perpetual problem for him. By that time—when she was talking about him not being passionate enough—Lee was desperately unhappy with Michael. I have no idea if she really did go out and have affairs, but she was certainly miserable and talking about it."

It was also becoming apparent to Lee just how unhappy Michael was, even apart from their marital problems. Publishing was never an expression of his real interests, nor was he able to find another niche that satisfied him. Michael told his friends that what he would really like to do, but that no one would ever let him, would be to run a "wonderful store" like the old MM Company on Park Avenue, which sold beautiful leather goods, little engagement books, certain articles of men's clothing—Michael loved all those things. Or else, he said, he would love to have an elegant wine shop with a distinguished clientele. (Later on, he did experiment briefly with owning an antiques shop.)

After several more unhappy months, Lee and Michael decided that a sojourn in London might get their marriage back on track. Michael would represent Harper's in London ferreting out books of interest to Americans, just as his father had done a generation before him.

Going overseas was really Lee's idea. Like Michael's officer in the Marines, she was always a kind of drill sergeant to him. Her eagerness to go abroad also bespoke a restlessness that went deeper than her dissatisfaction with her marriage. "I am afraid that I knew what I didn't want better than what I wanted," Lee confessed later. "The world I grew up in—of family business and bridge playing and special schools—that was something I wanted out of, although I am grateful for having had it. It couldn't have been more pleasant, you understand, and yet it had no meaning for me. Or maybe I should say nothing I was doing had any meaning. That's the point. I got married and out quite early, but I still floundered. I knew what I was running from, but not to."

Michael, too, had his own motives for wanting to leave New York. Aside from placating Lee, he wanted to get away from the pressure of being Cass Canfield's son. Canfield was one of the preeminent figures in all of publishing and one of the great publishers of the twentieth century. There were only half a dozen in that category—Knopf, Delacorte, Bennett Cerf, Harold Guinzburg—who all helped develop a conscience for American letters that vanished with them. Cass Canfield was also a significant figure in Democratic politics and an adviser to presidents and presidential candidates. Being the son of somebody of that stature was not easy.

In the hectic early weeks of 1955 as they prepared for their departure, the Canfields celebrated the Russian New Year with Serge Obolensky and then went down to Palm Beach for several days to visit Jack and Jackie. Before she left, Lee was photographed with Jackie for *Vogue*. The women's magazines looked upon the Bouvier sisters as two beauties in the news. The photo, taken by Horst P. Horst, was for a fashion spread on sweaters worn by socialites. Pretty, well-bred girls stunningly photographed was part of the formula of the magazine, and Horst was considered a master of portraits of social creatures who were not models but who wanted to look as though they were.

At the end of January, after an exhausting round of farewells, Michael and Lee relinquished their apartment and stayed with the Canfields until their departure February 18 on board the SS *United States*. Like a coiled steel spring, Lee Canfield was off to England and her dreams of adventure. Michael Canfield was going home.

14. *A Visit from Jackie*

It was close to midnight five days later when the Canfields arrived at their rented mews house in the Belgravia section of London. The very next evening had them socializing with friends, setting the hectic pace that would never let up. In the early weeks of their arrival Lee busied herself during the daytime hours with fixing up the little house at 14 Chesham Place with wonderful pieces of Regency furniture—just exactly what one would imagine a mews house should have—while various authors joined Michael on a busy round of lunches as he settled into his job at the Harper & Row office on the premises of Hamish Hamilton. At one point Michael took Lee to drinks with the very literary but rather grand Sitwells, who presumably were more to her liking than his Brooklyn-based authors.

The Canfields were an immediate social success. With their looks and charm, they were considered by London hostesses to be an asset and many invitations were extended to them. One couple they saw in London with some regularity at this time, Ambassador and Mrs. Winthrop Aldrich, were friends of Lee's who had been family friends at home. When Lee found out that Aldrich, the American Ambassador to the Court of Saint James, was in need of a social secretary, she pulled some strings to arrange for Michael to interview for the position. Although they had moved immediately into a very social set,

Lee reasoned that if Michael got the job at the Embassy, they would get to go to a lot of important parties, which would make her more prominent on the social scene. It did not take much effort on Lee's part to persuade Michael to abandon publishing and try this new possibility.

The ambassador was allowed to hire one assistant. His job was to take care of the social and some of the personal needs of visiting officials from abroad, usually from the United States, while his wife looked after their wives. Michael got the job and went on a leave of absence from his publishing house. "I think Lee was finished with Michael and that's how he got her to stay with him a little longer," said Tony Hail, another applicant for the position and a social acquaintance of the Canfields who is now a well-known West Coast decorator. "Their marriage was on the rocks, and he induced her to not leave him with the thought that they would have this wonderful job at the Embassy. It was pretty glamorous to have that job."

Michael joined a number of fashionable clubs in order to be able to entertain the ambassador's visitors, and he prided himself on being one of the few Americans allowed membership in White's. He happily ran around meeting Aldrich's friends at airports, getting them into the right clubs, and buying them tickets for the theater. It was an absurd job for a Harvard graduate but he loved it. Living in England brought out Michael's Henry Higgins quality—he adored the club life, the sporting life, the elegance of it all.

As Lee anticipated, Michael's position as Special Assistant to the Ambassador to the Court of Saint James really did put them on the social map, and they went to a good number of very grand parties and balls. As a newcomer, though, Lee had yet to learn the nuances of British etiquette and custom. Tongues wagged at her faux pas when she wore a borrowed tiara in the presence of the Queen Mother and Princess Margaret, who were the honored guests at a formal Embassy function.

Another time, she and Michael spent a weekend at Blenheim, the great ancestral home of the dukes of Marlborough, as the guests of the Marchioness of Blandford. Afterward, Alastair "Ali" Forbes, a Boston Brahmin who was living in England at the time, inquired of her: "How did you get on,

Lee?'' "Oh, it was all right,'' Lee replied, "except that the duke went to the bathroom in the fireplace." "No, dear, not in England, he didn't,'' Forbes corrected her. "One doesn't 'go to the bathroom' in England or France. They poof or have a pee. And the duke, like many lazy English people, often either pees into the fireplace, which is very big at Blenheim, or more commonplace, he simply opens a French window and pees on the lawn outside, and this is ordinary English practice.' But, I mean, Lee just didn't catch on. She never did fit into English society, because she remained hopelessly un-European."

Yet another time, Lee was the object of some disparagement when she left a drawing room at a party where she had just been gossiping about The Rumor (of Michael's royal roots) to one of the guests. Michael was not actively spreading the gossip of his royal antecedent, but he was certainly the original source of it in their circle—it flattered his ego to perpetuate it. Lee, too, was putting the word around London that Michael's real father was—shhhh! don't tell anyone!—"a member of the Royal Family who had an affair with a chambermaid or someone." On this particular occasion, when one English dowager heard the story, she retorted very sniffily to the other guests present: "Every year someone comes to town, usually an American, and makes a claim to being an illegitimate child of someone in the Royal Family. When will they understand that it's just old hat to English society, and we don't pay much attention to it?"

At the beginning of July, Jackie came to visit without Jack, and the next day she joined the Canfields for a weekend at Hermongers, a house in the English countryside belonging to a Kennedy friend, Frankie More O'Ferrall, followed by the Aldriches' Independence Day reception at the Embassy. The trio's nonstop social whirl included a cocktail party in Jackie's honor given by Michael and Lee, lunch at Ascot, a boating party in Devonshire, and a weekend at Blenheim with Sunday afternoon polo.

The sisters went off to Paris by themselves later in the month. Lee was very happy to be with Jackie, even relieved. Their lives were oddly parallel: Jack's never-ending infidelities humiliated Jacqueline, so they were both, albeit for different reasons, unhappily married and childless. When not commiserating with each other, they amused themselves with fashion shows, shopping, and parties —always parties. Interestingly enough, a stateside friend who ran into Jackie and Lee at one of the gatherings they went to said that their carefree behavior "denoted an absence of husbands."

After Paris, "Les Girls," as Michael called them, traveled down to Antibes, where the Canfields had rented a villa for the month of August. The vacationers led a lazy and casual daytime life shuttling between beach and villa. For a change of scene, they were joined by an English friend, Peter Ward, and his girlfriend and future wife, Claire Baring, at Eden Roc, the chic swimming place about a mile west of Antibes made famous in the twenties by the Murphys and Scott Fitzgerald; the group also spent an idyllic day sailing on Ward's boat to Nice.

According to Ward, who is the brother of the Earl of Dudley, when Jackie showed up in London weeks earlier without Jack, it was because she had walked out on him. "We were all together in the south of France," said Ward, and "Jackie left Jack Kennedy at that time. They were split. Jack was having trouble with his back, and Jackie had rather a bad conscience about that, but that was all. She said, 'I'm never going back' in my presence several times. She wasn't the least upset and seemed to be having a very good time."

Whatever Jackie's resolve at that particular moment, in no time flat, in just a matter of days, in fact, she was back with Jack. The Canfields joined the Kennedys for dinner on August 18, and then they made it a foursome for a gala at Monte Carlo. "That was because Jack persuaded her to come back," Ward insists.

Michael and Lee maintained the same nonstop social pace on their holiday as they had in London. They got together with friends they often saw at home, traveled up the coast to visit George Plimpton at an Italian villa, and saw a lot of Jayne Wrightsman, the wife of the oil and gas millionaire Charles Wrightsman, who gave a dinner the Canfields attended for Queen Soraya of Persia; the day after the dinner, Lee, Jackie, and Jayne went on an excursion to Venice; and there were forays to Cannes and Monte Carlo for gambling, and dinners in Saint-Tropez too.

One evening, Lee and Michael joined Stavros Niarchos for

drinks and dinner on his yacht, which was anchored in the nearby harbor. An Anglophile, Niarchos used to invite a multitude of the vacationing English aristocracy for cocktail parties on board his boat, and the Canfields were attached to one of the groups.

In just a few short months, Lee had made a rite of passage from being a relatively obscure American girl newly arrived on Europe's shore to circulating in some of the highest reaches of the British aristocracy and international society. To the shrewd observer, though, she appeared too impressed with her newfound company, a dead giveaway of her outsider status. Ali Forbes, who met up with the Canfields when he was passing through Cap d'Antibes on his way to Italy, remembered, "We had lunch at the Hotel Descartes, and Lee was in a great state of excitement because I had Diana Cooper with me. She was so excited simply because Diana was a big name. She and I were on our way to Ravello to stay with Grace and Stas Radziwill.

"The thing I noticed about Lee was that she was so extraordinarily provincial, really. She was so excited about everything in more of a Judith Kranz, rather than a Henry James, way, if you know what I mean. Lee was like a French concierge reading about Princess Caroline or Princess Stephanie in *Paris-Match*. That's what excited her. She used to say to Michael, 'Oh, listen to Ali. He's known so many famous people. Let him talk about them.' She would get so overexcited about it all. Lee said to herself, 'That's the world I must get into,' and by golly, she got into it!

"You see, both the Bouvier sisters longed to be what the Italians call *prominente,* people who get talked about. They wanted to be in what used to be called the jet set and to know a lot of very rich and important people. Lee was a terrible snob, and in the end she settled for the demimonde, which is what you have in New York—the restaurant world, people who are gossiped about. Lee longed to be talked about, and in the end she was.''

15. *Le Beau Monde*

Both the John F. Kennedys and the Hugh Auchinclosses came to visit the Canfields in October. Michael proudly took Jack Kennedy to White's for lunch, and Hughdie and Janet and Michael and Lee made an excursion to Canterbury, then flew over to Paris for a few days. "I spent an evening with them," said Blair Fuller, who was in Paris writing a novel, "and Lee and her mother treated Hughdie just something terrible. Oh, man, I found it shocking how they bullied him! He just took it."

The Canfields went to Longchamps for the races and attended the wedding of Dolores von Furstenberg to Patrick Guinness before returning with Lee's family to London for a week, after which the foursome went on to Dublin for some Irish hospitality from Frankie and Angela O'Ferrall and an evening at the Abbey Theatre; then the Auchinclosses headed home. By now, Lee was beginning to make other trips to the Continent without Michael. "She turned up in Paris several times," Fuller recalled. "The idea was she was looking for furnishings for their house. Michael would write me a note beforehand and say Lee was coming on such-and-such a day. So on that day I'd call her up at her hotel and ask her for lunch or a drink. For a while there we did meet sometimes, but I quickly saw that she had, shall we say, a rich social life, so I dropped that. When I'd call, Lee would tell me, 'Oh, gosh, I can't do that.' She had to meet so-and-so, or do such-and-such. She was playing around, I'd say. And I didn't want to discuss it with Michael. Once he said to me, 'Did Lee call?' I said 'No.' "

At home in London, the Canfields continued with the routine of their marriage as though nothing were amiss, often spending weekends at Bruern Abbey, the country home of Michael Astor, Lady Astor's third son; another favorite weekend place belonged to William Douglas-Home, the brother of Alec Douglas-Home, the former Prime Minister, in Hampshire. Stavros Niarchos and Douglas Fairbanks, Jr., became two of Lee's social favorites during the holiday season, which was cut short when she flew to New York in mid-December to see family and friends. Joining her a week later, Michael spent Christmas at Merrywood.

At the end of January, Michael and Lee relinquished their rented mews house and moved to a six-month sublet at 120 Mount Street in Mayfair. Lee was back in New York in February and went to a party Peggy Bedford Bancroft gave for Fiat magnate Gianni Agnelli. Michael's preference for ordinary family life always held few attractions for Lee. No matter how boring the party, she genuinely loved the social whirl of the beau monde and was out virtually every night wherever she was: drinks with the Maharajah of Jaipur, dinner with Gore Vidal, a dance given by Gilbert and Kitty Miller, the Queen's Garden Party, Wimbledon, and the Newmarket horse sales were some of the highlights of her spring-to-summer season. And it was about this time that she began to mix noticeably with celebrities from the entertainment world, attending a dinner given for Leslie Caron in May and David Niven in July. Prince Sadruddin Aga Khan, the younger brother of the present Aga Khan, became a frequent companion of Lee's at this time. He found her as charming, fresh, and delightful as did most of the English gentlemen she knew, and rumors of a flirtation made the rounds.

Such surface gaiety helped to mask the disappointment Lee was feeling at the time over her failure to begin a family. When she and Michael were trying to have a child, Michael underwent tests which showed a low sperm count. "It was nothing extraordinary, but it was perhaps why Lee wasn't getting pregnant," Blair Fuller acknowledged. "And on the advice of some doctor, Michael told me—this is absurd—that he was supposed to heat up his balls before he went to bed. He said to me, 'I am supposed to get a little pan of hot water and stand there and poach myself. Actually, I couldn't do it. It was just too humiliating.' So that tells you how much Michael wanted or didn't want children, although if Lee had become pregnant, he certainly would have gone along with it.''

The Canfields continued to pursue doctors' counsel in both England and America. Several physicians concluded that Michael was sterile, and the realization that she was married to a man by whom she could never have children was a severe blow to Lee. What's more, Michael's drinking had ominously worsened since their arrival in England. After coping with an alcoholic father for most of her life, she now had an alcoholic husband on her hands, and many of the couple's mutual friends, such as Lord and Lady Lambton, openly sympathized with her. They said Michael was a terrible drunk, a very nice man but a rather weak character, and a difficult person to be married to.

Friends from home, Chauncey Parker and Philip Geyelin, the husband of Sherry Parker Geyelin, were given a bleak, yet affecting glimpse into the dark gulf which had opened in the marriage when they came to visit the Canfields in the late spring of 1956. "My brother-in-law and I went to their house for dinner," recalled Parker. "I was working in Paris, and Phil had just come over to take over the Paris Bureau of the *Wall Street Journal*. It was a very unhappy evening because Mike had had too much to drink, and he just sat at the end of the dining table looking kind of vague, while Lee was very vivacious and full of beans, and she showed no hesitancy in making it clear to us by the way she talked to him that she thought he was a perfect fool. Both Phil and I were struck by how Michael just sat there and took it. We didn't think in such terms in those days, but today he would have been seen as being overly sedated.

"Well, the evening ended with Michael going upstairs to bed and Phil and me taking Lee to a bunch of nightclubs for an evening on the town. I never understood, ever, why those two got together. It may be that Lee married Michael for the very same reason that she seemed to prefer the company of homosexuals later on—she liked the companionship and there was none of the threat."

With her marriage now so obviously faltering, Lee began to pursue her extramarital interests more openly. Ali Forbes, a dapper and attractive man-about-town, paid her a visit at home one time, and, he says, "Lee did not want me to leave on that occasion. She chased me around a room and locked me in the bedroom, and she got so worked up, it was really quite funny. I called Michael at the Embassy and said, 'Michael, what am I to do? Your wife's locked me up in an upstairs bedroom!' And Michael said, 'Whatever next!' And I said, 'Come and get your wife!' Then he made a joke of it and said to me, 'If you open the window, you might be able

to get along the ledge and let yourself into some other house.'
And I told him, 'It's pouring rain, Michael. I'm not going to
do that!'

"There were many other times like that, and by the standards of English married women, Lee's behavior was quite
mild. When Michael first came to England he became a close
friend. I used to see a lot of them both. The point of my story
is that in my old-fashioned Bostonian way I regarded myself
as Michael's friend first. I could have screwed Lee until the
cows came home, but it's a great complication sleeping with
one's friends' wives just because they want you to.

"And then Lee went and told people that she had slept with
me in order to make them sleep with her, as it were, to show
she was available, or so the Duke of Beaufort told me. He
said that Lee told him, 'I had lovers before,' and he said, 'Like
who?' and Lee replied, 'Ali Forbes.' "

"It was clear Michael was having his affairs too," confirmed Blair Fuller. "I was back in New York in late 'fifty-
six and Michael was full of all this sophisticated talk when he
came to visit about going on these Greek cruises where everybody paired off behind the curtains—he was quite amusing
about So-and-so behind the curtains. I got the impression from
him that they were in a society where everybody was doing
it, that it wasn't even discussed." Michael was referring to the
Mediterranean cruise the Canfields had taken with Stavros
Niarchos the previous summer. Actually a year into their stay,
Michael told John Marquand, Jr., who was living in London
at the time and getting married there (to Sue Coward): "Here
in London, as soon as you are married, you can get anybody
you want in this town. You are going to have more women
than ever before."

It was Lee's clandestine liaison with the very married David
Somerset, on and off over a long period of time, that really
turned her head and made her conclude that Michael was ter-
minally inadequate by comparison. Somerset was descended
from King Edward III and succeeded in 1984 as the eleventh
Duke of Beaufort, a seventeenth-century dukedom with a truly
magnificent family seat, the forty-bedroom Badminton House
set on fifty-two thousand acres in Gloucestershire. Well
dressed and handsome, and an Old Etonian with just the right
amount of arrogance, he was one of England's finest

horsemen, and a yachtsman and pilot into the bargain. As if those advantages were not enough, David Somerset was smart and successful and rich in his own right. Sport was the family obsession until he altered tradition by becoming an art connoisseur. In the years when Lee first knew him, when he was still only in his twenties, Somerset got in on the ground floor of one of Great Britain's most profitable postwar enterprises: Marlborough Fine Art, the international Bond Street gallery which made contemporary art a really big business. Then a director and an art dealer—really more of a contact man selling masterpieces and lesser works to the international crowd, he is now chairman and co-owner and reputedly worth millions of pounds.

In England in those days, moreover, the nobility still had a powerful voice in the nation. Unlike the highest social echelons in America, its authority, by dint of the monarchy and the House of Lords, was officially recognized. It would appear that Lee Bouvier, who more than anything preferred someone with perfect genealogical credentials, had finally met the object of her desire.

Lee's glorious trophy may have been already spoken for, but in village-small social London, marital dalliances were and are completely accepted as long as the rules of discretion are observed —rules which are a necessity in the thicket of an ancient aristocracy's dense network of kinship. In accordance with upper class English custom, when a married woman and her current flame want to spend time together in public, they are careful to have chaperons with them, usually their own spouses. That way, they can enjoy each other's company in full view of society without upsetting the status quo. So it is no surprise that in the Canfields' social calendar for the waning months of 1956, the Somersets' names appear quite often.

Not that Lee was David Somerset's only interest at that time. "The two gentlemen in England who are famous for their love affairs are Beaufort and Lord Lambton," said a lady in his circle. "Everything is well known in our small world. They are definitely known as the lovers of England, known internationally, the numbers are so huge. The duke has always had a lot of charisma with the ladies. He's very good looking, dashing, strong, bright, amusing, witty, and there's no question he's had as long a list of mistresses as anyone can have. Wasn't it always the case that Lee had affairs with men who had a lot of affairs with women? Lee's affair with him was no big deal would be my guess. The big ones are very few.''

16. *Prince Radziwill*

The Canfields moved again in August, this time to a more spacious house at 45 Chester Square. The Chester Square house looked elegant rather than charming in its total effect. On display in her new digs was her collection of narwhal ivory—quite rare pieces. ''It's a curious coincidence. Onassis collected it too,'' said Ali Forbes.

Jackie came for another visit in November. She had given birth to a stillborn child in August and was feeling very depressed. Lee invited her sister to England to help cheer her up. Michael took the opportunity of Jackie's visit to confide in her his own frustration with Lee. He was desperate to try to hold on to her, and it seemed that no matter what he did, she was not satisfied. Michael was bewildered. Had he not taken her to London as she wished? And had he not gone to work at the American Embassy as she wished? Why then was she so discontented? he wanted to know. He asked Jackie what he could do to make her happy. ''When Michael talked to his sister-in-law about it, she did not give him very good advice about how he could improve things,'' attested Ali Forbes. ''Jackie responded with, 'Get more money, Michael!'

''Michael had a modest trust. He also had a salary from the Embassy, and one from Harper & Row, too. I, for one, would have been desperately happy with his income. And when Michael explained to Jackie that by comparison with most couples their age they lived very well and had a very reasonable income—which I expect at that stage was probably tax free, since Michael was working for Aldrich—Jackie said, 'No, Michael, I mean *real* money.' ''

When Lee went to live in England, the balance in the relationship between her and her older sister shifted. Gone were the days when Jackie would write home to Lee from Paris of her exciting adventures, while Lee sighed and longed to be there too. Now it was Lee's turn to write to her sister from London of *her* adventures, while Jackie opened letters and felt envious. With Jackie's day-to-day circle of acquaintances made up mostly of her husband's Irish cronies and relatives, she envied Lee her glamorous life with the international set, and when she came to visit her in London, Lee provided her with an entrée to people she would not have met otherwise.

Jackie's autumn visit coincided with an invitation to the Canfields from Lord and Lady Lambton for a shooting weekend at Fenton, a country house of theirs often used for hunting, which was located not far from the Scottish border in Wooler, Northumberland. Also invited for the weekend were Prince and Princess Stanislas Radziwill.

The entire house party, including the Lambtons, the Radziwills, and Jackie, traveled on the train together for the long ride to the border. The group occupied its own compartment and an atmosphere of merriment prevailed, setting the tone for the weekend. By the end of the journey, the Radziwills and the Canfields had become well acquainted. "The weekend was great irresponsible fun and very lighthearted," remembered Belinda ("Bindy"), Lady Lambton. "We had charades. Stas was very amusing. We all got on terribly well. That's a start, isn't it, if you have a really nice weekend together?"

It was indeed a start. "Stas was so brooding, so serious, I was absolutely terrified," Lee would say later of their first meeting. "I didn't say one word to him the whole weekend, but then our hostess organized a game of charades and dressed him up in one of her old slips. He wasn't so terrifying any-more—this very dignified, masculine figure in all those pink lace frills. And I discovered he had a marvelous sense of humor, a great sense of the ridiculous."

The house party took time out from all the weekend levity to ponder the gravity of international relations when they went to hear their host give a speech in his constituency, Berwick-upon-Tweed, about the Suez Crisis, which had just taken place. A born-to-rule Tory, Lord Lambton was then Parliamentary Private Secretary to the Foreign Secretary, Selwyn Lloyd, and a hardliner on Suez.*

*In 1973, Lord Lambton was the subject of the biggest scandal in the British government since the Profumo affair a decade earlier. The sixth Earl

For both Lee and Michael, the Suez Crisis had been very affecting. When the Egyptian leader, Gamal Abdel Nasser, nationalized the Suez Canal, Great Britain and France readied troops and naval operations to seize it back. The United States under Eisenhower opposed the use of force, and the political situation became critical. For a time, virulent anti-Americanism surfaced in Britain. As Washington dignitaries trafficked in and out of London daily for the duration, Michael worked overtime at the Embassy for weeks in an atmosphere of great tension, until a settlement by diplomatic means ultimately prevailed.

During the crisis, Lee found her homesickness suddenly coming to a head in an unexpected way. She said: "People I had considered my friends would suddenly whirl on me with the most incredible venom, as if I were personally responsible! Well, that sort of experience just makes you care less, doesn't it?"

When Lee sailed, it had never been her intention to stay permanently in London, and over the past several months she had found herself really missing her family and friends. Her homesickness only added to her uncertainty about her future. So it was not a coincidence that the Canfields left London at the beginning of December for a long holiday visit home. Midway through all the homecoming and celebrating, they flew down to Round Hill, Jamaica, to join Jack and Jackie for a week in the sun, returning in time to spend Christmas Eve at Merrywood and Christmas Day at Crowfields in a rare spirit of marital compromise.

With the onset of 1957, everything was in flux at 45 Chester Square, and Michael's career was in transition along with his marriage. Winthrop Aldrich retired at the beginning of February and was replaced by John Hay Whitney. Michael stayed on at the Embassy long enough to ease the transition and then

---

of Durham who disclaimed his peerage for life when he succeeded to the title in 1970, Lambton was caught with a prostitute, Norma Levy, and had to resign. His cousin, William Douglas-Home, proffered this comment to the author: "Most government ministers would have made such visits of ill repute in a taxi, but he went in a big government car with the flag flying, so that was why he was caught. He was very sporting, you see."

returned to his job as Harper & Row's London representative.

Lee had shut all her doors on Michael by now and was scornfully open in her indiscretions. When speaking of this period years later, Michael confessed in a resigned and laconic way to his friend John Appleton, "In those days I never knew when I got home after work whose hat I was going to find hanging on the peg downstairs."

In the shifting minuet of Lee's liaisons, Stas and Grace Radziwill at first overlapped with, and then supplanted, the Somersets as the couple of choice for the Canfields to socialize with—a sure sign that Lee's affair with Stas had begun in earnest. After their November outing, the Lambtons had the Radziwills and the Canfields back to Fenton a number of times, providing Lee and Stas with the opportunity to get to know one another better and ultimately to become lovers.

"Stas took worldliness many jumps beyond Michael," said Jill Fox, "but there was something of a kind there—a certain shrewd and joking playboy quality. It was avoiding life in certain ways." But unlike his younger counterpart, Stas had Old World authority and prestige to offer. Descendant in the eighteenth generation of a preeminent Polish family of Lithuanian origin, the Radziwills had acquired the kind of wealth and influence over the centuries that the modern political revolutions were intended to rout. Such a heritage was reflected in Stas's tremendous presence, for the man was suffused with more than a touch of the ancien régime.

He was born Stanislas Albert Radziwill on July 12, 1914, at Szpanow, in Volhynia, Poland. One of four children, Stas grew up on a family estate about forty miles outside of Warsaw and led the typical life of an aristocrat of his generation, indulging his love of hunting and the land. His grandfather Ferdinand had sat in the German *Reichstag* as a representative of the Polish national minority, and his father, Janusz, had led the Polish Conservative Party in restored Poland after the First World War. Upon completing his secondary studies at local schools, Stas attended the Catholic University in Fribourg, Switzerland. He wrote his thesis on the Ukrainians in Poland, and after graduating in 1937 as *licencie es arts,* he was appointed deputy governor of the province of Stanislawow, which had the largest Ukrainian majority in Poland. He, too, expected to spend his life in government service.

The Nazi invasion of Poland changed his plans and his fate. Stas managed to flee the oncoming German Army, but the subsequent Russian Occupation left him penniless, and after the war he set out to regain some of the fortune his family had lost. When Stas arrived in London in 1946 "much too frightened to be homesick," as he put it, there was easy money and big money to be made in the development boom of post-war London reconstruction if one only had the right connections. It was hardly a coincidence that a landed aristocrat like Stanislas Radziwill would be drawn to making money off "real estate," the modern concept of land ownership.

The ambitious Polish refugee formed an alliance with no less than Felix Fenston, one of England's great property kings. He did reasonably well for himself and was eventually given British citizenship. When Stas became a British subject, he forfeited the right to use his hereditary title of Prince of the Holy Roman Empire, a title conferred on his family in the sixteenth century. His continued insistence on being addressed as Prince Radziwill always remained controversial in Britain.

At the time he met Lee, Stas (pronounced "Stash") was married to his second wife, Maria Grace Kolin, the daughter of Michel Kolin, a wealthy shipping executive from Dubrovnik, Yugoslavia. Many people thought Stas bore a noticeable physical resemblance to Jack Bouvier. They had the same stocky physique, broad face, and thin mustache—and nineteen years Lee's senior, he was closer to her father's generation than to her own.

Certainly Lee found the colorful and talkative Polish patriot fascinating and unlike anyone she had ever known before. "There was a special kind of glamour to Stas. He was older, in business with Felix Fenston, and he was someone with a well-known name," said a London friend. Stas's generosity and decency also impressed Lee, as did, needless to say, his supposed wealth and ancient title. Stas, in turn, thought Lee beautiful and bewitching. Most important, the two shared the same element of fantasy in the way they related to the world. Stas had continued to play the grand Polish nobleman even when he was broke in England, and Lee habitually romanticized her attraction to the good and the great. By the beginning of summer, events had progressed rapidly enough for Stas to start thinking of whether or not he should leave his wife for her.

A cruise the Canfields took in June for several days along the Italian coast on board the Wrightsmans' impressive yacht, *Radiant,* served as a distraction from the evolving romance; the sailing party put in at Capri and Positano, among other destinations. Back in London, nonstop fashionable parties, including an affair given by Mike Todd to celebrate the success of *Around the World In 80 Days* and an Embassy reception for Adlai Stevenson—the man of the hour—served temporarily to divert Lee's attention from her decision when and if to leave Michael.

The more involved Lee and Stas became with the passing weeks, the more time Lee and Michael and Stas and Grace spent together. It reached the point where Stas's social life almost preempted the Canfields' life together. At Lee's prodding (Lee-the-drill-sergeant) Michael often found himself going to dinner parties with the likes of real estate tycoon Charles Clore and Sir Francis Peake, another two of Stas's business associates. The two couples even went on double dates to the movies; one July evening the Radziwills brought their young son John along with them to see *The Prince and the Show Girl,* and he could not help but notice how Lee went out of her way to be nice to him.

Stas had a very disconcerting way of teasing his friends. He would make the most outrageous declarations in the nicest and most charming way. For example, Bindy Lambton tells the story of how they and some other friends of theirs were once in Nassau on their way to a nightclub when Stas put his arm around one of the group, Jerry Zipkin, and in a friendly voice said: "Do come with us, and when we get there, we shoot you!" "A very alarming thing for a Pole to say, wasn't it?" Lambton asked. "Zipkin looked discomfited."

One time Stas said to Michael, who repeated it to Jill Fox: "I really think your wife is absolutely delicious, and I am pursuing her!" "Michael thought it was very amusing," Fox recalled, "and then he said, 'You know, he is quite something and reminds me of Black Jack.' Michael laughed as he told me this. Then he was full of regret later. But I think he felt powerless. Radziwill meant it, of course. He did pursue her and take her."

In August, the Radziwills invited the Canfields to their villa in Sicily for a holiday. They had taken a lease on the Castello di Trabia, the family seat of the Lancer di Trabia family located in a little town about twenty miles outside of Palermo. "It's not so much a villa as a bloody great palazzo," reported Ali Forbes.

No sooner had the Canfields arrived in Sicily than Lee received a telegram notifying her that her father had died. She and Michael left immediately for New York. Stas was keenly disappointed at the sudden loss of his special guest, and he confessed to Ali Forbes, who had also gone there to stay with the Radziwills, how much he had been looking forward to seeing her.

"After she'd gone, Stas asked me what I thought of Lee," said Forbes, "and whether I thought she would make a suitable consort for him. He was obviously quite smitten with her, because on the whole Stas only wanted money. But in that case he was really in love with Lee. I was hardly likely to list her possible faults if his mind was going that way, so I said nice things to him."

When Lee arrived in New York, Jackie, who was close by, had already made all the arrangements for their father's burial. The funeral took place the morning of August 6 in the Bouvier chapel at Saint Patrick's Cathedral. In addition to the handful of women friends who sat conspicuously at the back of the church, only two dozen friends and acquaintances, besides family, attended the service. Jack Bouvier was sixty-six years old.

He was laid to rest in midafternoon at Saint Philomena's Cemetery in East Hampton. During the burial ceremony, the mournful whistle of a passing Long Island Railroad train could be heard distractingly in the background. The sound brought back to Lee a flood of childhood memories of times with her father.

She would always remember him in an affectionate way shaded with great pity and sorrow. "We were his life. He never created another life for himself, except us," she said. "His children grew up and went their ways. He became more and more of a recluse. My father always felt he was a failure in some way. In the end he was a heartbreaking figure."

17. *The Bolting Coat*

Michael and Lee decided that as long as they were home they would make the most of it. After the funeral, they visited Hammersmith Farm, then went on to Fishers Island and Martha's Vineyard to see Katsy, then back to Newport for a formal dinner and Michael's thirty-first birthday celebration.

In the late autumn, Lee and Jackie posed again for a women's magazine, this time separately. Taking its cue from *Vogue, Ladies' Home Journal* ran an article entitled "There's Something About Them." Described in the piece as "intensely feminine," Lee articulated her ideas about clothes, a fashion philosophy which has remained remarkably consistent through the years: she preferred, she said, "terribly simple clothes," interesting handbags and shoes, and pretty jewelry. Ever mindful of the gray English climate, she chose a wardrobe aflame with color, as many colors as could be found in an English garden, because, she said, they cheered her up. After Lee and Jackie posed for the photographs, they insisted that they be given the clothes they had modeled, a demand the magazine found brazen.

The novelty of living abroad had begun to wear off, and Lee began to make trips to New York on a more frequent basis. On one such visit in mid-December, she attended the service at Saint Patrick's Cathedral for the christening of her godchild, Caroline Bouvier Kennedy, born to Jacqueline a few weeks earlier—a reminder, if yet another was needed, of how empty her life was with Michael.

In February, Stas indicated to Lee that he wanted to marry her, giving her the signal that she had been waiting for. She felt enormously relieved. The months of drifting, uncertainty, and deceit were finally at an end. All there was left to do was to tell Michael the bad news. When Lee announced to him that she was leaving him for Stas, he opted to let her go with a flourish. Coincidentally, he had just purchased a new coat for her. A romantic at heart, he decided to present it to Lee as a "bolting coat." This was something he had picked up in an English novel, Nancy Mitford's *The Pursuit of Love*. A lover of the heroine gave her a bolting coat, that is to say, a coat with which to leave him. For the moment, at least, Michael was quite pleased with himself for making what he saw as a gesture of the ultimate sophistication.

Once Lee had gone, however, and Michael had time to digest the full impact of the dissolution of his marriage, he no longer felt so cavalier. In fact, he was devastated. "I saw Michael cry a few times," acknowledged Jill Fox. "He had great regrets and Lee was certainly one of them."

Having already found her next-in-line, Lee, meanwhile, just sailed right along, with a touch of guilt perhaps, but with her ego relatively unscathed. In the ultimate put-down of her first marriage, she would say later: "Everything serious in my life happened to me after the age of twenty."

"Lee did not ever see that he was really a lovable man, Michael," said Blair Fuller. "His lovableness had to do with this gloomy, vulnerable soul putting on a perfect suit of clothes so that he could move through the world, and then one discovered the disparity between the perfect suit of clothes and what was inside. Back then, it seemed as though Lee knew how to make the world right. Michael never thought any such thing. His perfect suit of clothes was defensive.

"But in a way, you see, Lee was not wrong to choose him. With Michael, she went in the direction she wanted to go, which was to London to be received in the sort of society she wanted to be received in. Michael had the elegance and the charm for it. And then she wanted to go further, so she left him behind. They were right for each other at that time in their lives, even though it didn't last."

Michael never returned to America to live. He went on to become quite well known in Anglo-American social circles and his second marriage, to Laura Dudley (the sister-in-law of Ian Fleming), was a solid one. She gave him the comforts of home he always wanted, and the rich, ritualistic English country life he shared with her suited him well.

He never resolved the conflict of his dual heritage, though, nor did he ever get rid of his demons, and they claimed him in the end. Michael drank more than ever in his last years and was taking medication to combat depression. On a flight to London in December 1969, at the age of forty-three, his death wish was at last fulfilled: He went into a coma and his heart stopped. Michael died from a lethal combination of drink and pills.

Michael Canfield always had an enormous sense of irony about his life and would have been the first to appreciate the cruel symbolism of his death: he died in the sky between America and England, neither quite in one, nor the other. He died as he lived.

18. *In* VOGUE

In anticipation of the 1958 World's Fair to be held in Brussels, the State Department wrote to *Vogue* magazine some months before the spring opening and asked it to select American-made clothes for the fashion showings to be held in the United States pavilion. The fashion show was intended to be both an appealing bit of Americana and a boost to the American fashion industry.

At one of *Vogue*'s many planning sessions for the show, Lee's name was proposed to represent the magazine at the Fair and to lend cachet to the project. The editors felt that she transmitted a certain American quality; her on-the-scene European residency was the other reason she was selected. Lee gladly accepted the invitation and the challenge. She was to help get the show going and give it its rhythm and discipline.

The magazine did a tie-in spread on the World's Fair for its mid-April issue, which included a prominently displayed picture of Lee, describing her as its permanent representative at the Fair, on the spot to "cue" the show from its opening in April until the last round of fireworks in October. Lee's selection by *Vogue* was another example of its policy of utilizing well-known society women for their publicity value.

Lee now had even more reason to make return trips to the United States, and in the early months of 1958 she was often in New York to attend *Vogue*'s planning sessions for the fashion show. "On the American side, in the beginning, Lee was very enthusiastic and gung ho," noted fashion editor Catherine McManus di Montezemolo. "She was very sharp and on top of everything. I remember her working hard and being very enthusiastic and talking to me about Jackie's new baby."

The fashion show exhibit at the American pavilion attracted an enormous crowd. At Lee's direction, spectators watched the models wend their way from the balcony of the pavilion to "living areas" of the display, negotiating the pool there by boat or float. By the time the show closed, Lee had directed four different fashion shows to allow for changes in the seasons. Behind the scenes, she helped select the models and which outfits they wore, and as time passed and they changed the clothes, she would report to *Vogue* what was really working and how good the system was over there. But her main contribution was her presence. "She was a conversation piece, and a good one," said *Vogue*'s former executive editor, Mildred Morton Gilbert. "When we needed her to be a front, we could call on her. She was a wonderful front, very gracious and nice. Lee used her name. I mean, her name stood for something, you know?"

In later years, Lee gave the impression of having had more clout and responsibility for the fashion show than was actually the case. Enhancing her résumé once again, she told a reporter that she spent six months putting on a continuous fashion show in the American pavilion at the Brussels fair. "Not so," said Mildred Gilbert: "I was sent over from New York to be in charge of running that show, to keep it going smoothly, and to see to it that things got done politically and financially right, and Susan Train, who was under me, was sent over from the Paris office to run it day-to-day. Lee was sent to Brussels as a glamour person and to represent an editorial point of view. She was not in charge. She wasn't there all the time. She only stayed in Brussels on and off. She was busy going back and forth from England to the States."

As Cathy di Montezemolo remembers it: "My impression came from Susan Train, but when Lee got over to Europe after the New York meetings, where the real work and drudgery was, there was this sloping off on her part. She really dragged her heels at the end of it. She was considered a dilettante on it. The show went on forever, and who's to blame her? Maybe she got bored with the whole thing."

It is possible that the staff in New York may have had one expectation of Lee, and the hands-on Brussels contingent another, causing some confusion. At any rate, Stas came there often to see her, and when Lee was not busy with the show,

they strolled the cobblestone streets of Brussels and toured the
slate-roofed villages of the scenic Belgian countryside. Besides
Stas, several of Lee's friends came to see her handiwork at
the Fair. Even Michael made an appearance, spending a couple
of days with her in August and dining chez Lee afterward at
her place on the rue de l'Industrie.

American fashion had not yet come of age, and Brussels
was too close to Paris for American clothes to make the impression they might have made in another setting, but the fashion show was very popular with the Fair's visitors and judged
to be a big success. It was also considered a success in the
propaganda war raging between the Soviet Union and the
United States. One American newspaper reported: ''Garnering
most of the attention in the Soviet exhibition hall was a model
of Sputnik II. The attraction across the way was a fashion
show. The size of the crowd suggested that pretty girls and
high fashion could hold their own against models of satel-
lites.''

19. *The Pauper Prince*

''Shit! I've been robbed!'' Stas used to love to say. This observation often took place while he was sitting up in bed,
eating a boiled egg, and counting on his fingers in Polish. Stas
was always counting his money, money he thought he should
have and knew he lost somewhere. It was all fantasy and done
as a joke, of course—the poor boy who arrived in England
with nothing. It was more complicated than that, but Stas liked
to keep it simple. He would love to have been immensely rich
the way he used to be. Those who knew him well say that
Stas did not think people could like him just for himself and
that only wealth gave him a feeling of confidence.

Stas's family stood at the very peak of the dispossessed
Polish aristocracy. Originally a Lithuanian boyar family who
traced its roots to medieval times, the Radziwills were related
to the Piast dynasty that reigned over Poland for several centuries and, through marriage, to almost all the reigning dynas-
ties of Europe. Over the generations the family produced

generals, statesmen, and dignitaries of the Catholic Church, who collectively represented a formidable political power. They held the highest government offices and exerted a significant influence over the decisions of their sovereigns and the course of political affairs. They even maintained their own private armies, dispensed justice, and sent ambassadors to the Courts of Europe.

The family wealth in great landed estates was consolidated between the end of the fourteenth and the middle of the sixteenth centuries. The Radziwills virtually owned Lithuania, and their possessions, even in terms of eras past, were stupendous. But as the generations rolled by, the Radziwill fortune began to wax and wane. One generation might do nothing to increase the family's wealth and allow it to seriously diminish, then in the next generation someone like Prince Janusz, Stas's father, would come along and make it back. Extremely land-rich, Janusz's wealth derived principally from a vast forestry enterprise of timber exports to the rest of Europe.

On the day of the Nazi invasion, when the Radziwill fortunes would change forever, the whole family, except Stas, was at the family castle at Olyka, near the Russian border. Janusz, who had been appointed Duke of Olyka during World War I by the last Czar and was considered the dean of the Radziwill family in the present generation, was arrested by the Russians and taken to a prison in Moscow. The intervention of King Victor Emmanuel III of Italy got him released the following year, and he was allowed to return to his country palace at Nieborów in German-occupied Poland.

Shortly after the "liberation" of Poland by the Soviet Army, Prince Janusz was deported to a camp near Krasnoyarsk. His wife, Princess Anna, was deported along with him and died there. Stalin's murderous henchman, Lavrenti Beria, paid Janusz a visit at the camp and asked him to head a provisional government in Poland. (One cannot fail to appreciate the great irony of such a scene: the ultimate Communist asking the consummate aristocrat to lead a government.) Janusz declined. Upon his release from prison Janusz refused to leave

Poland. His homes and property confiscated, he lived out his days in a two-room flat given him by the mayor of Warsaw and paid for by Stas, while his Warsaw residence became the Lenin Museum. Not insignificantly, the Communists, in recognition of his patriotism, gave him a state funeral when he died in 1967.

Stas had been mobilized into the Polish Army and was on the western front the day the Germans came. He fought in the war as a cavalry officer before the Polish Army was routed (a cavalry charge against German tanks!), and in the general confusion when Poland collapsed he managed to get out of the country, escaping across Hungary and Yugoslavia to Paris. The Sikorski government-in-exile sent him on to Geneva as the representative of the Polish Red Cross at International Red Cross headquarters (his father had been president of the Polish Red Cross). Stas remained in Geneva for the rest of the war and married a Swiss woman, Roselyne de Monléon, whom he had met while at the University of Fribourg.

Stas's marriage to Roselyne was of brief duration. He walked out on her when he courted Grace Kolin, herself a refugee like Stas who was living in Switzerland at the time. They came to London together and married in 1946. Both were stateless people and had a hard time getting British citizenship. In the war's aftermath, there were thousands upon thousands of refugees in Europe looking for homes. After much struggle, the Radziwills went to the Bahamas and obtained British passports by the back door: they had a house in Nassau, which was still a British colony. Stas's Bahamian-British passport ultimately worked out very well for him for tax purposes.

Stas met Felix Fenston, the prolific and charismatic London developer and property impresario, in Nassau right after the war and each immediately sensed an opportunity. Fenston thought they could develop an interesting relationship based on his property know-how and ability to raise money, combined with Stas Radziwill's charm, princely background, and connections. Stas, too, thought it would be an unbeatable combination. ''They may have thought that, but it didn't prove to be so at the end of the day. The things they got into never really worked," said Fenston's tax consultant, Sidney Morris, who advised the pair on their joint ventures. "But it was a relationship where both sides had something to contribute, and they worked together for twenty years or more." Fenston always remained the main engine of the partnership, however. Whatever money Stas made, it was almost entirely through his relationship with Fenston. Stas was just a status emblem for him.

Stas became the black sheep of the Radziwill family because in those days real estate was not the business of the nobility. Essentially, Stas sold his connections for money, and he was quite open about it too. There were so many people he knew, that if one wanted an entrée anywhere in London, right up to the Queen, one simply asked him and he opened the door. In exchange for his effort, Stas took a cut in the equity.

One project Stas developed in his early years with Lee was named after her: Lee House was an eighteen-story office block erected in the City of London. Profitable but truly hideous, it eventually had the distinction of being the first postwar office building to be torn down.

During the course of their history, the Radziwill family developed the expedient of having one son live in Russia and one in Germany, as well as keeping one son in Poland, so that they could lay claim to their inheritances, since only Russian and German subjects could inherit land. They always saw to it that they had protection and influence so that whichever way the political wind blew, they were covered. Stas was a player in that consummate circle of the old European aristocracy—the King of Bulgaria, the Pretender of France, that sort of crowd. He preferred the old loyalties and was very much at variance with the modern world.

Stas played his princely role to the hilt, sometimes to comic effect, or to an extent that indicated a removal from reality, depending on one's point of view. Once, after he had been living in England for more than two decades, he and a business associate, Gerald Smith, arrived at London Airport after a business trip, and Stas invited Smith home for lunch. As he needed to inform his chef, they went to a public telephone.

Stas stopped in front of it, stared at it, then turned to Smith and said, "How do I work one of these?"

Stas Radziwill may have been regal but he was not a snob. Friends describe him as having a big Polish heart and great human warmth, someone who often laughed until the tears rolled down his cheeks, and who, to the embarrassment of his close male British friends, liked to walk down the street with them arm-in-arm, in continental fashion.

"Even after they had lost everything, many of those old-family Russian and Polish emigrés kept a certain nobility in themselves and a way of having fun," observed a friend of Stas's, Elisabeth, Lady Ampthill. "Anything and everything was a reason to rejoice. It was a marvelous quality of 'Let's make it a party,' but in the good sense of celebrating life. Stas had that quality to the gills."

"Stas's social life was one thing, but he had depth and a great sense of people and values. He knew exactly what was right and wrong," said his niece Isabelle, Comtesse d'Ornano. "He really had values which made him original in the world he lived in, a world which can be very superficial. And he was wonderful to his family in Poland. He saw them go through so much. They all lived thanks to him. Stas was a great personality, someone you would not forget. But Stas could be outrageously abrupt when it suited him, and a lot of people did not like him because he would dismiss them completely if he disliked them or thought they were superficial. Stas could be quite rough."

Stas's traditional Polish education and upbringing gave him a peculiar slant on life. He was very much prone to the grand gesture and had an immovable trust in people to a fault. When the Germans were pouring into Poland and he was trying to get out, he recognized a friend from his university days who was by that time a German Army officer. Stas jumped on the running board of his car, he told friends, and asked his old friend for a lift! The officer simply knocked him off the car with his gloved hand. Years later they met again in London. Both behaved like gentlemen, and Stas made it plain to the German that he bore him no malice. It was just an affair of the moment, he said.

*   *   *

When Stas left his second wife to marry Lee, he moved into a duplex flat in the Belgravia section of London for several months as an interim measure, and when Lee returned from Brussels, she rented a tiny house on Walton Street, close by Harrods department store in Knightsbridge. As if to underscore the absence of any male influence for once, the drawing room in her house was pink. Her father had left her his writing desk and a bequest of approximately $80,000 after taxes in his will. That money came in handy now that she was on her own.

One of the first hosts in London to receive Stas and Lee as a couple in the waning months of 1958 was David Metcalfe, one of social London's familiar figures and partygoers.* He and his wife had a house on Swan Walk and one night they gave a big dinner party. That same evening they had been around the corner at some cocktail party first and were a fraction too late in getting back. Some of their guests had already arrived. Lee, for one, had arrived alone. Stas was a bit late himself. The Metcalfes had a rather big drawing room and a small group of women stood at one end of it and Lee was alone—and quite uncomfortable—at the other. She said to Metcalfe later, "It's a good thing you came when you did because the other women wouldn't speak to me."

"A lot of people saw Lee as having seduced Stas away from Grace because Grace was enormously popular," said Metcalfe. "She was a very good hostess and entertained a lot, so she was somebody social London knew very well. Actually, it was a big scandal when Stas left Grace. Oh, God, she was terribly upset, and not only upset but very bitter. I've never known anyone to carry on like that! God, yes, it was a big, big deal!

"When Stas was married to Grace, I knew them very well, and that marriage wasn't doing very well anyway.

---

*An insurance company executive, David Metcalfe is the grandson of Lord Curzon and the son of Edward "Fruity" Metcalfe, one of the Duke of Windsor's inner circle when he was the Prince of Wales and best man at his wedding to Wallis Simpson.

Then he met Lee and that was it. It was a bit tough for them, but I don't think Stas cared. He didn't give a damn what people thought. I would say Lee felt uncomfortable for a period.''

Lee had broken one of the unspoken rules of London society in those days: it was all right to sleep with someone else's husband, but not to snatch him away. Grace's enmity toward Lee lengthened into a feud when the latter became an influential and rival society hostess in the sixties. A certain hairdresser was advised to see to it that the two women did not come into his salon at the same time. Their mutual dislike was something that was whispered about in the drawing rooms of London, and traces of the ill will that Lee generated for herself in London society when she stole her second husband away from a popular hostess stayed with her all her years there.

On another front, some in her set whispered behind her back that her husband's occupation as a real estate developer was not that of a gentleman. Granted the English can be very snobbish, but even Harry Hyams, the big-daddy developer of them all, and with whom Stas had done some deals, conceded at the time that ''the image of the property man is of a land speculator and shark,'' and Felix Fenston was referred to scornfully around London as ''the man who tore down the St. James Theatre.''

Lee was also plagued by the persistent snickering over her and Stas's preference for using the technically defunct Radziwill titles of Prince and Princess. Moreover, many in London thought she overplayed her princess role. For all of these reasons, Lee felt she had a tough time getting fully accepted into English society, if she ever was.

She had an easier time of it socially when she and Stas visited the States. One evening when they were in New York, the couple gave a party at the brownstone apartment where they were staying. ''A friend of mine and her husband had an apartment in the same brownstone,'' said Lee's old school friend Vale Asche Ackerman. ''Lee and I ran into each other in the building's teeny, tiny elevator. We had not seen each other since Farmington, and she said to me, 'Please, we are having a few people over for cocktails. Join us.'

"So we went down to her flat. It was a typical New York cocktail party with no place to sit. Then at one point a guest came up to me and said, 'Now if you don't have to go to the bathroom, you must make it a point to go anyway.' So I said, 'What do you mean?' and the guest said, 'Well, you just go in there.' So I did, and when I flushed, I noticed a little baby gardenia going down. Well, when I left the bathroom I stepped back to see what was going to happen next. Suddenly, a little maid rushed by me and dropped another baby gardenia in the toilet bowl. I thought that was carrying exquisiteness to the extreme."

When Stas and Lee got back to London, Stas continued with the protracted fight he and Grace were having over their marital assets. Stas had not realized what difficulties he was going to get into with Grace about money: at first she wanted to keep it all. True, he had nothing when he met her. True, by the time of the divorce he was living extremely well, and true, he had used some of her money in his real estate investments. But Stas's lawyers were able to argue that since a fortune had been made by his property activities, a more fair division of the spoils should take place, which it did.

When the Christmas holidays came around, Lee was thrilled to discover that she was pregnant, and for this reason she was now in a big hurry to be remarried. Her divorce from Michael was quick and Stas's divorce from Grace became final on March 6, 1959. He did not contest his wife's petition on the grounds of "his adultery in Paris the previous July with a woman whose identity he refused to disclose," and he was ordered to pay costs. Lee and Stas flew to Virginia the following week to be married. With only her immediate family present, she described the March 19 affair as "the quietest quiet little wedding at my parents' home." The Radziwills left for New York right after the small dinner Hughdie and Janet gave for them, and they were quickly back in London after that.

The following year Michael Canfield was to marry Laura Charteris, whose last husband was the Earl of Dudley, whose next wife was to be Grace Kolin Radziwill, who, of course, had been married to Stas Radziwill, who had left her in order to marry Michael's previous wife, Lee. There was much trans atlantic gossip and comment about the marital merry-go-round and Laura once penned a fair comment of the whole affair:

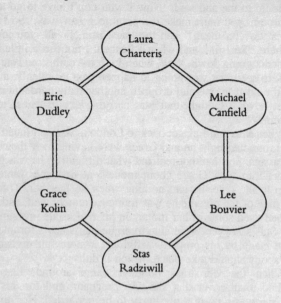

20. *Holy Matrimony*

On November 12, 1967, the Italian police confiscated all newsstand copies of that week's issue of the now-defunct magazine *ABC*, because it contained a very detailed account of the Vatican's role in the annulment of Lee's marriage to Michael Canfield. Why the Vatican felt such drastic action was warranted is an interesting story, and it began in June of 1958.

The pursuit of Lee's annulment was Stas's idea. The Roman Catholic faith teaches that marriages blessed in heaven cannot be dissolved on earth, and it does not permit divorce. But it will concede in rare cases that some marriages were null and void from the beginning. As a practicing Roman Catholic, Stas himself had spent years getting his own marriage to Roselyne de Monléon annulled while he was married to Grace Kolin, and since Stas's marriage to Grace was a civil one, it was not recognized by the Church. With his annulment from de Monléon in tow, Stas was free to wed Lee in a church ceremony. But since Lee had wed Michael before a priest, the Church could not accept her divorce, nor did it recognize, of course, the validity of her subsequent civil marriage to Stas. Technically speaking, Lee was an adulteress living with her Prince in a state of sin. An annulment of her marriage to Michael Canfield would enable her and Stas to remarry in a religious ceremony and to resume receiving the sacraments.

Stas's motive in wanting Lee to obtain an annulment was to placate his disapproving father, whom he greatly respected. A stern patriarch who believed passionately in observing tradition, Prince Janusz was not only disapproving of his son's three marriages, he disapproved of his whole way of life in the West. He showed his displeasure by remaining polite but distant to Stas's second and third wives.

"Stas's father was a devout Catholic for whom principles were very important," said Stas's niece, Isabelle d'Ornano, "and what his father thought of his behavior was very important to Stas. He was profoundly attached to his family."

Janusz appealed to Stas's conscience by setting an example of someone living a more morally worthy life: though Stas had tried to persuade him to come to London to live, the Prince had chosen to stay in his homeland, suffering acutely under the Communist regime but remaining true to his Radziwill heritage. These convictions had been shared by Stas's mother, Anna, neé Lubomirska, right up to her death in a prisoner-of-war camp and whose grave was never found. "My grandmother had never wanted to leave Poland," d'Ornano explained, "because she thought that if people like her and my grandfather left the country, people who knew the history of Poland and belonged to the aristocracy, then Poland would become just like Russia, without its history and without roots."

Stas admired his family enormously for the courage of their convictions, and he felt deep compassion for them for what they endured. (His older brother, Edmund, was ordered to be shot during the war by the Communists. Only the workers on his estate, who interceded on his behalf, saved him.) Stas's comfortable expatriate life in the West left him feeling guilty by comparison, and he wished to compensate in some way. The least he could do was to appease his father by getting recognition of his marriage from the Church, particularly since, like Janusz, he sought refuge in his religion as a stabilizing influence in the midst of agonizing upheaval.

In June 1958, while Lee was residing in Brussels, she wrote to Cardinal Spellman of New York asking him to undertake the necessary preliminaries on her behalf to initiate an ecclesiastical trial to have her marriage annulled; Spellman was a Kennedy family friend, and Lee wrote to him apparently at Joe Kennedy's suggestion.

Now that Lee was an American living permanently abroad, the question of which jurisdiction was appropriate had to be dealt with first. With that problem in mind, Spellman wrote to a Roman Cardinal, Pizzardo, about the feasibility of choosing a European jurisdiction for Lee's annulment proceedings. Pizzardo answered that there would be no obstacle. Later in the proceedings, Lee would say that a European jurisdiction was Spellman's idea, not hers, and she believed that his motivation in choosing it was political on behalf of the Kennedys.

Lee's next step was to hire a lawyer, Fernando Della Rocca, an expert on Vatican law and a lay advocate who argued cases before the Church's high court, the Sacra Romana Rota. In the fall of 1958, the Westminster Tribunal began its examination of Lee's case. An annulment is technically a ruling that no true marriage had ever existed, because of an essential flaw in the marital contract. In her application for a declaration of annulment, Lee stated that she was not convinced at the time of her nuptials of the "indissolubility" of the bond of matrimony, and that she possessed "a mental reservation" toward the formation of a family, considered by the Church to be one of the primary aims of a Roman Catholic marriage. (This line of reasoning is commonly used by Catholics to obtain an annulment.)

Lee was interrogated in London and her first witnesses, Rue Hill, her sister Jackie, and a Bouvier cousin, were interrogated in New York. "I had to go before that tribunal and answer intimate questions. They wanted to know about Lee's attitude toward marriage at that time," Rue Hill Hubert recalled. "It was a nightmare, absolutely ghastly."

Just as Lee's case was being examined by the London Tribunal and was taking its course, she made a colossal mistake: she and Stas married in that civil ceremony in March of 1959. When the Church heard of this civil marriage, they called it an "indignity," suspended the pending rotal judgment, and sent the suit to Rome. A long silence ensued. Unlike the London Tribunal, which is more akin to a conventional court of law, the Supreme Tribunal of the Holy Office does not assemble evidence for a trial but deliberates in absolute secrecy, without hearing the two sides of a case or witnesses. Della Rocca believed Lee's civil marriage was disastrous for her annulment proceedings, and he warned her not to be hopeful, but she was determined, justifying the civil marriage ceremony on the grounds that she was pregnant.

After months of "prayerful waiting" by Lee, a ruling was handed down in the spring of 1961: her petition was refused with no possibility of appeal. The Canfield marriage was valid, and were it not for the fact that her brother-in-law had been elected the first Catholic president of the United States in the intervening three years since she first made her application, the matter most likely would have ended there. But obviously the thing to do now, the Radziwills and Della Rocca reasoned, was to take advantage of the new situation and devise a strategy using President Kennedy's influence with the Pope, the only exponent of the Church who could reverse the decision of the Holy Office.

Della Rocca approached a Milanese friend and colleague, Ulisse Mazzolini, who had a contact with Pope John through the international Balzan Foundation, of which he was vice president. Della Rocca sold the idea to Mazzolini by saying that the Foundation's intervention on Lee's behalf would elicit the Kennedys' gratitude and promote useful contacts for it in Washington.

On May 10, Della Rocca met with Mazzolini and a prelate, Monsignor Bruno Vittori, and examined their options to reopen the case in the Vatican, and the following week the Radziwills made a visit to Rome to help plan the new strategy, which Della Rocca referred to as "the battle plan." According to this "battle plan," Mazzolini was to prevail upon Philipp

Etter, an "illustrious personality" and the former President of Switzerland, to "hit the target in the best way possible." Etter was the head of the financial committee of the Balzan Foundation and through its auspices was to make the official contact with "the target," Pope John XXIII. In order to motivate Etter to be helpful, the proceedings were cast by Della Rocca as a favor to the American First Lady, not to Lee. In return for such assistance, Etter, like Mazzolini, was told he could expect influence in Washington for his foundation.

On May 18, Stas and Lee, whom Della Rocca referred to as his "simpatico and ebullient friend," met with him at their hotel and in his office and together they drafted Lee's papal petition. It was written in French in letter form and dated two months ahead to July 18, 1961, to allow time for it to come to the Pope's attention. Highly dramatic in tone and expressive of harsh judgments and opinions toward the London Tribunal, Lee's petition referred to the First Lady over and over again to underscore the political connection: "My sister, Mrs. Kennedy, was my most important witness . . . ," it read. "My sister, Mrs. Kennedy, was interrogated by the Ecclesiastical Tribunal of New York. . . . After my sister testified. . . . I was fervently hoping that one day I would be admitted again into the Church, that my husband and my children would no longer be unhappy because I was the source of their pain and of the pain to my sister, Jacqueline Kennedy.

"I know that my sister is as desperate as I am," the petition continued. "She tells me that, in a way, as the wife of President Kennedy, she feels responsible for the apparent injustice of my trial. I would really like her to feel unloaded of all responsibility, but, still believing in the justice of the Tribunal, I have to admit that suspicions of a political nature torment me. . . . If I could have the right of appeal, then my suspicions and those of my sister would be dissipated." Lee was engaging in a bit of double-talk here. It was entirely as a result of political considerations that she had been able to make such a pitch with any effect in the first place. Yet when the outcome was not to her satisfaction, those same political considerations were blamed.

Referring to the illness she developed in connection with the birth of her daughter the previous year, Lee went on to say: "Faith and hope in justice gave me unquenchable strength and saved me twice in my lifetime. I was gravely ill, mortally ill, in these last two years. Perhaps my faith was the miracle that saved me.'' She asked the Pope to ''enlighten new judges'' and grant her ''the grace of a revision of my trial in front of an extraordinary Tribunal constituted by . . . Your Holiness.''

On November 7, after several more months of back and forth among all the parties involved—most notably Jackie keeping the pressure on Etter by writing to him and voicing her concern—Etter led a Swiss delegation to Italy. The delegation was to present good wishes to Pope John on the occasion of his birthday, and then Etter was to take advantage of the opportunity and submit Lee's petition to him. (That same morning Etter had met with Mazzolini to pick up the petition and a copy of a memorandum prepared for the ''Sacred Desk,'' which informed the Pope in advance of the meeting what Etter would personally request.)

The afternoon audience with the Pope at Castel Gandolfo, which was supposed to mark the final triumph of Lee's three-year attempt to get her marriage annulled, turned into an unmitigated disaster. It had gone along pleasantly enough until Etter tried to give Lee's letter to Pope John. The Pope's facial expression, cordial until that moment, darkened, and he said to Etter, ''It is the law that must play its role. It is not me personally who can deal with this matter, but the competent authorities.'' Etter realized from Pope John's reaction that he already knew about Lee's petition previous to that day, a piece of information the parties involved had carefully neglected to tell him. Highly indignant at the position he had been placed in, Etter fired off an angry letter to Mazzolini a few days later, describing the meeting as ''really unpleasant''—the words were underscored—and accusing him of having set him up. After this, he refused to have anything more to do with Lee's annulment, telling Mazzolini, ''It seems strange to me that the Balzan Foundation should be mixed up with this matter. Such commitments can have very embarrassing developments for us.''

Still, the Radziwills and Della Rocca refused to be deterred by their failures thus far, and the next strategy mapped out by Della Rocca with his clients' cooperation was even more defiant and bold than the one which preceded it. In the same

manner as they had previously tried to circumvent the decision
of the Holy Office through the Pope, they now planned to
circumvent the clearly expressed indignation of the Pope by
means of a lobby of the right clique of cardinals in the Vatican.
"Evidently there are avenues in the Vatican through which it
is possible to overcome even the will of the Pope," reported
ABC. Such an avenue was laid out by Cardinal Cicognani, the
Vatican Secretary of State, and a Kennedy family contact from
his days as the Apostolic Delegate in Washington.

At the end of November, Cicognani made a visit to Washington and while there, not coincidentally, called on the White
House, where the Kennedys continued their lobbying efforts
on Lee's behalf. Described by Cicognani afterward as a "long
and amicable conversation," a plan was apparently hatched on
that occasion to have Jackie visit the Pope with Lee in tow
under the guise of an official papal audience for the First Lady.
The visit was to be a Rome stopover on a trip that was already
in the planning stages of a semiofficial visit by Jackie to India
and Pakistan in early 1962. Lee was to accompany her both
to Asia and to the papal meeting, where she could subtly but
directly confront Pope John XXIII with the favor she desired.

Once Cicognani had met with President Kennedy and
Jackie, events moved toward their inevitable conclusion. Extraordinary pressure was now brought to bear on Pope John
by the White House through its planned papal audience for
the First Lady and Lee, and by the Vatican clique organized
by Della Rocca, so that on March 8, in the wake of Cicognani's visit, and four months after the disaster at Castel Gandolfo, Della Rocca was able to write a triumphal letter to
Mazzolini announcing the decision by the Pope to permit the
reexamining of Lee's case, as if the first two judgments and
his own refusal to get involved had never taken place.

In his letter, which contained the heading, "The Announcement of the Victory," Della Rocca said to Mazzolini: "I believe that an intervention by the Cardinal Secretary of State
was very useful after his return from the United States based
on an exhaustive meeting that I was able to have with him
before the pontifical decision."

Clearly some heavy dealing had been going on. It is hard
to imagine that Stas's father in Warsaw, religious traditionalist
that he was, would have approved of such tactics as coercing

the Head of the Church against his better judgment for any reason, much less to obtain a favor for his son.

Lee and Jackie arrived in Rome on March 10 for their papal audience the following day. When they arrived at the Vatican after spending the night as guests of the American ambassador at his residence, the Villa Taverna, they were ushered by two cardinals, one of them Cicognani, into a small, spare room where Pope John awaited them with great calm, and, one is tempted to say, resignation. To the world it appeared that Jackie's visit to the Holy Father was undertaken to increase President Kennedy's prestige with American Catholics. In deference to the delicacy of the situation politically (Jackie could not be seen engineering a favor denied other Catholics), Lee was not present for any of the press photographs taken of the papal visit.

Negotiations continued that summer when the Radziwills rented a villa at Ravello and Jackie came to visit. With the Italian villa as their base of operations, the party went sailing on Gianni Agnelli's yacht. Between bouts of sunbathing, Lee met with a special Vatican emissary who arrived on a high-speed motor launch for their seagoing rendezvous. Together they worked out the final details of her case.

In September, a favorable preliminary judgment was issued by the Sacra Rota, Rome's final court of appeal for most annulment claims, and on November 24, 1962, a determining one was issued: Lee's marriage to Michael Canfield was finally declared invalid. And so, over four years after their civil marriage ceremony, Lee and Stas were wed at long last in a religious rite by Monsignor Gordon Wheeler at the Roman Catholic Cathedral of Westminster.

ABC speculated that Lee must have been subjected to some tough conditions in order to obtain her annulment, specifically, that she promise to wait to be remarried and not to make her nuptials public. It was thought to be a strange coincidence that Lee remarried Stas in a religious ceremony on July 3, 1963, exactly thirty days after Pope John died. "It makes one think that the Holy Father, even if subjected to the pressure of the Kennedy clan, never completely forgot the indignation he had shown to Philipp Etter," said *ABC*.

Only JFK's assassination caused the story of the religious ceremony to be leaked to the press a few months after his death, in February 1964, so that a clarification from the Vatican became necessary. Della Rocca issued a statement which said in part: "It was a hard and difficult battle . . . four years were necessary . . . hundreds of pages [were] written in Latin and many witnesses [called] to reach the goal. Perhaps if the President of the U.S.A. had not been killed, and his sister-in-law had not run to the side of her sister in such a terrible moment, the secret of the marriage in London, held closely for a long time, would not have been revealed, and we would not be here to speak about it."

It was widely reported in the press coverage that Lee had obtained her annulment on the grounds that Michael Canfield did not want to have children. In fact, the Sacra Rota's deliberations were shrouded in strictest secrecy, and it was never revealed which line of "reasoning" had been used to invalidate the Holy Office's verdict. And although the Roman Rota does publish its decisions years after the fact, there is no way of knowing the identities of the parties involved in a particular suit since pseudonyms are always used to protect the confidentiality of each case. The press had based its assumption on the fact that to help her case, Lee had gotten Michael Canfield to give a statement saying that when he married her he did not intend to have children. "It annoyed Michael that he had to play the part he did, that he had to go along with the gag that he never wanted children," said a relative of his. "And it annoyed him that he was doing it for Radziwill. Lee bullied him. She could be very persuasive, and she just wore him down."

Michael's indignation was justified. Absurdities whirled like so many snowflakes around the entire proceeding. Whether Lee claimed to have had a "mental reservation" herself on the issue of having children, or whether she badgered Michael into claiming that he had had one, the fact remained that both of them had made a great effort during the course of their marriage to seek out a medical cure for Michael's sterility precisely so that they could start a family. And while Lee wrote to Pope John of her "soul soaked in Christian faith" and her belief in the sanctity of marriage, by the time she achieved her stated goal of a church ceremony in the summer of 1963, she was heavily into a bit of extramarital entertainment with a Greek shipowner—Aristotle Onassis. Ironically, after all those years of travail, it was too late for Stas and Lee. Their union had already become a shell game.

Even London's Vicar General, suspecting the worst, made a comment on the affair: "These annulments are given on the basis of witnesses telling the truth. The rest of the matter lies between them and God."

21. *A Blissful Beginning*

Buckingham Place is an unpretentious little side street tucked away in a neighborhood of office buildings and town houses near Victoria Station. Randomly planted plane trees and Victorian gas lamps with blue-painted standards add nice touches to the narrow, sleepy road. Only a small number of the eighteenth-century houses that line the street are still used as private homes. One of the few such historic enclaves remaining in London, many of the dwellings on Buckingham Place have had their facades rebuilt and most have been converted to offices. In Stas's day it was an ideal locale for someone who preferred to live quietly in a modest neighborhood handy to the heart of London. But the district of Victoria was not Belgravia or Mayfair, and the Radziwills' new address in this less fashionable neighborhood testified more to the reality of Stas's finances than to a deliberate preference for the quiet backwater.

With a new bride and a child on the way, Stas purchased No. 4 Buckingham Place, a terraced house located in the middle of the block, soon after he married. Originally two houses with some later architectural additions, it featured a small backyard, white facings, black shutters, and a gleaming white front door. When the new Mrs. Radziwill moved in, she immediately set to work to give her new home her imprint. Lee's years with Michael in London had always had a transient quality to them. Now at last she was putting down roots.

This time, apart from the top floor, which was set aside for children, she was able to make use of an exceptional collection of Radziwill family treasures. The many dinner parties the couple gave allowed her the opportunity to set an opulent table utilizing her husband's fine collection of eighteenth-century

Polish silver, and among other touches, a portrait of one of Stas's ancestors, a Radziwill princess who became Louise of Prussia, was placed strategically over the drawing room fireplace.

Lee always spoke of those early days with Stas as some of the happiest of her life. It was not unusual for them to get together in the middle of the day, so eager were they for each other's company. On those occasions, Stas would come home for lunch, or Lee would join him at fashionable restaurants like Wilton's, the famous seafood restaurant around the corner from his office on Arlington Street.

"They were very close at the beginning of their marriage," said David Metcalfe. "Stas was crazy about Lee, and she put herself wholly into it. For a period of time, he exercised a very strong influence over her." Another friend noted, "Stas was immensely proud of Lee, and in a curious way she had great respect for him. They had a mutual respect and admiration for each other which was rather exciting for both of them."

On August 4, 1959, their first child, Antony (changed later to Anthony), was born. Lee chose to have her baby in Lausanne, both because Swiss doctors were considered to be excellent and because she wanted to deflect attention from the date of conception. The Radziwills announced the birth of their son as three months premature. There were complications in the pregnancy, and the birth of Lee's first child was not an easy one.

After she recuperated, she resumed the rhythm of her city-and-travel life of auctions and art galleries—often in search of the fine eighteenth-century French and Italian drawings she liked to collect—and fairly frequent trips to France, Italy, and the United States. When it struck her fancy, the new bride took her pug Thomas with her for tea at the Ritz. She even started to ride again now, at Windsor, in her perfectly-tailored riding habit. During the winter months, Lee accompanied Stas on shooting weekends, a passion of his, and "joined the guns for lunch," lovely affairs in shooting lodges, followed by even more magnificent dinners.

"My husband bought or took a shoot in Yorkshire and Prince Radziwill often came," said Felix Fenston's widow, Greta. "Lee sometimes came too, and I recollect one time when she was there, we had David Somerset and Michael

Tree, and I remember thinking how amazingly alive they all were. They all had a lot of very amusing stories to tell and stayed up quite late enjoying themselves. I remember, too, Stas absolutely adored backgammon and his Polish vodka chilled just so.''

On her own, Lee attempted to express her powerful but still unfocused creative urge by painting flowers and scenery or doing stage designs. ''I got terribly critical and lost patience with them,'' she would say later. ''They're all tucked away in drawers or closets somewhere.'' She enjoyed writing little essays too. When there was something she found funny or something she just couldn't stand, like the extra-stiff British nannies and gynecologists, or the horsy-faced women she saw at balls, or people who read *The Tatler,* she wrote an ''article'' about it to amuse herself and Stas.

Once Lee did write an article with the intention of publishing it. It was entitled ''The Anxiety to Distinguish Oneself,'' a quote from Edmund Wilson, and when she finished it, she showed it to John Kenneth Galbraith, the author-economist and Kennedy friend. ''He put in a lot of lengthy asides about economics and changed the whole thing,'' said Lee. ''I ended up throwing it away.''

Lee had more success with the parties she gave. When the Radziwills entertained at Buckingham Place, guests sat on delicate antique French dining chairs upholstered in olive green velvet and they dined by candlelight, for Lee allowed no electric light in the dining room. In sharp contrast to the elegance of these occasions was Stas's habitual display of ribald humor, schoolboy remarks that usually had something to do with the ''loo'' and always made the English laugh. A host who enjoyed teasing and truth-telling in social situations where neither was acceptable, Stas would gaze out from half closed, heavy-lidded eyes and put his workable wit to good use.

Old friends who knew Lee when, and now came by for dinner in her new setting, found themselves feeling out of place. ''When my husband and I moved to London, Lee and I resumed our friendship,'' said Sherry Geyelin. ''Lee had a perfectly beautiful house and beautiful things. She always did have wonderful taste. But she was clearly happy in the demimonde, the Cecil Beaton crowd. She loved that life, and we were not part of it at all. It meant a lot to her to be married to a prince, I don't care how worthless the title was in England. Radziwill was a very nice guy, but I thought he was on the make just as much as she was. They made a good pair.''

In the early years of their marriage at least, Stas and Lee liked to tease each other in an affectionate way, and when they were in good form, friends who witnessed it found their banter entertaining. Stas's conversation was often preceded by the word "Shit!" To tease Lee, he would say things like, "Shit! The little girl is very, very small. Not very big. It is fantastic how much she costs to dress!" "Stas's command of the English language was curious for someone who lived in England for so long," said his friend Nicholas Cobbold. "He spoke in broken English and used no grammar at all. A typical sentence of his was, 'Wherefore shitty man does this.' I am sure he did it on purpose." Lee teased her husband about the way he spoke; she liked to mimic his Polish accent, and she could be very funny when she did her imitations of him.

Both Stas and Lee were very interested in the political fortunes of John F. Kennedy. At high summer in 1960 they went to the States for a prolonged visit, with plans to attend the Democratic Convention in Los Angeles and to go on to Hyannis Port and Newport from there. Marginal figures both, they attended the Democratic Convention as observers, content to follow the Kennedy operation and enjoy the euphoria of Jack's first-ballot victory on July 13 strictly from the sidelines. From her suite at the Beverly Hilton, Lee talked often about each day's events by telephone to Jackie, who was pregnant and had remained behind in Hyannis Port.

Lee was expecting another child too, and when she arrived at Hyannis Port, had much to gossip about with her sister. In the continuing parallel developments of their lives, both were expecting babies in November.

On a routine visit Lee made down to New York City from Cape Cod in August, catastrophe struck. On the night of the eighteenth, she was picked up in an ambulance and taken to the emergency ward of New York Hospital, where she gave birth three months prematurely to a baby girl who weighed less than three pounds. Put in an incubator, tiny Anna Christina remained there for months and survived against grave odds.

Lee herself became dreadfully ill, a victim of a crushing postpartum depression that left her at times during the next several months in a deeply despondent state, without even the will to live. Medication to bring the illness under control was not widely used or available in those days, and she vacillated wildly between periods of recovery and relapses that paralyzed her. Jackie was a great help to Lee during this episode. With her own history of problem births, she greatly empathized with her sister.

When Lee was feeling better, she showed up at some of the campaign meetings in Washington offering to help out. Stas, meanwhile, had cheerfully put his aristocratic charm at the disposal of the Democratic process. He was drafted by Jack into the campaign and assigned to galvanize the Polish vote for him. Although terrified by all the public speaking and almost fainting before each event, he stumped the country from Boston to Los Angeles making speeches in Polish to Polish-American communities. "There are an awful lot of Poles in America," Lee remarked afterward, "and Stas must have spoken to most of them." Stas's contribution in the swing state of Illinois was very significant in that extraordinarily close presidential election. (Robert Kennedy once said his brother owed his election to the Poles in America.) After the election, Jackie presented Stas with a drawing she had done featuring a map of the country with a figure representing him crisscrossing it, and with the words, "You really did do it, Stas."

Shortly before the election, Lee relapsed again and Stas took her home to London to recuperate. On election eve in November, she was almost too ill even to follow the returns. Added to her other physical problems, she was having difficulty speaking and catching her breath. She had been separated from her baby since the moment she was born and her anxiety over her infant's condition weighed heavily on her, making her feel even worse. Tina, as she came to be known (she was nicknamed Tina because Anthony could not pronounce Anna Christina, and the name stuck), was still in the hospital in New York, too weak to travel. Lee was up and about again after a few days, but she was still not well enough to fly to New York on December 12 to collect her infant. The nurse went in her place. Too excited to wait at home for their baby's arrival, the Radziwills went out to the airport to meet the flight. Baby

Tina, now six pounds, arrived home sleeping peacefully in her pale blue carry-cot. When the party arrived at Buckingham Place, Lee picked her baby up and held her for the very first time, saying with evident feeling, "This is really the most wonderful Christmas present I have ever had."

Lee's poignant reunion with her newborn child was not, unfortunately, the happy ending to the story of her birth. Events in the lives of Stas and Lee relating to their daughter, both before she was born and in the immediate aftermath of her birth, were responsible for the turning point in the Radziwills's marriage, causing the couple's happiness to be extremely short-lived.

Stas had pressured Lee into having another child almost immediately after Anthony's birth, and she conceived her second child only six months after her first baby was born. Lee felt that having them so close together put too much pressure on her and was responsible for her devastating illness and the condition that caused her to give birth prematurely. She not only blamed Stas for what happened to her and their baby daughter, she also deeply resented him for abandoning her when she needed him most. Preoccupied with his brother-in-law's campaign, Stas left her to face her trauma and their infant's crisis alone while he traveled the country. Then, when they were back in London, during her relapses, he was preoccupied with the business affairs he had left unattended while in the States. Lee's anger was so deep that it developed into emotional and physical withdrawal: she simply refused to have sexual relations with her husband again. Ever.

Stas remained with Lee for several reasons: It had always been customary in the high European circles to marry primarily to preserve the purity of the family's bloodlines, and one found one's day-to-day sexual pleasure elsewhere, and Stas was nothing if not the epitome of Old World mores. He also could not abide the idea of another divorce; he was on his third try, and he now had two young children to consider. Most important, Stas was deeply in love with Lee. It was as simple as that.

22. *First Lady and Second Sister*

Lee felt well enough to travel with her family to Palm Beach for Christmas to join her sister and Jack at his father's mansion, but she relapsed again at the time of Jack's inauguration. Jack cared enough for Stas and Lee to take time out from his extremely hectic schedule to telephone the Radziwills, who were back in London, twice on the day of his swearing-in ceremony to say how much he missed them.

In February, Lee made it to Montego Bay in Jamaica for a few weeks, staying at the same cottage at the Half Moon Hotel that Jack and Jackie had stayed in the previous winter, when the Radziwills had also been along. Much to Stas's annoyance, he found that the cottage's rates had been arbitrarily increased for his stay there this time simply because his brother-in-law was now the President of the United States. There would be many such irritations—the Radziwills had to change their telephone number within days of the election because of all the crank calls, for instance—and they quickly learned the downside of fame.

From Jamaica, Lee and Stas flew to New York. During what Lee later termed "the political years," they spent a lot of time in the States frequently shuttling back and forth between the White House and the Carlyle Hotel in New York, where Jack kept an apartment. These jaunts were sometimes coupled with visits to the Kennedys at their weekend homes, whether it was up at Hyannis Port or at their leased estate in Virginia, or at Jack's parents' house in Palm Beach. For a change of pace, Jackie would join Lee in New York for a few days of shopping and ballet and theater.

Lee was seeing more of the Kennedy clan now than she might have liked and she found most of them boring company. She once said: "Why do they always write about the Kennedys? They are so dull." Jack, of course, was an exception. She developed her own relationship with him, and so did Stas. Lee would often speak of her brother-in-law as a serious and thoughtful man who cared greatly about what he was doing, but for the most part the relationship they shared was breezy and gay. Actually, she once confessed to her writer friend, Truman Capote, that she had "a crush on Jack," a feeling she otherwise kept to herself.

The President was certainly very fond of Lee. One could see why. They both had the same wry, spontaneous, prodding sense of humor. Kennedy loved to tease and Lee was a good teaser herself. They enjoyed a lot of clever repartee. Jack thought his wife's younger sister was "full of beans, imagination, and spark." Referring to the amazing White House telephone operators who could get almost anyone in the world on the line in minutes, not to say seconds, he once said to Lee: "You know, Jackie's got no imagination. Do you realize what we have at our fingertips here? We can do *anything* we want, and Jackie is so unimaginative, she just has no idea!" The President knew that was not the case with Lee.

Lee used to save up amusing anecdotes to tell her brother-in-law and sometimes she gave him political gossip and comments on other developments. "I always told him everything," she acknowledged. Once, at a dinner party she gave in London before Jack's election, the journalist Philip Geyelin and other guests were discussing Kennedy's candidacy, and Geyelin offered the opinion that he thought Jack Kennedy had not been a very conspicuous member of the Senate, that he had not introduced any particularly interesting legislation, and that others who wanted the nomination— Johnson, Humphrey, and Scoop Jackson—all had better credentials. "My wife and I were subsequently invited to a White House dinner," Geyelin recalled, "and I heard that when President Kennedy found my name on the guest list, he said, 'Why should I invite that son-of-a-bitch who's been bad-mouthing me all the time he was living in Europe?' The only person he could have heard that from was Lee. She meant it jokingly, of course, as a funny story."

The President also had a great rapport with Stas, who was amused to find himself related to this man whom he considered to be a very nice person as well as a powerful world leader. He, too, provided the President with reports on the British scene as he saw it. Actually, he did so with enough regularity that officials at the American Embassy in London complained that the White House was often tipped off by Stas about events in Britain before their official reports arrived.

Although being part of the presidential entourage afforded Lee the opportunity to meet many dignitaries and celebrated artists, her primary reason for spending so much time in Washington was to keep her sister company. Jackie had a confrontational relationship with the Kennedy women, especially during her White House years, and she relied heavily on Lee for support.

To show her appreciation, in mid-March Jackie gave an elegant dinner dance in the Radziwills' honor. She looked terrific in a white sleeveless sheath, and Lee, her dark hair loose down her back, was equally striking in a red brocade gown. Jackie's intriguing guest list, an eclectic mix of the fashionable and the powerful—from Ali Khan to LBJ—was revolutionary for political Washington. Much discussed and envied afterward, the stylish affair set the tone for the Kennedy White House, while simultaneously proclaiming to the world that *here* was the group that mattered.

Lee would benefit enormously from the media's relentless mythologizing of the Kennedys, who captured and made over their era perhaps from that very moment on, and she would, correspondingly, pay an exacting price. Not content to be merely a bit player on the world's stage, yet with no legitimate claim to a larger role, she could only watch and dream and try and fail until that time, many years hence, when she set more modest expectations for herself during her bout with alcoholism.

Problems with the Inland Revenue awaited the Radziwills when they got back to London at the end of March. Stas may have required an apprenticeship to learn real estate development, but he was apparently a natural at the pay-no-taxes game practiced by many of the wealthy. As his personal tax adviser, Leo Backer, explained it: "Stas had an enormous expenditure. Between 1957 and 1961 approximately, he had a yearly turnover of a million pounds, five hundred thousand coming in and five hundred thousand going out, and nothing was income. The Inland Revenue did not believe he had no income and they gave him a hard time. They said: 'On what does this guy

live? Doesn't he declare his income?' It took us *years* to convince the Revenue that Stas had no income.

"You see, the idea of a property tycoon having ready cash
is absurd. Like most people in business, they all live on credit
and their reputations. Stas's income all went to his companies.
He held shares in companies which rented properties, and they
never paid him anything. Stas pledged his properties and lived
on loans. Money was no object as far as he was concerned
because there was always plenty of money available to him
by credit. But in the philistine sense, Stas could not afford to
breathe because he had not a single pound of income. He
always lived on the accretion of capital. And when the increase
of capital became a decrease in capital, well then, there would
be no way for him to continue, would there?"

At the end of May 1961, Lee got her first opportunity to par-
ticipate in official affairs of state when she took her seat in
President Kennedy's motorcade as it made its way through the
jammed, flag-draped streets of Paris on the first leg of his State
Visit to Paris and Vienna. In the more familiar role to her of
bystander to her sister's success, Lee trailed behind Jackie's
bubble-top Citroën with the other ladies-in-waiting and
watched as great crowds of people pressed close to Jackie's
limousine just for a glimpse of her.

Lee's Paris visit, which included an evening of dazzling
pomp at the palace of Versailles, did afford her one small
surprise: a family reunion. While standing in the receiving line
at a formal reception given by General de Gaulle at the Elysée
Palace on the evening of her arrival, she encountered her
cousin and Lasata playmate Michel Bouvier, whom she had
not seen much of since her first marriage. "We spent the rest
of the night chatting with her," said Michel's wife, Kathleen,
who marveled at how beautifully turned out Lee was in her
embroidered turquoise taffeta gown. "She had quickly become
accustomed to being the toast of Europe. Lee was absolutely
thriving, looking young and happy and beautiful and terribly
successful."

The President and Jackie went on to Vienna without Lee.
On their return trip they stopped off in London for a brief
private visit as guests of the Radziwills for Tina's christening
ceremony, which had been postponed until the time when the

President could be there. That same evening, the Radziwills joined the Kennedys and Queen Elizabeth and Prince Philip for a dinner in the state dining room at Buckingham Palace. The Radziwills were listed in the Court Circular for the event as "Prince" and "Princess," and a big fuss was made in the press once again over the fact that the Queen had never granted Stas, let alone his wife, a royal license to use his title.

In truth, Stas had been referred to as Prince Radziwill from time to time in the London press ever since his arrival after the war, and, prior to the Kennedy presidency, no one seemed bothered by it. Only when he obtained a proximity to real power did it suddenly become a relentless issue. Stas was hurt. In public he feigned indifference, but privately he told friends that since he came from generations of a great family the press should not have been so intolerant.

One of the advantages for Lee of being the President's sister-in-law was her rapid emergence as a fashion leader. She had been well on her way to becoming a tastemaker before the Kennedy presidency anyway. During the summer of 1960, in a series it ran on fashion personalities, *Vogue* magazine did a feature on Lee celebrating her "one enchanting, instantly visible asset: her beauty." Lee had spent two days posing for the layout. With JFK's election the following autumn, her role was consolidated, and the fashion press began to report her clothing choices.

In another indication of her growing influence as a tastemaker, an invitation was extended to Lee and five other socialites with "beauty, wealth, and chic" by Wilhela Cushman, the fashion editor of *Ladies' Home Journal,* to form a fashion panel and critique the fall 1961 Paris collections. Lee went to Paris in late July, and, eyeing some of the outfits enviously, particularly the evening dresses, recorded her reactions for the magazine's readers. Not afraid to voice an unpopular opinion, she found Christian Dior's collection, which was the hit of that fashion season, "extravagant, exotic, and not for me."

Fashion was one area where Lee always knew who she was, and she created a style for herself—a perfect marriage between the chic and the casual—that put her on the Best Dressed List in 1960 and kept her there year after year, eventually landing her in the number-one slot later in the decade. Her fashion signature was young, simple, never fussy, yet feminine and elegant clothes. Five foot six, slim as a sliver, and a more finely drawn version of Jacqueline, Lee possessed a sophisticated style which was unassuming yet emphatic. "She could wear a twenty-shilling sweater and make it look good," an English designer once remarked.

"Lee was very dégagé. She had the nonchalance that only comes with dressing well in a casual way," observed the fashion designer Oleg Cassini. "She had the elegance within and refinement of spirit that translated externally into the clothes she wore. She was a very chic woman." Cassini, who knew Lee through his Kennedy connection, designed some clothes for her trip to India and Pakistan.

In November, Lee was back in the States traveling the northeast corridor between New York and Washington for another round of social engagements, while Stas remained in London. "She felt a little out of it in England," said an English friend. "It was unusual for anyone that well connected to power not to be part of it. For Lee, that whole connection with the Kennedys was very strong. They met very interesting people and knew what was going on in the world, but that was mostly in America. At the same time, her Kennedy connection played a very large part in her role in England. She got used over and over again for it. On the other hand, it opened doors for her."

Lee attended a dinner on this visit that the Kennedys gave for the President's ambassador to India, John Kenneth Galbraith. Oleg Cassini was also a guest, and, in fact, frequently found himself at Kennedy affairs at which Lee was also present. Having had ample opportunity, therefore, to observe both the Bouvier sisters' behavior at these functions, he noticed time and again that although their smiles were warm and their manner attentive, their spirits remained detached. "Lee's good manners made her look casually indifferent to things. She gave the appearance of flowing through these events," Cassini said. "She wore an elegant mask. I could imagine both her and her sister at the court of Louis XV. Destiny had separated them. It was Jackie who became the historic figure and Lee the society woman, but their roles could have been reversed."

The evening following the Galbraith dinner Jackie gave another one, this time in honor of Lee. The author Gore Vidal (whose mother had been married to Hugh Auchincloss before he married Janet) apparently had too much to drink. He managed to antagonize Bobby Kennedy by his behavior and annoy Jackie, and was escorted back to his hotel by some of the guests. This incident would come back to haunt Lee in years to come.

After another holiday season in Palm Beach with her family and the Kennedys, Lee had occasion early in the new year to have lunch in New York with Truman Capote. Straightaway, Lee felt Truman was someone she could confide in. She spoke to him of things that had been troubling her and she admitted to him how unhappy she was. It was uncharacteristic of Lee to open up like that, much less to someone who was still a stranger, and her behavior testifies to their extraordinary rapport. Afterward, Truman wrote of the event to his friend Cecil Beaton: "Had lunch with your new friend, Princess Lee. My God, how jealous she is of Jackie. I never knew. Understand her marriage is all but finito."

Truman's biographer, Gerald Clarke, who had talked to Truman at great length before he died about his relationship with Lee, said: "Lee was very depressed and lost at the time Truman first knew her. At least he saw it that way, and all the evidence points to it. He said she was a lost woman, and she did not have any purpose. She felt very much eclipsed by Jackie. She seemed to have everything, but it wasn't enough. She told Truman that Stas did not understand her."

It had not taken Lee long to discover that she and Stas really had very little in common. Each had married the other for the appeal of their surface attributes. When compelled by the demands of married life to reach deeper, she was forced to realize that their different generations and cultural backgrounds gave them widely divergent perspectives on life, which often left them feeling alienated from one another.

Lee found marriage to Stas difficult for other reasons. Intense, brooding, and very demanding, he was someone who had to have things his way and was quick to lose his temper. "If Stas did not like what you told him, he was quite capable of flaring up. He could not hide his feelings," said Leo Backer, who had many occasions to see this side of him. "Stas was a very friendly man, but like all Poles, he was very temperamental."

A Kennedy intimate who spent a lot of time with the Radziwills observed: "Those rages of his just came out of the
blue. He'd be high and then low. It was just the tone of his
voice or his mood. He'd swing. Stas was just born that way.
He was so Polish. And Lee was as volatile as he was. They
would just drift into arguments. They asked me to come to
London once when they weren't getting along, and I had to
spend my visit walking in between all that. The two of them
had absolutely no conception of or concern for the other.

"And anyway, an exiled Polish nobleman would be about
the last person to turn to for understanding about the kind of
struggles Lee was having with herself. It would be like going
down to the city jail and saying 'Help me' to the inmates. Stas
was preoccupied with his own monumental problems. He was
struggling with his own black spells. I don't know if Max
Jacobson's injections had anything to do with it. I suppose
they didn't help."

Dr. Max Jacobson was a highly controversial doctor Stas
saw whenever he visited the States or whenever Jacobson
came to London, who gave him injections laced with amphetamines, and who later lost his license to practice medicine.
"Stas took quite a lot of Valium and that doctor in America
was responsible for some of the things that happened to him,"
noted another English friend.

With so little common ground, it is doubtful Stas understood
the complex feelings Lee had toward her sister's great success
as First Lady and how much it haunted her, which may be
why Lee felt the need to talk to Truman about it.

As close as the two sisters were during this period, Lee
could not bear it that the press and the public, in their idolatry
of Jacqueline, gave Jackie far greater credit and attention for
the very taste and style Lee knew she had always excelled at.
Lee complained bitterly to Truman that *she* was the one who
was considered the beauty, who was chic, who was clever,
who had the fashion and decorating know-how, yet it was
Jackie who got all the adulation and publicity for those talents.
Of course it was her sister's status as a public figure that ac-
counted for this discrepancy, but Lee was not necessarily
thinking rationally. She only knew that she stood to be permanently eclipsed by Jackie's rapidly emerging prominence.

For up to now the sisters' lives had continued to progress

with a certain synchrony in spite of Jackie's many small triumphs. That harmony dissolved instantly with Jackie's ascension to the White House. From then on, her historic role sealed Lee's fate and made it official that she would be defined forever more as Jackie's kid sister not only in the mind of the public, but, far worse, in her own.

Seeing Jackie with so much influence made Lee envious and, more than ever, she longed to find someone or something, as her sister had, to launch her on the world stage in other than a supporting role. She would not find it, and she would always remain resentful that it was Jacqueline the world had dreamed.

23. *Role Playing*

One weekend in the fall of 1961 at Hyannis Port, the President brought up the idea, at his ambassador to India's suggestion, of Jackie making a semiofficial visit to help smooth over strained American relations with that country. Jackie agreed to go, and wanted Lee along for support. "We'd always wanted to go to India and Pakistan," Lee acknowledged. On this trip she would be sharing the spotlight with her sister a good deal of the time.

On their arrival in New Delhi on March 12, the sisters stayed in a charming little Embassy guest house before moving on to Prime Minister Nehru's residence as his guests. Nehru spent an hour or so each day walking in his garden with Lee and the First Lady, and Lee was quite taken with him. "He was possibly the most fascinating, certainly the most gentle, intriguing, sensual man I have ever met," she said later.

One evening, they sat on lawn chairs under a canopy of flowers in Nehru's garden and watched a concert of Indian folksinging and dancing, described by another guest as "like watching a whole series of Moghul miniature paintings sprung to life." Throughout the performance, however, the loudspeakers and the lighting system kept breaking down with a predictable regularity. The incident, a celebration of ancient traditions juxtaposed with the harsh economic reality of modern India, was a microcosm of their entire Asian tour.

Still, the sightseeing was glorious. A romantic train journey to see the Taj Mahal at Agra took the First Lady and Lee at a leisurely pace across the Ganges Plain; the train, brilliant red on the outside and a pleasant fawn color within, once belonged to the last viceroy of India and had its own drawing room, dining room, and bedrooms. In Lahore, two thousand men with flaming torches marched in their honor. Jackie and Lee watched several ancient rituals performed just for them, rode elephants and camels, visited ancient Moghul palaces and gardens, and cruised the sacred Ganges River in a marigold-decorated boat. Everywhere they went, masses of Indians crowded in for a glimpse of them, and their hosts showered them with gifts: saris, books, silver daggers, carpets, and jewels.

Eventually tedium and fatigue took over. "There were times when we were so completely exhausted by our schedule that at the end of the day laughter overcame us, and we exchanged stories of whom and what each of us had to cope with," Lee reminisced. "Then it was back to smiles and nectarine juice at the banquet table until I thought I would collapse."

A planeload of reporters had accompanied the First Lady on her Asian tour. Seasoned foreign correspondents from all over the globe suddenly found themselves covering what they dolefully called "a glorified fashion show." The press had come on a long, expensive journey and their editors expected something exclusive, something substantive, but they could not even get near the object of their assignment. Nor did Jackie say anything as she went along that could be turned into a decent news story, even if they had. "It was an impossible situation," said one of her staff.

Frustrated, the reporters turned to Lee for information whenever they got the chance, hoping she would say something about the First Lady that they could use. But Lee remained aloof and protective of Jackie's privacy. To make matters worse, she had a condescending manner toward them, "and, in fact, most strangers," as one of them put it. Her phony English accent further exacerbated the feeling that she was a snob.

Lee behaved quite differently with the never-ending procession of functionaries that she and Jackie met throughout their journey. Decorous and gracious at all times, even when she was rudely pushed into the background, as she often was, she was otherwise a great credit to her sister. "I was so proud of her," Jackie told Joan Braden. "Nothing could ever come between us."

In June, Lee spent three weeks of reviving calm with her family at a rented villa in the south of France, near Cannes, followed by a stay at another rented villa, El Episcopio, in Ravello, Italy, a tiny, cliff-top resort about twenty-five miles south of Naples, near Amalfi in the Gulf of Salerno. The twelve-room eleventh-century villa (the same one Stas had stayed in with Grace in 1955) was perched on the top of an eleven-hundred-foot cliff, and it was a long, steep walk—three hundred uneven steps to be exact—down to the sea; El Episcopio had its own private beach and beach house across the bay.

The Radziwills filled the villa with guests. Gianni and Marella Agnelli were there. So was the journalist Benno Graziani, who friends described as an extraordinary wit and the historian of *le tout monde*. Another houseguest was the former British model Sandra Paul. "Lee was not a girl another girl could get to know well," Paul said in observation of her hostess. "She doesn't know how to chat. She was slightly regal at all times. I think if Lee had relaxed, she'd have been a lot more lovable. She tried to be on her best behavior all the time, I suppose." That was one thing those who knew her well in those years always noticed about Lee: her position as sister-in-law to the President of the United States somehow prevented her from being wholly herself.

About forty-eight hours before Jackie was due to arrive with Caroline for a two-week stay, Lee became visibly edgy. She sacked the chef, a local man, and sent to London for a more sophisticated French chef; she personally supervised the local security arrangements—a ten-car procession with a motorcade police escort—and generally turned the household upside down to ensure that Jackie would be comfortable and well served.

If Lee were guilty of overreacting to her sister's position as First Lady, she was merely reciprocating for the royal treatment Jackie always provided for her when she visited the White House. "When Jackie entertained her sister, it was always a production, as if [she were] entertaining a visiting dignitary. Princess Radziwill would sleep in the Queen's Room, her husband in the Lincoln bedroom," testified J. B. West, the White House majordomo.

Once Jackie settled into her visit to El Episcopio, however, "the two sisters stayed together for hours talking of their youth like two little girls," said Benno Graziani. "It was a wonderful time in Ravello."

Just before Lee went to Italy, she spent a week in Paris as a fashion judge again, this time on her own. She was asked to cover the 1962 fall-winter fashion openings for *McCall's* magazine and to model some of her favorite choices. "It was fun to be doing something independent," said Lee, "and Mark Shaw [who would take the pictures] was a friend."

McCall's cabled the Chambre Syndicale in advance of her arrival and asked for "a front-row seat and preferential treatment" for their special correspondent, saying that it planned to do a four-page spread on the showings. Other fashion publications wondered sniffily how "journalist Radziwill" rated such preferential treatment when every season they devoted much more than a paltry four pages to the coverage of the Paris couture.

When Lee got to Paris, she telephoned from her hotel to reserve a place at Givenchy's private show for buyers. But because of past disagreements with reporters, both that house and Balenciaga were not allowing the press to see their collections until a month after the other houses had shown theirs, and until after the buyers had made their selections. Lee was informed that since she was a "reporter" working for an American magazine, she would not be welcome until the press showing. The couture house was adamant, even when she promised to attend as a private individual together with Jayne Wrightsman.

A flap ensued and made the newspapers. Lee was quoted as saying: "I haven't been buying Givenchy's clothes for months. I much prefer the designs of Yves Saint Laurent." This snippy remark was gleefully exploited by the press, who pointed out that her retort was not one that a working journalist would make.

Since Lee had been a prominent client of Givenchy's for many years, the couture house extended the olive branch to her in haste, and she was buying from him again in no time. But she never forgot the incident and took the opportunity several years later in an interview to present her version of the controversy: "Givenchy made a big statement about barring me as 'a member of the press.' I was amazed. It's rather disappointing when people you know—and have helped—behave badly just to get attention, but I suppose the publicity was more important to him."

At the other couture houses, meanwhile, Lee made more news than the fashions she was assigned to cover. With her looks and wardrobe, she was as arresting-looking as any of the models in the shows, and she stole the spotlight wherever she went. It was at this moment that she became prized as a real trendsetter by the fashion industry.

Lee was one of the very first to appreciate the special talent of Yves Saint Laurent, who was showing his second fashion collection that season. In her article for *McCall's,* she wrote: "By 9:00 P.M., there was nothing I wanted more than to fall asleep and never hear the words 'cape' and 'culotte' again. At least not until the next morning, by which time I hoped there might be another word to add. There was more than another word: there was Saint Laurent, the young genius who makes you feel as shy as himself. I had a sneaking feeling—the same kind of hunch as when you bet on a horse, only many times more certain—that his collection would be a knockout." At the climax of his showing that season, she joined the audience's excited dash to embrace and congratulate him. Lee saw what Saint Laurent was aiming at and attached herself to his rising star.

She was also quick to eye the creative coups of other-up-and-coming couturiers, like Courrèges and Ungaro. She would periodically comb through their racks, pick out what she liked, and, without trying them on, order clothes in her own size and colors. Courrèges was the designer who more than any other was credited with giving the sixties its look, and Lee did more for Courrèges than any other woman, or so an industry spokesman once said. In clothing, as with so many things, she felt she had "a certain instinct, almost animal, for what's worthwhile." But when a designer's clothes became a rehash of his former inspirations, as Givenchy's and Saint Laurent's eventually did, she moved on.

Mark Shaw found working with Lee on their *McCall's* assignment "terrific, but exhausting—that woman worked around the clock." At Ravello, Lee spent days finishing her story, polishing and rewriting and fretting about phrases until they were perfect. Then she read it out loud to her guests for reassurance.

John Mack Carter, *McCall's* editor, thought Lee's Paris report was well done and that she demonstrated a real skill for the snap of fashion language. In his words: "Lee was just beginning to explore fashion journalism and get more interested in the idea of writing and editing about home furnishings, decorating, and style in general. She had not been trained to do any of this, but she came in with a high taste level, and she turned out to be a much better writer than I expected her to be. She really did have a great deal of ability."

In her piece, Lee wrote of clothes "as straight and assured and as dignified as a Greek column," of dresses "as delicious to look at as a dessert you know you shouldn't eat," and black velvet suits that looked to her "out of a dance from *West Side Story*."

"Ah, Paris," as Lee's article was called, led to the offer of a guest editorship. "*McCall's* wanted to make her a correspondent, and the magazine paid very good money," said a former editor. "But Lee demanded some astronomical figure, and they were appalled." *McCall's* did not meet her asking price, and the idea was dropped.

Earlier in the year, Lee had less success at *Ladies' Home Journal*. In her ongoing effort to consolidate her role as a tastemaker others might learn from, she wrote an article on manners, which ran in the February 1962 issue. "Jackie's name on the cover was astonishing magic," recalled Curtiss Anderson, then the *Journal*'s newly named editor. "It could increase newsstand sales by five hundred thousand copies. The magazine's former editors [Bruce and Beatrice Blackmar Gould] had negotiated for Lee's piece. They thought the Jackie magic might work with her as well. They wanted to bill her as 'Jacqueline Kennedy's kid sister,' but she strongly objected. I inherited the inventory for that issue from the Goulds, so we ran that one article of Lee's, but I did not think it was skillfully done, so I did not want to use her again."

Another person who dealt with Lee in a professional capacity and ran afoul of how to refer to her was the television personality and broadcast journalist Barbara Walters. Walters interviewed Lee in Paris for the *Today* show. (She held up the segment for airing to coincide with Lee's fashion report in the November issue of *McCall's*.) Lee protested politely but firmly when she was introduced by Walters to television audiences as "Jacqueline Kennedy's sister." Nor did "Princess Lee Radziwill" make her happy. "Mrs. Lee Radziwill," Walters's third try, was accompanied by groans of exasperation from the crew. Ultimately they settled for "Lee Radziwill."

Once over the hurdle of how to refer to and address her, Walters was struck by how at odds with herself Lee seemed to be. When she mentioned the kudos Lee had received from the fashion world, Lee reacted with annoyance, obviously resentful of the "clotheshorse" label. She told Walters that she didn't spend much time thinking of clothes; she had her husband and two children to consider. "Yet Lee was clearly not ready to settle down, if ever, to that role," Walters wrote afterward in an article for a magazine. Similarly, her attempt to pull rank at Givenchy's fashion show indicated a confusion on her part between her roles as a journalist and socialite. "Here again, her conflicts got in the way," said Walters.

"Unwilling to settle for simply being the First Lady's sister, and unable to decide what other role—homemaker or international butterfly, career girl or society matron, princess or just plain Mrs.—will suit her best, she is currently giving them all a fling," Walters wrote in conclusion. "It seems ridiculous to feel even fleeting sympathy for a married, titled . . . young woman whose only problem is deciding what she really wants out of life, but sympathy is what I feel. I hope that when Lee Radziwill finally makes up her mind where she wants to go, she will be able to go there."

24. *Ari and Bobby*

"Nothing will ever come between us." That prophecy of Jackie's about herself and her sister proved to be incorrect. Something did come between them—or rather some persons: Aristotle Onassis and Robert Kennedy.

Back in the 1950s, a familiar sight at the restaurant in Claridge's Hotel was Aristotle Onassis, the Greek shipping tycoon, and Stas Radziwill holding court. The two men used to sit at lunchtime on the raised portion of the restaurant floor, while a steady stream of VIPs and impressionable ladies walked up to the table to say hello. "It was great fun," said Stas's business accountant, Sidney Morris. "The restaurant was very fashionable in international circles then, and Stas often went to Claridge's because it was across the road from his office. Of course, Onassis always had his table there."

Apart from sharing tables at Claridge's, it would have been difficult for anyone in the international set, as Stas was, not to come across Aristotle Onassis in those years. "One met Ari everywhere, he was here so much," said David Metcalfe. "Stas would see Ari in a thousand places. He was at people's dinners. I saw him all the time." The two men had their foreigner status, their eye for women, and their continental urbanity in common, and they formed a friendship which lasted until Ari's death in 1975.

When Lee married Stas, she fell into the routine of entertaining her husband's friend together with his mistress, the married Greek opera singer Maria Callas. "There were many dinner parties given for Maria Callas and Onassis when they were in London," recalled Lady Lambton. "Lee was the hostess at several of them. We were their London friends, and they would have dinner with us when they were in town for no particular occasion."

The Radziwills' hospitality was reciprocated by Onassis with many invitations to cruise on board the *Christina,* his floating hotel of a yacht. In the early sixties, Lee and Stas were the guests of Onassis and Callas on a number of uneventful and pleasant cruises, and over the course of time, Lee and her Greek host came to know each other well. Somewhere between the winter and summer of 1963, their relationship took on a new dimension: it turned into a casual affair, and Lee would now sometimes see Ari privately at his suite at Claridge's Hotel.

"The two flirted with each other harmlessly," said Jacques Harvey, a French friend of Ari's. "They were bound by a type of friendship, a rather improper one. I know that Lee and Ari held each other in high regard. Ari himself said to me on several occasions that the Princess Radziwill was, in his opinion, one of the most *spirituelle* women he had encountered in the course of his life." By that Onassis meant Lee was a woman with a uniqueness, not only of wit and style, but in her approach to life, someone whose intuitive grasp of people and events indicated a vital intelligence.

Ari was also name hunting. One of the richest men in the world, he built a tanker fleet larger than most navies and virtually owned the principality of Monaco. What mattered to him, once he had acquired his vast wealth, was to be noticed and envied. He needed an audience, so he played host on board the *Christina* to heads of state, tycoons, Hollywood stars, and the international set. The presence of the famous at his table confirmed his status and told him he had arrived at last.

Ruthless in business and tyrannical in private, the Turkish-born Greek was exceedingly charming and generous to those who only knew him in a social context. He was also a primitive man, lacking in education and cultivation, who relied completely on his intuition and instincts. He used to think that the Impressionists were artists who wanted to impress people. He believed in mermaids. He once told a friend that he would take him to a place near the Suez Canal where he knew "for certain" there was a stuffed mermaid.

"Onassis was an outstanding man, not only as a financier, but also as a person," said Lee, explaining her fascination with him. "He was very active, with great vitality, very brilliant and up to date on everything. He was amusing to be with. And he had charm, a fascinating way with women. He surrounded them with attention. He made sure that they felt admired and desired. He took note of their slightest whim. He interested himself in them—exclusively and profoundly."

Lee's new relationship with Aristotle Onassis brought an unexpected benefit to Stas. "Ari made Stas a director of Olympic Airways, and that was, I am convinced, because he was having an affair with Lee," said David Metcalfe. "One always used to notice that when Stas started doing a business deal with someone, it quite often seemed to be at the same time that Lee was having an affair with that same person. Stas loved being director of Olympic, and he formed a much closer friendship with Onassis as a result of Lee's affair with him." (Stas was so thrilled with his directorship of Olympic that he joked: "Now I can live on an airplane with my secretary and keep going around the world, and I won't have to pay any tax!")

In June of 1963, Stas and Lee, along with their fellow guest, Winston Churchill, went on another routine cruise party on the *Christina* with Onassis and Maria Callas, this time along the Italian coast. Lee left the cruise at the small port of Fiumicino, where the Tiber runs into the Mediterranean, to fly to Germany to join President Kennedy for part of a European tour he made that summer to Great Britain, Italy, Germany, and Ireland. Since Jackie was pregnant and had remained behind, he was accompanied in relays on the tour by his sisters and sister-in-law. Lee joined the party in Bonn for the President's dinner for the president of Germany, and then she continued on the trip as they moved around. She was present during John Kennedy's electrifying visit to West Berlin. She was there at Berlin's city hall and caught the crowd's emotion when he shouted, "Ich bin ein Berliner!"

"Lee came with us to Ireland too," said Dave Powers, JFK's political aide, "and I can remember her looking so beautiful in a white coat when she got off the plane. She had a remarkable presence. When Lee walked into a room, it just lit up. At the same time, she was just one of the gang, so down-to-earth and full of fun—a joy."

The three days of JFK's sentimental visit to Ireland was one long party. The whole country stopped, and laughs and high spirits were everywhere. After the President's plane left Ireland, Lee accompanied him and other members of his party on a private, unscheduled visit to England to his sister Kathleen's grave at Chatsworth, the estate of the Duke and Duchess of Devonshire, and then flew with him back to the States. Then she went home to London for her secret, Catholic rite wedding to Stas in early July, and on to Deauville, France, with her family for the wedding of Stas's niece, Isabelle Potocki. (The two Radziwill children were in the wedding party.) While a thousand guests from the most illustrious families in Europe joined in to celebrate Potocki's marriage to Count Hubert d'Ornano, Lee spent a good deal of time off to one side talking to her favorite guest, Aristotle Onassis.

"I saw them together very often," said the bride. "Lee had an affair with Onassis, but I never had the impression it was serious. All those people led complicated lives—everything moved very fast."

After the wedding Lee spent some time in the south of France, and then, accompanied by Dame Margot Fonteyn, the ballerina, flew from Nice to Athens during the first week of August to rejoin Onassis on the *Christina*. Life on board the *Christina* was casual and guests did pretty much what they wanted. The yacht's actual voyages were often accomplished in short hops, with the majority of time devoted to amusements on shore. Lee was only aboard four days when she received the news that Jackie's newborn child, Patrick, had died three days after his birth. She interrupted her vacation to fly to Massachusetts to attend his funeral and to be with her sister, who was convalescing at the Otis Air Force Base hospital near Falmouth. Before returning to Athens, Lee stayed on for a week at the Kennedys' rented summer home on Squaw Island, where Jackie continued her recovery.

When Onassis went away on business for a few days, Lee remained behind at a villa he had purchased for his sister, Artemis Garofalidis, in the Athens suburb of Glyfada. One day she contacted a friend of hers, Taki Theodoracopulos, to suggest they have dinner together. The heir to a Greek shipping fortune (and known simply as "Taki" in his profession today as a right-wing journalist and columnist), Theodoracopulos was then a self-described "young good-for-nothing playboy and professional athlete."

"I had gotten to the finals of the Greek tennis championships and had taken a bungalow by the sea so I could sleep in the afternoon," he recalled. "I don't know how Lee found out I was there. It was the middle of August and very hot. Lee was living in Onassis's villa by the airport, and the planes were driving her crazy. She said, 'Please, let's have dinner.' So we had dinner by the sea right next to my house.

"Lee was going nuts. She was very lonely and wanted company. Onassis used to park his women and go do his business, or go off with friends. I said to her, 'Where's your boyfriend?' She got very angry. She replied, 'What are you talking about?' Obviously Onassis had just left her and was cruising somewhere. He turned her over to his sister."

Ari often did exactly that. He did not have a home in Greece, just the *Christina*, and rather than play host all the time, he had his friends and girlfriends stay in the Glyfada house and let his sister entertain them. "She used to make little parties and take them to the theater and museums and so forth because Onassis didn't want to bother," said Maia Calligas, an Athenian friend of his.

Ari was back in Athens and on hand with Lee to toast the opening of the Athens Hilton on August 22. He was seen dining with her alone in public at this time, and rumors began to circulate in the international press. A *Washington Post* columnist, Drew Pearson, wondered aloud: "Does the ambitious Greek tycoon hope to become the brother-in-law of the American President?"

Drew Pearson in private life was a liberal and quite sympathetic to the Kennedy Administration, but he would do anything for a story. It is possible that the Onassis-Radziwill gossip item was given to him by Giovanni Meneghini, Maria Callas's husband, whose motive would have been to expose Ari's interest in Lee to disillusion Callas about Onassis. Much more likely, though, the item was a plant from the publicity agent Onassis hired to keep his name in the press. Ari had a great talent for self-advertisement. He believed that the publicity his social exploits generated helped his credibility with his bankers; it also increased his recognition as a celebrity.

Lee was taken aback at the leak to the press about her dalliance with Onassis. "She made a good effort to be discreet. It was Onassis who was indiscreet," stressed Taki, who said he had his own "fling" with Lee at a later date.

David Metcalfe made a similar observation: "Lee had quite a lot of affairs. It was all very discreet. But Ari was very much out in the open because he reveled in publicity. One couldn't be discreet with Onassis."

In light of later events, namely, Jackie's marriage to Onassis, Lee's escapade with him was embellished in the heat of gossip and blown up out of all proportion to what actually took place. Pearson's one insinuation about the nature of their relationship was subsequently spun into an entire scenario. It was repeated as a certainty that Lee and Ari's "romance" had reached the stage where marriage was being discussed. This had never happened. The rumor mill even had the Kennedys asking Lee to wait to marry her tycoon until after Jack's re-election bid in 1964.

Lee ignored all the talk and continued to do as she pleased. When she returned to Athens after her visit to her sister, she mentioned to Ari that Jackie had taken her baby's death very hard, and she suggested that Jackie join them on a cruise to help lift her spirits. Onassis agreed, and when Lee relayed the invitation to Jackie, she accepted. The early October cruise retraced a path the *Christina* had followed many times: it touched at Lesbos and Istanbul and then sailed along the coast of the Peloponnesus.

The story of Jackie's effect on Ari during that cruise has been told many times. Lee would tell her intimates later that she was only trying to do something nice for her sister when she brought her along on the *Christina,* and that Jackie co-opted Onassis on that cruise, and moved in on him *very soon* after Jack was assassinated.

"I know there was a lot of bitterness about what happened with Onassis. That's definite," said one person close to Lee. "There was a lot of resentment there. Even when Lee saw how unhappy her sister became when she was married to him, she still preferred to hang on to the resentment and the competition."

Jackie's expropriation of Onassis drove a deep wedge between the two women which, when coupled with a parallel development between Jackie and Robert Kennedy in the aftermath of the assassination, was the beginning of a profound change in their relationship, one that would last.

Lee was at home early that Friday evening, London time, when she heard the news that President Kennedy had been shot. Nancy Tuckerman, Jackie's new social secretary, dealt with a bewildered inquiry from her. It was Robert Kennedy who called her afterward and told her that the President had died. Lee immediately rang the American Embassy for help in getting on the first available flight to the States the next morning. Until her departure, she kept in touch with events in Washington by talking at intervals with Bobby.

When Lee arrived at the executive mansion, a friend of JFK's, LeMoyne "Lem" Billings, told her that it was nice of her to come. She whirled on him and cried, "How can you say that?! Did you think I wouldn't?!"

Stas was at the Saint James Club when he heard the news, and the shock of it, he said later, brought back to him that same feeling of dread he had on that black day in 1939 when the Nazis invaded his country. He arrived at the White House a day after Lee (and was "reminded of Versailles after the king had died"). When told that Jackie had placed remembrances in the President's casket, he donated his most treasured possession, an old Parisian rosary. Lee's contribution was reportedly a sapphire bracelet, one of her favorite pieces of jewelry.

Later that evening, Lee led her husband into the Chief Executive's suite and told him they would be sleeping there. Stas demurred. It was Jackie's wish, she explained. But the more he looked at the familiar four-poster and bedside table with the President's pill bottles and bric-a-brac, the firmer he became. "In the end, they compromised," wrote William Manchester in his account of the assassination. "A cot was brought over from the White House dispensary and set up at the foot of the huge bed. With his old-fashioned European dignity, Stas stiffly insisted he would be quite comfortable there. He even refused to use the bathroom. No one knew where Stas shaved; razor and toothbrush in hand, he wandered through the mansion for ablutions elsewhere."

The day of the funeral, Lee retained her composure until the moment at the burial ceremony at Arlington National Cemetery when the presidential aircraft, Air Force One, made a fine wing-dipping salute in tribute to the fallen leader. Lee wept because she knew "how much the plane meant to Jack."

Her mood changed considerably by the time she returned to the White House after the funeral service. Lee's cousin John Davis recalled later that she acted "a bit too carefree for the occasion." He speculated that Kennedy's death might have been, for her, something of a psychological relief. Stas, too, he said, had taken on a new dimension: "Now he was the only husband of the Bouvier sisters left and he need not defer anymore to the mighty Jack Kennedy."

Before retiring that evening, Lee wrote her sister a note of admiration and love and pinned it on her pillow. After Jackie left the White House and moved into Averell Harriman's Georgetown house, which he made available to her and the children, Lee remained in Washington for the next several weeks to give Jackie support and to help her pick up the broken thread of her life and begin over.

Jackie grew very close to Robert Kennedy during this period, and Jackie and Bobby, and Lee by extension, spent a good deal of time together. As Jackie grew closer to Bobby day by day, so did Lee, who felt he mellowed after Dallas. When she went back to London in January, she even gave luncheon parties on two successive days for the Attorney General, who was passing through Europe on his way to the Far East.

The sisters had many discussions early in 1964 about the logic of both of them purchasing apartments in New York City. Lee was the first to do so. On March 1, Stas bought an eleven-room cooperative apartment at 969 Fifth Avenue and put it in his wife's name because British Exchange Control Regulations in effect at the time prevented the removal by British subjects of substantial amounts of capital from England. As Lee had always retained her American citizenship, she was free to do so. Jackie followed her sister a few months later with a co-op she purchased a few blocks along Fifth Avenue from Lee.

Over Easter, Lee and Stas, and Jackie and Bobby together with Chuck Spalding, a friend of Jack's, flew down to Bunny Mellon's house in Antigua to try to jump-start their lives again and work their way out of the overwhelming gloom that all of them were feeling. Jackie and Lee water-skied and, with the others, went for picnics on an uninhabited nearby island. They played pop records and turned the volume way up in the hope that it would shake their pain and lift their spirits. Bobby in particular kept playing the same records over and over again.

When the moment came for Lee to return to London, Jackie

began to be more dependent on Bobby as that relationship evolved in her absence, until it was Bobby, and no longer Lee, who was Jackie's most intimate confidant. Most likely, the resentment Lee felt over Onassis in the months ahead gave Jackie further impetus to move away from her sister emotionally. In any case, the assassination brought forward a successor to Lee, and from this time on, Jacqueline and Lee began to grow apart.

25. *Restlessness*

By the mid-sixties, the Radziwills made separate lives for themselves, while their children, mutual friends, the absence of anything better on the horizon, and sheer force of habit served to hold them together.

As with her first try, Lee remained physically present in the marriage but spiritually gone from it very quickly. It was that elusive quality of hers which always kept Stas enthralled and formed the basis of her hold on him. On the surface, Stas appeared the stronger personality, but Lee controlled him by holding back. She learned to manipulate him by remaining just outside his reach and making him feel vulnerable.

Their good friend David Metcalfe said as much: "In the beginning, Stas was the dominating personality, but as the marriage went on Lee became the stronger of the two. Stas liked to control people, but he simply could not control Lee. He was crazy about her, and in a way, Lee could not do any wrong for quite a long time. Stas put up with Lee's obvious infidelities because he was almost mesmerized by her. She had some sort of spell over him. It was fascinating really. There was always something about Lee he could never get hold of, something beyond him, something intangible. Lee let a distance grow between them, and in a funny kind of way, he was always trying to impress her. Maybe he wasn't so impressed at the very end, but Stas always kind of looked up to Lee, because she did things so well and she looked so marvelous. He was proud of her, his Princess Lee—he really was, you know. Lee is the kind of woman one could so easily be proud of. But it was quite true the marriage wasn't happy—maybe at the beginning. I spent a great deal of time with them, and I saw how unhappy Stas gradually became.

"One always hears a lot of confusing things about Lee because she is a very confusing person, and very complicated," Metcalfe said in conclusion. "Lee is a hard person to know well. Speaking personally, I never knew where I was with her, but I always knew exactly where I was with Stas."

"Lee always found it difficult to make the people around her happy," attested another London intimate. "I rather doubt she could make anybody happy. She is an astonishingly selfish woman, immensely self-involved, but frightfully attractive into the bargain. If the world is made up of givers and takers, Stas was a giver and Lee was a taker."

Another friend who came to a similar conclusion about Lee was Taki Theodoracopulos. He got to know her well, traveled with her to Kenya, went on trips together with her and Stas, and even lived at Buckingham Place at one point. He was able to observe the Radziwills on intimate terms unvarnished by dinner-party manners. "Stas was always up very early and off to the office," he recalled. "He had a wonderful butler called Stanley, who took good care of him. Stas was bright red all the time from the speed he took from Max Jacobson. It was high blood pressure from whatever on earth it was Jacobson gave to him. Stas was very tight, too. He wasn't a big spender. He spent money on the house, but why should he spend money on a woman who constantly betrayed him and wasn't very nice to him either? Lee was very pouty all the time, always in a bad mood. She was always looking for something to do—Lee had nothing to do. And she was always going to doctors and complaining that she was sick. She was never very healthy. When I knew her, the English thought her a bit too affected in the way she spoke, which is ridiculous because half the country is affected in speech.

"Lee and I had a fling. It started in 1964 when I was twenty-seven, and it went on for a couple of years. I had a mad crush on her. When I was alone with her, she couldn't have been more charming and nice. When she wasn't in a bad mood, she was perfect. But the moment Lee got in a crowd, she became everything one dislikes—arrogant, superficial, snotty. She became insufferable. She suffers from great insecurity. She doesn't have the authority that Jackie had.

"Once we were staying in Monte Carlo together, and it was very sweet. Lee played all of the female tricks. She gave me The Gaze. She looked at me with 'lock-in eyes,' you know, like they do in the Jets [the football team] when they lock in the enemy. She had come to watch me play tennis in the Monte Carlo tournament. This was in March 1965, and after she watched me play the first set, which I won, she left.

"When I arrived at the Hotel de Paris to join her for lunch, she was going on about how wonderfully I played to all the big shots who were there—Gianni Agnelli and some others. After I sat down, Lee asked me the final score, and when I told her I had lost, she turned on me. She said to the others in my presence, 'What a worthless life Taki lives. He just sits around all day and does nothing and then he goes out at night.' And she went on and on about it, embarrassing me. And here this woman was my guest. I don't know what she was trying to prove. But a lot of people have noticed that same tendency in Lee, how she becomes a completely different person in a crowd.

"Look, Lee is not a real person. If a person is real, she is not fifty percent real, and there is a definite pattern of behavior with her that changes according to the people she's with. A lot of people see Lee as a phony. Her manner is phony—like her mother, who pretended to be a Lee from Virginia when her own mother was a maid from Ireland. Lee is not a warm, nice person. She never looked after her children. She bullied them, and she uses people. She's bitchy, frustrated—I wouldn't want to go to her when my heart was breaking. I wouldn't want to rely on her. Lee always wanted to be someone, and it made her desperate.

"People would make fun of me. They used to say, 'How's Lee? How's Lee?' I was sleeping with the person who was seeing everybody. It was an unholy mess, and I realized very early on how jaded and false all those people were.

"Incidentally, when I was seeing Lee, I shared an apartment with Peter Lawford at the Sherry Netherland Hotel [in New York]. I left because Lawford was a drunk and a bully.* Any-

*Lawford's good friend and manager, Milton Ebbins, revealed to Lawford's biographer, James Spada, that Lee once "made a big play" for Lawford in the early sixties while they were strolling through Hyde Park in London.

way, Jackie and Bobby Kennedy used to come to the bar in the hotel sometimes and have a drink, quickly and rather discreetly, and Lawford was telling me at the time—this was in January 1965—that Jackie was sleeping with Bobby.* The press always knew about Jack's affairs, they just didn't reveal them. But Bobby played altar boy and the press bought it."

Taki's sighting of Jackie and Bobby's tête-à-têtes was hardly an isolated observation; in the months after Dallas, there were many such incidents. But so unwilling was the public—and the press—to cock an ear to anything that would diminish the Camelot myth, that no one ever wondered if Guinevere and Lancelot were sleeping together now that Arthur was dead. Even the redoubtable Kitty Kelley in her 1979 biography of Jackie dismissed as "vicious rumors" the fact that "Bobby and Jackie were being seen together in New York so much that people began to gossip that their friendship might be more than familial." Kelley said that Jackie not only ignored the rumors "but fueled them by embracing her brother-in-law in public, holding his hand, and kissing him."

A Republican stronghold like Glen Cove, Long Island, had not a moment's hesitation, however, in drawing the obvious, though unpopular conclusion. Out there, where Jackie had rented a four-bedroom fieldstone house for weekends, the pair were the talk of the town and the gossip was cynical. "Many people often saw Jackie and Bobby off by themselves, heads together, or looking fondly at each other in various hotels in the area, so they got the idea," said Bruce Balding, at whose family stable Jackie boarded her horses. He himself saw the pair in an amorous-appearing context: "They were holding hands or walking arm-in-arm, I don't recall which now," he testified. "Their relationship was the talk of the Piping Rock Club."

There are others who have come forward now and say that Jackie and Bobby were having an affair. And it defies common sense that a man and a woman who were exhibiting that kind

---

Lawford said he turned her down because "he had too much respect for her husband."

*The news of John Kennedy's relationship with Marilyn Monroe and of Jackie's marriage to Aristotle Onassis were initially greeted with hoots of disbelief.

of body language in public, and who were spending that much time alone together, would be sitting at opposite ends of a sofa in private. Obviously, the emotional framework of their relationship was a powerful one. Whatever else they meant to each other, being together was a way for each of them to try to hold on to Jack.

Lee was with Jackie at her Glen Cove house on the first anniversary of JFK's assassination. Her global wanderings that year had included a visit to Monte Carlo later on in the spring after her Easter visit to Antigua. She attended a concert there conducted by her friend Leonard Bernstein, afterward joining a crowd that drove up to Prince Rainier's palace for a glittering evening reception "where all the Bourbons in Europe were."

She also stayed with her new friend, the legendary premiere dancer, Rudolf Nureyev, for a few days at his first house, Villa Arcadie, in La Turbie, high in the hills above Monte Carlo. Lee was always one to respond to domestic beauty, and the enchanting atmosphere of the house, with esoteric music wafting through monasterylike white stucco rooms linked by exquisite wrought-iron gates, left her feeling transported.

The Radziwills rented another Italian villa that summer, this one at Porto Ercole, a coastal resort ninety miles north of Rome on the west coast. They interrupted their August stay for a few days to cruise the upper Adriatic Sea along Yugoslavia's Dalmatian coast, with Jackie, as guests of the Wrightsmans.

As much as Lee enjoyed all these jet set jaunts and glamorous happenings on one level, on another, she felt caught in an eddy of meaningless movement, "so pointless" in her words. After thinking it over, she concluded that an existence of endless indulgence unleavened by any other goal for oneself was a life devoid of purpose, unless perpetual motion in itself could be called purpose. Her chronic restlessness and boredom, so obvious to those around her, and the frustrations that were roiling her spirit, all had the same source: she had no center. She was merely a fabulous armpiece, the ultimate token of a man's success. Her survival strategies had backfired. It was a personal judgment: the deal she had made for herself was the wrong one.

The catalyst for this momentous revelation was her exposure in recent months to the artistry and dedication of her new creative friends, the architect, decorator, and stage designer Renzo Mongiardino, and the acclaimed dancer Margot Fonteyn, as well as Rudolf Nureyev, and of course, Truman Capote, all of whom found in their work an entire universe.* Up to now, money had been the prop and stay of all Lee's dreams, and the perfect surface of things her adventure. Lee's firsthand observation that a life of creativity gave one the greatest satisfaction made her want to enrich herself in the same way. But what should her effort at self-realization be? And how would she deal herself in?

A chance remark at a party in New York by the actress and television panelist Kitty Carlisle Hart gave her the answer: "You are a natural for the stage," Kitty said.

26. *Seeking the Spotlight*

As a professional actress Lee could star in an area not already staked out by her sister. Passionately wanting a life of her own now, she made up her mind. To be known as an actress "of quality" would be her stated ambition, while secretly, one suspects, she desired to attract attention to herself on a scale competitive with her sister's klieg-lit celebrity.

"I did say to Lee she should be on the stage," said Kitty Carlisle Hart. "I thought she'd be marvelous." Early in 1965, Hart took it upon herself to discuss Lee's interested response with the producer Lee Guber, who owned a string of summer playhouses up and down the eastern seaboard and Florida. "He and I talked about Lee coming out with me in summer stock in a play I was doing with him, *The Marriage-Go-Round*, but we decided it wasn't suitable. So I suggested that Lee audition for him because he did a lot of summer stock, and if she were interested, he would put her in a cameo part

*One could disagree with such an assessment in the case of Truman Capote, who, after his success with *In Cold Blood*, once said to a friend, "Why should I bother to write books when I can get my message across to millions in five minutes on the Johnny Carson show?"

and protect her with good actors. Lee auditioned for him—I came along too, of course.''

Guber had Lee read for him from the Morosco Theater stage and was extremely interested in her. He saw an indefinable something, a strong urge, a ''charming obstinacy'' that somehow inspired confidence. ''I thought the Princess terribly attractive in that well-bred Dina Merrill style,'' Guber later recalled.

''At the audition, she was excellent,'' said Hart. ''Several conferences followed, and Guber was perfectly happy to engage Lee—but not in a leading part to start with. He didn't think that was sensible. She'd never been on the stage. He suggested a smaller part, and then perhaps the next season, a big one.''

Guber told Lee, ''I could sell out instantly if I announced your name, but I think it important you don't go out and fall on your face. Do some studying first and acquire technique.'' Lee took his advice gracefully. She approached her friend Alan Jay Lerner, the musical-comedy writer who wrote the book of *My Fair Lady,* and told him of her hopes of a stage career. Lerner contacted the London impresario Binkie Beaumont on her behalf, who, in turn, referred her to a drama coach, Elizabeth Wilmer. Wilmer taught at the London Academy of Music and Dramatic Arts and she instructed Lee in breathing, moving, and extending her voice.

''I think Lee was talented, actually, and very keen on becoming an actress,'' Wilmer recollected, ''but she started rather late. She was good for someone just starting out, but it was hard for her to compete with actresses who had started much earlier who were the same age as she.''

Wilmer worked on helping Lee to project her soft-as-powder, small-girl voice for the stage. ''I discovered from voice tapes that I hated the way I spoke,'' Lee acknowledged. ''I sounded so breathless, so la-di-da, that I clenched my fists and winced. My voice is much less affectatious now.

''Elizabeth Wilmer helped me a lot. The minute I went to her tiny room at the London Academy, I knew she didn't know or care who I was, that she was without preconceived ideas, and only my work in that room counted. When she did begin to care, when she was touched by something I had done, it was so satisfying for me because it was impersonal and professional—not like Stas's approval, who got tears in his eyes when he watched our daughter dance. Once, when I finished reading a passage about Chesterton given to me as an exercise, I looked up, and she had tears in her eyes. I can't tell you how much that meant to me. She was maybe the first person in my life who ever gave me confidence. And yet my time with her was so brief.''

Another instruction Lee took, called the Alexander Technique, was to help make her think out each move before she made it. ''You imagine how you will sit down, how you will light this cigarette or reach for that glass,'' Lee explained. ''Really, I understand why actors are always said to be so egotistical. The work demands such terrifying self-awareness that they just can't help it. Anyway, the classes helped with my nerves and somewhat straightened out my way of moving.''

Lee studied with other acting teachers besides Wilmer and even persuaded a few big-name director friends of hers like Michael Cacoyannis, who made *Zorba the Greek*, to coach her occasionally. ''She had great determination and passion,'' Cacoyannis said, ''and that's a large part of talent right there.''

Indeed, Lee was fervently resolved if not to become an actress, to at least find out what her capabilities were. ''What I am seeking is self-expression,'' she declared at the time. ''I need some kind of personal satisfaction. I want to be involved in something I have a passion for, rather than to just go on existing. I have always loved the theater and wanted to be part of it. I don't want to be a star. My ambition is to be a working actress who is offered things of quality. I feel I have an intensity to bring to acting—it is just something I feel I can do. I'd like to do new plays or films. Tennessee Williams, Capote, interesting older women, alcoholics. I have the greatest sympathy for those who end in despair.''

Lee told a reporter that she was ''ambitious and ambition is killing.'' Needled in the press for that remark, she responded, ''I can't see why people try to make ambition a derogatory word. Perhaps it's because they have nothing they care strongly enough about to go out and do. I am such an obvious target. I have no respect for people who say things like that. I know how fleeting everything is. Power. Fame. I was an observer long before I became a participator, and around me I saw how secure some of the people at the top thought they were, and they were not. I know a lot of very rich people and none of them are happy. They contribute nothing to life. They get nothing out of it.

"I've benefited enormously from knowing people who are in love with their work. Truman. Rudolf and Margot. I have such admiration and respect for them. They seem to create from nothing. Renzo Mongiardino can make something beautiful from two scarves and some paint. They'll stay up all night working because they care. They're obsessed. But it's only in the past five years that I've come to know people like that. If I could have changed one thing in my life, I would like to have known creative people in my childhood. If I had, I might have found work I cared about much sooner and so had time to develop it.

"There is a quote of Edmund Wilson's I thought applied to me. It is from his story 'Glimpses of Wilbur Flick.' I've always thought his stories were much better than his criticism, though no one would agree with that. Anyway, in the story, he tells about how there's no necessity of doing anything when nothing is demanded of you. One may be able to function just as well as any employee, but one can't *create* the necessity. Then the character says, 'Well, maybe fate will come to get me.' That may be a little dramatic, but I do think it is important that I've finally begun some work I care about. Nor do I have any illusions about the glamour of it—I've had all that. It is just that I am not happy any longer to be on the outside while most of my friends are on the inside."

By the autumn of her second year of acting lessons, that is, in late 1966, Lee was doing mostly "reading, reading, reading," and she felt that she was wasting some of this time. The moment had come, she decided, to get some real acting experience. Searching for the right way to begin, she talked it over with some of her friends. Rudolf Nureyev urged her to get experience in repertory. Cecil Beaton, the photographer-designer, wanted her to "nag on with lessons and small roles." But Truman Capote told her that her natural star quality would only be diminished with too much training and he offered to introduce her to Milton Goldman, the New York mega-agent whose clients included Laurence Olivier and John

Gielgud, to see about placing her in a starring role.

Cecil Beaton strongly disagreed with such a move, and he admonished her: "Laurence Olivier spent two years learning to walk around a table. Not even *he* began as a star."

Always insecure about how people might perceive her, when Lee sought the counsel of others she usually ended up taking the advice of the person who spoke the loudest, rather than ultimately deciding things on her own. On this occasion, unfortunately, that person was Truman.

The pair had fallen more completely under each other's spell in recent months. Part of their growing attraction for each other flattered their egos: Truman had become an international celebrity based on the extraordinary success of his nonfiction work *In Cold Blood,* published that year, and his star was very much in the ascendant. Lee's attraction for Truman, at least in part, was her connection to the Kennedy family, although he would never admit it. More important, she seemed to represent an idealized woman to him, a much-desired heterosexual perfection, someone totally beyond his own capacity.

Some strange force field got constructed between the two of them. "I wouldn't say we had an affair," Truman would say later. "It was never romantic love, but it was a very emotional friendship, an intense emotional relationship." So close had they become that Truman, a well-known homosexual, indicated to his biographer, Gerald Clarke, that he and Lee got in bed together on one of their trips to Morocco.

Truman made Lee his protégée. He was convinced stardom was within her grasp. He deluded her into thinking that she could sail to the top of a profession as easily as she had become a celebrity, without the proper apprenticeship or peer recognition. He brushed aside the knowledge, gleaned from his own personal experience, that only years of hard work got him where he was.

Lee had tea with Milton Goldman and asked him to please keep an eye out for an appropriate vehicle for her. Afterward, he announced in a talent meeting at his agency, Ashley Famous, that Lee Radziwill wanted to be an actress. (Lee would say later that Goldman did nothing for her, and that she owed everything to Truman and David Susskind.) Various inquiries followed, and Lee considered several options, some of them in television. She was asked if she was interested in doing narrations, sitting on panel shows, even doing a talk show. "But the trouble was if I did those things I'd have to be *me*," she confessed. "It's much easier to be someone else, if you are a private person."

A screen test was arranged for her in London which was considered by her handlers to be successful. "I'd probably come across a thousand times better on film than on the stage," she said at the time. Still, she did not want her first professional appearance to be in a movie either because, she reasoned, "there wouldn't have been the desperate feeling of 'this is it' in a film," and if the film turned out to be a disaster, "it could just be discarded, and no one would have to know." After much thought, Lee chose to make her debut on the stage. To her it seemed "more honest that way."

It was another agent in Goldman's office, John Sekura, the rep for the Ivanhoe Theater in Chicago, who fixed Lee up with the stage role of Tracy Lord in *The Philadelphia Story*. He created and sparked the interest and followed through with the actual production. "Lee had a lot of people advising her outside the agency as well," Sekura noted. "It was suggested that if she were serious perhaps she could begin her career at a smaller, nondescript theater. However, the final decision was that no matter where Lee would make an appearance, there was still going to be notoriety. So rather than try putting her in, say, Podunk, Idaho, it was decided to go ahead and do a play at the Ivanhoe."

The Philadelphia Story was a comedy by Philip Barry about the Philadelphia Main Line which opened on Broadway in 1939 and became a hit motion picture. Katharine Hepburn starred in both as the spoiled but spirited divorcée who, after a fleeting romance with a newspaperman, was won back by her ex-husband. The play was scheduled to run for four weeks, a long time for a stock production, beginning on June 20, 1967.

Lee was given a guarantee and a percentage of the take. She held out against her backers who wanted her billed as Princess Lee Radziwill and insisted on using "Lee Bouvier" for the stage. A number of theaters asked to have the play after its Chicago run, but she would not make any commitment until she saw how it went.

When it was announced that Lee would play Tracy Lord, many said that nothing could be easier for her than to play someone as much like her own shadow as Barry's heroine, both "attractive, rather spoiled, ultra-privileged eastern seaboard postdebutantes." Annoyed by the comparison, Lee retorted that she "could not agree less" with such an assessment, adding, "Tracy is a charming, pleasant, attractive, amusing girl, but I don't think I have much in common with her. Not many ideas have crossed her mind. And she's a little too conventional for me. I haven't had a very conventional life. Conventions are probably needed, but I never liked them very much. I hate special schools and big weddings, for example. I don't like many of the things you're supposed to like.

"*The Philadelphia Story* is nice, but it's really just frivolous, charming nonsense. Tracy Lord has none of the feelings I understand of sadness or despair, or of knowing loss. It would be much easier to get involved in a role like something in Chekhov, as somebody who could really have naked feelings. That's what the theater is *for* after all."

To play her heroine, Lee worked on the role with a coach in London, studying diligently and making periodic hops over to Paris for fittings with Yves Saint Laurent, who was designing her costumes for the play. "I got a friend of mine who owns a London theater to let me practice on the stage and two young actors to read lines to me now and then," she recalled. "Of course, the theater was completely empty, and it had a huge proscenium—nothing like the little in-the-round stage we were to use in Chicago—but it helped a little, just to get the feeling. Rehearsal time with the cast was exactly one week, so I needed all the preparation I could get."

On the eve of her departure for Chicago, Lee found herself rattled by mixed emotions. Speaking later of those feelings, she said: "I knew how lucky I was to have such an opportunity, but there was a price to be paid. I was walking into an incredible barrage of criticism—much more than most actresses onstage for the first time—and it was very frightening. For weeks before I went to Chicago, I couldn't sleep a whole night through. Every two hours I woke up. Terrified. I *knew* everybody would be out for skin and blood. Of course, I got discouraged. The work was difficult. I had two lives to keep going at once, and I knew people were waiting to laugh. But it would have taken more than that to stop me. If you want your dreams to come true, it is much better to stick it out. To fight and persist. There is no escape. Unless it's love.''

27. *The Cast and the Critics*

"It may have been naive of us," Truman Capote said, "but we just did not expect all that attention to be focused on this. After all, the Ivanhoe Theater is not Broadway, or even the Loop." The place where Lee chose to pursue her dream was a six-hundred-seat neighborhood playhouse (now renamed the Wellington) located in a déclassé neighborhood on Chicago's North Side, which she commuted to from her hotel across town.

The precaution of booking this tryout engagement far away from Broadway was fruitless. From the moment Lee arrived in early June, several days before rehearsals officially began, it was clear that her acting debut was going to be a media event. National newsmen hung around the theater during rehearsals in an attempt to report what was going on. Nervous enough, Lee made a decision at the outset that she would ignore them as much as possible in order to concentrate on her acting.

One of her agents, John Sekura, came to Chicago for the first day of rehearsal. "I was asked to appear, and she and I took a private walk together," he recalled. "Lee expressed her fears and reservations to me. I really admired her guts because she had the courage to step on a stage in front of hundreds of people who were going to dissect her every performance. In my experience with her, she was gracious and lovely."

Unfortunately, the folly of placing a theatrical production on the shoulders of an untried novice playing the lead was obvious to the cast from the very beginning of rehearsals, although most of them gave her credit for her daring and spunk. "Lee wanted to do a good job but she was untrained," said Bob Thompson, the actor and drama coach who played Tracy Lord's father. "There were a few telling scenes with the father. I taught her what to do with her hands, where to look and all that. I helped her from a selfish point of view. I wanted some response instead of arguing against a stick. Otherwise, one doesn't tell the star how to stand and move. But this girl was so innocent, she said, 'Oh, my God, Bob, help me! Tell me what to do!' ''

Matters were not helped by Lee's relationship with her leading man, John Ericson. As he saw it: ''The show was done strictly for her publicity and enhancement, and I have never worked with anyone in my life so unprofessional or rude. When I told her she had a lot to learn about acting, she didn't want to hear it and she cut me. I hate to say this, but Lee seemed to me like a real airhead. We members of the cast used to say, 'Come and see the freak show.' I couldn't wait to finish the run.''

There were other problems. According to some members of the cast, the director was not up to par. ''Sidney Breese knew what theater was all about, but I was disappointed in his treatment of that whole play,'' Bob Thompson acknowledged. ''He didn't tell anybody where to move, which you have to do in a theater-in-the-round. Anytime an actor is standing in one position, all the people in the back see nothing but his behind and vice versa. And Sidney never told the cast, 'Now we've got to move here and come out there.' Basically, we all felt it was a disaster.''

''A lot of people were making a big fuss over Lee, which didn't help either,'' said Erika Slezak, who had a supporting role in the play. ''Nobody really let her do her acting part or let her learn. They wanted her to do so much more—to become Jackie Kennedy overnight on stage. During breaks, she would ask us on her own to rehearse with her. She rehearsed a lot, but all of her friends were coming to see her, distracting her. Lee didn't socialize with the cast very much. She had a lot on her mind, and she was, quite frankly, very nervous.''

At the same time that rehearsals were not going well, there were comic scenes taking place off stage rivaling anything in Barry's play. Some of the cast asked the director if they were supposed to curtsy when they met Lee. And when Stas arrived on the scene, he would show up at rehearsals accompanied by an entourage, so that when he kept moving to different sections of the theater in order to see Lee's performance from every angle, his entire entourage would noisily move with him, distracting Lee and making her crazy.

Then one morning when the cast came into rehearsal there was a little man slouched down in a chair in the back row with a hat over his face. At first no one knew it was Truman Capote. "We all made fun of him," said Bob Thompson. "He was so taken with Lee he was blind. We said to each other, 'He's trying to make a star of Lee and she doesn't have it.' Sometimes he would sit up at the top of the balcony, and if she turned in a certain way, or said a line in a certain way, there would be these strange little sounds of adoration coming from up there like, 'Yesssss! That's right! Oh, it's wonerful, Lee, wonerful!' "

Meanwhile, bedlam prevailed in Lee's penthouse suite at the Ambassador East Hotel. Bellmen brought her endless bouquets and telegrams and packages wishing her good luck; secretaries and other supernumeraries went in and out; Chicago Poles that Stas had wooed and won in 1960 for JFK kept calling. "I love Poles, but they are so intense!" Lee remarked. And when Truman wasn't consoling and coaching her at rehearsals, he was back at the hotel dancing with abandon, and by himself, to his favorite phonograph records.

To complete the three-ring circus, Zsa Zsa Gabor arrived at the hotel. She was there to star in a play following Lee's run. "When I asked for the suite I wanted, I was told that Mr. Onassis had arranged the suite for Lee, that she had it," said the actress. Wherever Zsa Zsa went, a blaze of publicity followed her, and she felt the need to make as much noise as the production currently there and to find out as much about it as she possibly could. "She drilled everybody like crazy about Lee," said a cast member.

On opening night, newsmen persuaded some teenagers to block the road by the entrance to the theater so that they could photograph Lee as she was driven up to it in her rented car. With her hair in curlers, she grimaced obligingly for the press as she simultaneously poked her finger at her driver to move on to the stage door. Lee's makeup man, George Masters, came from California to do her face. He arrived at the theater quite drunk that evening, and as he stumbled across the lobby on his way to her dressing room, he dropped his makeup case, spilling pots of color and brushes and other tools of his trade in all directions. He was said to have expostulated at that point: "Oooh, there goes the Princess's face all over the floor!"

"Lee threw him out of her dressing room because he was drunk," testified Erika Slezak. "Apparently he arrived very late to do her makeup, and she just asked him to leave, and he got very upset. She had an apprentice do her makeup. Lee was so breathtakingly beautiful, there was very little you could do to hurt that face—very little."

Outside the theater chaos reigned. "We had to show proof we were in the cast in order to get into the theater," Bob Thompson said. "There were TV cameras and lights everywhere. It was like a Hollywood opening, there were so many people around to see the girl. I had never experienced such a thing as that."

When the curtain went up, a critic from New York who was in the theater that evening, Chauncey Howell, reported his impression of Lee's acting debut: "The ill-starred play began late. The lights came up on Lee Bouvier, actress, in a smashing Saint Laurent outfit. Applause greeted the dazzling sight. Lee spoke her first lines, revealing an unmistakable Miss Porter's lockjaw. She looked gorgeous, but she seemed ill-at-ease. . . . The performance was slow and agonized. The acting, for the most part, was on an amateurish, stock company level. The Princess, to do her credit, was one of the few in the cast who really knew her lines. Lee wore a few more Saint Laurent stunners, and Kenneth kept her lion's mane of hair at full flounce between the acts. Lee's performance, unfortunately, stayed at a consistently wooden level . . . but even though she can't act, she was goshawful beautiful."

"Lee made an uptight, wound-up Tracy Lord," observed her half-brother, Jamie Auchincloss, who had come with Janet to see her opening performance. "Her own psyche was coming through rather than her acting." The Auchinclosses joined Lee and Stas for a party they gave afterward at a restaurant next door to their hotel called Maxim's, which was an exact Corn Belt replica of the Paris original.

The Chicago drama critics were uniformly negative in varying degrees in their assessment of Lee's acting debut. Except for a notice in a Polish newspaper that gave the play two pages and tried to be enthusiastic, and a certain number of reviews that were unduly sarcastic, the consensus was that Lee came over the footlights as an eager beginner who was not yet an actress, but who might become one with time.

"One wanted the pretty lady and her friends to be good, but the snap, the sparkle, and the fun that should have been there never got moving," wrote one reviewer. Another praised her poise but said the spirit of her role "never came through for a moment." And a third critic said: "Miss Bouvier is only a lovely-looking amateur, an enthusiastic beginner who requires more experience and conscientious struggle to achieve professional acting skill. She has a certain assurance, but no style; her voice has a nice tone, but she does not know how to project it. And what is almost embarrassing to an audience are her inept little gestures. She doesn't know what to do with her hands or her arms."

Inwardly, Lee was hurt. Outwardly, she accepted her severe critical handling with rather good grace. "When the reviews came in, we crossed our fingers that Lee wouldn't quit," said Bob Thompson, "and we went out of our way to praise her."

"Lee was very professional about the reviews. She was aware that she wasn't just being reviewed as Tracy Lord, but as Jackie Kennedy's sister and Princess Radziwill—she was being reviewed for lots of reasons," Erika Slezak noted. "But she did one thing that did not endear her to the Chicago press. Her rehearsal time was precious and she refused to give local interviews beforehand. Then she gave an interview to the *New York Times* and made some mention in it of Chicago as being 'a small, out-of-the-way town.' I remember two headlines, 'Lee Lays Golden Egg' and 'A Star Is Not Born.' Very unkind. But I think they were just angry because she had refused to give interviews."

By now, Lee was getting used to the fact that the press was either at her throat or at her feet. In Chicago that night she received few of the allowances that might have been made for an unknown actress. Even though she had expected it, the penalties that high position carries along with its privileges were apparent to her as never before.

She was somewhat cushioned from the critics' blows, though, by members of the audience who took the trouble to write her letters of encouragement. "I had lots of letters after Chicago, all of them friendly," Lee said. "I got a lot of nice letters from people, teachers and college students especially, who said they'd come to laugh or out of curiosity, but had been surprised to find a real actress who cared about the part and gave them pleasure. I hadn't expected letters like that. They made me very happy.''

Certainly the audience loved her and paid no attention to the critics. *The Philadelphia Story* was standing-room-only the entire run and was very successful financially, which explains why, in spite of the bad reviews, the majority of other stock theater managements expressed an interest in having Lee.

In Bob Thompson's opinion, ''Lee got applause from the audience because the women didn't come to the Ivanhoe to see Laurence Olivier act. They came to see Lee Radziwill with her bouffant hairdo and her magnificent clothes and her nice legs and shoes. Anybody who acted scenes with her was ignored, the same way as when a dog comes on stage. They were going to look at her instead of any of us from Chicago—why the hell look at anybody from Chicago! I don't think the audience cared what she did as long as she kept turning around so that everyone could see her. They gave Lee a new costume every time she went onstage, and the women in the audience would start discussing it out loud each time. It was a ridiculous, ridiculous affair!''

Lee's glamorous friends filled the front rows of the theater every night anyway. One evening, Rudolf Nureyev came with Margot Fonteyn, and dashing back to his seat from Lee's dressing room after intermission, he bounded up the stairs four at a time. Jackie was conveniently out of the country for her sister's entire run. If she had come to see her, she might have caused an uproar, upstaging Lee, and if she did not come to see her, it would have appeared rude. ''Lee really resented Jackie a lot,'' John Ericson noticed. ''When we talked about her, the hairs on her arms would stand up.''

Stas left after opening night. ''He asked me what I thought of her as an actress,'' recalled Bob Thompson. ''He said, 'Do you think she'll make it? Do you think she has anything?' He had his doubts. That's why I told him what I honestly felt, which was that she started at the top and didn't know what she was doing. Stas said, 'Yes, I agree. She's no actress, but she's a nice girl.' That was the idea.

''And yet Lee had to do something in life besides be in the

shadow of others. I felt sorry for her because she was like a little child who should have been given more of a chance in life. She had no identity. I liked the girl. I could kid with her, talk to her straight, and I told her frankly I didn't think she'd make it.''

Lee sensed as much. While she was starring in the play, she was booked one evening as a guest on a local television talk show. It was a long wait to go on, and while waiting to be called, she had a heartfelt conversation with another guest, the columnist Dorothy Manners. ''I am serious about acting, and I have studied diligently,'' Lee told her. ''The drama critics here do not think I've succeeded too well. It is difficult for someone raised in my world to learn to express emotion. We are taught early to hide feelings publicly. I feel I have gone as far as I could with a drama coach. The rest I had hoped to get through training and experience, which I might have done if I didn't have a 'name.' I could learn in private. But I am finding that isn't possible. . . .'' And her voice trailed off.

28. *From Stage to Screen*

Final curtain on Lee Bouvier's *Philadelphia Story* came down on July 16. During the run of the play, Lee was continually sick to her stomach and suffered from loneliness and insomnia. Now that it was over, she felt only a pervasive feeling of emptiness.

''After the play finished its run, I came back to London with the most enormous sense of letdown,'' she said. ''Truman was waiting at the house because he knew how I would feel. . . . Besides being generous with his own talent, he understood exactly how and when I needed bolstering. . . . His friendship, his loyalty, his caring were something very special. Once in Chicago, Stas and I tried to thank him. He just shook me by the shoulders and said he hadn't done anything—it was only me. I've never had such a friend!''

Lee and Truman, who stayed for a week, had a lot to talk about. He was working on a television adaption of John Van Druten's romantic comedy *The Voice of the Turtle* especially for her. The project had been set in motion even before Lee went to Chicago. It had originated the month before, in May, the night Truman won an Emmy for an adaption he did for ABC of a short story of his, "Christmas Memory." He sat at a table with the president of the network, Tom Moore, and the independent producer and talk show host, David Susskind, and Susskind's colleague, Alan Shayne, and he said to them, "I think we should do something wonderful for Lee, and David will produce it." All those present said they were interested, and it went on from there.

Ignoring the critics, Lee's handlers felt that she had performed creditably for an amateur in Chicago and that she might do better on television, where the small screen would be a better medium for her beauty and a less severe one for her acting. "I saw enough of her in Chicago to convince me she would do all right," said David Susskind, considered at the time *the* television impresario and a spellbinder. "She wasn't very good, but I thought maybe I saw a glimmer of something in her performance. The television companies had noticed the publicity, so it looked like we could set something up."

Susskind almost didn't have any choice. He complained afterward that Truman Capote telephoned him at all hours and appeared in his office carrying a portfolio of photographs of Lee as Tracy Lord and badgered him until he gave in. As an added inducement, he even offered to write the script himself. "I did say to Truman, 'She may be Jackie Kennedy's sister, but how do we know anybody will want to see her?'" Susskind recalled. "'ARE YOU KIDDING?!' Truman shrieked."

Truman was a few weeks into his adaption when it was decided that Lee should instead play the lead in a remake of Otto Preminger's 1944 mystery-thriller, *Laura*. Gene Tierney had starred as the romantic and enigmatic Laura in the film classic based on Vera Caspary's best-seller. Once again Lee was to play a socialite heroine in a role previously made famous by a movie star. The idea for *Laura* belonged to Alan Shayne, Susskind's associate producer and casting director. "I suggested *Laura* because although she's pivotal, Lee would not have to carry the play totally the way she would in *Turtle*," Shayne recollected. "There were several other actors she could work with." Susskind agreed. Lee did not mind the switch, and Truman wrote a remake of *Laura* for his friend's television acting debut, updating the story by casting Lee as a successful advertising executive.

Truman's smartened-up version of *Laura*, for which Lee was paid a salary of $50,000, was a two-hour Movie of the Week to be shown both on the ABC-TV network and London television; rehearsals and taping for the Lee Bouvier version were to be done in the fall in London by Talent Associates with David Susskind in charge of production.

In August, Lee took a vacation from her acting chores at Amalfi, Italy, with her family. Pleasant as her holiday was, she was too excited to focus on anything except the tremendous adventure which lay just ahead of her. She wrote to Truman: "I wish we could begin tomorrow. My interests have narrowed down in such a violent way that now I'm just possessed. Thank you!"

Before Lee left Chicago, she posed for a ten-page fashion layout and advertising tie-in for *Vogue* magazine to help promote audience interest in her acting career. The spread appeared in their all-important September issue featuring the new fall fashion collections. The idea originated in *Vogue*'s promotion department with Diana Vreeland's blessing. Condé Nast liked to run thematic ideas in conjunction with Du Pont around the collections issue, and that season they featured multipage ads with the glamour of Lee Bouvier, actress, as the model. In return for the free publicity, Lee was not paid. The photographs were taken by Bert Stern, then under contract to *Vogue*. Smiling glossily, she modeled several au courant designer outfits made of Du Pont fibers.

"Lee did the Du Pont spread on the condition that I shoot it, but that was the second part of the story," said Bert Stern. "The first part was a note from Diana Vreeland asking me if I'd do her a favor and do a personal sitting with Lee Radziwill. Lee had said something to her about my work. She thought I was the only photographer at the time who understood women, and she wanted me to do her picture. It was a very flattering start, and when I did the pictures, they were fabulous because she reached out and wanted me to do her. Lee was like Marilyn Monroe to work with. Very sexy. Very sweet. I was surprised at how beautiful she was when I photographed her. She is better-looking than most of the pictures you see of her."

*   *   *

When Lee returned from her summer holiday, she again practiced her lines on a real stage belonging to a theater-owning friend, and hired two actors to feed her cues. John Moxey, the director of *Laura,* came by her new country home, Turville Grange, near Henley-on-Thames in Oxfordshire, to work with her prior to rehearsals. Every effort was being made to make the fledgling actress as good as she could be in her next performance.

Another visitor to Turville Grange was the painter Jan De Ruth, who came to do sketches of Lee for the all-important picture of her needed for the story; in *Laura,* the detective falls in love with Laura's portrait. The painting was to be a combination of Lee Bouvier and the heroine. The artist spent some time with his subject "talking, not painting or sketching, just finding out," and said of her afterward: "She's extremely emotionally strong. I liked her. And, you know, I don't think she's a woman who's had an easy life. You can see definite experiences of suffering in her eyes."

During one of their sittings, De Ruth asked Lee if she ever had her portrait painted before. "Yes, a couple of times," she answered. "We keep them in the basement." Stas liked the sketches De Ruth did of his wife so much that he wanted to buy them. He told the artist, "You brought out the inner strength in her."

When rehearsals for the television show began in mid-September, David Susskind came to London to promote *Laura.* He invited photographers and reporters to an evening reception at the Savoy Hotel and told them in typical Susskind style, "Laura . . . was a Mona Lisa dame you never really knew—and that's Lee Bouvier."

Susskind was very keen on drumming up even more publicity for his costly show, and he wanted Lee to appear on television as herself to help him do so. "David wanted to do a show at home with Stas and me and the children, but Stas wouldn't think of it, and I wouldn't think of asking him," Lee said at the time. "This new work of mine should not interfere with his privacy."

Excited by the idea of playing Laura, yet not a little afraid, Lee confessed to her producer that she had "butterflies" in her "tummy." If she were seeking simple reassurance from him, she did not get it. "Listen," Susskind told her, "you damn well better be scared. This is a butterflies-in-the-stomach game, *Miss Bouvier*. It's a tough, scary business you're in now."

After Susskind returned to New York, Lee was left in the hands of Dick Blodget, the agent at the London end of Milton Goldman's talent agency who saw to it that the contract for *Laura* and all the demands of the deal were met (Ashley Famous represented Susskind too). Blodget's association with Lee was not a happy one; her eternal role-confusion offended him. As he remembers it: "The first time I went to see her, I was greeted by a butler in a white coat who said to me, 'The Princess will see you in the Green Room.' Perhaps it was nerves, it might have been standoffishness, but I got the feeling that I was received with a great deal of hauteur and condescension. 'You will do this, please. You will do that.' There was no friendly rapport. I come from a theater background,* and my feeling was that there are princesses, and I presume they belong in palaces, and there are actresses, and they are either on a stage or on a set, and they behave in quite a different way." (Dick Blodget knew Lee from their days on the debutante party circuit, though she did not remember him when they met again here.)

"I also felt that Lee was overly interested in publicity and too particular about who she was going to speak to and how it was going to be done. Several columnists called and asked to do interviews, but she didn't want to grant them—this one had done this and the other one that. Her focus should have been more on the actual production."

During both the rehearsals and the taping, uninvited journalists never stopped snooping around the set, asking everyone from the janitor to the dialogue coach for tidbits of gossip about Lee Bouvier and her acting. Lee did end up talking to a slew of them, and even made the cover of *Life* (for *The Philadelphia Story*) and was the subject of a major feature in *Look*. But she was positively spiky if any of them implied that her acting career was just a passing fancy, saying defensive things like "I sometimes suspect people think I am doing this as a whim. But I have a lovely home in the country where I

---

*Dick Blodget is the son of Cornelia Otis Skinner.

could be relaxing today. I could have slept late and enjoyed a leisurely breakfast, and instead, here I am [at the studio]. I got here at eight o'clock this morning, and I'll be here till seven or eight tonight, standing under the lights, making sure my feet are on the marks, checking my makeup and doing wardrobe fittings. I come home at night so exhausted that I fall into bed. Does this sound like a whim?''

The four weeks of rehearsals for *Laura* took place in Chelsea at the Duke of York's headquarters, a splendid classical barracks rented from the War Office by the production company. The fine setting, alas, did little to alleviate the unfortunate turn of events, for the making of the television special turned out to be a tense, difficult, and frustrating experience for everyone involved in it, Lee most of all. The same problem of a novice who was supposed to carry the show thrown into an ensemble of professional actors played itself out in London as it had in Chicago, only this time the stakes were much higher. *Laura* was a high profile, $600,000 international venture starring George Sanders, Robert Stack, Farley Granger, and Arlene Francis, all veteran actors at the peak of their craft. David Susskind packed a solid phalanx of professionals around Lee—all of whom gave her a great deal of cosseting—with the intention that the strong cast would help her to perform better, but they only succeeded in showing up her glaring inadequacies and making her feel even more of an outsider than she already did.

At the outset, Lee decided she would get through the ordeal of being in way over her head by not showing any of the qualms of a beginner. ''What Lee chose to do was to brazen it through,'' said Alan Shayne. ''She played her role with a kind of authority that didn't make for acting but did make it possible for her to handle it. And the fact that it didn't come out well was a lot of people's fault, not just hers.

''The whole situation was bad. The production started out on the wrong foot. We discovered we had the wrong script very close to going into rehearsal, but when we asked Truman for a rewrite, he either couldn't or wouldn't help us by then. Some of the cast weren't happy with their parts, because they weren't happy with the script. Even the scenes Lee wasn't in weren't going so well.... If an actress has years of experience behind her, she can cope with this very difficult process of

having to do a show in a short time. Otherwise, all those distractions will serve to make her stiff, and that's what happened
to Lee.''

"There really was a lot of tension on that set, a lot of un-
dercurrents and all kinds of vibrations going on with everybody, not just Lee,'' said Farley Granger. "Then Moxey and
Lee, who seemed to get along, suddenly didn't get along at
all.''

"What Farley saw,'' Moxey explained, "was my final realization that Lee wasn't going to cut it. There was a tension
that grew between us which was the frustration of my trying
to get her to do the job and her being unable to do it.''

The problems with Lee's performance worked to Farley
Granger's and Arlene Francis's advantage. "What happened
was that as time went on they kept making Arlene's and my
parts bigger when they realized that Lee couldn't cope with
carrying it,'' said Granger, who played Laura's boyfriend.
"But the show was called Laura, not Arlene or Farley. Lee
understood what was going on. She was very frightened, and
so was everybody else.

"And then they were going to replace her. Other actresses
were contacted to stand by, which happens often in television.'' The decision to replace Lee was made between Tom
Moore and David Susskind, and then Moore discussed it with
Truman. Truman's reaction now was that maybe it was for the
best, and he, in turn, spoke with Susskind about it. Lee had
by this time exhausted Susskind's patience. "What really an-
gered me was her attitude,'' he said. "She was constantly late
for rehearsal because of late-night doings at her home. Into
the final weeks of rehearsals, she didn't know her lines, didn't
know her cues, didn't know where to enter or exit.''

Susskind had connections to the Kennedys and was uncomfortable with firing Lee outright. Instead, he instructed his director to make it so miserable for her by attacking her acting
so mercilessly and so often that she would quit rather than go
on. Moxey says he did not follow Susskind's orders and that
he took the position that no matter how bad Lee was, she
should not be humiliated. But Lee did not perceive Moxey's
behavior in the same way. To her, he was riding her much too
hard. "He loved to humiliate me in front of everybody until
finally I was just getting ill,'' she complained.

Unaware of Susskind's plan to force her to quit—"Oh, no way did I tell Lee!" Moxey exclaimed—Lee complained to Truman and Cecil Beaton about Moxey's treatment of her. Then she called Dick Blodget to talk to him about it. "Lee said she had been up all night being sick because she was being victimized and pressured by John Moxey," Blodget recalled, "and that she had talked to her two best friends, and they both told her to walk off the set. And I said to her, 'You do that, Lee, and you'll be a Princess for the rest of your life.' And the moment I heard myself say that I expected her to either hang up or have a good old furor." Lee did neither. She went back to work instead. But she did tell Moxey that he had to stop riding her. "I told him that I'd be no good in it if he carried on that way," she said later.

If Lee had established more of a rapport with the cast, they might have been able to advise her sensibly on how to deal with her dilemma, but she kept her distance. "She had the impression that she was different from them because she was who she was, Princess Radziwill," John Moxey observed. "Internally she pulled rank."

Lee did establish a friendly rapport with one of her co-stars, George Sanders. In fact, she was sometimes so relaxed before the cameras with him that they ruined a couple of takes by erupting into laughter over a private joke. "Sanders was a dear, sweet, funny man. He helped to keep things going," said Farley Granger.

One day, the production company had quite a laugh at Lee's expense. After a necking scene with Robert Stack, she forgot that her mike was still on and she whispered seductively into his ear, "Farley kisses well, but I think you kiss better." The control room broke up, and Lee's face turned red.

After Tom Moore's conversation with Truman and Truman's bad advice to Lee to walk off the set, he made himself unavailable to the company from then on, more or less washing his hands of Lee's acting career. "Truman wanted to be a star-maker, and he was supposed to do rewrites, and he never did," Granger recalled. "He just disappeared. Susskind was in New York all the time we were rehearsing. We were just left on our own."

The actual taping was done at Intertel Studios in Wembly in north London. Like any film or TV set, it was hot, chaotic, and crowded during shooting. The confusion made Lee so uptight that one of the studio girls whispered to another as she was walking by: "Walk, walk, walk. Even when she's sitting down her eyebrows are nervous."

"It was very difficult to remember all the little things for television," Lee complained, "the chalk marks on the floor, the very precise movements you have to make. And there's no continuity as there is on a stage. It was very hot, and there were all these people everywhere. I just got numb with tiredness and hardly knew what I was doing anymore."

Susskind, who arrived back in London for the taping, chopped the shooting into many brief scenes, presumably so Lee would not have to sustain any extended display of emotion, and a lot of her performance ended up on the cutting-room floor. "We had to do as many as thirty takes in some instances, and the only way to get it done was to focus the camera on anything but Lee," he said. After ten very trying days, taping was completed on October 26.

"The morning after we finished filming was a great letdown," Lee told a reporter at the time. "I'd been keyed up for so long I just felt, 'When can I start again?' Then I realized I needed a bit of time for reappraisal, a time to see the children."

David Susskind gave a preview party for *Laura* in New York and showed it to his friends. "There was a moment when Truman and I were alone watching one of the monitors," John Moxey recalled, "and just by the look on his face I realized that he was desperately unhappy and that he felt it had all been a terrible mistake. But when asked about it, he tried to jolly it along and put his best face on it."

Ingrid Bergman and Johnny Carson and some of the other guests walked out on Susskind's party. "Johnny was offended by the command of the rich and famous," the producer said when speaking about *Laura* with Truman years afterward on one of his talk shows. "It had more to do with his professionalism," countered Truman. "He resented the idea of a young lady who was not a professional being starred in an expensive production like that." "And justifiably so," declared his host.

The night the teleplay was aired on American television, January 24, 1968, Lee and Stas gave a small party at their apartment. Jackie was there. "I watched *Laura* at Jackie's with John and Caroline," said Jamie Auchincloss. "They were so excited. There were oohs and ahhs at seeing their aunt kissing on the screen. But Lee couldn't come out of herself and be Laura either."

Lee suffered a further volley of punishing criticism from the reviewers of *Laura*, who for the most part demolished her performance. They stated that her acting had not visibly improved since *The Philadelphia Story*, and that she attitudinized stiffly rather than communicated any real emotion, and that although she did her level best, "the vital core was not there." Nor did they like the production as a whole. One critic called it "an exercise in theatrical frustration . . . the occasion was just a labored walk-through for the entire company."

Viewers disregarded what the critics had to say just as the audiences in Chicago had ignored them. The program drew very high ratings. Presumably, they tuned in either for the Bouvier mystique or to watch Lee fail, depending on how they responded to her personally. "That was another thing," said Alan Shayne. "The camera did not really love Lee. She is a much more beautiful woman in life than on camera, although part of that was probably the lighting. It was still the early days of taping then, and the lighting techniques were not so wonderful."

After Chicago and then *Laura*, Lee's moment as an actress came and went. At first, this was not obvious to her. She was still eager to explore any new offers that came along. "I did not go into this as a whim," she again insisted fiercely. "There's just no question of my giving up if I can find work to do." One of the film projects she considered was a western, *Shalako*, being produced by the Briton, Euan Lloyd, who said he eventually decided she wasn't right for it. A second possibility was the offer of a *small* role in Roman Polanski's *Rosemary's Baby*. That option came about because Polanski was a friend of Lee's, and she declined the part after reading the script. The third possibility, to co-star at a Phoenix dinner theater in a play, George Kelly's *The Torch-Bearers*, greatly interested her. Yet neither the film nor the drama projects went anywhere for Lee. According to her, it was because she was wrongly advised to turn them all down.

Many years later, when being interviewed by Andy Warhol, Lee gave her version of these events: "One lesson that I did learn from my experience in *The Philadelphia Story,* as well as in television, is to follow your own intuition. Because the 'professionals' always say, 'We are here to help you. Be sure to ask our advice before you do anything.' So many interesting project possibilities came in, and I knew that I should do something in the same field immediately, because the people I would have been working with would have taught me a lot, but this professional man said, 'What? You do a western? Why that would be perfectly ridiculous and offensive!' Well, it turned out that Brigitte Bardot and Sean Connery did it, so I could have kicked him for his great advice.

"And then there was another play that I wanted to do in Phoenix, which was with Cornelia Otis Skinner and Maureen Stapleton, and this man said to me, 'It's all wrong for you,' and I said, 'But it's only going to last six weeks, and I'll learn so much by doing it.' But I didn't." (The unnamed advisor Lee refers to here is David Susskind; apparently she was afraid to antagonize him any further, so bitter was he with the whole experience of *Laura*—as indeed was she.)

It is questionable whether Lee would have followed through on these projects even if she had decided she wanted to do them, because by now her husband was implacably opposed to her acting career. It was one thing for Stas to be supportive of her, however reluctantly, if she was doing well, but after the debacle of *Laura* he saw no point to it. "He just never understood," said Lee. "He always felt why expose oneself when it's not necessary."

With no one left now to cheer her on, and apparently unable to continue on her own, Lee reluctantly let go of her dream. Her failure at acting was a spiritually violent climax for her, one that left her more discontented than ever, and one that she would never entirely overcome. Ironically, in trying to fashion a bulwark against her sister's fame, she had succeeded only in making herself more vulnerable.

One interesting and unexplored aspect of Lee's acting experience was touched on by Truman when he was a guest on David Susskind's talk show years later and the painful subject of *Laura* came up. He said that Lee got much tougher scrutiny than she might have got otherwise because she was the whipping post for the underside of the public's feelings toward Jackie Kennedy. "We've got to admit," Truman told Susskind, "that we had not foreseen the extent to which no matter what Lee did, the press was going to come down on her like hell . . . because they really wanted to say nasty things about Mrs. Kennedy and never could at that time because Jackie was still the widow lady, a little saint. There was underneath all that adulation—we're pre-Onassis now—a tremendous resentment and envy for this beautiful girl who had everything. And here was this other girl who wouldn't have got the part if she weren't Mrs. Kennedy's sister. Naturally it was going to have a whole thing come down on it—bang! I didn't realize it would be quite as severe as it was. Lee was aware of it, but she was willing to take the risk because she very much wanted a life of her own."

Ever one with an apt remark, Truman told Lee: "The dogs bark and the caravan passes on."

29. *Changes of Scene*

During the years Lee diligently pursued a career as a professional actress, her personal and social lives were by no means slack. In June 1965 she wrote to Truman from London of a trip she had just taken to Belgium and Holland with Marella Agnelli: "In spite of the paintings I prefer the south! The weather is suicidal here, so it will be nice to change." The change of locale Lee had in mind was Setúbal, in the Portuguese countryside, where she and her family spent two and a half months beginning on July 1.

Shortly before she left for her summer holiday, Lee met with Renzo Mongiardino to discuss the redecoration of selected rooms at 4 Buckingham Place, which he was to accomplish in August while the Radziwills were away. Because Lee spent a good deal of her time in her drawing room, she wanted an atmosphere there that would be "warm, comfortable, strange, and mysterious, something completely removed from the kind of room Stas and I usually saw around us." She and Mongiardino came up with the bold idea of a Turquerie room. Lee's decorating style had evolved by now into one of

whimsical historicism. In all of her homes that she would decorate from this point on, she blended a variety of styles and
periods into a highly individual whole, and the rooms she created were cozy and enchanting. Her real gift was her use of
color. One could see that talent at work very clearly in the
new look of her drawing room. The room's walls, tables, sofa,
and cushions, and even the lampshades, were all covered in a
blaze of bright orange, paisleyed Indian cotton to very sensuous effect. When sunlight filtered into the room through the
vines outside the window, and through the flame-colored taffeta curtains, to "glance off logger-red flowers in turquoise-
blue Sèvres vases," the effect was dazzling and uniquely
Lee's.

Earlier in the decade, Diana Vreeland, Lee's former boss at
Harper's Bazaar, had become editor-in-chief of American
Vogue. She had always admired Lee's special style and when
she heard about her sensational new drawing room, Vreeland
had Cecil Beaton photograph it the following year, for the
magazine's 1966 Christmas issue. Lee's exotic decor was a
smash hit and it started a fad. "I did the first comeback of a
Turkish room, and then it got so widely copied that I was
disgusted," she admitted. "But still, it was so good that I left
it."

A number of other splendid details were installed in the
town house as part of the redecoration: finely laid floors, richly
carved woodwork, and for the dining-room walls, gleaming
old Cordoba leather. It could be said that many of Lee's
choices, particularly her use of French-château-inspired doors
on the ground floor, were inappropriate decoration for an eighteenth-century Georgian house. But this was the sixties, after
all, when the fashionable goal was bold effect, not historical
authenticity. Anyway, all the fancy work and redecoration of
the Radziwills' home went into the first two floors—the rooms
the visitors would see. The remaining floors remained quite
ordinary.

Behind 4 Buckingham Place was a second house, which the
Radziwills also owned. Reached through an entrance in the
garden, it was used for guests and servants, and, it was said,
Stas took his girlfriends there.

The London house was the first in a succession of interiors
for which Lee would become renowned. What is to the point

is that when she had her home conventionally done in creamy brocades with off-white carpeting and walls prior to her collaboration with Renzo Mongiardino, neither Diana Vreeland, nor any other magazine editor, for that matter, was interested in featuring it, no matter how pretty and charming it may have been, because it was not glossed over by a fashionable interior decorator. But then again, Lee's own tastes changed. She declared her home's simple, vanilla-painted walls a mistake, and they all vanished with the makeover. "The house was like a bowling alley. No genius could make it come together," she said.

One of the guests Lee invited to Setúbal that summer was the French actress Leslie Caron, who came with her two children for two weeks. Caron and Lee knew each other socially in London. Their children were schoolmates at the French lycée, and Lee invited Caron to stay at the lovely, comfortable house she and Stas rented in the country around Cascais because she wanted playmates for her children.

"It was the most extraordinary holiday because Truman Capote was there," Caron reminisced, "and in a small group like that all the meals with him were quite fascinating. He talked about his experiences on Death Row with the prisoners he knew intimately. I remember we all went to visit Lisbon together, and around five o'clock Truman would say to us, 'Oh, I ain't got no more pep.' He did drink quite heavily, and he didn't have the strength to go on touring the surrounding attractions, so at that point we would all go back to the house. What Truman liked was lounging around talking and drinking white wine.

"He and Lee were accomplices. They knew the same circle of friends, society people who, on the whole, I didn't know, and they had very much the same sense of humor, the same vision of the world. I could see they shared a lot together. But nevertheless, Lee wasn't your usual, spontaneous American girl. There was always a secret part of her—inhibition is something you can't let down. And Lee had a strange accent, too, which was part of that same distance, that same personality. She had a way of saying really—rahhhhhly— a very long drawn-out vowel which was unrecognizable. It wasn't like anything I ever heard before; it wasn't Canadian, American,

English, or Australian; it was entirely her own.

"When I met Jackie, I found her also very restrained. She, too, had that same polite distance and inhibition. Both sisters' characteristics were formed way before they became prominent on the stage of the world—a person cannot be fashioned so late in life. It had something to do with their upbringing.

"But Lee was a very lovely person with a fine way of expressing herself. Her dinners and interiors were always surprisingly exquisite. She was a woman of distinction and a very prominent social figure in London, very successful and sought after, and much admired and followed by the press.

"And Lee was well read, too. One could see that when she talked about books. I always admired her turn of mind. She would think about things and give a smart answer. Then there was the athletic side of her: she was in great shape and could water-ski very beautifully—she was really quite good at it. Nor did I ever see all those things people said about her suffering on account of her sister. I never saw that Lee was in Jackie's shadow at all. She certainly was a star in London, and she did that all on her own, before Jackie became famous.

"Yet at the same time, Lee was unsure of herself in every way, timid even. She was never someone to step first in front of a door, for example, and her opinions about books and plays were often given with some hesitancy. She was a very tactful person, essentially polite to a fault—all part of that breeding. And once in a while she would reveal a vulnerability that was touching in someone so accomplished and who appeared to have resolved everything, and a very sensitive nature that needed protection, and this is why I think she chose an older man like Stas. I understand that, because he was such a warm teddy bear. There was an amused quality on his part, as if he were dealing with a child, and Lee looked up to him as a protector.

"Lee was protected like Nora in *A Doll's House,* and I had the feeling that she wanted to try out her wings and be independent in the same way. This is contradictory, of course, because, on the other hand, she needed that protection. Most women are frightened of facing life all by themselves. This was just my instinct about her because she never confided in me."

Leslie Caron's view of Lee Radziwill is obviously a gentle

one. By contrast, Stas's property broker and close associate of
many years, Gerald Smith, who was instrumental in the purchase of the Radziwills' country estate that same year, acquired such a different impression of Lee's personality and
manners in his dealings with her that it is hard to believe he
is talking about the same person. Finding her warmth highly
selective and her manner "incredibly offhand," the comparison serves to underscore Lee's confounding, two-sided personality:

"Lee could be very direct and persistent when she was on
a quest of something that she wanted, but once she got what
she wanted, in the very next moment whoever had helped her
get it became invisible. She would walk right past you. Either
she was all over you or you didn't exist for her. When Turville
Grange came on the market, I worked very hard to negotiate
the deal, and I got a snowshower of cables from her with
instructions. Soon after the deal was closed, I saw her in the
office, and she ignored me. Lee doesn't add up to much on
the human scale, unlike Stas, who was a real person."

When Lee returned from Portugal, she and Renzo Mongiardino drove out to Turville Grange to plan its resurrection. Set
in fifty acres of gardens, orchards, woodlands, and fields, the
eighteenth-century mansion, which was once a bakery house,
had a Queen Anne facade that incorporated two centuries' additions. It was situated, secretive and seductive, above the gentle and spectacular sweep of the Thames Valley in the village
of Turville Heath, near the busy sailing town of Henley, forty-
five miles west of London. Stas bought the estate from Vis-
count and Viscountess Esher in Lee's name and gave her a
fair sum of money to completely rebuild and enlarge it.

"I told Renzo how I imagined it," Lee recalled. "He and
I worked together, planned together, and pulled it together."
Turville Grange was Lee's "irresistible mistake," her toy and
refuge and pride and joy for the remaining years she spent in
England. Tucked behind formal hedges, the house itself had
seven bedrooms and three reception rooms and every typical
English house vice. "Indeed," Lee said ruefully, "the place
had no architectural points whatsoever. I thought initially that
we had made a mistake in buying the house. The rooms
seemed small and hard to do anything with, and I wondered

if perhaps we might have built a new house, one that would have overlooked the Valley. But there wouldn't have been the eccentricities, the charm, the way the floorboards creaked. I liked the way the house strayed and rambled about and how the rooms opened off each other, and because of its tranquility, its atmosphere, and the unexpected way its silences were broken, it seemed of another time.''

One of the biggest jobs the Radziwills undertook, and one which occupied Lee well into the following year, was laying a cobblestoned courtyard behind the house and surrounding its other sides with a veranda, herb garden, and a stable and guest cottage made from the old barn and grain house. ''I want there to be a lot of *life* here,'' she declared. ''See those windows that face onto the courtyard?'' Lee asked a visitor. ''That's going to be the stable. Won't it be nice to have horses' heads protruding out of the windows?

''Stas and I were always repairing, painting, taking out floors, and decorating was the subject of a running battle between us,'' Lee said later. ''He liked to surround himself with little sentimental things, which I objected to. But I always won.'' As a result, there were few such objects in the Radziwill households. Only one family photograph was allowed at their house in town and two in the country, and all three of those pictures were of the same individual, taken with children. That person was John F. Kennedy.

30. *Rudolf and Truman*

''I am lonely and unhappy. She is gone again. May I come 'round?'' Stas would ask his Polish friends whenever Lee had once again winged away from her family on another of her global jaunts. ''We would always tell him, 'Come over and have supper, and let's talk about old times,''' said one of those friends. ''It was a matter of giving succor and friendship to somebody we loved.

''Stas would pop over and complain about various aspects of Lee,'' this friend continued, ''about how she was always traveling and gadding about. He wanted to settle down, go to church, see the children at school, and play the country gen-

tleman on weekends at Henley. Lee didn't want to do any of
that. Stas would make helpless remarks like 'She has gone to
see her sister,' or 'She's gone shopping,' or else he'd complain
about the money she spent. Lee was always redecorating the
house. It was unbelievably beautiful, but it was Lee's house.
He was upset about the cost of it all. Stas would throw up his
hands and say, 'Oh, God. She is at it again! The room has
been changed again!' Whereas in his own properties in Poland,
a room was decorated once or twice in a century.

"Stas never complained about Lee's infidelities—that was
a matter of pride—and he would only come by when she was
away. We felt sifted out by her. Perhaps we weren't grand
enough. But Stas did not have to compete with us or pretend
with us, and I think he found that refreshing."

Certainly Stas was used to Lee's absences; for that matter,
he, too, jumped around. Rather, his complaints were more a
question of degree. As the decade wore on, Lee began to go
farther afield more often, and for longer periods of time. During the mid-to late sixties, there were journeys to North Africa,
several to Palm Springs to visit Truman, and three visits to
Israel in as many years, all in addition to her routine trips to
the States and the Continent. Lee's capricious, last-minute
tours had become her means to escape what she increasingly
saw as the confinement of her marriage. Yet this freedom to
roam that Stas allowed her was actually their marital salvation.
Without it, their union would have broken up years sooner.
Of course, Lee never told her husband that she felt her life as
Princess Radziwill had become a narrow, cooped-up existence
for her. They did not share that kind of honesty with each
other. She left Stas to hope that one day she might quit her
search for "innocent adventure" and stay put.

In the meantime, insiders like Leo Backer took note of the
Radziwills' ever-widening rift. "As Stas's accountant I was in
constant touch with both of them," he said. "My feeling
was—and I had many occasions to see this—that Lee was a
cold woman. She was more friendly to strangers than she was
to Stas. The way she treated him was not the way you treat a
husband you like. I witnessed scenes where he was very amorous and Lee was absolutely like a glacier. It was a situation
that had been going on for some time. Stas would be physically affectionate, and she just had no reaction. She was for-

mally polite to him. It was as if he didn't exist for her.''

''After a time one begins to know the geography of people, and Lee had her limitations as a person,'' confided Gerald Smith. ''When her facade started to wear off, she was like a little girl pulling the legs off of flies. She mocked Stas because she enjoyed it, and Lee had a good master as well because Stas could also be sarcastic, and his sarcasm could be very cutting. His response to her sarcasm was to drink a lot of vodka. Stas was on his way to becoming an alcoholic, and it would have happened anyway, but over a period of time it really distressed me to see how much he was drinking.'' (How life repeats itself! Here was Lee, in a perilous echo of her former marriage, mocking a spouse who took solace in drink.)

Smith continued: ''Because of this ultraloyalty to people that he had, Stas wouldn't believe there was any malevolence in them, particularly in somebody he was married to. He might have known, but he wouldn't believe it—I am sure he did know. I am not saying he wasn't responsible for a lot of his own actions, but Stas was taken for a hell of a ride by Lee. And yet I am reluctant to chisel away at her because she was a very unhappy and insecure person. She had this never-ending conflict to live up to the various images of herself, her various personas, and that just doesn't work.''

While Lee ran around, Stas sought distraction from his marital misery in his friendship with Charlotte Ford, the daughter of the auto magnate Henry Ford II. So fond were they of each other that their relationship became the object of some speculation. ''Stas used to call Charlotte 'the Princess Margaret of America' before she married Stavros Niarchos, because he thought she was the number-one American girl,'' said David Metcalfe. ''She was young, unmarried, very pretty, and glamorous, and she was Henry's daughter. Stas was very proud of his relationship with her, and he thought it was a hell of a feather in his cap. Probably his relationship with Charlotte was his way of trying to handle the way Lee was carrying on. He thought it was one up on her, which to a certain extent, it was.''

''Stas and I were introduced at the Carlyle Hotel by Arkady Gerney [a Kennedy friend] immediately after Jack was killed,'' Charlotte recalled. ''It was a very innocent friendship, and it was nothing more than that, ever. We had a great affection for each other. He was a wonderful and loyal friend. He certainly never asked me to marry him, as people said.''

Stas felt he could let down his guard with the quiet, convent-bred, nondrinking Charlotte in a way he could not do with anyone else, not even his old Polish friends. "He was going through troubled times," she acknowledged. "I used to try to get him to stop drinking. He admitted to me how unhappy he was, and I kept saying to him, 'What are you going to do about it?' And he would say, 'I don't know.' "

The Radziwills kept the tension in their relationship under wraps for the most part in their social life, and they never missed a party if they could help it. Friends still found them great fun to be with. They were frequently spotted at Claridge's Grill and late at night at their favorite nightspot, Annabelle's, the fashionable and very hip Berkeley Square club founded by Mark Birley in 1963, which catered to the elite of the newly named jet set.

"We saw Lee often. Whenever there was a party, she and Stas were there," said Lady Annabelle Goldsmith (then Birley), the club owner's wife and, obviously, the inspiration for its name. "Lee was a very special woman in being beautiful, and she was quite clever and fascinating. A lot of men were crazy about her. She was the sort of woman who would spend all evening dancing with some man she found wildly attractive, absolutely wrapping herself around him, and that sort of behavior gives rise to rumors." Ironically, just such an evening occurred between Lee and the tycoon Jimmy Goldsmith, Lady Annabelle's future husband: she remembers that their flirtation was nipped in the bud when Lee left on a long vacation the following day.

At one time it was suggested only half-jokingly that Lee take over the selection of discs at Annabelle's, so avidly did she follow the top-ten charts. Both Stas and she loved pop music, and a record player blared throughout the house almost continuously when either one was at home. "Lee would have made a very swinging disc jockey," joked a friend.

At times Lee got tired of all the nightlife and preferred quiet evenings at home. She said, "It can be so exhausting to be polite, you know." When the Radziwills did step out culturally, they often went to Covent Garden to see Rudolf Nureyev dance. They had adopted the company of the runaway Russian danseur in 1962, a year after his defection to the West, when he came to London as a guest artist with the Royal Ballet. Lee met him socially and invited him to stay at 4 Buckingham Place, where he remained for seven months. "It wasn't easy," she recollected. "He had lunch at four or five o'clock in the afternoon before a performance, and after a performance it took him hours to wind down. We used to go antiquing about eleven and walk and walk until two in the morning. And Rudolf would inevitably become thrilled about some extremely dark, heavy piece of furniture, and the next day I would have to go and find out what it was."

Nureyev was often at the Radziwills' London house even after he got one of his own. Stas referred to him as "Lee's friend the dancer," and on March 17, 1966, they capped a recent spate of weekends with him at country-house parties and nightclubbing in Saint James's by throwing a twenty-eighth birthday party for him at their home. Sensitive to the jostling that went on among people eager to meet him, Lee invited mostly Nureyev's dance-world friends to the party.

Lee's friendship with Rudolf Nureyev was a great coup for her. He was the first pop icon of the sixties (and an unlikely one, since his achievement was to romanticize ballet) and Rudimania was in full force then, replete with "wild-eyed fans straining against the barricades." "It was Nureyev who ignited a new curiosity and passion for dance, captivating thousands who had never been interested previously," noted Lee, who had become a balletomane as a result of her friendship with him and Margot Fonteyn.

To most who knew him, Rudolf Nureyev exerted a pull beyond his gift and fame. "One of Nureyev's extraordinary assets is his tremendous curiosity about a thousand things totally unrelated to his work, from every field of the arts to history and politics," Lee once said of his fascination for her. "His hunger for knowledge is relentless, and that is part of the excitement of being with him. His acute and precise observations on almost anyone or anything are the most unusual, the most original. When I first knew him, the only language he spoke, apart from Russian and Tartar, was English—poorly—but then I have always found Slavic English with no prepositions more expressive and far more provocative than English spoken as expected!''

It was a testament to Lee's considerable charm and intelligence that superstars like Rudolf Nureyev and Truman Capote, whose company everyone sought, preferred to spend so much of their time with her. Nureyev, for one, said of Lee: ''She is very beautiful. Very bright. After all, she's not just a socialite. She attracts people of substance.''

Lee's friendship with Rudolf Nureyev, which endured through three decades, was very layered and complicated and fraught with innuendo. Certainly in the London years, they were very involved with each other, and the influence he exerted over her was a powerful one. Drawn to what she called his ''intense animal passion,'' in some deep recess of herself Lee was always in love with him and felt frustrated that he was a homosexual. She once told Truman how taken aback she was to discover pictures of naked men in the guest room when she stayed at his house in Monaco; the implication of those pictures was not something she wanted to accept. Lee described her own sexual experience with him, which she said occurred only once in England, as ''the most athletic'' she had ever known.

''They were an item. Nureyev was known,'' said a London friend of theirs. ''I don't think that was ever going to lead anywhere, but he was a tremendous friend. Whenever he danced, he picked up tickets for her. She went to Russia and visited his family. It went on for a number of years. Lee liked the stage, she liked all kinds of success, and he was the leading dancer.''

The summer of 1966 found the Radziwills back in Setúbal. Truman came again, along with another repeat guest, Stas's son John; David Somerset paid a visit, as did John Kenneth Galbraith and Benno Graziani. ''The sea was so cold that none of the guests wanted to swim,'' remembered Graziani. ''It was really freezing. Even Lee's husband forbade her to water-ski. But to give courage to everybody, she plunged from the yacht and swam in the cold water—thirteen degrees!—for fifteen minutes. She was blue when she came out.''

After a cruise down the Dalmatian coast of Yugoslavia as guests of the Agnellis with Truman and others (a voyage which got off to a bad start because Lee became dreadfully seasick—"Oh, oh, oh! Hold on to the wall!" Truman wrote of the trip), she was back in London in September and then on to New York. Modeling outfits by Courrèges for a two-page spread in *Vogue* (it enabled her to get a better deal on his clothes) and Truman's Masked Ball were the highlights of her fall visit.

The writer's shindig for 540 of his friends—all wearing black or white—in the Grand Ballroom of the Plaza Hotel was the largest private party ever given. *Esquire* magazine described it as "a spectacular occasion that served as an eye in the storm of the sixties and was Truman's greatest creation." "I think Truman was more excited by the preliminaries of it, by who he'd invite, and who he definitely would *not* invite," said Lee, spite being a sentiment Truman relished (as Lee would find out firsthand one day). Spending most of his time in the shadows at the back of the ballroom just watching his party, he danced only with his guest of honor, Katharine Graham, and with two other guests, Lee and Lauren Bacall. Lee had a difficult time of it that evening; the dramatic dress she wore was completely covered in white beads and each time she moved a few more of them slipped off and skittered over the floor.

In late January Lee joined Truman for several days in Morocco, traveling south with him from Rabat to Marrakesh to the luxurious Hotel Gazelle d'Or in Taroudant. The hotel's circular Berber-style bungalows with their shimmering silks and baths of rose water were a grand respite from the biblical simplicity of the town. In early March Lee was in Paris to take in an art show, and she made a day-trip to Milan to shop for clothes, ordering a score of ensembles, some of which she planned to wear in her upcoming acting debut in Chicago. Later that month she was on to Acapulco for Easter week with Jackie and their respective families, vacationing in a hacienda near the beach.

When Lee flew back from Acapulco to New York, she taxied to a fashionable East Side boutique straight from the airport to splash a fast $450 (a considerable amount in 1967) on dresses, sweaters, culottes, and kilts. She bought the clothes not so much from need as from an unhealthy compulsion to shop. A former shoe salesman at Bergdorf Goodman said that

in a typical scenario Lee would go there and buy a dozen pair
of boots at a time and then have them all brought back the
next day. She was a shopaholic in those years, and she shared
the disease with her sister. The two of them would raid stores
together and then compare notes over tea and sweets at La-
fayette, a favorite restaurant of theirs.

One weekend in the autumn of 1967, an unusual visitor came
to stay at Turville Grange. Gloria Steinem, later the celebrated
feminist, at that point in her career had an assignment to interview Lee for *McCall's* magazine. A previous interview
Steinem had done with Truman Capote influenced Lee to decide to talk to her about her private life. She told Steinem that
even though she received numerous requests for interviews,
she had strong feelings that her private life should remain so,
and as a result, had only given two in-depth interviews since
her debut in Chicago and none at all before that. Lee said that
she hated what was written in the press about her, complaining
that it was "so limited, so jet set, empty, cold, and not true."

The two women hit it off. Over lunch and dinner and long
walks in the countryside, and, most of all, very late in the
evening when the house was quiet, Lee opened up to Gloria
Steinem for publication in a way she had never done before.
Presumably, Steinem's intelligence was the catalyst for Lee's
extraordinary departure from her customary attitude toward the
press.

In addition to a frank interview, Steinem asked a volley of
provocative questions, such as if she thought life in another
century might have suited her better. "Well, the music, the
painting, the *atmosphere* I'm most drawn to is always the nineteenth century," Lee answered. "It was wild, romantic, soar-
ing, out of control—oceans booming, horses galloping. Not in
the least cold and pretty like the eighteenth century. I love all
the dramatic composers, Debussy, Scriabin, Mahler, Ravel,
and painters like David and Delacroix. They had such power
and vitality, and such warmth. I like the same period in the
theater. Ibsen, Strindberg, Chekhov, Pirandello. It was the beginning of a great changeover to character analysis, but in a
most subtle and astute way. I like contemporary plays, too—
stark, bare ones, like Pinter's.

"As for novels, I'm not an avid reader. I hardly ever completely lose myself in a book. I prefer poetry. It has a tranquilizing effect on me, as if I've entered some very different world. Yeats, Housman, Rupert Brooke. I'm still barely out of the nineteenth century, am I? Well, at least I am consistent."

At one point, Steinem asked Lee if there were any historical or fictional women she might identify with, adding that, personally speaking, Lee reminded her of Natasha Rostov in *War and Peace*, "not after she married Pierre and settled down," Steinem said, "but before, when she was still uncertain about her future, still full of moods and enthusiasms."

"If I were a man, I'd identify with Alexander the Great," Lee said. "Not because of his power, but because he was romantic, daring, impractical. The only woman I would vaguely have wanted to be is George Sand. She must have lived an interesting life, throwing convention to the winds. But really, she wasn't *feminine* enough for me. And the trouble with all the interesting women in the past—or in novels for that matter—is that they came to a tragic end. Maybe I like living now for that reason. It's the first century that has allowed women to be interesting without exacting some terrible price. So you see, my romanticism only goes so far, doesn't it?"

When Lee was asked how she would like to be described to someone who did not know her, she said she needed the weekend to think that one over, finally confessing: "I'd like them to say that I'm kind, but without sounding insipid, and that I'm *original*. That's the most important part, originality. It has nothing to do with the way one looks, good or bad. I'd rather that be left out completely. Just that I'm original. Not on the outside, but the *inside*."

After the time taken to pursue her ill-fated acting career, Lee resumed keeping company with her eternal flame, Rudolf Nureyev. In mid-November 1967, a few weeks after she finished taping *Laura*, she went with him to Stockholm at his invitation to see his staging of Tchaikovsky's *Nutcracker* at the Swedish Royal Opera. They checked into the same hotel, where photographers waiting to get a shot of them caused a melee.

Nureyev stayed with the Radziwills for several weeks during the Christmas season. "He and Tina got to be great friends," said Lee. "For Christmas, he went to the most incredible trouble to find exactly the right present for her. Finally, he gave her slippers that he and Margot had used in performance, and that they both had written on. They were tied with long satin ribbons, and Tina kept them hung over her bed. Rudolf was an inspiration.''

Lee went public with her affection for the dancer the following March in Paris. Lunching at the Plaza Athenée, the hotel off the Champs-Élysée where she usually stayed, the couple caught the eye of a British reporter who described their meeting in a press report: "With temperatures in Paris yesterday hovering around 40 degrees and spring only just around the corner of the Étoile, I found even the platonic embraces of Rudolf Nureyev and Lee Radziwill setting my adrenaline circulating." Later, at some dress-up affair, a photographer caught Lee clinging suggestively to him as they danced.

Shortly after the Radziwills' return from a trip to Israel in May, Lee sublet her New York apartment for a year under pressure from Stas to curtail her gadding about and spend more time with her family. She reasoned that by leasing the apartment she would not have the expense of its maintenance and could use the added income. She sublet it to John Revson and his wife, Ricky; Revson was the son of Revlon founder Charles Revson, an occasional escort of hers. "Lee was paying maybe twelve hundred dollars in maintenance, something like that, and we were paying three thousand to sublet it," Revson said. "Even though it was eleven rooms—eight rooms and three servants' rooms—that was a lot of money then.

"Lee's attorney was always coming to the apartment to inspect it, to make sure that we weren't destroying her possessions, and the truth of the matter was, it was a nice apartment but it wasn't decorated with such valuable antiques to justify such concern. They were absolutely paranoid about it.

"The apartment was a duplex, and the master bedroom was on the upper floor facing Fifth Avenue. Right in back of Lee's bedroom was a second, smaller bedroom, more like an anteroom, where Stas slept—he had one of those big English sleigh beds. The size of that room spoke volumes about their relationship."

Revson used to see his pretty landlady around town both before and after he sublet her apartment. "I'd see Lee and her sister at all the best French restaurants and the like, and I remember thinking that Lee was the more intriguing personality,'' he said. ''Her relationship to life was totally different. Lee was always lively, laughing, having a good time, whereas Jackie was just the opposite. She was stuffy, square, and boring. I mean, Jackie was a power, she was bright, but she was not somebody who was inherently fascinating. Jackie was never going to go out and live a life that took a few chances. She didn't even rock the boat when she was married to Kennedy, and she had plenty of reasons to, with all those women he had. Instead, she played perfect Mrs. John F. Kennedy and let it all slide by.

''Lee was much more straightforward and honest. She said what she felt, and she was willing to admit she made a few mistakes. Jackie would only say what was politically proper. She was married to the world's worst husband, and her attitude was, 'How can you say anything is wrong?' She was much more concerned with the image she portrayed, and Lee with the life that she led, and that's a big difference—it totally changes the psychological perception that Lee was always the second sister.

''Lee was the more interesting even in the way she dressed. She was always loosely elegant, whereas Jackie was always uptight elegant, and the choice of designers and the clothes they wore reflected that strongly. There was a flair to Lee. She was less constricted.''

It is certainly true that Lee led the life of wider risk and greater embrace. Several people who knew both sisters well enough to penetrate beyond their facades made the same observation that Revson did. As one friend of both women put it: ''Just because Jackie is the bigger story, it doesn't make her the bigger life.''

31. *Turville Grange*

As long as Lee, under pressure from Stas, was hunkering down
to focus on her domestic life, she concentrated on the joys of
Turville Grange and English country living. "Although I came
to England too late to be profoundly influenced by the English
way of life, I love it," she said. "I love all the things the
English love—their passion for animals, the country, flowers,
books, and the theater."

Gardening, in particular, became a fascination. To her, a
garden was like a home and required even more planning than
her house did. Approaching the gardens at Turville Grange
with her customary gusto, Lee had them ramble and meander
absently into each other, like the rooms in her house, and they
often displayed idiosyncratic touches: a copse of rhododen-
drons made a border for a croquet lawn, for instance, and in
her kitchen garden, serried rows of peonies bloomed next to
cabbages and carrots.

In the house, the Impressionist-like garden room was Lee's
favorite. Used for relaxing and listening to music, it was filled
with birdsong and had a through-the-mirror sense of being
another part of the garden it faced. There were bright, flowery
fabrics on the walls and sofas, a profusion of flowers in bowls
and jars, and carrot-colored canaries in an airy Victorian pa-
goda; framed nineteenth-century watercolors of fruits and veg-
etables hung on the walls, and in one corner, suspended from
the ceiling, an antique cage was home to a myna bird; in the
opposite corner in an identical cage, an enormous, lime-green,
Polish-speaking parrot looked very picturesque against the
flowered walls.

"I wanted my house to be warm and colorful and full of
flowers, unlike the coldness of most English country houses,
so that one wouldn't notice the weather if it were dull," Lee
explained. "I wanted rooms that would dance, a place that
would always be gay to walk into. . . . The eye changes the
soul. *Everything* is in the eye. . . . It's the difference you feel
when you see a brilliant blue sky and sun and shadows in

comparison to a heavy gray rain. It affects one's mood enormously—too much."

A feature writer at British *Vogue*, Polly Devlin, wrote an article about Turville Grange for the magazine, singing its praises, but privately she sniped: "That house was so overdecorated by English taste!"

On Sunday mornings, the Radziwills would all pile into Stas's big American limousine for the ride to the local church, though one suspects that Lee's churchgoing, like her annulment, was more of a professed interest to accommodate Stas than any real religious conviction. In the same spirit, she once told a weekend visitor, "I do love Catholicism. I couldn't belong to any other religion. Protestant churches always seem so cold and empty—all locked up until the hour of the sermon. In Catholic ones, there's such a feeling of love and suffering, as if the walls have witnessed and comforted all human emotion."

After church, the children would change into play clothes and dash outdoors, Stas would retire to his masculine retreat in the library, and Lee would sip hot mint tea in her pretty pink, batik-walled bedroom while she mulled over her list of things to do. Lee ran her homes like a seventeen-jewel Swiss clock; many considered them among the best-organized in England.

When there was any kind of sunlight outdoors, she seldom stayed inside and would often stroll the grounds with her dogs; a favorite walk was the mossy Edwardian path that stretched the breadth of a nearby wood. In back of the house, a rustic, ring-shaped bench with wildflowers growing underneath it and a shade tree in the center was a popular place to pause and relax. What Lee loved to do most was saddle her mare, Topaz, and ride across her property at a leisurely pace, surveying her manicured acres. "I love going out to see what's happening in the country—how it's changing—and to appreciate the beauty and peace of it," she said.

Anthony and Tina had a garden and pony stable of their own and a favorite place to visit: across the gardens and beyond in the fields, under giant elm trees, stood a gypsy caravan, a gift from their parents one Christmas. There Tina gave tea parties to her favorites.

Visitors to Turville Grange had the sensation of entering a

special, private place, a magic kingdom. "We were there once and strolled through the gardens and we couldn't get over how beautiful the place was," said Brigitte Gerney, the wife of Lee's longtime friend Arkady Gerney. "I remember thinking that if I lived there, how could I ever be happy anywhere else? Because it was like paradise. Everything was perfect and Lee was so efficient in the way she ran it. She had the most wonderful style."

"The place really is like a fairy tale, isn't it?" Gloria Steinem asked Lee when she visited her. "Even that herd of sheep looks as if it had been painted on the hillside." "I know," Lee agreed. "I love it. One of the first things Stas did was to bury all the electrical wires and pipes so nothing would break the spell."

"Aren't you afraid Tina and Anthony will never find anything so perfect again?" Steinem asked her. "I hope if they're completely happy and confident now, they won't have to look for perfection when they grow up," Lee told her in reply. "They'll have it with them always, inside."

On a typical weekend at Turville Grange, there would be three or four houseguests, and four or five friends would come for Sunday lunch. Guests stayed in Lee's red and blue toile-hung guest apartments overlooking the courtyard. In addition to simply relaxing, they had the choice of riding, tennis, and croquet, or swimming and a sauna in the pool house. Built at the time the estate was purchased, the pool house featured an immense heated pool, white Hollywood-style furniture of the thirties, and a jukebox. Lee called the pool house "Stas's folly." "I don't think I ever saw anyone use the pool," said one frequent Sunday visitor, "and I never saw Stas play tennis."

That's because he usually played by himself. One weekend when John Moxey was out there, Stas said to him, "Come and watch me play." "He stood in the middle of the court," Moxey recalled, "and made the tennis coach on the court with him hit the ball precisely to him so that Stas *never moved* his feet. He just stood there, planted, and hit the ball back! And if the coach threw the ball so that Stas couldn't reach it from where he was standing, he yelled at him. Stas was the prince of the tennis court."

In another amusing tennis game, Sammy Davis, Jr., the

black entertainer who converted to Judaism, was a guest one time at a weekend house party right after Stas had just had the grass court sprayed with a green chemical of some sort. "There was a crazy game of tennis going on," recollected another guest, Gerald Smith. "Sammy couldn't find tennis shoes to fit him, so he played in his bare feet. At the end of a particularly hilarious game—which was funny because he had only one eye and therefore his tennis wasn't very good — Sammy sat down on a bench, looked down at his feet, and said to no one in particular, 'It's bad enough being a one-eyed black Jewish comedian—but who needs green feet?!'

"Most of Stas and Lee's weekend guests at Turville were so sycophantic!" Smith continued. "Talk about effete, two-dimensional hangers-on! They were posturing and strutting, fairly ordinary people. An exception was Rudolf Nureyev. He and Lee would go strolling off into a meadow during the sunset. To the outsider, one would have thought from their body language that they had been lovers for quite some time. They were very much together."

On June 5, 1968, it was Stas who rang Jackie from London in the middle of the night, New York time, with the news that Robert Kennedy had been shot just moments after his victory speech in the California primary. Stas learned of the shooting from a telephone call to his home. While Lee remained behind for the time being, he flew to New York to be by Jackie's side and to go with her out to Los Angeles. Ever since her husband's assassination, Stas felt very protective toward Jackie, and he made it a point to be available when she needed help. "Jackie was vulnerable and could make mistakes," said a friend. "In that period after Jack died, and for a time afterward, Stas was really quite close to Jackie."

Lee took the news of Bobby's shooting badly: "It is terrible, horrific! I really can't believe that it has all happened again. It is beyond belief!" she cried. She was so distraught that later in the day she plowed into another car near Henley. She said afterward that she could not even recall the accident. No one was hurt, but Lee was charged with careless driving and failing to stop or report the accident. She pleaded guilty to the charge and was fined a small sum.

As upset as she was, she did not cancel the dinner plans

she had that evening with Cecil Beaton, who wrote in his diary that, most extraordinary for her, Lee spoke to him freely about Jackie. She could not get her sister off her mind. Lee left London soon after for Bobby's funeral in New York and the burial at Arlington.

The Radziwills took their holiday that summer in Mykonos, an Aegean island off the southeastern coast of Greece. Caroline Kennedy visited her aunt for a spell, since her mother was spending a lot of time on nearby Skorpios, Aristotle Onassis's private island. By now Jackie and Onassis were planning to be married, but had not made an announcement or set a date. One day, with photographers dogging them, Lee played tourist and took her niece on a donkey ride around the island.

Before leaving London, Stas and Lee had made plans to meet up with David Somerset and his family on Mykonos. An Athenian yachtswoman, Maia Calligas, recalled the Somersets' unusual arrival on the island: "David Somerset was a great friend of mine, and he and his wife, Caroline, and their children took a cruise with me from Athens to Rhodes that summer. We encountered a terrible storm along the way, and David kept saying, 'But we must go on to Mykonos. We must.' Because he had arranged to meet the Radziwills there, we sailed on. We arrived in Mykonos more than half drowned with all our sails torn. Suddenly, in the harbor we saw the *Saita,* the Rothschild boat, and to our surprise, it turned out that Stas had rented it. We all had dinner together that night— the crew, the sailors, and all the people from Mykonos I knew, even the fishermen. There were violins playing and dancing. At one point, David disappeared with Lee. . . . But David is a very loyal friend and a nice person. He left with me when I sailed away at dawn, leaving the Radziwills behind."

Lee's primary amorous entertainment those days was the politician Roy Jenkins, who was Chancellor of the Exchequer in Harold Wilson's Labour Government at the time. "I wouldn't call it a big affair, Roy was very easy to sleep with," said a mutual friend of theirs. "There again, Lee wouldn't have slept with Roy if he hadn't been Chancellor of the Exchequer. Like lots of people, Roy liked talking to Lee—he enjoyed her funny little breathy voice and her very pretty face. But don't misunderstand, the heart was not engaged. Lee was a starfucker, and Roy was a very considerable star in those years.''

Indeed, he was. For many of his parliamentary years, Roy Jenkins's star burned brightly. A man of the moderate center, he had a fine track record as Home Secretary and was one of the most able Chancellors Britain had since the war. When Lee knew him, he was widely considered to be the next leader of the Labour Party at a time when the Left still had a grip on the average Briton. Jenkins possessed the ambition to push on to the top in British politics, and if Labour had won the general election in 1970, he probably would have been Foreign Secretary and inherited the Prime Ministership when Harold Wilson retired. As it happened, the Conservatives were returned to power, and his moment was lost. When Labour regained power in 1974, Jenkins had resigned the Deputy leadership of the Labour Party two years earlier over the issue of Britain's entry into the Common Market. Eventually despairing of the course on which Labour was embarked, he left the party to become the first leader of the unsuccessful Social Democratic Party, causing one of the biggest upheavals on the British political scene in a generation. He is now the Chancellor of Oxford.

Literate, bookish, a prolific diarist and writer (notably of political biographies), Roy Jenkins was the darling of the intellectuals, yet many people remained leery of him, even inside his own party. They accused him of the vice of aristocracy— very unfashionable in the radical sixties. This croquet-playing, gourmandizing, elegantly dressed, aloof owner of expensive cars was, in fact, the son of a miner-turned-Labour MP from the Welsh border country. who refused to remain true to his roots.

"Typically, Jenkins's affair with Lee followed a pattern," said Taki Theodoracopulos, who was still on the scene and knew of the relationship. "He came from a working-class background but affected upper-class mannerisms and cultivated upper-class friends. He was a climber, which was par for the course for Lee. Jenkins is a smart, worthwhile man who has done a lot of good things, but he's a snob. So he was perfect for her. He's reached the top now, he's become a lord, but I would have much more respect for him if he wasn't such a snob. You can't compare Roy Jenkins to a bunch of buffoon

Jack and Janet Bouvier, 1929. (*UPI/Bettmann*)

Lee with her dog "Cappy" at a pet show in Southampton, 1940. (*Globe Photos*)

The Auchincloss family at Hammersmith Farm: Yusha, Nina, Hugh, Jackie, Tommy, Janet, and Lee. (*Lloyd S. Pauley*)

Deb of the Year, 1950.
(*Glogau*)

Lee and Michael
Canfield on a
London street.
(*Express Newspapers*)

Was he or wasn't he? Prince George, the late
Duke of Kent, is on the right.
(*Syndication International*)

The sisters share a confidence, 1959. (*Globe Photos*)

Fashion plates: Lee as well as Jackie popularized the Camelot look. (*UPI/Bettmann*)

Above: Prince and Princess Radziwill heading home to London, 1961. (*UPI/Bettmann*)

Left: The Radziwills and Tina at the wedding of Isabelle Potocki, Stas's niece, in France, 1963. (*Globe Photos*)

Lee departing the *Christina* in Italy to join up with JFK on his German tour, June 1963. Lee's host, Aristotle Onassis, is on the right, Stas is on the left. (*AP/Wide World Photos*)

Her friend Aristotle Onassis. While Lee looks on, Ari toasts the owner of the Athens Hilton, Stratis Andreadis, at the hotel's opening in the summer of 1963. (*AP/Wide World Photos*)

Turville Grange. (*Express Newspapers*)

Her eternal flame: Lee with Rudolf Nureyev in the 1960s. (*Globe Photos*)

Below left: Peter Beard. (*NYT Pictures*)

Below: Truman Capote and Lee in happier times. (*Ron Galella*)

Lee took the eroticism she felt for Peter Tufo out in public. (*Oscar Abolafia*)

Newton Cope. (*Mickey Pfleger*)

Richard Meier. (*Time/Life: Ted Thai*)

On the job. Lee with Giorgio Armani (left) and Martin Scorsese. (*Globe Photos*)

Tina and Anthony Radziwill.
(*Brian Quigley*)

The happy
couple. Lee
and Herbert
Ross, 1991.
(*Jim Smeal/
Ron Galella*)

dukes who know nothing except how to fart loudly in public and shoot. He's a much better person, but in one respect, he's a worse person because he's such a snob.

"Lee bet he was going to be the next Prime Minister. He wasn't, because he was too busy sipping claret with the swells instead of sitting around the working clubs with the lads, as they say, and making friends."

Lee often met Jenkins for lunch in public places, and their affair went on for a few years. Each found the other highly diverting. "Lee's affair with Jenkins was pretty open in the sense that people knew about it," said Lady Ampthill. "At quite a lot of big dinner parties, they were seen talking to one another and had a certain way of looking at each other, and people knew what was going on and would gossip about it. One day they stopped seeing each other, just like that. It fizzled out. Jenkins had a lot of ladies in his life. He was a jolly, convivial person.

"If Roy Jenkins had been a Tory, the affair would have been known to the public. Because he was a Labour minister, it wasn't. The press never understood that a Labour minister can have something on the side—they only looked for it in the Tory Party. Look at the number of Tory scandals Britain has had. We have never had one in the Labour Party, and, God knows, they have just as many affairs."

If the Radziwills' friends noticed what was going on between Jenkins and Lee, surely Stas must have. He considered Roy Jenkins a friend of his. What was he to make of Lee's infidelities within his own circle? Most of the time he just set his jaw tight and pretended not to notice; once in a while, though, he let his real feelings slip out. As Sidney Morris remembered it: "Stas was cut very deep and raw by what was going on. He was terribly, terribly hurt."

Lee was traveling in Tunisia in October 1968 when Jackie decided on short notice to marry Aristotle Onassis because news of their engagement had just leaked out. Lee and her family were among the last of the two dozen or so guests to arrive for the wedding on Skorpios. After the ceremony in the island's tiny chapel, family and friends departed in jeeps and later boarded the *Christina* for the wedding dinner. There were toasts and tears all around as one guest after another, Lee included, wished the bride and groom peace and happiness.

But one afternoon the previous spring, Eleanor Perry, a writer who collaborated with Truman Capote on dramatizing some of his short stories for television, was at his apartment working with him when the telephone rang. It was Lee. She had just learned that Onassis was going to marry her sister and she was hysterical. Truman went into another room to take the call, but Lee was screaming and crying and carrying on to such a degree that even in the next room Perry could hear her voice coming through the receiver: "HOW COULD SHE DO THIS TO ME!" she screamed. "HOW COULD SHE! HOW COULD THIS HAPPEN!" Truman tried to calm her but with no success. When Perry related the incident to a friend afterward, she remarked that she did not understand how the sisters' relationship could ever survive such bitterness.

In public, of course, Lee never let on. She stolidly told a reporter the day before the ceremony: "I am very happy to have been at the origin of this marriage, which will, I am certain, bring my sister the happiness she deserves."

Years later, when Truman and Lee fell out, he made the comment, "Lee really thought she had Onassis nailed down. She pretended to have great contempt for him and the marriage. She wasn't in love with him, but she liked all those tankers."

A few weeks after the wedding, Jackie and Ari came to stay the weekend at Turville Grange. Another guest at that same weekend house party (which included Dame Margot Fonteyn and Rudolf Nureyev) spoke to Jackie in a firm and critical way over some small matter, and Lee said to him, "It is about time someone spoke to Jackie like that and put her in her place." This sort of thing happened very often—Lee noting that her sister was in the wrong and hoping someone else would notice, too. To her, Jackie was not this figure on a cloud that no one could touch.

Actually, Lee was utterly impatient with the public's sentiment that had turned her sister into a monument. As Jackie's sibling, she knew all too well the weak spots in her character and the chinks in her psyche. If the key to Lee was held by her relationship to her sister, then the reverse was true, and one could never truly know the one without knowing the other. Once, in an unguarded aside, Lee told a friend, "You should see that woman! She wakes up in the morning and goes through all the newspapers looking for her name, and if she doesn't find it, she just throws them all away, and when she sees her name, she cuts it out immediately!" Such an indiscretion where her sister was concerned was very rare. Yet Lee could, if she wanted to, reveal to an extraordinarily curious world all those shared secrets and fears and hushed confessions of Jackie's that she had stored away in her memory. It was a fatal knowledge, a weapon, and a temptation. That she never did, even after they lost their closeness, was the greatest benevolence she would show her sister.

32. *Misfortune*

A visit to a clinic in Lausanne in February 1969, reportedly to undergo a treatment to increase her weight, ushered in a particularly rough patch in Lee's life. Her fashionably slim figure sometimes hovered dangerously near downright emaciation, and this was one of the times she crossed the line. "I am always trying to gain weight," she said. "It's terribly annoying to be described as 'fashionably gaunt' or 'chic and bony' as if it were on purpose. I have a weight problem in reverse, and I've always had trouble sleeping. I guess I am what one might call high-strung."

That same season, on a visit to Truman Capote in Palm Springs, his pet bulldog, Maggie, got hold of Lee's sable coat and chewed it up. "I could have heard Lee's screams a mile away," Truman said.

In April, a fire at Turville Grange endangered the manor house and caused a lot of smoke damage and heartache. The blaze broke out in one of the adjoining outbuildings. The alarm was raised by Anthony, aged nine at the time, who was playing in the courtyard and saw the flames shooting through the roof. He ran into the house shouting "Fire! Fire!" "I always thought he exaggerated, so I did not hurry at first," Lee recollected. "Then to my astonishment, I saw the fire was going very strong. We got some of our things out of the house, and people started throwing buckets of water on the fire." A shortage of water hampered the firemen, so they had to pump it from the swimming pool. There was a great deal of damage to the kitchen and the cottage at the back, and Lee and her family had to move into a staff house for the night.

The following month Lee was in a serious car accident near Henley and she got her second road conviction in a year. After lunch in a local pub with her family, including her stepson, John, she and Tina headed home while Stas and John stayed behind to have coffee. Driving at a high speed on the wrong side of the road in a brand-new Aston Martin, she hit a family-filled smaller car, also going very fast, injuring two of the passengers. The driver of the other car, William Hay, of Holmer Green, Buckinghamshire, sustained serious head and body injuries. He was pulled unconscious from the wreck, and remained in the hospital for over two months. His sixteen-year-old son was also hospitalized with serious injuries; his wife escaped unharmed. Both cars were totaled.

On his way home from the pub, Stas came upon the scene of the accident and saw Lee sitting in the road, crying and covered with blood from a broken nose. Their daughter also suffered a facial injury and lost some teeth. He took them away in his car. One good thing came out of the accident for Lee: the expert reconstructive surgery done on her nose gave her a far softer, prettier profile.

Her woes continued at the end of the year when she sued the French magazine *Marie Claire* for alleged libel over an article in the December 1969 issue about her sister's new marriage, which stated that Aristotle Onassis and Lee were once intending to marry, and that she had been "liberated from her marriage to the Prince" in order to do so. The magazine had a substantial circulation in Britain, and Lee alleged that as a result of the article, she had been "gravely injured in her credit and reputation." Through the years, both she and Jackie had grown used to the avalanche of nonsense that was written about them in the press ("How Ari Helped Bring Jackie Back to Jesus" was one story circulating at the time). But obviously this story struck a nerve, and presumably it was Stas's honor that was at stake. The matter was settled out of court.

After a relaxing Christmas at Turville Grange with Jackie and their respective children and spouses (an arrangement which repeated itself for the duration of the Radziwill marriage), Lee went to New York and did some redecorating at

969 Fifth Avenue with the money she had made on her sublet.

In March, Stas and Isabelle and Hubert d'Ornano went on safari together in Kenya, with Lee joining them a bit later on. "Stas loved safaris. Every year he went, often alone," said his niece. "He was not a great killer. He loved the atmosphere, the night, the jungle." Later still, Taki Theodoracopulos joined the group down on the coast. "I felt even Stas knew," d'Ornano remarked of Lee's obvious relationship with the young Greek.

"We had a very nice holiday but after a week Stas left and I stayed behind with Lee," said Taki, "and even then we met a nice young zoologist, Iain Douglas-Hamilton, and Lee got very, very excited by *him*."

By the summer of 1970, Lee was floundering between worlds passing and worlds coming, her life in England long since become an outworn wish. She spent several weeks in June and early July summering in the country at Turville Grange. "I felt this terrible claustrophobia . . . these trees closing in on me," she lamented. "I longed for the sea." Her longing led to a notebook of memories about her years in East Hampton.

The balm of time's passage and selective memory had erased the effects of her parents' bitter feuding from what were essentially recollections of innocence lost, for at a later time she wrote an article based on her notebook and in it she mused: "Picasso said, 'When I was fourteen I knew I could draw like Michelangelo, and I spent the rest of my life learning to draw like a child.' I understand that so well, because in growing up we lose, and are forced to lose, all our originality, all our simplicity. That is why I look back with such love on those precious days. I like to recall those days because of the carefreeness I once knew. Those years were a time to laugh. Complication, confusion, wounds, suffering hadn't entered our lives. I suppose if I had never left I would have taken every summer for granted and never been haunted by sea smells and images of winding tar roads."

Lee's nostalgia for East Hampton was shaded by a more general homesickness that had always run like a continuous current beneath the surface of her life in England. Admitting that she missed the "energy and enthusiasm" of America, there was some private part of her that always wanted to go back, both because she had always remained very American and because neither she nor Stas were ever accepted as English. She once said of the breakup of her marriage: "I was a foreigner married to a foreigner, and that is very difficult in a way. We *both* missed our own countries a lot."

Lee's yearning for the sea, at least, was satisfied in mid-July when she and her family rounded out the summer on Skorpios, where she spent many contented hours swimming, diving, snorkeling, and sunbathing. Ari's island home, approximately 175 miles from Athens, was the gathering place, as was the *Christina*, of three generations of Kennedys that season. With Lee on board in August, the converted Canadian frigate cruised lazily along the Italian coast, stopping in Capri and other ports to allow her and Jackie and some of the other guests time to go browsing.

An event occurred in September which, in retrospect, was the beginning of the end of Stas Radziwill's life: Felix Fenston died of a massive heart attack on a train returning from a shooting weekend. "With the death of Fenston, the swan song of Stas's business career started because he wasn't the tough businessman Fenston was," said Sidney Morris. "He was too generous. I myself witnessed one or two instances of softness in his business dealings. His willingness to concede certain terms led to a great extent to his downfall.

"There was another factor which led to his troubles. When Fenston died, the property market was booming, so Stas thought, 'I'll carry on and make a fortune.' Then came the great property crash of 1973 that he was ill equipped to deal with. At no time was Stas a particularly wealthy man."

"Stas knew my husband wasn't well," said Greta Fenston, Felix's third wife and widow, who was pregnant when her husband died at fifty-five years of age. "He had a heart condition for several years previous to his death. Anybody else might have taken precautions financially and tried not to spend so lavishly. In a way, I feel very sad for Stas because he tried awfully bravely to carry on the business, but he was too nice.

"Stas was as particular about living as Lee was. He liked beautiful things too, and he adored Lee because she was so beautiful. He treated her just like a baby. He would say, 'She's a child. She hasn't grown up yet. She hasn't had a chance to find out about life yet.' He wasn't patronizing. He loved adoring her. Lee was absolutely the child-wife. She might have got thoroughly bored with it. And he was weak. If Stas had been stronger about the house, about not giving her so much, he might have had more of her respect.

"Stas gave Lee everything—beautiful dresses, decorators, money to travel. She wanted the house in Henley, so he bought it for her. We said she was mad. I think Lee ruined him! All one had to do was see her clothes. My husband was in business with him. We *knew*. We could tell just by looking at Lee's house and the staff they had: cook, butler, nanny, maid, and valet-chauffeur. It went on and on. At dinner everything was beautifully done. Every plate had its own half bottle of claret, all the silver and gold was perfectly arranged. Besides the splendid sight of the table, we were always served a fabulous dinner. They had a wonderful butler and chef, always. Stas was the first to put wood surrounds to the bath and have a wooden lavatory seat, an old-fashioned thing in wicker. Stas's bathroom cost a fortune! And then we went down to Henley and they had a house which was perfectly done, although it appeared to be small. They showed us the cottage they were doing up with top designers.

"But Stas's ruination was of his own making, I suppose, because he was a Polish aristocrat who did not understand money. He had this wonderful fund at the back of him that was producing all this money for him, and he didn't know when to stop. The problem came in 1970 when my husband died and Stas lost his bank, in addition to which Lee was also doing all that spending—1970 was at the height of their spending—and he realized then that he had to slow down.

"When I say Lee ruined him, he was not financially ruined at the time. The way of life that she was continuing to expand on was a way that could only lead to ruin. Stas wasn't a big company. He was just a partner in a small, private business."

Stas's friendship with the Fenstons was maintained for the most part separate from his wife. He usually entertained them when she was away. On the whole, Lee avoided his business and shooting friends, particularly at Turville Grange on weekends, when she made it a point not to be there unless it was with her own crowd. Actually, by the final years of their marriage, Lee had become fairly invisible in England. Then, on Skorpios in the summer of 1971, Lee met a Peter Pan character who became the igniting force for the inevitable change in her life. His name was Peter Beard.

33. *Lee and Peter*

Adventurer, photographer, author, heartthrob, party boy, wildlife conservationist: so many bits and pieces make up Peter Beard's persona that it is hard to know which most defines him. His multifaceted and elusive personality has always begged and defied explanation. "Half Tarzan and half Byron" said one who tried to put a name to it. A captive of Africa, Beard made the leap from Pomfret, English boarding school, and Yale to the Dark Continent through the writings of Karen Blixen, a.k.a. Isak Dinesen, whose book *Out of Africa* he credits with altering his life.

In the summer of 1954, during a family trip to England when he was still a teenager, Beard read Blixen's tales, and the following summer made a pilgrimage to Kenya to retrace her steps. While doing so, he became permanently enthralled with Africa and, in a sense, has never returned from there. He succeeded in meeting his heroine, and after her death he saw himself as the keeper of her legacy: her classic memoir echoes throughout his own books on Africa.

Before his youthful conversion, Peter Hill Beard grew up in an affluent, nominally Catholic, old New York family, the second of three sons. His father was a stockbroker and also a graduate of Yale. For reasons Peter has never adequately explained, he was estranged from his parents for most of his adult life. His great-grandfather, James Jerome Hill, founded the Great Northern Railway and left a large estate Peter himself estimates to have been $53 million, although he says the remains of the fortune never filtered down to him, or, rather, did so only in readily squanderable amounts. "I haven't got a dime," he once complained. "I have tiny little bits coming in, and several little tiny trusts, but it's like being on welfare." At college he studied art history and he retains a knowledgeable interest in the subject.

After he left Yale in 1961, he divided his time between Africa and New York and took on fashion photography assignments to support himself, treating it as an avocation rather than a full-time occupation. The endeavor provided him with a steady supply of great-looking models, who, along with an array of dazzling socialites, were often seen clustered around him at popular nightspots and fashionable parties, as if they were so many props in one of his photographs.

Early on in his series of trips to Africa he understood the threat of encroaching civilization as it played itself out on the continent, and, blessed with a keen eye for the grotesque as well as the idyllic, he photographed the evidence for posterity, documenting African wildlife at "its very annihilating edge."

If Beard's nomadic life lent a certain glamour to his reputation (he reportedly once spent an isolated summer alone in Africa, on the back of a zebra), two events which took place in the late sixties only added to his growing legend: he spent five months in a New York psychiatric clinic following an overdose of barbiturates after his marriage to the beautiful Newport socialite Minnie Cushing failed; and an incident with a suspected poacher on his Kenya property, whom he left temporarily entrapped in his own snare, left him with a shaved head, twelve strokes of the cane, and a nodding acquaintance with a Nairobi jail.

So who is Peter Beard? "Peter is the great impresario and archivist of his own life," said his friend and sometime editor, Steven M. L. Aronson. "His life is an open scrapbook but one that is oddly untenanted by its subject. Not that he isn't everywhere, he is, but only in a series of vignettes bolstered by a glamorous cast of characters. Who he really is, he's made it hard, if not impossible, for anyone to know." That is because for all of Peter Beard's bravado and adventures the vital dimension is not there: he is a person without a center.

"Peter Beard has created himself as a great celebrity and, no question, there has been hard work involved," offered another friend. "Yet for all that he is still an amazing creature— a dynamo, a powerhouse. He has a touch of genius but it's hard to pin down."

Many who know Peter Beard are of the opinion that his genius has been channeled into his diaries, huge, obese, leather-bound books, one for each year, phenomenally crammed with maxims and notations, torn snapshots, records of phone calls and appointments, newspaper clippings, center-fold porn, dried blood, dead insects, fingerprints, doodles, and his own minute drawings—collages, actually, of his life and times.

"In those days Peter had his diaries thick as the Manhattan phone directory under his arm wherever he went," said his friend and old college chum Porter Bibb. "He was always grabbing things and slapping them in. And it was so telling. Peter was fixated with the Kennedys—he would have pages and pages of Jackie, Caroline, John-John, and Bobby. Peter was Jackie's biggest fan. Hanging out with the Kennedy women was almost a fixation with him.

"What I saw from Peter when he was around Jackie was that he was coming on to her, and I thought she was amused. Peter's ferocious energy and his sense of commitment to the right things must have impressed Jackie, since she was so in-volved with people who were compromisers necessarily."

Jackie invited Peter to Skorpios in 1971 as her houseguest. Staying the whole summer, he was there primarily to amuse, babysit, and endlessly photograph her children. Because he was childlike himself, he was able to relate to Caroline and John—and Lee's kids too —at their own level and Lee picked up on it. He tapped in to a sense of playfulness in her in a way that her relationship with Stas never did. Suddenly this young American happened along who was, quite simply, a lot of fun.

When Jackie introduced Peter to Lee, their mutual chemistry was so great that it was instantly apparent to others. "I saw it happening, how they responded to each other and how excited they got," recalled a visitor. But so careful were they to keep their affair from view, no one assembled on the island had any idea that Lee and Peter had already become lovers. They would get together secretly at night, making love in Peter's room in the villa, in close proximity to Lee's husband, chil-dren, sister, niece, and nephew. It was all nip and tuck, and there were some close calls. Peter often worked long into the night on his diary, and Jackie would occasionally stop by when she saw the light on. In a couple of instances, Lee man-aged to scurry out of sight just in time when she heard Jackie approaching.

Lee had gone to Skorpios that summer to help recover from a hysterectomy she had just undergone. The experience was a horrifying one for her and it left her feeling desperate. "The whole thing with Peter, who was five years younger than she, was from her end," said an observer. "She made her pent-up desire obvious to him, and he had no hesitation in responding."

Stas considered Peter a friend, mostly from knowing him on safari in Africa. Peter's attitude toward his betrayal of him was that surely Stas was too old to seriously care, as if advancing age by itself banished passion or love.

Poor balding, stocky, aging Stas! Peter Beard was so handsome, so fresh and irreverent, so vigorous and invigorating, in no time, he had swept Lee up in his enthusiasms as well as in his affection.

One of those enthusiasms was a book he was working on that summer, *Longing for Darkness.* It was a retelling of some of the tales from *Out of Africa* recounted by Kamante Gatura, the Kikuyu who had been Karen Blixen's cook and a central figure in her story and who had, after her death, become a permanent resident of Hog Ranch, Peter's camp in Kenya. Lee encouraged Jackie to write an introduction to the book, which eventually appeared as an afterword.

Peter's preoccupation with his work did not stand in the way of his enjoyment of the considerable merriment and light-heartedness among the group gathered on the island (with the exception of Ari). Also joining in the fun were guests who stayed on the *Christina,* which was anchored nearby. David Frost came at Lee's invitation, bringing the entertainer Diahann Carroll with him. "He mostly stayed on board with her. They were pretty much making out the whole time," said a guest. "We never saw them." Ari groused that Carroll was drinking too much of his Dom Perignon and his good vodka, and when he learned of his daughter Christina's hasty, surprise marriage to a Los Angeles realtor, Joseph Bolker, in Las Vegas at the end of July, he became so volcanic in his eruptions that some of the guests on the *Christina* fled.

Even without that bad news, Ari was shouting the whole time. "Lee and Jackie were terrified of him when they were on his territory," said a source. "I suppose if you are staying in someone's little empire and are totally dependent on him, you feel vulnerable. I must say that Skorpios was so small it looked as though the island was anchored to Ari's yacht rather than the other way around!''

A disturbing incident occurred when Lee took some of the photographs she snapped to a shop to be developed. "Like everyone else on holiday we took lots of pictures for our own amusement," she recalled. "We simply left them to be developed. They must have kept a set of the negatives, because they were sold to magazines all over Europe. I found that most offensive.''

Both she and Jackie, who were consumed by the media, never got entirely used to it. Actually, Lee was full of fear at the vulnerability her celebrity placed her in. "The hatred, the danger are so tangible," she lamented. "Every time the phone rings, I fear it is bad news. Nine times out of ten it is. Then there are the letters. There is always someone who wants to see more of the family killed.

"One time a few years ago, when a bed was being moved into our London house and we were away, a couple of reporters posed as moving men. They took pictures of everything, even wrote down the titles of our books and records. For all I know, they read the letters in my desk. We knew nothing about it until the pictures appeared in the newspapers, and then it was too late. If you sue, it only makes it worse. There is a terrible price and burden that go with fame.''

"Whatever is complicated in our world was a thousand times more complicated in theirs," said a source close to the situation, "and Jackie and Lee were experts at handling the horror that was all around them—the press always trying for a cheap interview, making up total lies about them. With everything they did, they had so much scalding experience and paranoia in the background, I frankly sympathize.

"At the same time, Jackie, for one, was totally uninterested in delving beneath the surface of anything. If you look at some of her drawings, it's like reading a Rorschach test. They are the drawings of a little girl in her desire to escape, with their light colors, light drawing, light handwriting—light involvement. The complexities of her life were just too ugly and pushy around her all the time. So you can't fault her—or Lee for that matter—if what she was doing was escaping from that and just trying to do the best she could.''

* * *

At the end of August Stas's brother, Edmund, died, and Lee, Jackie, and the children accompanied Stas to Warsaw for the funeral, while Peter went back to Kenya. But no sooner was Lee home in London than she began to write him impassioned, erotic letters. Beset with longing, she was desperate to see him again. The opportunity did not present itself until the following February when Stas went to Kenya on a safari he had planned. Trying to make it look as if she were casually joining her husband, Lee wrote Peter that she would be coming, too.

Lee left a week ahead of Stas and went for a holiday in the Seychelles with a close friend of hers, Karen Lerner, the widow of Alan Jay Lerner. After the Seychelles they flew to Kenya. Peter met them at the airport and took them out to Hog Ranch, about seventeen miles outside Nairobi, where they had a ball until Stas showed up. Peter was used to playing host at his camp to international socialites and other luminaries who wandered through. His written record of the "beginning of the end" of Africa, a book entitled *The End of the Game,* published prophetically in 1965, had greatly improved his status as a tourist attraction in Kenya.

When Stas arrived in Nairobi with Baron Ashcombe, Henry to his friends, everyone went on safari together. Then, when the Radziwills continued on their hunting safari to Hell's Gate without Peter, Lee managed to break away and join up with Peter again at his camp a great distance away. It was a very risky endeavor, and Peter was surprised at her recklessness, since both were concerned that Stas should not learn of their affair. When she again joined up with Peter, mutual declarations of love were made, and it was clear then that her marriage would never be the same.

Like most people who fall under Peter Beard's spell, Lee was once again swept up in his enthusiasms. In this instance, he was engaged in a stealthy, airborne photographic mission over Tsavo National Park (photography was banned inside the park) to document the great die-off from starvation taking place there of thousands of elephants, a result of their being hemmed in the confines of the park. Lee was there when Beard took photographs of an elephant, famous locally for its 148-pound ivory tusks, as the creature kicked dirt around in a kind of a last hurrah. His gruesomely beautiful photographs were utilized as a visual aid in the war on poaching.

That was the thing about Peter Beard: he remained devoted only to witnessing the spectacle. Solutions held no interest for him. In his work for environmental policy he was just a goad to other people's actions. *His* action was the message itself. "People like Peter serve as catalysts. That's their principal role for everybody who comes into their orbit," said Porter Bibb. While it is true that Lee was actively searching the horizon for her own future when she met Peter Beard, it was no co-incidence that it was his influence that finally propelled her to take control of her life and end her marriage. Exposed to his qualities of imagination, courage, and conviction, she re-charged her spirit on his vigor.

Peter rejoined the Radziwills in London only a short while after their departure from Kenya, staying at 4 Buckingham Place for about ten days before traveling on with them to the Caribbean. Combining business with pleasure, he peddled his dead elephant pictures during the day and went out on the town with the Radziwills and Ari Onassis at night.

On one of his daytime appointments, Peter visited his friend the painter Francis Bacon, an artist with a view of the apoc-alypse similar to his own.* Peter got a call from Lee from her car phone while he was there, and he proceeded to guide her to Soho to join him at Bacon's cramped and chaotic, light-shunning studio-cum-living quarters, rarely seen by outsiders. Arriving in her big, fancy automobile to pay a visit to someone decidedly unimpressed with consumer goods and who, it was said, disliked women, Lee succeeded against formidable odds in charming Francis Bacon.

Down in Barbados, a favorite vacation spot of the Radzi-wills, Stas and Lee rented the same house (actually a com-pound) they had stayed in the previous year as guests of Baron Ashcombe. Jackie and the children regrouped with Peter, Stas, and Lee in a replay of Skorpios, however this time the ending was quite different. After two weeks, Stas flew back to London and the rest of the crowd headed for New York on Ari's pri-

---

*Peter Beard and Francis Bacon had a symbiotic relationship: Beard got the idea to do *The End of the Game* when he saw a haunting painting Bacon did of an elephant; when Beard showed Bacon his masses of dead elephant photographs, Bacon used some of the images in his work.

vate plane. Stas did not know it then but it was the last time he and Lee would be together as a couple. Lee stayed in New York in one prolonged absence until finally he got the message.

Lee left Stas not only because she had had enough of England and their marriage, but because in America she could live the life that she wanted. It gave her more freedom. Lee wanted her children brought up in America too. Under the influence of their Kennedy cousins, they were eager for more exposure to it.

At long last Lee had come home, and, more significantly, for the very first time in her life, at thirty-nine years of age, she was on her own. "I still have a chance to change things," she declared. "What I really fear is realizing one day that it's too late. Too late to change relationships I've spoiled. Too late to be happy with the children. Just too late. But that moment hasn't arrived yet, either for them or for me. I still have a chance to start something new."

34. *Andy and the Movies*

One of the first things Peter did when he and Lee got to New York was to introduce her and Jackie to Andy Warhol, the bizarre and fascinating exponent of Pop Art and underground film. It happened one night when he invited the sisters to come along to dinner in Chinatown with him, Andy, and Jonas Meekas, the avant garde filmmaker. At first, Jackie and Lee were reluctant to go; like many people at the time, they thought Warhol was a monster. He associated with drag queens and drug users, even though he himself didn't use drugs, and the release of his shocking film, *Chelsea Girls,* followed by the incident at his studio in 1968 when he was shot by a disturbed, so-called radical feminist, helped to create an image of him as demonic. One prominent art critic dubbed him "The White Rat" (Warhol had very pale skin and wore a silver wig). Peter managed to allay Lee's and Jackie's fears, and then at the end of the evening, when Andy gave them all the Polaroids he had shot of them during the course of the dinner, he finally won them over.

A few weeks later on a cold early spring day, Lee, Peter, Andy, and Paul Morrissey, Andy's business manager and friend, drove out to Montauk, the easternmost town on Long Island, to see if Lee would be interested in renting a house that Andy and Morrissey had recently purchased. The house was actually one of a compound of five white clapboard houses, a five-bedroom "lodge" and four smaller houses dramatically set on the edge of a cliff. Known locally as the Church estate, the dwellings were built in the thirties by an Idaho family who used it once a year to go bass fishing. The main house was simple and charming in a Spartan way and had magnificent views. Most of all, the property was very secluded. Surrounded by twenty acres of grounds and situated a long way off the main road, it would afford Lee the privacy to carry on her still-secret affair with Peter Beard undetected. She loved the place and took it immediately; then Peter moved in with her.

Andy came out occasionally on weekends to visit them, staying in one of the other houses on the property. Friends say that was the only time he ever spent any real time there. Ultra-fair-skinned, he hated the sun, and the sea breezes blew his wig off. He purchased the estate solely as an investment. Andy used to say that he was going to frame the toilet seat in the main bedroom of the house Lee rented because, he quipped about her and the visitors she'd been having, "Who has a toilet seat that Mick and Bianca [Jagger] and Jackie and Lee have all gone to the bathroom on?"

Whether Lee and Andy got together for meals in the big, old-fashioned kitchen with its stone floor, or they sat around on the worn leather couches in the living room, the easy, relaxed atmosphere at Montauk formed the setting over the next several months for a casual friendship that evolved between them. "I am all for people not taking themselves too seriously," Lee remarked. "That's what is so charming about Andy—he's such a treat." Contrary to his monosyllabic image, Warhol loved to gossip, at least with some people, including Lee, and he was just beginning to seriously hunger after glamour and power and to make the transition from the underground into higher levels of society. One could almost say that he could not afford to ignore his new tenant. At that time he was doing a lot of commissioned portraits, and he depended on social climbing to meet and associate with the kind of rich people who could afford them, always hoping that they would either commission him to do a portrait or buy one of his paintings.

When they weren't exchanging gossip about the growing number of New York's major players they knew in common, Lee, who respected Andy as an artist, sought his advice on the making of a documentary film about her childhood. Her relationship with Peter Beard had been given a major boost when they began to plan that documentary together almost immediately after her return to New York. The decision to do the film was a synchronistic formulation of plans and reactions that began with a dinner one evening at Jackie's, when Peter brought along Marvin Israel, a versatile photographer and book designer who was helping Peter on the design of some of his books. Lee had come back to Manhattan with her notebook of childhood memories of East Hampton in tow, memories which were revivified when she returned to Long Island that spring for the first time in twenty years. She struck up a conversation with Israel about the experience, the outcome of which was she decided to write a book about her childhood, which would include lots of pictures. Israel was to design it, and Jackie, who was very enthusiastic about the idea, offered the use of her many scrapbooks and photograph albums for the project.

At the same time that Lee was beginning her memoir, Peter had a pet project of his own fall through, a movie about the "end of the game" in Africa with the Rolling Stones doing the music for it, so he just shifted his focus and together with Lee they hatched an alternative project: they decided to do a film special for television about her and Jackie's childhood summers on Long Island with their father, which would echo the book she would be writing and which would include scenes from their present life. The documentary, which was essentially Lee's idea, would allow her to become totally involved in the making of the film with Peter and, they reasoned, since the movie would probably be a good two-year involvement, she naturally would have to remain in the locale where she lived as a child to film it. Hence the project would make her separation from her family more acceptable to the outside world. For the time being, Lee did not want to make any final decisions about her marriage.

Convergent with these events, articles had begun appearing in the newspapers about Lee's aunt and cousin, Edith and Edie Beale, who were threatened with eviction by local health authorities, on grounds of unsanitary conditions, from Grey Gardens, their dilapidated twenty-eight-room mansion in East Hampton. The two women, who were unstable eccentrics, lived with no heat or running water in rooms littered with excrement from stray cats and raccoons, and their garden had deteriorated into an overgrown jungle of weeds.

While Lee spent a good deal of her time that spring overseeing workers as they cleaned out and refurbished the mansion to bring it up to health standards (with money provided by Aristotle Onassis), Beard saw an opportunity to rework his own obsessive theme: their film would also be about the sweeping changes that had taken place in the Hamptons and the erosion of life there, contrasted with the very romantic ambiance of early Long Island when it was still unspoiled, the Long Island of the Bouviers when Lee and Jackie were children. Grey Gardens and the Beales, whose thirty years of Christmas and Easter cards, along with other memorabilia, remained lined up on the mantel and walls, untouched for decades, were to be included as a time capsule of that past.

For the moment, the film project preempted Lee's memoir, which she only worked on intermittently anyway, and she began to make the rounds of the television companies in pursuit of the financing that she and Peter needed above and beyond the cost of the test shot, which they themselves would absorb. Lee did not hesitate to exploit her sister's name in her effort to obtain the money: it was always she and Jackie as subjects.

Peter, meanwhile, asked Jonas Meekas to shoot some preliminary footage. Meekas was a highly respected steward of independent film who had worked with him on other projects, including a movie of his in which Peter played the leading role, *Hallelujah the Hills,* an effort Peter saw as a tribute to cinema.

"All my films are diaristic. They are like little sketches of people, friends, locations, even the weather," explained Meekas of the kind of films he made. "My style is very condensed and intense, glimpses and bits of scenes. It is not a traditional filmmaking style with people sitting around and talking.''

Peter intended to have Meekas do the single-frame, romantic, intimate family shooting necessary beyond the test shot, and, with the financial backing he and Lee hoped to secure, an additional filmmaker was to come in and do the free-running footage on the larger theme of the movie and then put it all together.

''I think the film will be totally unexpected from what people expect,'' said Lee at the time. ''It should have fantasy as well as a simple lyrical quality and . . . a feeling of timelessness, because in all these photos and flashbacks of my sister and me it was always us together, and now there are so many photos of our last few summers together and both our sons together and our daughters together, it's nice to see how it continues.'' It was Lee's intention to round off the film's nostalgia with the reactions of her children to her life at a similar age.

''I thought Lee to be very talented and smart when I was working with her,'' Meekas pointed out. ''There was a lot of grace in her, and generosity. She has learned to be clever and to handle the difficulty of being Jackie's sister with tact and finesse, sometimes under very demanding circumstances and great pressure. Lee is not a grinning or a merry person, but there is a lightness and style to her. She can fool around.

''To tell you the truth, her relationship with Peter Beard didn't make much sense to me. It was very sweet. They respected each other, but I did not believe it would last. Peter is very strong and obsessed. I don't think he can really lose himself completely in another person. He is so much into his own thing that the other person has to surrender to him to sustain it, and, of course, Lee was very much her own person. She would not give up who she really is. I don't know if Peter can sustain a long relationship with such a person. And then, her life is in New York and Peter cannot leave his Africa no matter what.''

Meekas was only given a few thousand dollars for his work, just enough to meet expenses. Peter did not have much money at the time and was constantly having financial problems. After Meekas shot some of the film and made a rough cut, some television producers with whom Jackie had dealt got wind of it and they expressed a possible interest in putting it on television. "They told me they wanted to see some of the footage," said Meekas, "and when they saw about ten minutes of what I had filmed, they did not hide their feelings. 'No one will show this kind of film on television,' they said. They thought my style was too difficult and demanding for television audiences. I told them, 'I don't give a damn what you think! I don't need you!' So I walked out on them and bowed out."

Some of the sketches Meekas shot were incorporated into his film short, *Scenes from the Life of Andy Warhol.* Released in 1990, it had a certain "keyhole-peeping charm" and was dedicated to Lee Radziwill for the film they never made together.

The episode with Jonas Meekas left Peter feeling leery about the project's outcome, but in the interim he had contacted his old friend, Porter Bibb, who fixed him and Lee up with the Maysles brothers. Bibb was Albert and David Maysles's former partner and he had produced *Gimme Shelter,* the brothers' very successful free-running documentary on the Rolling Stones' 1969 U.S. tour, which included their notorious concert at Altamont.

By now Truman had become involved. The idea was to have him narrate the film. "I told them, 'Ah, you put Jackie and Lee and Truman together, and it will definitely appeal to the networks, and it could be a real winner,' " said Porter Bibb. "With my mind's eye I could see that a narration by Capote made sense, one that would talk about these two girls growing up with this unusual father and having this extraordinary pair of lives.

"It was my understanding that the project was to talk about the Bouvier sisters as having star-crossed lives—lots of tragedy unforeseen. I think by association Lee saw herself as sharing her sister's tragedy. And Lee was always the magnet, but everybody understood implicitly that it was Jackie as much as she who was the real drawing card. I thought it was a great story."

Lee had the Maysles brothers pick up where Jonas Meekas had left off. "I got a call from her describing her purpose in going back to her childhood and her hoping to put it into film somehow," Al Maysles recalled, "and it surprised me that she was calling us, because normally one would recapture the past by recreating scenes with actors, and Lee said, 'No, no, these people still exist, and life is still going on in many instances the same old way. We can go back to these people, and I have a list of some forty or fifty items that would be relevant to the film.' Her list of items indicated the places to go as well as the people to see. The family cemetery was on the list. So was a friend from the local newspaper who knew the Bouviers — he was wonderful. The golf caddy was still around. I remember very well that item number thirty-four was her eccentric aunt and cousin, Edith and Edie Beale.''

Al and David Maysles began shooting. ''One of the most memorable things that we shot was in the cemetery,'' said Al Maysles. ''Lee was walking around the graves in a very sad mood and she was telling me about her family. All of a sudden, she heard the sound of a train whistle in the distance. That haunting sound transfixed her. It must have brought her back to her childhood and the memory of her father's weekend arrivals on that same train. As the cry of the train came roaring through, there was a captivated look on her face that I had never seen before. It was not a public look—I don't think it has ever been captured by a photographer or a paparazzi. It was a private moment that got inside her soul, and it was beautiful.

''If I weren't filming, I would have been moved to tears. I became totally vulnerable. I began crying in my heart. Lee was very tender and fragile, and something of great beauty came across in that moment, in the cemetery of all places, surrounded by death. Had we been able to find that again at other moments, the film would have been as fine as *Grey Gardens* [the acclaimed documentary film they subsequently made about the Beales that came out of this project].

''The scene in the cemetery reassured us that we could get a very good film. Then at one point Lee called us and said that it was quite likely she'd be getting together the next weekend with Jackie and Caroline and could we film that? And the problem arose once again of our not having the money to do it. We were having a running battle over the financing of that film.''

Jackie's walk-on role in Lee's extravaganza never came to pass. At this juncture, the money ran out and the project ground to a halt. Lee and Peter got into a bitter and unresolvable dispute with Al and David Maysles over exactly what the $20,000 Peter put up for the test shot was supposed to cover. Basically, he and the Maysles brothers operated on very different financial levels conceptually and for that reason could never come to terms.

Lee and Peter's dream film never did get made. In retrospect, it was for the same reason many such projects fail: an unresolvable power struggle over creative control and money. "Some TV people eventually did offer Lee a very big deal," said a friend of Peter's, "at least half a million, but Peter, who stayed out of the money deal, thought they were big-time sleazy people who just wanted to buy out the rights. And once they had Lee's ear and gave her a limousine, the whole thing started getting away from what they were originally doing. It fell apart in a domino way, because when it gave more power to the big TV people, Peter withdrew, and Lee was incapable of carrying something like that to completion on her own.

"But a lot of why it didn't go through ultimately had to do with Lee's neurotic wheeling and dealing with the TV producers. Her dreams of glory allowed her to become seduced by them, and the moment Peter saw it coming—this moth to the flame business—he just looked the other way. Lee just lives for the idea of some great, glorious thing happening to her that is going to salvage what she sees as her superior talent and beauty. But the moment it got out of the hands of Peter, Jonas, and the Maysles brothers and it went over into big promises and big contracts with those crude people, it became a tasteless mess. Lee thought she could have the integrity of an artistic production *and* a big Hollywood power play, but you can't have it both ways, that's all."

35. *Living Large*

To compensate for their movie deal falling through, Mick Jagger invited Peter Beard and Lee, whom the Stones nicknamed "Radish," to come along on the Rolling Stones' 1972 North American concert tour. They joined the tour in Kansas City in late June in the middle of its eight-week, thirty-city engagement and stayed in the entourage when it went on to Dallas and Fort Worth. Truman also came along to cover the story for *Rolling Stone* magazine, and Peter was to do the photographs for the article.

It was Lee's first time in Dallas, and her visit to Dealey Plaza unnerved her. The Texans had made a museum out of the bottom floor of the Book Depository where President Kennedy had been shot, and she was horrified to see that what was on display there were the newspapers where Dallas was conspicuously mentioned, as if it were a source of pride. She always spoke of John Connally with scorn, saying that the Texas governor "just screamed his head off" when he was shot and never contacted the family afterward. Lee was haunted by memories of John Kennedy: "There are scenes I remember as if they were last night," she has said, "and it will always be that way."

After Dallas, Lee needed to return home, and she expected Peter to come with her. A flaming row ensued when he refused. He intended to continue on with Truman. Lee kept saying over and over to him that Truman wanted them to break up, and that it was his fag dream to break up any heterosexual relationship. Peter Beard was the first serious male claim on Lee's attention since she and Truman had become friends, and it seems he reacted with jealousy to this formidable new rival.

When the tour got to New York at the end of July for its finale at Madison Square Garden, Mick Jagger stayed out in Montauk at the Church estate with Lee and Peter before they all flew into New York, where a waiting limousine took them to the Garden. The tour was capped with a birthday party for Jagger given by Atlantic Records owner Ahmet Ertegun, with hundreds of guests in the rooftop ballroom of the St. Regis Hotel. Lee, Peter, Truman, and Andy Warhol sat at a table together with some other guests, including Bob Dylan.

Lee was traveling in a circle now that was a far cry from that of Princess Radziwill. "She never wanted to miss anything. That was part of her appeal to Peter," said his friend John Revson. "Through him, she entered a whole other world. Peter represented a socially accepted link from her world to the major players of the counterculture. He filled a niche. He was her launch boyfriend. Peter was the right person for that moment."

*   *   *

Lee had Anthony and Tina to stay at Montauk for five weeks in August and September. "Lee had nice, nice children—a very good reflection on her," said Paul Morrissey, who would see them on and off over the summer when, like Andy, he stayed in one of the other houses on the grounds. Lee kept her Montauk summer a low-profile, strictly family affair, except for Truman, who often came to visit. He and Lee and Peter liked to go to a favorite restaurant of his in Southampton, Herb McCarthy's, and shoot the breeze.

Often when the trio got together Truman used to love to bad-mouth Jackie. She did not pay enough attention to him. He used to say that the way she treated friends reminded him of a little girl who had a lot of toys in her room, and one day she's playing with this one red ball and it rolls under the bed, and then she doesn't notice or think about it again until a few years later when she happens to find it and starts playing with it again. Lee was delighted to hear Truman's negative comments about, and a more realistic appraisal of, her sainted sister. With Peter and Truman she could drop the gushing sister act and voice a few complaints of her own.

In Manhattan, the trio frequently joined Alan Schwartz for lunch, and some of these occasions ended unpleasantly. It seemed that Truman was getting advance after advance from his publisher and various magazines without ever writing anything, so he owed large sums of money. Schwartz, who, of course, had negotiated Truman's contracts for him, would use these occasions to tell him about the repercussions of his delinquency. The bad news caused him more than once to literally spill his meal in front of everyone on the sidewalk outside the restaurant.

When Lee and Peter were in town, they would stay at her apartment. Her Fifth Avenue duplex was a vast improvement over the station wagon with its rattlesnake skins and animal bones on the dashboard that Peter had been known to sleep in prior to moving in with Lee. When the couple entertained chez Lee, Peter cut an amusing, if disheveled, figure: attired in his traditional, ancient preppie garb and sockless moccasins, he was in striking contrast to the formal nineteenth century opulence of Lee's drawing room, with its magnificent rich reds, English hunting paintings, floral Bessarabian rug, and flowering orchid plants. "Peter always looked like he had just been sleeping in his car, but he was so damned good-looking and appealing and visceral that he was irresistible anyway," said Porter Bibb. "He loved the ability to drop out of the sky into Lee's life and then go back into his own life, and in that sense I saw him as being in control. Peter was desperate to be in control of every aspect of his life."

By the fall, word was out on Lee's romance with him, and it is probably no coincidence that it was at that moment that Stas decided to file for a divorce. "Stas would never have abandoned Lee if she had not led such a completely selfish life," said Isabelle d'Ornano. "He loved her for what she was, and he knew her." It was Peter whom Stas felt very embittered toward and betrayed by, and whom he chose to make the scapegoat in the divorce papers. "Stas was very hurt by Lee's relationship with Peter Beard because he thought of him as his friend," said David Metcalfe. "Peter was one of the people Stas would never speak to again. But then again, Peter Beard was just an individual. Maybe if he'd had Olympic Airways it might have been different."

The Radziwills' formal split was a slowly evolving mutual decision. To deal with the enormous guilt she felt at having run off, Lee would complain to her intimates about what a wreck Stas was, how he was just an old man who shuffled around without much vitality and relied on a lawyer to make decisions for him, and how he would fly all the way across the Atlantic so that Max Jacobson could pump him full of amphetamines to give him energy. "Lee kept talking about what a wreck Stas was because that was her way of justifying having ditched the poor old guy and run off with Peter," said Jay Mellon, a former friend of hers. "She was quite tense about Stas, and he was mad as hell at her for leaving, you bet. He cut her out of his will. He was angry, I am telling you!"

"All I have to say," Lee lamented, "is that it is more than difficult to say good-bye to fourteen years of one's life together, with children one deeply loves."

One evening in November, Peter rang up his old African hunting buddy Jay Mellon, and invited him over for a drink at 969 Fifth. Mellon was an heir to the vast Andrew Mellon industrial fortune, a courtly, arrestingly handsome graduate of St. Paul's and Yale, intelligent and good-natured, but totally eccentric, and possessed of a Teutonic streak and a bloodlust for killing animals. His relationships with women resembled Peter's in that he was often seen with a showpiece girlfriend on his arm with whom he had no real intimacy or connection. Mellon's wealth allowed him the freedom to pursue his own interests, and at the time Lee met him he was at work on a book about the African hunter and living out the experiences in its text. Later, he published two other books: one on antique photography featuring photographs of Abraham Lincoln, and the other a critically acclaimed work on the American slave experience called *Bullwhip Days*.

"After drinks at Lee's place, we all went out for dinner," Mellon recalled. "Peter and Lee were obviously in love, but they were chafing at each other. Peter was incredibly informal. He'd arrive at a dinner party with no socks on. Lee was more uptight, more conscious of appearances. She was always pecking away at him about his slovenly behavior, and he didn't give a damn. They quarreled a bit here and there.

"Anyway, about a week after that Lee telephoned me out of the blue—I didn't expect to see her again at all, frankly— and she asked me to come over and have a drink with her, which I hastily did, believe me. She was thirty-nine, but she was awfully attractive at that age. Lee had something. There was a femme fatale quality about her.

"Lee and I became friends. I knew right from the start that it wouldn't get physical because she was involved with Peter, and hell, she was nine years older than me. I gave her a few kisses and that was it. That didn't mean we couldn't have some fun together. I saw her maybe once a week or once every other week for the next year and a half or so. Lee has quite an interesting way of talking. She can make lively and intelligent conversation on all kinds of things, and she's good company. She's not terribly well-educated, but she's fairly fast in lots of ways.

"If she started on that business of the stage or anything to do with it, she went bananas. If she saw some big stage personality in a room full of people, she would get all nervous and it would set off her drinking. Lee really wanted to be a great actress more than anything. She was always talking about acting, but in a pained way. She would say to me, 'I wasn't so bad as an actress.' She was already drinking too much. I heard it got much worse later, but it was pretty bad even then.

"Some people make a great first impression, and then the more you get to know them, the more disappointing they become. Lee was a person who made a much better impression than the substance behind her. As I got to know her better, I backed off a bit. I tend to judge people by their values, and I wasn't crazy about hers. She was fascinated by just plain money, high living, big names, all the cheap values that are out there, and so was her sister. Peter saw through Lee more and more too, as most people do after a period of time, although with him, he is a man without a profession and he uses people all the time. He lives on PR. But there is a serious and brilliant side to Peter, and with her there isn't.

"Nevertheless, I had the feeling quite often with Lee that there was another person inside of her who was really quite a nice person, actually. And Peter would often say to me that if you get Lee out to the country and put some blue jeans on her, she becomes a completely different and a much nicer person. The problem with her starts after a few days when she gets the itch to go back to the city, because she feels that things are happening and she's missing them, and that she isn't being seen in the right places and going to the right parties. Then this uptight quality of hers asserts itself and she has to go back to that scene again where the other side of her takes over, the publicity-conscious part that wants to build up her image in various ways. Those values would always reassert themselves in Lee because she couldn't really stay out of that world. She was helpless to resist. There were always those two sides to her. The good and the bad in Lee are mixed inextricably."

Steven Aronson confirmed Mellon's statement: "Peter once said to me, and I am quoting exactly: 'When Lee is around the fancy city people, she graduates from the honesty of good rural living and real experience to manipulation and cunning.' He will still say she will go anywhere to make a fool out of herself but that she is a marvelous and genuine person if you can get her away from the strobe lights."

Steven Aronson was Jay Mellon's friend and sometime editor, just as he was Peter Beard's. One day when Mellon was visiting Aronson at his home, he spotted a chapter from a

manuscript lying on his desk written by the landmark decorator Billy Baldwin, and he picked it up and read it. The chapter was called "La Princesse Manqué," and, although Lee
wasn't identified by name, he recognized immediately that it
was about her. Aronson had published a best-selling how-to
book of Baldwin's, *Billy Baldwin Decorates,* and had asked
him to do a sequel about his personal experiences as a decorator, *Billy Baldwin Remembers.* The first part of the book was
to be called "Stars in My Crown" and was about clients he
had worked with whom he thought were sublime, like Babe
Paley and Cole Porter.

The second section, to be called "Thorns in My Crown,"
was about the most appalling clients he had ever encountered.
The identities of the prickly "Thorns" were thinly disguised
and the titles of their chapters were can't-miss hints: "Unfin-
ished Symphony" was obviously about Leonard Bernstein,
and "The Lady Playwrite" could have been no one but Clare
Boothe Luce. The chapter Baldwin wrote about his experiences with Lee, which was the lead chapter in the section,
described her as an "American woman who was married to a
Polish prince and who was related by blood to a First Lady
who wore pillbox hats." Aronson remembers that the chapter
was written "in piss and vinegar, and it was devastating."

In "La Princesse Manqué," Baldwin revealed how Lee had
come to his office one day to discuss the redecoration of her
New York apartment. Together they went around to his fabric
and furniture sources and she took notes on everything he said
he planned to do. Then she never hired him but instead proceeded to work with all the sources he had just introduced her
to, getting everything she needed at the big discounts she was
able to negotiate for herself because of her celebrity status.
Baldwin, by then long considered to be the dean of decorators,
told Aronson flatly that nothing like that had ever happened
to him before over the course of his very long career. He said
he felt that he had been plagiarized, and he considered her
behavior reprehensible and practically actionable.

Meanwhile, without Aronson knowing that he had seen it,
the irrepressible Jay Mellon told Lee all about the "Princesse"
chapter. A short while later, Aronson found himself at a small
dinner party seated across the table from Lee. She behaved
cordially toward him until the end of the dinner when the other

guests had just gone ahead to the living room and he found himself bringing up the rear in step with her as they exited the dining room. As Aronson remembers it: "Lee turned suddenly and took my hand and her hand became a claw, her fingers became talons, and she hissed, 'You tell that little fag'—this from the bosom friend of Truman Capote and Rudolf Nureyev!—'that if that chapter ever appears in print, I am going to sue the shit out of him!' I left out the 'fag' part when I later relayed her threat to Billy. Even without it, his response was that she was such an awful person, with such a history of making trouble for people, that it was worth it to scrap the chapter just so he'd never have to think about her again."

Stealing Billy Baldwin's "to the trade only" contacts (not to mention his ideas) was not an isolated episode. Lee routinely circumvented middlemen by first going to them, and then going around them and buying things wholesale. "Lee was full of little schemes like that, nickel and dime stuff," reported a friend. "She was a person who lived way beyond her means. Her image as a jet-setting princess took a lot of dough to keep up, and it caused a kind of desperation in her. She was always worried about the maintenance of her apartment and the cost of living. She was very money-conscious and always ready to drive a deal or do a trade somehow. Lee has always had a penchant for using people and living by her wits."

Contrary to what one might expect, the time Lee spent in the company of Jay Mellon did not make Peter Beard in the least jealous. On the contrary, he sometimes would tag along as an extra man when Mellon was taking Lee somewhere, causing Ari Onassis once to make the wisecrack, "There are a lot of Ping-Pong balls in the air around here!" "Peter doesn't care enough about anybody to be jealous," said a friend.

In line with Beard's indifference to whom Lee might see or not see, he himself continued to see other women. In fact, he continued to see everyone. "Peter had all his women at the same time. He never dropped anybody," said Jay Mellon. "Lee found out about a whole lot of them. Peter is just so outrageous. He would just laugh it off and say, 'Oh, it's nothing.' Lee didn't agree with that. I know damn well that she was upset whenever she saw or heard about him being with anybody else, and she was furious whenever things got in the gossip columns, or if there were pictures in the press of him with other women. She didn't like the *appearance* of it, you know.''

While Lee played sexual politics with Peter, she wrote a short article for the January 1973 issue of *Ladies' Home Journal* culled from her in-progress memoir, which she continued to work on intermittently. As with everything else she undertook, there were always too many social invitations and other happenings to distract her from focusing on her work alone. "I don't want to be stuck in any frame," she once remarked appropriately. In her piece for the *Journal,* Lee informed the reader of her nostalgia for her childhood summers in East Hampton, the only time, she wrote, that she was truly carefree.

Taking advantage of her famous name, *Ladies' Home Journal* gave an overblown "literary launching" cocktail party in Lee's honor just before Christmas to celebrate the one-thousand-word first serial from a book she had still only just begun to write. As with her directives to Dick Blodget concerning her interviews for *Laura,* Lee was overly concerned with who would be attending her party. *Vogue* was banned from the scene as "too fashionable," and the columnist Suzy was considered "too social." The *New York Times* and United Press International were allowed in the door, and so were a string of book publishers, who, it was hoped, would nibble at the bait and offer her a big contract. Lee's friends, the contentious Norman Mailer, the towering John Kenneth Galbraith, and, of course, the quotable Capote, were all invited to give the occasion a veneer of literary respectability. "She wrote it herself," the ever-loyal Truman enthused on the scene. "I see the book going to forty thousand words. The title, 'Opening Chapters,' is good."

The party took place at The Four Seasons, a fashionable and expensive restaurant in midtown Manhattan. While *Journal* staffers spent most of their time at the gathering wondering if Jackie would show up, expenses for the affair were kept down by serving cheap champagne in very narrow glasses. Lee was presented with a cake made to look like a book, as if it were standing in for the missing thing. She chose not to eat the book-cake and instead took it home to her children, who were staying in New York with her before they all went out to Sun Valley, the Idaho ski resort, for the holidays.

"I scribbled on a long yellow pad, sometimes in the middle of the night," Lee told a guest reporter about her writing experience. "It was difficult to get it down to a thousand words, but in the end it was the easiest thing I've ever done. I did all the captions for the pictures too. I want my article to be taken seriously—not that it's serious—but as writing. I am serious about this."

"That's what she said when she tried acting," joked one of the guests from the publishing crowd.

36. *Breaking Up*

Almost a year into her return from England, Lee was still in her "resettling phase." Her routine first nights and black-tie affairs were kept to a minimum in order to better suit Peter's lifestyle. More typical of her social life in this period was the party she happily gave for Peter's birthday—his thirty-fifth—in January of 1973 in the privacy of her home, with Andy Warhol, Jonas Meekas, and other members of her new crowd in attendance.

Birthday boy Peter had just purchased a very secluded, six-acre woodland property in Montauk, less than a mile away from Andy's compound. The place came with a small stone cottage, and it was Peter's intention to live in the cottage until he moved into a refurbished replica of an old English windmill that he was planning to relocate onto his land from its original site several miles away.

During the early months of 1973, Lee and Peter would shuttle back and forth between the Church estate and the cottage. Lee disliked Peter's humble little cabin. It was too much of a comedown for her after the perfection of Lasata, Merrywood, and Turville Grange. Her effort at trying to talk him into purchasing a very expensive property in fashionable Southampton, even though she knew perfectly well that he was unable to afford it, was one in a series of warning signs that convinced Peter that he and Lee were traveling on inevitably different roads.

Their entanglement waxed and waned over the year. Each
sent out contradictory and confusing emotional signals to the
other. They enjoyed a couple of romantic vacations together;
the first during the early winter at a chic resort in Haiti, and
the second in the spring for a leisurely two weeks at the Coton
Bay Club on the Bahamian island of Eleuthera. Yet back at
home Peter became increasingly preoccupied with laying the
foundation for his windmill and then moving it, while Lee
came to see him at his cottage less and less—but not before
she managed to either stumble on or rifle through a bureau
drawer of his and take back the sexy letters she had written
to him in Kenya.

Lee remained in love with Peter in spite of her absenteeism,
until a very rude awakening early one morning in May when
she found him in bed with another woman. She and Jay Mellon had stopped by Peter's place to say good-bye to him as
they were leaving Montauk to drive to Manhattan. Mellon
went into Peter's bedroom first and found Peter lying there
with a young woman from Bermuda; both were fast asleep.
Thinking to defuse the situation, Mellon came hurriedly out
of the bedroom and told Lee that Peter was still sleeping and
that they should just leave. She ignored his suggestion and
went into the bedroom to wake Peter. When she saw the girl
in bed with him, a big commotion followed. Lee was crying
and leaving and then not leaving and talking to Jay and not
talking to Peter. Ultimately she left for New York in a very
big huff.

"She just wanted to be distressed, you know?" Peter said
to Jay afterward. He thought her indignation a shade peculiar
when she had made it clear to him that she did not enjoy being
with him at his cabin home.

Before it was all over between them there were some
strange transition times. After the incident with his Bermuda
friend, Peter became very involved with Barbara Allen, a sloe-
eyed, slinky, and seductive sometime model and dazzler-
about-town, who like Lee, was mad about him. Allen worked
at *Interview*, Andy Warhol's magazine. Her estranged husband, Joe Allen, was the magazine's co-owner, so she was
part of the Warhol crowd that frequently went out to Montauk.
Allen was younger and more unformed than Lee, but she came
with the same expensive price tag. She had the same penchant

for men who could keep her closet full of designer dresses, and, like her older competitor, Peter Beard was a departure for her in that regard.

When Peter began spending a lot of time with Barbara, and it was obvious that she was his new main interest, Lee actually went over to Allen's apartment in New York to try to seduce Peter into leaving there with her. She confronted Barbara and made irrational scenes to the effect that Peter was *hers*. Lee pestered her on the telephone as well and in so many words kept nastily repeating the same warning: Peter was *hers*. Barbara thought Lee's behavior was as odd as it was offensive. There was almost a cat fight between the two of them as each claimed the same territory. What a funny scene! These two talked-about beauties of New York acting so possessive over someone as indifferent and unfaithful as Peter Beard. Typically he told a reporter at the time: " 'Dating?' 'Going steady?' I don't even know what those words mean!"

But it must be said that whatever Peter's loyalty was to any given woman at any particular moment, Lee would always remain his sexual favorite. Peter could be extremely indiscreet about his affairs, and he once told a friend that Lee was "a very sexually oriented person and wildly erotic whenever there was someone who echoed back to her." Similarly, in far less elegant language he told Steven Aronson, "Man, Lee was the best fuck I ever had." "That's a direct quote," Aronson attested.

Lee's love affair with Peter Beard came to a whimpering end when she moved away from Montauk and rented a Southampton beach house for several months beginning in January 1974. They remained friends on and off for a while, and then, nothing.

On her fortieth birthday, Lee was in England working out some of the terms of her separation and divorce with Stas. He timed the press announcement of his divorce petition for that day, March 3, 1973. After Stas got over his initial outrage at his wife's desertion, he fell into a deep and ongoing depression. For years afterward he would say to his friends mournfully, and in all seriousness: "Why did Princess leave? I can't understand why Princess left." "Self-honesty was not his strong point," conceded a friend of his.

What distressed Stas even more than Lee's departure was the breakup of his family. Both he and Lee desperately wanted custody of their two children. Stas did not want to lose both of them, so, after much anguish all around, an arrangement was agreed to that allowed Lee to have care and custody of Tina, while Anthony would remain with Stas. (Anthony was attending Millfield, an excellent progressive boarding school in Somerset which catered to the special needs of children of the rich.) But the arrangement satisfied no one, least of all Anthony and Tina. They loved each other in that special way that siblings with absentee parents do, and because they were so close to one another, they were heartbroken at the prospect of being separated by such a great distance. Stas was bitter that the children were being separated at all. Everyone involved was extremely upset, and it was this guilt over the pain she unleashed in her family that helped trigger Lee's problem drinking.

Stas enlisted Jackie to his futile cause to try to persuade Lee to return to him. Jackie had very critical things to say about her sister's decision to get a divorce, and she bad-mouthed Lee to their family and intimates. Worst of all, she undermined Lee's relationship with her own children by not always being supportive of her to them. Lee was absolutely furious that Jackie would run interference on a decision that was hers alone to make, and she was sick and tired, as she saw it, of Jackie always having the upper hand with her in ways that were destructive. It was all well and good, she raged, for Jackie to say that she should remain with Stas when she did not have to rub up against his black moods day in and day out. "Divorce is a fifty-fifty thing," she said. She wondered aloud how long Jackie's own marriage to Jack would have lasted had he lived.

The episode caused the two women to turn yet another corner in their relationship. From that time forward they showed no hesitation in expressing an overt hostility toward one another whenever they thought the situation warranted it, which was often enough. Their slow disengagement from one another, ongoing over the past decade, now began to rapidly accelerate, so that by the time Lee and Stas were divorced, Jackie spent more time in the company of her former brother-in-law than she did with her sister. And by the time of Stas's death a few years hence, their relationship had deteriorated to the point where they were merely polite to one another. From then on, they would get together for important family occasions and keep up appearances for the public, but their youthful closeness was gone.

With the exception of selling Turville Grange, the rest of the divorce matters that needed to be dealt with went relatively smoothly. Stas gave Lee a very generous settlement. He was suffering acutely by then from the effects of the 1973 property crash and was deeply worried about business conditions in England. He reasoned that the more Lee had, the better, since his assets would then be outside Labour England and would ultimately go to the children. So generous was he to Lee that his attorney said to him: "You are really giving away a lot here, Stas. Why don't you at least take back the [Francis] Bacon?" The reference was to Stas's great painting by the artist, *Man in a Cage,* which remained in Lee's possession.

Stas allowed Lee to keep the family jewelry he had given her, in addition to the considerable new jewelry she had accumulated during their marriage. Turville Grange was sold in Lee's name early in 1974 to Henry Ford II for approximately £400,000, the top of the market at the time.* Lee got the cash from the sale of Turville Grange, plus 969 Fifth Avenue and all its contents, a settlement of about a million pounds altogether.

Stas, who did not have the money to buy out his wife, was heartbroken at the passing of Turville Grange, and he was never the same again. The loss of the house, Lee's labor of love, broke her heart, too.

Stas was granted a divorce by consent decree in July 1974 on the grounds that he and his spouse had lived apart for two years, and the award became final the following September.

Immediately upon Lee's return from England, she and Jay Mellon flew down to Palm Beach to join Jackie on board the *Christina,* which was docked in the harbor. Lee's friend Karen Lerner was along. After a few days Ari got restless and wanted to get out of there, so they sailed over to the Bahamas.

---

*The Fords made a family affair out of the Radziwill properties. Henry's daughter Charlotte bought No. 4 Buckingham Place when Stas died in 1976.

"Lee didn't like Onassis very much by then," Jay Mellon stressed. "He was just a pathetic old man and had been for a long time. Both those girls were always knocking him and making jokes about him behind his back. I remember Lee said to me one time, 'You know, we Americans think of Greeks as Europeans, but having known Ari as long as I have, I can promise you they are not. They are really a Middle Eastern people. They are like the Turks, and they are on a totally different wavelength from us.' Even Caroline would refer to Ari as 'my Turkish stepfather.'

"I have to say I did not find Jackie to be as attractive as Lee, who was a very pretty woman, but Jackie was a person who impressed one in a completely different way. What I liked and admired about her was her hard core of inner sanity. The wheels turned with a smooth hum inside her, and with Lee, they don't at all. Jackie kept herself together very well, whereas Lee was a mess basically. She was not happy, she was so screwed up.

"I never felt that Jackie as a woman was as attractive as Lee because she didn't have a certain quality that Lee has. It's an intangible, but it's important, because it is one of the most interesting things about her. A couple of other men I know who knew Lee well also noticed this fascinating quality of hers, this peculiar and fatal but very appealing vulnerability, a defenselessness, if you will, which draws a man to her, mixed with enough intelligence to make you feel for the person.

"Peter used to tell me that Lee really needed love, but that her values prevented her from getting that love because she had such a checklist, with money and glamour and all that. He thought that if she could just let go and get rid of the phony side of her life, she could be a happy person. But Lee was someone who all her life could not find fulfillment in anything, no matter what she did. She is a person who has never and will never get her life together, and one can tell this about her fairly quickly.

"At the exact center of Lee is a quintessential confusion. With anything she undertakes, be it one project or another, it can be pursued only so far and then this confusion takes over, and it just dissolves. Lee can't follow through on anything, and the fact that she never got her life together is related to that somehow. There is a dilettantism in her that cannot be overcome. And right at the middle of Lee, along with her confusion, is a lack of self-respect and confidence in herself. She doesn't really believe in herself very deeply. I had that feeling about her many times, and believe me, it did not begin yesterday, and it will not change either."

In sensing Lee's profound vulnerability, at least, Mellon saw in her that same quality of *douceur* that her admirer Chauncey Parker noticed in her all those years ago. It was part of her essence, and, as an adult, it formed the core of her femininity. That special compound of poignancy and suggestiveness she embodied was seductive to the majority of men who got to know her well.

Jay Mellon kept his harsh assessment of Lee pretty much to himself. She continued to see him at regular intervals until one evening the following spring when he invited her out to dinner and their friendship went up in smoke. As he remembers it: "We went to her favorite restaurant, Quo Vadis, one night in May, just at the time the soft-shell crabs are coming out, and a stranger came up to our table and sat down. He began chatting Lee up and said to her, 'I knew your sister,' and he dropped a whole string of names. Lee started shoving me under the table and egging me on to get rid of him, until finally I simply grabbed the guy and slugged him and that was that. Maybe I am a brute, but I just got sick and tired of the bum, you know? They took him out of there and put him on the street. Lee got pretty mad at me, I can tell you. She thought being involved in brawls in restaurants violated the image people had of her, to say the least."

The incident set off a screaming match between the two of them: "YOU HAVE NO RESPECT FOR MY POSITION!" Lee yelled at Mellon. "YOUR POSITION?! LADY, WHAT ARE YOU TALKING ABOUT?!" he shouted back. "YOU ARE JUST SOME STOCKBROKER'S DAUGHTER. JUST WHAT THE HELL IS YOUR POSITION? START TELLING ME ABOUT IT! START TELLING ME!

"We had other arguments along those lines before that," Mellon admitted. "Sometimes Lee would give herself airs, and that's usually what pissed me off, until finally, not too long after that last encounter, we just didn't see each other anymore, and that was it."

37. *A Clean Sheet*

With Lee's marriage ended and her affair with Peter Beard over, she began to spend a lot of time alone, a new situation for her. Rising every morning at seven-thirty, she spent her days working on her memoir. Evenings she lost herself in books, especially biographies and books on psychology, with a taste that ran to the works of Robert Graves and Willa Cather. Watching old movies was another preferred activity before bedtime at eleven.

Not that Lee stopped going out in the evening or traveling. In a departure for her, she took her nephew, John Kennedy, Jr., to a heavyweight fight early in the year and they saw Muhammad Ali defeat Joe Frazier, even visiting Ali in his dressing room before the bout. She continued to hang out with Andy Warhol, whom she had to her place for dinner countless times. One night they stopped at a popular East Side eatery, Melon's, for a meal and were told it would be an hour before they could be seated. Visibly shaken by the nonpreferential treatment, they quickly left and were tagged "melon heads" by the other restaurant-goers waiting in line.

In March, she made it down to Lyford Cay in the Bahamas. "It's beautiful here, and I should return outrageously fit if I don't get the bends from my underwater life," Lee wrote a friend. The press sighted her at the wedding of her stepsister, Nina Gore Auchincloss, to Michael Straight in May, and at a party a few weeks later in France to celebrate the engagement of David de Rothschild to his childhood sweetheart, Olympia Aldobrandini. In between those last two events, she and Rudolf Nureyev were the most talked-about couple at a formal reception given for the Royal Ballet at the Metropolitan Opera House. A personality given to vivid displays of sartorial exuberance, Nureyev showed up in a snakeskin jacket and boots, to the amazement of the black-tie set, who speculated that it must have been very trying for a fashionable woman like Lee to be outdressed by her escort.

Lee was seeing a great deal of Rudolf Nureyev during this period. Her perennial quasiromantic affair with the Russian dancer flared up again in the void left by the end of her affair with Peter Beard and it helped ease her loneliness in the wake of his departure. Often dining privately together, the two continued in their habit of constantly teasing each other as a way of expressing their mutual affection. They were seen in public exchanging fond glances and they even went together to some wildly romantic Saharan oasis. Lee was crazier about the ballet star than ever, and she continued her crusade to make him go straight, but with the same lack of success she had had all along.

Yet no matter how much their relationship fluctuated over the years, it never altered her deeply-felt response to the man's extraordinary gift and talent. "Rudolf made me cry with a moment he created onstage," she once admitted, adding in an aside: "But anything that is incredibly beautiful touches me—not in nature though. I am only really moved by beauty that results from human effort."

Apart from Rudolf Nureyev, it was her relationship with her daughter that most occupied Lee's thoughts and energy in her still-unfamiliar life as a single woman in New York. Their relationship underwent a radical readjustment in the wake of the divorce, which apparently was harder on Tina than any other family member. Not only did she have to contend with her separation from her brother and father, but she also lost all of her friends and was forced to adapt to the customs and traditions of a new country and a completely different life—all this on top of the normal travails of adolescence, not to mention the competition between a pretty, thin mother and an overweight daughter with complexion problems.

Once resettled in New York, Tina began the seventh grade at Miss Hewitt's School, located a few blocks from her East Side home. She was a shy and sensitive child, solemn of expression and demeanor, and very much in her mother's shadow. Tina had that same quality of *douceur* that Lee had—even more so. Although she struggled with her schoolwork, she was gifted as an artist and could draw and sketch wonderfully. One of her friends and a former classmate at Hewitt's, Catherine Weinstock Rayburn, remembers Tina as someone who was "disheveled-looking in her overall grooming and pretty withdrawn, and very, very timid. Yet she was a lovely girl with a certain sweetness about her."

Many who know Tina Radziwill say that she was a neglected child. It was not that Lee did not love her children, she just seemed to always put herself first. Her maternal instinct came in spurts. Testimony to that effect was given by Catherine Rayburn, who spoke for several others when she said: "I always thought Lee was concerned about her daughter in a very detached way. Tina was not a happy child. This might have been because she was shuffled around a lot. But a mother who is actively concerned about her child spends more time around the home and is more involved in that child's life than Lee was. Lee was not a good mother, absolutely not. My mother really liked Tina and felt sorry for her. We thought of her as an orphan."

What Tina's friend did not see was the extent to which Lee used Tina as a whipping post for her own frustrations. She was very domineering and did not give her enough room to be her own child: She badgered Tina about her weight, her complexion, her indifference to clothes. Surely Lee meant well, and to a great extent Tina was enduring the perfectly normal growing pains of most adolescent girls. But Lee's interference went deeper than that. She saw a disappointed self in Tina. She wanted her to be more like she was: someone gay and energetic, sharp and quick-witted, and who got innuendoes rapidly, while Tina was just the opposite. She was quiet and undemonstrative, gentle and unpretentious, and not at all jaded, and she always saw the best in people and was by nature slower to respond. Down the road, Tina would run away. She did not go very far, only to her aunt Jackie's, but she would not come back for a long, long time.

One early spring evening, Lee attended a gala and struck up a conversation with her sister's nemesis, the paparazzo Ron Galella, who at the time was preparing for publication a book of photographs he had taken of Jackie. "Princess," he said to her, "we have something in common. We are both coming out with a book." "Yes, and I am writing mine *on my own*," Lee told him proudly.

In September 1973, she had finally signed a contract to publish her memoir. Alan Schwartz, Truman Capote's lawyer-agent, made a deal on her behalf with Eleanor Friede, an able editor who had her own imprint at Delacorte Press, for a whopping advance of $250,000—$35,000 upon signing—and a due date of June 1975.

A full reminiscence of her early years was a serious undertaking for Lee, who felt that she had much to say about time and change and why and how the joy of youth disappears. In discussions at the outset, she gave Eleanor Friede the impression that she would tell her story not only with a loving nostalgia but with complete honesty and intimacy, or so the editor wanted to believe. Once the book was well under way, however, Lee was reluctant to be candid. "If anyone expects it to be one of those sensational, revealing memoirs, I am afraid they are in for a disappointment," she declared in a comment to the press. "My book will be about the sweet innocence of childhood." To Delacorte, the "sweet innocence of childhood" was not worth $250,000, and her memoir was of little value if it were not sufficiently honest and revealing. Thus, the seeds of conflict were sown fairly early on between her and her publisher about what the book's contents would be.

In the meantime, Jackie came out to Southampton one weekend to help Lee to decide on what material to use. The two of them had gone up to Newport and scoured the attic at Hammersmith Farm to see what they could find. They slogged through a mountain of documents, earmarking possibilities as they went along—mementos from Chapin, a faded notice of the Christmas play, their school yearbook entries, and a wealth of letters from the distinguished and eccentric of the family. "The research was an immense piece of work," said Lee.

Janet Auchincloss also got into the act, and, while searching her attics, she came across her daughters' long-forgotten scrapbook of their grand tour of Europe in 1951. As Lee reread it, she thought it was too much of a separate entity to include as part of her book. Rather, she was excited by the possibility of having it published as a book in itself, and she immediately brought it to Eleanor Friede's attention to test her reaction. "We were very excited about it too," said Friede. Lee picked up an additional $100,000 for *One Special Summer*, as the journal was to be called, and a Book-of-the-Month Club contract with an initial press run of 100,000 copies; publication was set for some months hence, in October 1974. *One Special Summer* would turn out to be one of the flops of that publishing season.

Once Lee finished compiling the research for her memoir, she preferred to do the actual writing of her manuscript out in Southampton. "You know New York," she said. "There are so many interruptions."

Lee threw herself into the task with her customary early enthusiasm. Driving out to Long Island from New York during the summertime, she would suddenly pull over to the side of the road and jot down "things of the senses—foods, smells, burning leaves, flowers." When she got to her house, she would leave the children and go to the beach and "just write, write, write," and when a brain wave came, it was "usually in the middle of the night." She said she finally understood why so many writers took to drink and that the experience taught her she could never be one. The isolation was just too desperate.

But the logistics of writing were nothing for Lee compared to the agony of expressing her personal feelings publicly. She said later that she learned a great deal about herself in the process of grappling with those feelings. "Suddenly my whole life opened up before me, and I could see what kind of person I was, my complexes and confidences," she confessed. "It was a rather frightening experience but much better than psychoanalysis." If Lee's life did open up to her as she claimed, she chose not to share those revelations with her readers.

Nor did what she was willing to share constitute writing that made any sense. Lee wrote wispy bits of thoughts, sometimes beautiful little gems, even an occasional chapter that was coherent, but they were not connected. Her writing did not constitute a book with a beginning and an end.

"At first, I started editing what she wrote," Friede explained. "But then Lee would go and put it right back the way it was. She wanted to sound like herself, and that's fine, but herself wasn't publishable. Many times I said to her, 'Lee, you have things to say. If you let me, I can get somebody who can make a real exciting chapter out of what you just told me because you are not doing it. 'Oh, no! No! No! Oh, no! It has to be my words!' she cried. So there was a strong need for self-expression on her part. On the other side of it, there was a strong need for a book that could be understood, and that was the problem."

Friede often got together for working sessions with Lee in

Southampton. "There was never anybody there when I was around," Friede observed, "and Lee always looked so sad. I think the only happiness she got during this period was from her children."

Lee worked on the book with Friede for well over a year. By then, Delacorte had half the manuscript and there was another payment due, so it was time for a reckoning. A meeting took place in Delacorte chairman Helen Meyer's office. "Helen, myself, and Ross Claiborne [the editorial director] were there and then Lee came in," Friede recollected. "We talked about the book, and apparently they had gotten together beforehand and not liked it. They said to Lee, 'We don't find this manuscript acceptable, and we don't want to continue with it. It will never work.' It was a shock to Lee, I know it was, and a big disappointment. That's a very tough thing to take."

"Lee wouldn't say enough about her family," said Helen Meyer in explanation of her decision. "She was very hesitant. I tried to get her to open up. Lee felt she had done all she could."

"That was one of her big problems in my view," Eleanor Friede acknowledged. "Lee couldn't make up her mind about whether what she was doing was right or not. And I knew that when I wasn't around, she asked whoever the next six people were she saw in her life—whether it was Truman or Jackie or whoever—whether they thought it was. Lee came to it with a kind of shyness, perhaps a kind of privacy, an attitude of 'I don't want to tell anything about what really happened.' The lovely memories of childhood are okay, but when she got into marriages and events like that, she balked. She was very reluctant to even discuss them. I think the whole idea of her life on the newsstand would be frightening to her. It was that fragility of hers that, again, was part of her sadness. She could not have taken too much of her life coming out. There is something there that scares her."

What was Lee so afraid of? Surely, she feared the exposure of the great disparity between her carefully orchestrated public image and the actual stuff of her conflicted inner life. Lee did not want anyone to discover that, like the heroine of a nineteenth-century novel that she imagined herself to be, her life yielded the portrait of a casualty: no matter how much she changed direction and milieu, she always remained a soul of

bluff and illusion, someone whose talent it was to stir up just
enough dust to create a beautiful facade. And therein lay the
great paradox of Lee: while passionately desiring success, in
the delivery, where it counted, she hid herself.

"Lee was constitutionally unable to confront the truth about
herself that she was hiding from all those years, to maturely
face herself with grace and get it all down," offered the filmmaking former psychologist, Al Maysles. "In a big way, it
took a certain amount of courage for her to even *think* that
she could do anything on her childhood. She thought she could
still keep the lid on the truth about her life and present it as
a fairy tale, not a profound revelation of what actually took
place. Unless that changed, we probably could not have made
a good movie of her either, even if that project had gone forward. Opening up is a requirement for doing a film of one's
life as well as a book. But for her own happiness, that repres-
sion is a terrible handicap. At some point in her life maybe
she will break through that. I always had that kind of hope."

38. *Talk Show*

"If something interested me enough, and I thought I could do
it, I'd make a stab at it. I've never been sorry for anything
I've done, and I'd do it all again. I'll never find myself just
staring out a window." So Lee declared in her dauntless determination to express herself in some medium.

Her search for self took yet another twist when she chose
television for her next attempt at self-realization. Once again
Lee's big-time ambitions took her back to the small screen
when she now decided that she wanted to establish herself in
the medium as an interviewer or talk show hostess. With her
fabulous network of connections she felt that she could book
her own guests, famous personalities from differing walks of
life who were certainly newsworthy and who would not appear
on television except as a favor to her.

Lee did not hide her feelings about the fledgling crop of
talk show hosts on the air in that era and was convinced she
could do better. "They're literally offensive," she complained.
"They're so glib, and they have done so little homework on

their guests' backgrounds. Their questions have no substance or value, and they seem to have no interest at all in their guests. The one exception is Barbara Walters, who is absolutely great."

Lee asked her good friend William Paley, the founder and chairman of CBS television, if he could help her. Paley thought her suggestion was an interesting idea and wanted it developed and put on the air for a tryout. In June 1974, it went down the pipeline at CBS to Sam Zellman, the Stations Division news chief, to produce a pilot of six interview segments with her and her chosen guests to be called *Conversations with Lee Radziwill*. "We just wanted to do it and then see where it would fit," said Sam Zellman. "At the outset we needed to see if Lee were a talented interviewer. She certainly had excellent contacts. That was the biggest thing going for her."

Lee cajoled four of her friends into appearing with her in the pilot—Harvard economist John Kenneth Galbraith, Rudolf Nureyev, fashion designer Halston, Gloria Steinem (a quid pro quo for the interview Lee gave her a few years back)—and one stranger, Peter Benchley, the author of the phenomenally successful first novel and hit movie *Jaws*. They were each to be taped carrying on a conversation with her in her red velvet living room in order to make it seem as though viewers were "eavesdropping on friends." A sixth interview was to be done in Concord, Massachusetts, at the home of Dr. Robert Coles, the author and Harvard child psychiatrist.

Sam Zellman flew in from out of town to do the assignment. He telephoned Lee from the airport in New York to get her address out in Southampton. "Your driver will know where I live," she told him. As a veteran newsman, Zellman knew that he was lucky to get a rented car on his typically tight production budget, never mind a limousine with a driver. Her naive remark made him chuckle and became a favorite story to pass around to the boys at the station.

After he prepared all the questions for the interviews, Zellman gave them to Lee for her input. On her own, she did a fair amount of homework on her guests' backgrounds; Nureyev, for one, found her knowledge of the ballet impressive. But, typically, she groused about the hard work involved, saying: "It's amazing the amount of work that goes into an interview. It's so demanding, so time-consuming." Zellman said that as the interviews worked out, Lee seemed to have the best rapport with Halston. He assumed that she felt more at home with her couturier than with people at an intellectual level. Clothes were the one topic under discussion in the series that Lee knew as much about as the person she was interviewing. She asked Halston, whom she bought both day wear and evening clothes from, what a woman could buy with $25. "Nothing," he said.

Looking back on the filming, TV veteran Galbraith remembered his experience as thoroughly rehearsed spontaneity. "Ken is the only man I ever met wearing a nightgown," said Lee. "It was madras with long sleeves, a Moghul idea he got when he was in India. We talked about that, about women as consumers, and inflation." When she asked Nureyev if he ever planned to get married, he blushed and retorted, "One doesn't expect close friends to ask silly questions."

It was the author Peter Benchley whom Lee managed to charm the most on the air. "Doing that interview was one of the most delightful afternoons I ever spent," he enthused. "I thought Lee Radziwill was one of the most charming, solicitous, sweet women I ever met in my life, and she framed interesting questions and was well prepared. But the experience was so low key and pleasant it was like too much vanilla. Lee was inherently polite and wanted to avoid controversy, not the right formula for a successful talk show host in the counterculture, hard-edged seventies."

After much dickering back and forth between Lee and CBS programming executives about where and how to place *Conversations with Lee Radziwill,* it was decided to try the series out on the daily news programs of the five locally owned and operated stations. Beginning at the end of August, CBS stations in New York, Philadelphia, St. Louis, Chicago, and Los Angeles, whose broadcast schedules varied, were to televise one interview a week for six weeks, with each of the conversations being edited into five short daily segments. If the pilot worked, that is, if the series clicked with the viewing public, Lee would get her own syndicated interview program.

As it happened, *Conversations with Lee Radziwill* was received with little enthusiasm by the local stations' news departments because it was considered "soft news," and in those days broadcasts did not have the time to do soft news. The local news ran for only thirty minutes—all hard news—and then went right into the national evening news with Walter Cronkite.

Apart from the core issue of hard news versus soft, there was a long delay after the interviews were finished and before they actually ran on the air. "Lee was unhappy with the way I cut the segments," Zellman admitted. "She thought I did a lousy job, so someone else took a crack at it. I don't know what happened to them after that because I turned my back on it. But I am sure that Lee would be more than eager to tell you how she is so talented and the stuff got screwed up by the professionals."

That is exactly what Lee did say. She thought the results that aired were destructively pared down from her original conversations, and she was bitter about it. "I am rather tired of people ruining things that could be good simply because they say they are 'pros' and know how to handle it," she lamented later. "Several of those interviews were good. Many people said so who didn't know me. But the company insisted on cutting them up like little daily commercials instead of having the continuity of one interesting conversation with someone quite special in his field."

Sam Zellman thought the real problem was that Lee's interviewing style was too convoluted. "She asked questions that didn't grow out of the previous answer. There's a flow to an interview and you have to roll with it. It was almost as if she weren't listening to the answers. I chopped it up because if a question doesn't grow out of the previous answer, you have to either truncate it or eliminate it.

"Lee Radziwill did not prove to me in those interviews that she was a born journalist, that it was in her bones. She was a celebrity who had friends in high places and was able to get a tryout in a news broadcast. For a purist in journalism, that isn't the way you become a journalist—just by having important friends."

Ray Beindorf, the CBS programming executive who developed the series and whose judgment of Lee's performance was far less severe than Sam Zellman's, said, "Talk television had not surfaced yet. It was still in its early stages, so we didn't know how to present it properly. I thought Lee was coachable, and certainly we all liked her personally. The consensus was

that she had a quality that was attractive. She wasn't Barbara
Walters, but she held her own. The problem was not her performance. The problem was that the form had not established
itself enough to create a place in a station's schedule yet.''

"When you don't want to offend someone, you give a tech-
nical reason for something not working out," insisted Sam
Zellman. "Paley didn't take a flier and give Lee her own show
because they didn't think she was that good. There is no other
reason for rejecting something from a broadcast—you find
places for really great pieces. Frankly, Lee just didn't have
charm on the air."

Nevertheless, if the series had run as it was originally conceived—as full half-hour conversations, or longer, between
Lee and her friends, it might have played very well as they
were done. And with more on-camera experience, she could
have easily competed with some of the scores of talk show
hosts who are on today. As it was, they did head shots, mostly.

At least one fan watched *Conversations with Lee Radziwill*
and was not unhappy with what he saw. In a column he did
for *Esquire*, Lee's old friend Taki said of her, "When compared to the infantile level of people like Merv Griffin, Lee
came on like a genius."

39. *Mood Swings*

Lee's thwarted ambition to establish herself as a star outside
the social firmament ran headlong into the same roadblock
every time: allowances for inexperience are not made at the
top, and Lee never wanted to begin at the beginning.

There was also the delicate matter of explaining away all
her creative failures to others without losing face. Once, when
someone came up to her at a social function and asked her
whatever happened to the memoir she was writing, she said,
"I finished it, but I decided it's not the right time to publish
it. It would abuse other people's privacy."

Lee knew that she had to recover her starting point, her lines
of force, once again, but what that starting point was remained
frustratingly unclear to her. "I've painted but I am not a
painter," she admitted in an interview at the time. "Nor an

actress. Nor a writer. I was reading Tom Wolfe, and *he* said he was not a writer. I understand that. I know people who have written books, but they aren't writers either. It would be presumptuous of me to say I could direct, but I certainly could do some producing," she pondered aloud in a new twist. Nor would she rule out the possibility of being a news commentator. "Or who knows," she said, "I just might go into journalism, newspaper journalism."

Lee was all over the place. Not only had she thrown out the possibility of pursuing three different career options in that one interview, but she made it four when she told Andy Warhol only a few weeks later in an *Interview* cover story that she should have been in the decorative arts, since she was "a very visual person." Apparently her mood had swung back into self-doubt by then, because she went on to say: "My deep regret is that I wasn't brought up or educated to have a métier. I am mainly interested in the arts, but because of my kind of education, my interests were never channeled in any particular field until it was too late to make use of them except in a dilettante way."

Yet the fact that Lee's life, so far, anyway, read like a book of first chapters—or a series of apprenticeships, if you will— had less to do with not developing her artistic bent early enough than it did with that "confusion at the exact center of her" that Jay Mellon spoke of. And just as she could never make up her mind conclusively about which avenue of life she wanted to walk down, she still could not decide what her true priorities were and which values were most deserving of commitment—the same unsolved problem that Barbara Walters noted after that interview she had done with her back in the sixties.

This ambivalence of Lee's was clearly evident in her attitude toward money; she expressed scorn for people obsessed by money, while she made life choices over and over again exhibiting that same obsession. "The rich are really scared to go out into the world," she said, "and that's why they cling together so much. They miss a great deal. Their circle is narrow, and they don't dare break it. Wives are terrified of their powerful, moody husbands. They are women in bondage whose weeks, months, and years are spent in acquisition. Shopping becomes a disease, an everyday necessity to keep up with the latest and to fill empty time. I know this because I did the same thing for a while until it made me feel useless and disgusted with myself. Now I realize how precious time is. Life is all we have, and you don't want to look back when it's too late feeling that you have done nothing but collect junk and overburdened closets.

"To me money means freedom and comfort. What more is necessary? Living well doesn't have anything to do with money. Take a bottle of wine, some cheese and bread, and go on a picnic to some charming place. What could give you more pleasure if you are with someone you like? That's living well."

"Lee is a very complex character," said a friend of hers and one of the very rich that she was complaining about. "She has two levels of thinking. She may know who she is by now, but she was quite mixed up for a long time. She could make those remarks about the rich and genuinely mean them. It would depend on what sort of mood she was in. But her need for money was always the dominant thing with her, and it ran through everything she did, making a mockery of her other sentiment. There is no way she would be happy in a small apartment tucked away somewhere."

At the same time, one could say that Lee's apparent change of sentiment was in part the normal mood and mind changes of any maturing life, and in part her unusual ability to think and observe in the uncoordinated way we feel, on various levels at once. This is why Lee was so complex. Not only would she vacillate constantly in her preferences, but her ability to see her life in a detached way and at one remove—as if through a camera lens—provided her simultaneously with great insight and a feeling of alienation, for it meant that that same quality of detachment would always prevent her true participation or involvement in anything she might undertake.

Despite Lee's continuous confusion on which creative endeavor would best focus her talents, the possibility of becoming a professional interior decorator had been on her mind on and off for many years. How something looked had always been the first thing she responded to, and the more she reflected on it, the more she came to accept the fact that it was her eyes that worked best for her, and that her root strength was in working her vision in a clever way. Even so, her recent failures at finding the right career made her wary enough not to be in a hurry to jump into the fray again. She preferred instead to take her time deciding if interior decorating was what she really wanted to do.

With that in mind, she contacted an old acquaintance of hers, the San Francisco decorator Tony Hail, and told him that she admired his work and, since she was thinking of becoming a decorator herself, she wanted to get to know him better. On a trip she made to San Francisco for no particular reason in February of 1975, Lee gave Hail a call, and he invited her to come along to a party at Gordon Getty's place, a stylish residence he thought she might enjoy seeing. When they got there, they took a look around and then, at her insistence, went and sat down by a window and chatted.

"Lee never liked to be standing up or in a group," remembered Hail. "She wanted to be off on the side, so we sat on the side. She was afraid of being mobbed, of everyone coming up to talk to her. She always felt that she was going to be grabbed or taken advantage of, and she thought that she should be protected from that—very much the Princess, you know, very celebrity-conscious, always thinking somebody was watching her, and, of course, they were to a certain extent." It was true that Lee had a formidable claim on people's attention in the seventies, and those in the same room with her seldom lost a special alertness to her presence. She was defined by that special kind of celebrity, one not bestowed by achievement but rather by lending her presence—by showing up.

"If you want to look at it in a certain way, Lee could be quite a pill," Tony Hail went on. "She took herself quite seriously and was very self-satisfied and enormously conscious of her sister and always trying to keep up her side of things. She was skin and bones and airs and attitudes and many things that do not appeal to a man who wants a nice wife to spend the rest of his life with. It's so easy to say naughty things about Lee. She's strange that way. But one can easily take the other side of it and argue the other way:

"I think Lee Radziwill is a genuine icon of her time, a good-looking and very vocal, articulate member of her group, a true woman of the world who knows everyone from her life in London and New York. And she has lots of good qualities, even if sweetness and light are not two of them. She's much more interesting than Jackie, who was marvelous at the funeral and didn't do a damn thing since. Lee is less full of shit than her sister was. You could talk to her better, man-to-man and straight on. And she's such a wonderfully glamorous, terribly attractive woman. When Lee Radziwill walks into a room full of people, why then you know *somebody's* there, somebody that you're dying to talk to. Here she was a woman who still looked eminently good at fifty and even sixty—like a woman a man would still want to go to bed with. And Lee's still got allure and personality. I don't think you could have said that about Jackie."

While Tony Hail and Lee were chatting by the window at Gordon Getty's house, Blair Fuller walked in, and Hail said to her, "Look, there's your ex-brother-in-law." Lee replied, "No, it's not." He said, "Yes, it is. He's a good friend of mine." She said, "Don't you think I know my own brother-in-law?" And with that, Hail went and got Fuller, who came over and embraced Lee. They had not seen each other since the mid-fifties in Paris and after an enjoyable time talking about the old days, Fuller promised to get together with Lee the next time he came to New York.

Back in Manhattan, Lee made preparations to go to Paris to attend the funeral of Aristotle Onassis, who died in the middle of March after a long illness. But Jackie would not hear of it and a bitter row ensued. "Jackie was brilliant at photo ops and public relations," said an insider. "She was as shrewd about understanding how the press works and about what people want to perceive as anyone you could ever encounter. She wanted to be the center of attention, and Lee's own relationship with Onassis was a distraction that she did not want others to be reminded of." Alas, Jackie's will prevailed, and, much to her regret, Lee stayed away from paying her last respects to her old friend and lover, Aristotle Onassis.

It is perhaps hard to believe but true that Jackie could be just as jealous of Lee as Lee was of her. Jackie sensed with envy that the men in their circle were attracted to Lee for herself rather than for her position. Not only was Lee the more sensuous, some of them considered Jackie to be asexual altogether. "She would sleep with a man only if he were useful to her," was how one put it.

A colleague of Andy Warhol's, the journalist Bob Cola-cello, accompanied Andy and the two sisters to a museum one afternoon to see a show of Egyptian art, and he had this to say about what he saw of their relationship: "Lee seemed to know everything there was to know about the exhibition. 'Oh, look, Jackie,' she would say, 'that bowl is just like the one we saw in the Cairo Museum.' She could list the Pharaohs and the dates they ruled. She seemed to have the mind of a curator and the taste of an aesthete. Jackie looked at her the way a pupil looks at a teacher, intently, taking it all in. Lee talked. Jackie listened. Lee led and Jackie followed."

Lee, moreover, was a more natural and human person than Jackie was because, said a source close to Lee, "her range of emotional responses were more those of what a normal and open person's might be than were Jackie's. But Jackie, as a result, remained the more powerful of the two because she had fashioned a persona for herself that had a coldness and ruth-lessness to it that made her far less vulnerable."

Even their way of speaking gave them away. Lee's husky voice was an attractive, lilting, and expressive instrument, whereas Jackie's baby-doll, whispery voice was a put-on, cal-culated to achieve a certain effect. She could, when she wanted to, speak in a perfectly normal voice, a fact remarkably over-looked in the great many profiles written about her.

And Lee was a loyal person, too, and Jackie was not, at least not in Lee's opinion. She had wanted very much to renew their close sisterly relationship in spite of all the recent friction between them, but Jackie wasn't interested. As Lee saw it, or as she came to discover and complained to intimates, Jackie valued people in proportion to how much she could use them, and since she had her own life in New York and no longer needed Lee for her contacts or her solace, as she had when Lee lived abroad and she was in the White House, Jackie just brushed her aside and went her own way.

It was "not at all surprising" that Jackie would drop her sister, in the opinion of Chauncey Parker, who said, "I have always thought Jackie had a real mean streak in her and that she inherited it from her mother. I remember vividly in the old days at Merrywood how she would make these cruel remarks in a smiley, sing-songy way, usually accompanied by a little twist in her mouth, as though she rather enjoyed it, watching the hurt exact its toll. But then, maybe I am being unfair in singling Jackie out, because so many women who came through the college ranks at that time seemed to have acquired that same dulcet, self-effacing approach under which lay a very sharp rapier. It was particularly evident in Vassar graduates. Those rich women came out of there so polished, but underneath they had all this anger. They were all so damn mad as hell about something, and with Jackie there was plenty of it. Whatever the reason, she figured out somewhere along the way that she could camouflage that fury and still get what she wanted. But if you look at photographs of Jackie in later years without her dark glasses on and without her knowledge, her facial expression was that of a very, very angry person."

Since Blair Fuller had not had a chance to talk to Lee in any depth at Gordon Getty's party, he was looking forward to seeing her again when he arrived in New York in April. He took her out to dinner and was surprised to discover the extent to which Lee had changed in the intervening years since she left Michael. "It was a bad period in her life," he recalled. "She was melancholic and very thin and ill with some unnamed thing. I had the strong feeling that she felt she had made a very big mistake in leaving Radziwill. She said words to that effect, really. Not that she said anything great about Stas—it was just better than being alone. I had that feeling of regret from her, and she seemed like a burnt-out case. She had lost her vitality, which was her most attractive quality. Lee had gotten herself worn out and didn't know quite how it happened, and thus she was vulnerable and tired. She didn't seem to have any wisdom about this, and I am not saying that anybody else would. But she didn't, she hadn't. I really felt quite sorry for her."

"It was her breakup with Peter Beard that really shook her to the rafters," said Truman Capote, who traveled that autumn and winter with Lee to New Orleans and Mexico. "That was the beginning of this period of hers of feeling totally undone. It was the first time that anybody had ever dumped her, because she had always done the dumping, and she was really devastated by it."

Lee's struggle with herself was always much more obvious than most people's. She gave off sparks, and one could easily see how tension-ridden she was beneath her external charm and cordiality. "I don't rage," she confessed. "I am pretty well closed in, but by temperament I am very melancholic. My sign of the zodiac is Pisces the fish, and fish swim both ways. Fish are supposed to be oversensitive, but that's all right with me as long as there are toughness and balance along with the sensitivity." Still, she conceded, "I am very sensitive to other people's moods, too much so. It's much easier to be happy if you don't feel for them so much."

Lee once said that the man in history she would have fallen in love with was Lord Byron, "not for all the obvious reasons, but because he was vulnerable." Then, obviously thinking of herself without saying so, she added, "There is something extraordinarily appealing to me about people who aren't quite in tune with the world. Everything about them may seem like perfection, including their achievements, but they suffer terribly. They are usually very sensitive people who find that life is too fast or too tough for them to keep pace. That quality of being slightly lost, slightly out of step, always makes me cry."

Poor Lee. There was an essential emptiness to her, her psyche maimed not only by an overcritical mother and powerful sister, but by her two failed marriages and the emotional dead end of her lifestyle. She did what she could to create a surrogate personality out of those materials which lay at hand; that is, she exploited her natural glamour and beauty, but she was lost and she knew it. Without a powerful distraction to occupy her, she would repeatedly sink back into her resident sadness, crippled by some nameless unhappiness and restlessness, and captive to alternating fits of yearning and the doldrums. "What is so sad," said Chauncey Parker, "is that the Lee I knew really had some potential and where it went sour I don't know."

Nor was there any psychological reserve to prepare Lee internally for the news, come September, that Jackie had taken a job as an editor at Viking Press. Jackie had chosen not to tell Lee of her plans in advance, and when she learned of it through the grapevine, she reacted with red-faced ire. "She just lost it, she was so angry beyond all reason," said one witness. "It was one of those telling situations in which one realized that Lee wasn't angry about what she was saying she was angry about—that is, 'Why didn't Jackie tell me?' — she was angry about something much deeper, and this was symptomatic of and spoke to the odd tension that always maintained itself between them. Maybe the emphasis changed from time to time, depending on which one of them was doing what, and many people called it a rivalry, but it was really a kind of tension, and it was mutual.''

Jackie's career move unnerved Lee because she still had not had a chance to shine in her own right and thus build her defenses and mount a counterattack psychologically. It was now imperative that she make a decision on whether or not to become an interior designer. Decorating had always been her hobby, after all, and the homes she had done for herself were considered to be fabulous. After the passage of a few more months and a chance offer from a hotel group, she took the plunge, deciding it was high time to put her ability and great taste to professional use. "It's what my friends have been telling me to do for years," she said, "and I finally got it together."

40. *A New Career*

Before Lee decided to set up a decorating business, an even more significant change happened in her life: she fell in love. Well, almost. She had met Peter Tufo, a prominent New York City lawyer, at a luncheon the year before in Southampton, and it was mutual attraction at first sight. At the end of the lunch, when they had been talking a long time, they continued their discovery of each other with a walk on the beach, after which Peter drove Lee home. In the intervening year he escorted her to a movie from time to time but that was about all until September of 1975, when Peter ran into Lee and Tina at a Manhattan restaurant. He passed their table as he was leaving and stopped to say hello. Lee introduced him to her daughter and said, "Would you like to come to dinner Saturday night?" The invitation, which he accepted, was for Southampton, where Peter also spent his weekends. Tina, who was a teenager by then, made it a threesome, and they all had a raucous and merry time.

Shortly after that, Lee and Tufo started dating. He escorted her to so many social functions that fall—the fortieth anniversary party for the Hayden Planetarium, a gala at the Metropolitan Museum's Costume Institute, the theater, and various dinner parties—that they became linked in the public's mind months before their relationship actually became serious.

Peter Tufo was born in 1938 and grew up in Chicago, the son of a child psychiatrist and a ballerina. Very bright, he skipped a couple of grades at the private North Park Academy, majored in history at Beloit, a small liberal arts college in Wisconsin, then went on to Yale Law School, class of 1962. After joining a prestigious Manhattan law firm, Davis, Polk and Wardwell, as an associate, he headed up New York's Washington office under Mayor John Lindsay from 1966 to 1970 as a lobbyist for Federal assistance. Subsequently, he set up his own successful law firm, so that by the time he met Lee, he had achieved a good deal of recognition in the city as a skillful and influential negotiator. He did so through hard work coupled with political connections and the right friendships, some of which had begun at Yale, while others were made through a fortunate former marriage to Alexandra Gardiner Creel, a socially prominent New Yorker and heir to historic Gardiners Island, in Long Island Sound. Tufo lived in a six-room cooperative apartment on East Seventy-second Street in the same building as his former wife and only several blocks away from Lee.

Once on his own as a lawyer, Tufo continued his tradition of public service and did pro bono work in addition to his law practice. That same autumn, Lee came to his swearing-in at City Hall as the unsalaried but high-profile chairman of the Board of Correction, an entity which runs New York City's prison system. He was called upon to give a speech at the ceremony, and afterward Lee said of him: "Peter's so bright, he'd be good in politics. He has terrific guts. He reminds me of the early sixties—his style, his drive, his belief that things could be better."

An event occurred in November which made him a hero in Lee's eyes and gained him a good deal of additional prominence in New York as a cagey power broker. In his position

as chairman of the Board of Correction, Tufo had warned of
an impending riot at the Men's House of Detention on Rikers
Island. When it occurred, he and the Commissioner, Benjamin
Malcolm, crawled on their hands and knees through tear gas
and a three-foot hole the prisoners had made in one of the
prison walls into prisoner-held territory, where they established a truce, negotiated the release of the five correction
officers taken as hostages, and ended the rebellion. A former
reservist in the Marine Corps, Tufo credited his military experience with giving him the courage to mingle with prisoners
under such tense circumstances, and he seemed able to mix
such disparate worlds as New York's high society and its pris-
ons with ease.

Peter Tufo was also someone who had an extraordinary success rate with the women in Lee's circle. Before Lee, there
was Kate Paley, the daughter of William Paley, and after Lee,
there was Katherine Johnson, the daughter of the southern
newspaper magnate Anne Cox Chambers, to name two. The
ladies-who-lunch crowd sat around and gossiped about his affairs at length, while still others considered him an outsider
and suspected his motives. But Tufo, who was a wiry five feet
nine inches tall, intense, and rather average-looking, had something women liked. "He's had quite a history," said Jay Mellon, who knew him from Southampton. "What interested me
was that he hung in there with Lee longer than anybody else—
maybe it was his Marine training!"

Whatever it was, Peter Tufo quickened something in Lee,
and by the time they attended Midnight Mass together on
Christmas Eve, they had become very close. This new relationship inspired startling changes in Lee's mood and demeanor. What Peter saw was a lively, vigorous, and fun-loving
woman—unrecognizable from the person Blair Fuller had
taken to dinner only months before. Some of Lee's merriment
took the form of practical jokes: she would schedule a surprise
of some sort and then tell Peter or Tina it was something that
she knew neither of them wanted to do when she really had a
delightful happening planned.

On Peter's part, he was captivated by Lee. She always had
interesting firsthand observations to tell to him about people
he had only read about, and like many people drawn to her,
he liked the proximity to a big event. He summed up his feel-

ings about her one evening at a social function when he was heard to say: "Isn't she beautiful, intelligent, artistic, creative, and radiant? Lee is just so wonderful!"

In the early months of the new year, after they had discovered they liked many of the same things—books, ballet, the theater, movies—and lots and lots of walks on the beach, their relationship evolved to another level. By the time they returned from a skiing vacation in Klosters, Switzerland, in March, they had fallen madly in love.

Peter Tufo was very much of-the-moment, visceral, high-energy, and athletic, a worldly, upper-middle-class, committed professional with a very different view of life from many of Lee's spoiled, rich friends. She found him stimulating, exciting even, someone who gave her the opportunity to look at life in a different way. Lee was attracted not to what Tufo had but to what he was: as she saw it, a masculine, amusing, challenging person who lived life passionately.

Above all, Peter Tufo was another experiment for Lee. He was, as was Peter Beard, a threshold moment for her, a time of exploration to see if she could forego relationships dominated by her need for status and security in exchange for emotional and sexual fulfillment.

Peter and Lee discussed marriage, but only as a state in life. "It's the last thing on my mind right now," she said, and even though their relationship was very intense, it still wasn't a full-time occupation for either of them; they saw each other mainly on weekends. Between his law practice and his pro bono work Peter put in long hours, and by then Lee was deeply involved in her own decorating business.

On that front, the first thing Lee had done was to put out feelers to see if she could go into partnership with an established decorator. She tried to hook up with several of them. Her favorite possibility was Mark Hampton. There were some discussions, but he did not own his own business at the time. Another possibility was "the Prince of Chintz," Mario Buatta, but he related to her, through an intermediary, that he was very happy the way he was. Eventually Lee scrapped the idea altogether, saying, "Without a partner, I am not indebted to or irritated by anyone. I don't have to worry about disagreeing over taste or tempo."

With a partnership no longer an option, Lee started asking

her friends and acquaintances to connect her with potential clients. One of them knew Mario di Genova, then the president of the Americana hotels and resorts chain, and invited him to Lee's apartment, ostensibly to a cocktail party, but really to see how she had decorated it. To further help matters, di Genova was given some magazine articles to read beforehand, which featured the places Lee had decorated (her Manhattan duplex had appeared in *Architectural Digest* the previous year).

"I knew I was set up," said di Genova. "I was invited to Lee's apartment to see what she could do. I thought her place was extremely attractive yet very simple, and I got very excited about her approach to things, especially color, and her treatment of various materials." After some additional discussions over lunch, di Genova decided to try Lee out by giving her two sample suites of rooms to do (normally he would give a decorator a hundred rooms at a time), one suite at the chain's resort in Bal Harbour, Florida, and the second at another resort, the El Presidente Hotel in Acapulco. A third commission at the chain's very up-and-coming hotel in Palm Springs was included shortly afterward. If di Genova approved the sample rooms Lee did, they would be used as models in further redecorating.

The Americana chain was a mass market operation. Lee said they hired her because they wanted to upgrade their image a bit. "My giving her a commission had a lot to do with the person she was," di Genova acknowledged.

The Americana commission spurred Lee to set up shop. Her design firm, Lee Radziwill, Inc., was announced in mid-February 1976. For the moment she was a one-man band operating out of her office on the second floor of her duplex, a small white room dominated by a big table that would be piled high in the coming months with the tools of her trade—design renderings, dozens of cloth and marble samples, various written estimates, and so on.

Immediately after she announced the start of her design firm and before she had a chance to begin her Americana commission, the New York department store Lord & Taylor approached Lee to see if she would decorate a model room for them around their theme of "Celebrity-Decorated Rooms for Summer." She accepted, choosing to do a "barefoot" dining-

sitting room. Using pieces from the store's furniture department, she created a cool, uncluttered look for the room with
a peach and green color scheme, straw rugs, and rattan furniture; in a sentimental touch, she placed an oval window inspired by one at Turville Grange over the fireplace. The
official unveiling of the model room on March 2, to great
fanfare from the press and general approval from everyone
else, was Lee's debut as a professional decorator; the room
was also featured in *House and Garden* magazine—not a bad
start for a novice. Apart from these commissions, Lee im-
mersed herself in her new field by reading about interior design extensively, and she ultimately became quite
knowledgeable about it.

Down in Florida, she brought the outdoors inside for her
Bal Harbour suite, stressing continuity, with each room relating to the next by the use of similar furnishings, wall and floor
coverings, and the fresh blue and white color scheme of the
sea and sand outside. "While the suite radiated an aura of
brightness and shine, it had the warmth and comfort of home,"
Lee pointed out. "I wanted the definite quality of a residence,
as opposed to a typical hotel interior."

When the project was completed in September, Peter flew
down to Florida with Lee for the celebration party. "She was
so obviously an extremely elegant woman, and she gave parties at our hotels that brought national and international attention to them," said di Genova of this and her other decorating
jobs for the chain.

The Bal Harbour design was reproduced successfully, after
which there was a change in plans and Lee next did the presidential suite, a penthouse on the fiftieth floor, for the Americana Hotel in New York. All in all, she worked for di Genova
on design commissions for a period of two years, and in sum-
ming up his experience with her he said: "I was very impressed with her work. Lee's suites rented well. She designed
the kind of interiors that were well accepted by the upper
segment of our market, but her work was a little too luxurious
for the rest of it. It didn't hold up too well as far as the colors
and materials went. This was a problem we had with her,
because I tried to point out that some of her choices were too
delicate for the hotel business. She used light leathers, for
example, that were not treated for durability; they were too

delicate. We had a problem with the upkeep and the finish.

"Lee was very pleasant to work with, but she wanted to be different, to do rooms that would not be run-of-the-mill, and she was very adamant about maintaining the integrity of her design choices. I have worked with almost every major decorator in the world, and I have never dealt with anyone as extremely . . . well, not *stubborn*, but let's say 'determined' in her taste and opinions as she was. But Lee had a tremendous charisma that set her apart from the other decorators. At the same time, one had to be aware of the power of her personality or else she would tend to dominate you. She didn't win in the end, because the money came from us. It was very simple. Instead of her doing the large volume of rooms we originally discussed, we wound up only giving her a few sample suites to do. This is not to say that she wouldn't have ultimately been given a good volume of our deluxe suites to do if we hadn't run into cash problems in 1978.* The suites Lee designed were very, very attractive."

In September, as her commissions grew, Lee took space in the architectural firm of John Carl Warnecke and Associates, and, though still independent, she had access to the firm's larger resources. Warnecke was a client of Peter Tufo's, and it was he who had arranged the sublet. Primarily a San Francisco–based architect with an office in New York, Warnecke was a sometime escort of Lee's and a favorite Kennedy architect (he designed the JFK memorial grave at Arlington National Cemetery) who was instrumental in encouraging her and helped her get clients by having her do the space planning on some of his architectural projects.

The setup was perfect for Lee. The office was conveniently located on Fifth Avenue at Fifty-ninth Street, across from the Plaza Hotel, and it looked out on Central Park. Her office was just one room—an ultramodern space decorated with sleek Italian furniture—but clients could come up on the elevator to the firm's reception area and see her name listed on the door. By then Lee had hired an assistant and various freelance specialists to deal with the commissions that were rolling in: a residence in San Francisco, a club in Houston, a resort in Brazil. "If I had no clients, I'd certainly be apprehensive, but

---

*The chain, a subsidiary of American Airlines, was put up for sale.

that's not the case," said Lee. "It's no joke. I have been far more successful than I ever imagined!"

Of the half dozen or so clients she had had up to then, only one was someone she knew. For the most part, jobs came to her by word of mouth. She claimed to have turned down more of them than she accepted, both when she felt a client was going to be impossible to work with, and when it wasn't going to be "interesting" for her. Half of Lee's work was commercial (banks and offices in addition to hotels), which she greatly preferred because those jobs gave her more freedom in her design choices and allowed her to set her own hours, provided she met deadlines.

Although she insisted that interior decorators did not earn a great deal of money, Lee was impressed with the amount she was making. "I am not in it for that, but it does make me feel more confident," she acknowledged. She designed several living rooms with dining areas for between $25,000 and $35,000 each, and with her new professional arrangements she soon concluded that four jobs were what she could cope with satisfactorily at one time. But no matter what the budget was, her fees were the same: there was a consultation fee and a retail fee. She charged $500 a day for a consultation, and a "day" was about five working hours: her retail fee was simply the difference between the wholesale and retail price. "I had to learn all that," she admitted. "It was so complicated, how to order, how to get fifty percent down before you start."

It was Mark Hampton who played a crucial role in helping Lee set up her business logistically. He was her mentor with the vitally important trade contacts and contractors, and he advised her on how to bill and draw up contracts. "He and Lee were very sympathetic to and understood each other," noted Tony Hail.

Hampton and Lee's relationship was symbiotic. In exchange for his advice, Lee invited the decorator to parties where he met potential clients. "It would amaze me if Mark didn't take advantage of her," said one of his colleagues. "It's just his nature to use those people to be part of the scene. He and his wife, Duane, still play that whole Southampton game. Mark is amusing and titillates all those ladies with his tales. I don't know how he finds the time."

By the autumn of 1976, Lee had settled comfortably into

what would be her routine for the next few years. On a given day when she wasn't traveling, she could often be found telephoning a workman at six in the morning. "You've got to be up early to talk to plumbers and contractors," she said, "but then I always wake up at dawn, no matter how late I have been up." Later in the day, she would go to her office to make some more phone calls and do some desk work, or she might just as easily be found scouting the market for furnishings, or overseeing draftsmen and artists.

"I wanted a full-time job, and now I have really got one, and in this field I think I am as good as anybody," Lee declared at the time. "I expect to get well established, and remain and build on this [business]. I am very serious. In five years I'd like to see Lee Radziwill, Inc. essentially as it is now but with a larger staff and bigger projects throughout the world."

Her design philosophy? Light, comfort, the charm of personally collected objects, fireplaces going night and day, if possible. "It's like having a friend that you like to be with," she said, adding: "For me, the main pleasure of decorating is that I never use rigid styles. Every place I have ever done has been completely different from the last. I don't have any trademark, and I don't want to have one. I like to be able to do anything a client might want, whether it is very contemporary, nineteenth century, even eighteenth century—although that bores me now, because it's so uncomfortable and stiff. The surprise comes from watching the whole thing take on a style of its own—it's very exciting!"

In answer to criticism from other designers that she had no professional training, Lee said, "I really don't think formal training is necessary. If you are imaginative and have a good eye, you will immediately recognize something marvelous amid a heap of clutter. I know many designers who haven't had those degrees or courses who are far better for it because they have not been taught rules. Taste is something you are born with—and yes, I would call it an emotion."

41. *Changing Partners*

On June 27, 1976, Stas died suddenly of a heart attack. He was staying at the Essex home of a friend for a small weekend house party when it happened. After a very late game of cards on Saturday night, he went upstairs to his room and died instantly as he began undressing for bed. Around sunrise, sensing death, a dog belonging to another guest went out into the corridor and started howling. The guest woke and rang for the butler, who entered Stas's room and found him lying dead on the floor. He was just shy of sixty-two years old. His live-in girlfriend of the past few years, Christine "Chrissie" Weckert, was asleep in a room down the hall.

While it was true that Stas had a heart condition and that he had had a previous heart attack, his death still came as a shock to Lee. "Despite our divorce, we were very close," she said. She and Tina flew to London as soon as they heard the news and went to stay at the Ritz Hotel, where Anthony met up with them.

Jackie and Caroline joined the rest of the family for the funeral. "Jackie loved Stas," said Isabelle d'Ornano. "He and Lee were so different, they had nothing in common. Jackie had much more in common with him than Lee did. She understood him, and whenever she spoke of him, it was with enormous affection. Jackie always missed Stas. He counted in her life."

The funeral took place at Saint Anna's Chapel, a lovely little church that Stas had built and donated in memory of his mother on the grounds of the Grammar School of the Marion Fathers, a now-defunct boys school serving the Polish community that he helped organize at Fawley Court, near Henley-on-Thames. His coffin was draped in the Radziwill flag, which the Communists allowed out of a museum in Warsaw for the occasion. After the ninety-minute service, his body was laid to rest in an adjoining crypt. Jackie and Lee stepped out into the warm sunshine with their arms around Christine Weckert before parting from her.

Weckert was a pleasant but unsophisticated American girl

in her late twenties, a graduate of the University of Hawaii who dabbled in cultural pursuits and was, from all reports, crazy about Stas. His friends saw her as a poor imitation of Lee (it was a stretch, but they did look somewhat alike), and they considered his affair with her "not the most serious thing he had ever done." She put great pressure on Stas to marry her, which caused a strain. He finally succumbed to the pressure and had proposed to her reluctantly only hours before he died.

Stas's friends had been worried about him at the end of his life. He was drinking much too heavily and had become rather desperate. He had given up, essentially. His losses were too much for him, and he had a terror of being left alone. Stas never did get over Lee. To the end of his days he would still ask his friends mournfully, "Why did Princess leave?"

When Lee got back to New York after the funeral, she thought about how much her life had changed since she had left Stas. She finally had to admit to herself that it had been the right decision. Owning her own business was largely responsible for her change in attitude. It empowered her. "I think there is nothing that makes you happier than to be really involved in something," she said. "In the last few years I have really learned to take care of myself. It was almost like being reborn. Before, everything was done for me. I was totally incompetent, and so was my daughter—there were endless things one could not cope with. Suddenly I was on my own with two children. It was terrifying. These years have been a period of tremendous growth, and I have found the most important thing is to be self-reliant. Marriage is an extremely difficult relationship. It's nobody's business, but I am so happy on my own."

To be on her own with two children took on new meaning for Lee with the death of Stas. Not only were Anthony and Tina left without a father, but it did not take her long to discover that Stas had very little cash on hand. As it turned out, his estate went bankrupt and his children were left with absolutely nothing. The depleted state of Stas's finances took Lee by surprise. She knew he had been in financial difficulty but had always assumed everything would work itself out. The estate went bankrupt because Stas personally had guaranteed the bank debts of the companies he owned; with his death his debts crystallized, the banks called in their loans, and, as many had long suspected, his liabilities far outweighed his assets.

Stas owed colossal amounts, £15 million in 1976 money. His creditors only received roughly 7 percent of their liabilities, just under £1.1 million. A few years after Stas's death, Jackie came to his children's rescue by setting up trust funds on their behalf, but until then it was rough going.

With Stas gone, Anthony came to live with his mother. "My children have been deprived of a family life, and I am trying to make up for everything," she admitted. She enrolled Anthony at Choate, a preparatory school in Connecticut, and she worked hard at making him feel he had a home. Lee was glad to have Peter Tufo around. He and Anthony got along well and enjoyed masculine activities together.

The same month as Stas's death, June of 1976, Lee received a lovely valentine from Truman Capote in the pages of *Vogue*. He had been asked to write something on her as part of a feature they were doing on her Fifth Avenue duplex. Once again, Truman told the world how much he admired her. "I can't think of any woman more feminine than Lee Radziwill—not even Audrey Hepburn or a great seductress like Gloria Guinness. . . ." he wrote. What was noteworthy about Truman's latest love note to Lee was that it was written when they were no longer really friends, but he was ignoring, in print at least, the profound changes in their relationship.

About the time Lee started seeing Peter Tufo, she and Truman stopped seeing so much of each other. Truman did not like Tufo. He did not think he was good enough for her. But then, he felt that way about all her boyfriends. It was a matter of power: if she preferred Peter's company to his, then she no longer belonged to him. Still, the estrangement was wholly on Lee's part, and it had begun at least a year before that. Blair Fuller remembers that when he saw Lee early in '75 and asked after Truman, whom he knew, she was snide and contemptuously dismissive of him in response, and that they had already had their breakup. To another friend, Lee referred to Truman as "that little worm."

"That little worm!" They had such a deep friendship. Whatever happened? The answer is that Truman's self-destructive behavior in recent years had become too difficult for Lee to deal with. He just wore out her patience. The Truman Capote of the mid-seventies was not the Truman she had befriended a decade before. He was so heavily into a cycle of pills and booze by now, and then detoxing and drying out in hospitals, that his personal stock plummeted with a lot of his friends. What made matters much worse were his ruinous sexual escapades, usually with disreputable males his socialite friends did not want to have around.

And though Lee was spared the verbal rod in "La Côte Basque 1965," the much talked about excerpt from Truman's work-in-progress, the gossipy roman à clef *Answered Prayers,* published in *Esquire* the previous autumn, which lampooned many in their social circle and was never completed, she had long ago discovered what a fabricator and conniver he was. It was obvious to her that he had squandered his gift and was on an unstoppable slide to disaster. It is not incidental that Lee came to this conclusion about Truman in 1975, a time when she could barely cope herself. "He was sick, and there was nothing one could do about it," she said.

Truman was allowed entrée into the circle of the glamorous rich because he so greatly amused them. (The British wit Michael Tree once dubbed him "the rich man's Pekingese.") It was a world in which he was only a visitor, a status he acknowledged to no one but himself. To be amusing takes energy, and, increasingly, Truman had none. "He knew that everybody expected so much of him, to entertain them, and he became exhausted by that," Lee noted.

Just as Truman went on pretending that nothing had happened to his friendship with Lee, she, too, was not yet ready to go public about her disenchantment with him. On the contrary, when Gerald Clarke interviewed her around this time for his Capote biography, she still had nothing but the most glowing things to say about Truman.

In July, Lee put in an appearance with Jackie at the Democratic National Convention at Madison Square Garden, which was in the process of nominating Jimmy Carter for the presidency. Peter Tufo came along; he remained her constant companion. In September, she once again got to doctor her résumé when, in a testimonial to the fashion empress Diana Vreeland, at a dinner dance given in her honor, she stretched the time she had spent working for her at *Harper's Bazaar* from the several weeks it had been to "two years." "I never learned so much so fast," Lee said. That part was probably true.

In November, she exercised her option to buy the Gin Lane beach house she had been renting in Southampton for the past few years, paying $329,000 for it and using up a good chunk of her marriage settlement in the process. The owner, Mark Goodson, whom she knew socially, had been invited over to discuss the selling price. "I brought my new wife, Suzanne, with me," Goodson recalled, "and Lee was a little taken aback. She's a pretty good negotiator, and she thought she was going to bargain with me a little better if I was alone. I was a dummy to sell it. It had three acres of woodland, with a swimming pool on the beach side and two hundred feet along the beach, an incredible property right at the end of Main Street. But those were the days before properties went wild."

There was a problem with the realtor's commission. Legally, Lee owed it, but she was reluctant to pay, and the realtor, Charles Horowitz, had to resort to litigation to get it. "We were told we were the bad guys and how DARE we sue someone of her stature," Horowitz said. Another time, when Lee sublet the beach house during the high season, she complained to a real estate agent about the amount the agent had negotiated on her behalf with a tenant after she heard of a similar house renting for more, and she tried to wriggle out of their deal. "When it came to money, Lee was just impossible," said the disgruntled realtor.

Although the contemporary A-frame house Lee purchased was very modest on the outside—its value was in its oceanfront location—she set about redecorating its interior to bring it up to her level of taste, and, sparked by her customary panache, the Southampton house became another showcase for her reputation as a decorator, and for once the mood was not traditional. "I enjoy decorating any house," she said, "but I prefer decorating houses in the country, and most of all I enjoy decorating for myself. I wanted the house not for the summer only but for any time of the year, a house that focused on the natural environment, an unencumbered place that would constantly renew the spirit."

Lee transformed the house to more fully exploit its oceanfront site, using colors throughout that were perfectly keyed to the beach and sea. The shutters, wicker sofas, and sailcloth upholstery she chose were in sharp contrast to the elegant French and English period pieces and yards of exquisite fabric of her New York apartment; at the beach house there wasn't a sash or a medallion in sight.

Lee herself designed the dining chairs and the coffee table in the beach house and she had someone make them up. Sleek and simple, they were thought by many to be a great design, and there was talk of her expanding her business into a home furnishings line. But she made it known that she would only do it for a great deal of money up front, so nothing ever came of it.

The same thing happened when she was approached by a designer's rep, Peter Bradley, with the possibility of his representing her in "designing" a line of printed fabrics. It was to be a licensing arrangement actually. The public relations story would be that Lee was designing the fabrics herself, but all she would really be doing was selecting them. Lee was interested, but according to Bradley, the negotiations stalled because, again, she asked for too much money up front—about $100,000—and because she kept changing her mind about the designs. "I worked with Lee for a year and a half," he said, "and I couldn't get to first base with her. She kept holding at $100,000, and nothing seemed to get off the ground. Then she wound up keeping the design samples I had done on the outside at my own expense. I wanted them back. It wasn't a very pleasant situation."

One of the big social events of the New York season is the annual Winter Antiques Show, always held in January in the historic Seventh Regiment Armory on Park Avenue. Mario Buatta, the interior designer best known for popularizing the English country house look in the American market, was in charge of the show for its 1977 season and he asked Lee, who had done other showcases for charity, to do a room with a Victorian theme for the Armory show's opening night.

"Lee was a stellar name and had a following," Buatta said of his choice. "The public response was incredible. Her name sold a lot of tickets. She drew a crowd every day of the week the antiques show ran. 'I want to see the Lee Radziwill room. Where is the Lee Radziwill room?' they kept asking. Every-

body was so startled by it. Lee did a fabulous job; she did
bright spring-green taffeta sashes and ribbons and bows and
covered the poles—the columns—with it, and with the help
of Jean-Jacques Bloos, the floral designer, she used cut ama-
ryllis in glass vases on all the table tops in pale-shrimp-like
colors—pinks and creams and white. Lee had such a fresh
sense of color. Her rooms were very pretty."

In the spring, Lee got going on a much-delayed but equally
successful decorating project, the San Francisco residence of
the millionaire industrialist Bill Hewitt (the CEO of Deere &
Co., makers of lawn mowers and farm machinery) and his
wife, Trish (Patricia), who, though she knew Lee, actually
learned of her decorating business in a gossip column. "Not
many clients have had as much experience decorating as I
have," said Mrs. Hewitt, who owns several residences, "and
Lee was really neat about having our ideas conform to each
other. It was a mutual relationship, not a command performance. This is very unusual in decorators. The other times
when I used them it was instant war. I am a very opinionated
client, and Lee was special in that regard. We never got on a
'thou-shalt-not' basis. Lee did three rooms and then the traveling became very difficult for her, so I did the rest of the
house. But those three rooms are really nifty. When people
come in, they gasp."

Lee worked on the Hewitt house from April to August. On
one trip out to San Francisco in July, which she made with
Mark Hampton, who also had business to take care of there,
she was invited to a dinner party at the home of the socially
prominent rancher and vineyard owner Whitney Warren, an
old friend of her mother's. Seated next to her at dinner, not
by accident by any means, was Newton Cope, one of the city's
more eligible bachelors. It seems that Warren took it upon
himself to do a little matchmaking. Cope was the fifty-five-
year-old widower of Dorothy "Dolly" MacMasters, née Fritz,
whose father had left her a real estate fortune; she had died
the previous year of a heart ailment at just forty years of age.
Whitney Warren had been a friend of hers, and so he took
Newton under his wing after her death. Without mentioning
Lee by name, he told Cope there was a very interesting person
he wanted him to meet, and he invited him to the dinner party.

"We talked about our children the whole night. I have seven

children," recalled Cope, who would later confess it was love at first sight. "It was a wide table, and I suppose if Lee had sat across from me nothing would have happened." But fate and the seating plan intervened, and the two of them hit it off. "I didn't know it at the time," Cope went on, "but Lee's modus operandi was talking to one person all night if she liked or was interested in someone, and never looking at the other side of her.* We got up finally and went into another room and talked some more, and I thought, 'Gee, she is so interested in me,' and afterward I drove her and Hampton back to their hotel." Worried that he might never see her again, Cope did some fast thinking and asked Lee if she would be interested in decorating some rooms at the Huntington, a charming hotel on Nob Hill that had been left to him by his wife. Lee told him she would love to. "And that's how it all started," he said.

On her next trip out to San Francisco in August to wrap up the Hewitt job, Lee and Newton got reacquainted at another dinner party, also not by accident. That one had Tony Hail playing cupid. And when Lee was dining with Trish Hewitt in a local restaurant soon after that, at Cope's insistence she was once again reintroduced to him; it seemed that everywhere Lee went, she and Newton Cope were being introduced. When they finally started working together on the Huntington Hotel job a short time later, the hotelier finally got his wish, and Lee started casually going around town with him.

Also on that same August trip, John Carl Warnecke gave a party at his office on Montgomery Street for Lee, whom the gossip columns described as the toast of San Francisco. "We gave a huge party for her, and everybody was dazzled," said Warnecke's former wife, Grace. "Lee was really very big then, and I remember being impressed by how gracious she was to the endless stream of people who came by who she was never going to see again." Warnecke used Lee to help promote his business by padding his guest list with his business associates. "Celebrities like Lee Radziwill get used by people often for such purposes," said a friend of hers. "It's the other side of the coin from all the perks that come their way."

---

*"I know immediately who interests me and who doesn't," she once said.

CHANGING PARTNERS 255

While Lee was gallivanting all over San Francisco, Peter
Tufo kept up the same pace at his end, working on a field
project for television in addition to his usual hectic duties.
"Save Our Schools," which he narrated, was a thirteen-part
series on urban public education for which he would win an
Emmy the following year. To get away from it all, he and Lee
took a romantic ten-day holiday in Fez, Morocco, early in the
fall, but they would continue to be separated a lot due to their
heavy schedules.

All through that autumn and winter, Lee spent a good deal
of time in San Francisco working on the Huntington Hotel
commission. She stayed at the hotel when she was there, and
Cope went into overdrive trying to start a romance with her.
To be sure, Lee played down her relationship with Peter Tufo
when she was with Cope, and likewise minimized her involvement with Cope when she was with Tufo. But Lee really did
have her hands full with Peter, and consequently, she avoided
Cope's advances, so that when she and he got together, which
was often (she did not necessarily have anything else to do
out there in the evening, and Cope was a *very* friendly client),
she left doors open at the hotel and tried to have other people
around whenever they saw each other. She did not want anybody making suggestive comments about them. This was not
just for Peter's benefit but for Jackie's, too. As Tony Hail
pointed out, Lee always took her reputation quite seriously
because of her sister.

"That's when they started writing things about us," said
Cope. "I was not involved with her yet. It started out in San
Francisco and drifted back east. The press said, in so many
words, 'What's going on between those two?' My attitude
was, 'So what if they say those things?' But it annoyed Lee
that they were reading something into our relationship that
wasn't there. The rumors preceded the relationship, and they
started hot and heavy then."

Celebrities always have that added dimension to their relationships—the intrusion of the press, which, in turn, helps to
define those very same relationships. When Newton made a
trip to New York that fall, he and a South American friend of
Lee's, Patty Cisneros, made it a foursome with Lee and Peter
one evening for dinner. "We were just working together
then," Cope recollected. "I went there to buy some furniture

and so forth. I remember Lee and I went to lunch, Diana Vreeland was there and some others, and that night the four of us
went out, and I met Peter, an awful nice guy. Later on, after
I got back to my hotel, Lee called me up and told me that he
was mad as the devil. Apparently after I had left them, they
picked up a newspaper and went back to Lee's apartment,
where they saw this column item in the *Daily News* that said,
'What's this hot romance between Lee and Newton Cope?'
They made it up, but Lee said that Peter got so mad he stormed
out of her place.

"Lee would bellyache about Peter once in a while, about
how he was mad at her all the time for her coming to San
Francisco so much. Little things. It was jealousy. He got furious at our going out together. And Lee was always sort of
mad at him anyway. Evidently they used to fight."

Others noticed it, too. Tony Hail recalled that he joined Lee
and Peter for dinner one night at Quo Vadis, Lee's home-
away-from-home on East Sixty-third Street, not too long before Lee and Peter had gone to Morocco: "I always had a
little corner table and Lee and Peter were often there. You had
to look for them way back beyond the bar, and I sat there with
them more than once. They were mad about each other. But
one night when I joined them for dinner, Peter spent his time
putting Lee down. They certainly weren't getting along very
well. They were arguing about nothing. That's the point.
About nothing at all." Andy Warhol made the same observation in his infamous *Diaries*: how Lee and Peter, when out
on the town together, were seen fighting. More than likely,
the uncertainty of their situation fueled their bickering.

Their disagreements aside, Lee's bicoastal mischief with
Newton Cope may have annoyed Peter temporarily, but it was
not a determining factor in the dynamic of their romance: their
love affair was too intense to be set aside so easily. Nevertheless, by the end of 1977 it was clear to both of them that they
did not totally meet each other's requirements. Although they
found each other's company fulfilling and were very intimate,
Lee's effort at living with lowered expectations remained exactly that—an experiment. Like Peter Beard, Tufo just did not
have the finances to keep up with her needs. She was used to
a different kind of life and was oblivious to any standard of
living except her own. Peter was not in a position to provide

the kind of financial security that she craved. And because he was always going to have to work, he would never have as much free time as she would like him to: Lee was a high-maintenance woman. Then there was the matter of Peter's equally daunting reservations: to him, fullness of life meant having a family, and Lee could not and would not have any more children.

Just before Christmas, perhaps prompted by the nostalgia of the season, Lee and Peter had a serious discussion about the fact that they were never going to make a permanent life together. They took Anthony and Tina to Santo Domingo over the holiday to visit friends and enjoy themselves, but they knew that it would be their last Christmas together and that their romance was at an end. From then on they would lead separate lives.

There was an occasion when they saw each other once again. At the end of March, Lee asked Peter down to Washington on some pretext. The trip was a ruse arranged by Lee to try to get Peter to change his mind about their no longer seeing each other, because in the interim she had painful second thoughts about letting go. No, he told her, they had to stick to their decision. It was all over, he said. So Lee was left with Peter's rejection.

42. Newton and Gore

Lee kept losing ground, that was the thing. Only love kept her level, and when Peter Tufo slipped away, once she felt the full impact of what she had lost, she slid right back to where she had been just before she met him and then sank ever deeper into her own personal quagmire. She was turning a corner, and it was a dangerous one, drinking from the combination of guilt and loneliness that was plaguing her. This time when she and Jackie next went to St. Martin, it was Jackie who, in a conversation over tea, told Lucy Porges of New York, another visitor to the island and a stranger, how ''difficult, complicated, and unhappy'' her sister was.

With her nerves now drawn extremely taut, Lee, as usual, vented her feelings of frustration on her daughter by berating

her constantly, so that Tina, always very inward, became more
so. Patterns of emotional deficit are usually passed on: Tina
had exactly the relationship with Lee that Lee had had with
her mother. There was so much deprivation there for both of
them to share. Was it the pain of the recent past or was it
something deeper, her own childhood, that was driving Lee?
It is doubtful that even she knew.

Anthony fared better. He was turning out more like his father, whom he resembled, and he had a somewhat different
and easier relationship with his mother because of gender and
temperament. He was much more placating. The more Lee
drank, however, the more both he and Tina learned to tread
lightly around her. Particularly when she was feeling better,
they hated to say or do anything inadvertently that would upset
the balance or harmony.

There came a time during this period when, weary of all
the friction, Tina left home and went to live with Jackie. They
were close, and Tina had often spent weekends with her. At
first Lee was merely miffed, but Tina stayed away for months
and months. Lee grew bitterly resentful toward Jackie and told
her that whatever had happened, she had no right to usurp her
position and steal her daughter away like that, and for a time
they even stopped speaking.

"They must have had quite a row," said Newton Cope,
whose own relationship with Lee had heated up by now. "Lee
said to me, 'Tina and I aren't getting along and she is staying
over at Jackie's.' And every time I saw or spoke with her after
that, she'd say, 'Tina is still over at Jackie's.' It must have
cooled things off between them for a while, because Lee never
mentioned much about Jackie after that. I think she was hurt.
She didn't say much about it, and I didn't want to pry.

"But it was quite obvious to me that Lee wasn't much of
a great, warm mother. Tina always struck me as unhappy. She
was in the same relation to Lee that Lee was to Jackie—
she was living under a cloud. Something went wrong. Maybe
Lee was too interested in having a good time. Her father's
death must have been a terrible weight on Tina. It's too bad,
because she is a very nice girl."

What was interesting about Lee's depression and psychic
misery, and even her drinking, was how compartmentalized it
was. In the midst of all this chaos, she managed perfectly well

to keep her design business going and to maintain her evolving relationship with Newton Cope. When she went out to San Francisco to work on the Huntington Hotel job—approximately once a month until well into 1979—Newton, like Peter Tufo, never saw her drink and was unaware of her spiritual malaise.

That began to change when Lee grew more and more fond of Newton as they got to know each other better. It would have been hard not to like such an attractive, low-key, easy-going Californian. Lee enjoyed the exuberance of his happy-go-lucky company. He always gave her a lift, and he continued to be smitten, dazzled by her.

Newton Cope was born in Bakersfield, the son of a salesman for Anheuser-Busch. He dropped out of Berkeley, where he majored in psychology, to join the Air Force as a fighter pilot in 1942. After the war he married Marilyn Jacobs, the daughter of a Sacramento car dealer, and eventually he took over a share of the business. Later, in 1959, he bought an old 1853 firehouse on the city's skid row and remodeled it into a restaurant, an investment that proved very profitable when the area was later designated a historic district. "I went into the restaurant business as a joke, a fun idea," Cope confided. "The Firehouse is a very colorful place. Both of Governor Reagan's inaugural dinners were held there. Later, I gave it to my daughter to run—it's still around." In 1976 Newton was divorced and two months later he married Dolly MacMasters. "I bought vineyards in Napa and built a restaurant there and a hotel in Carmel and lots of other things," he said, recalling some of his investments.

When Lee's long-distance romance with Newton picked up speed, her malaise began to lift correspondingly. In describing the courtship that brought about the change in her, Cope said: "When Lee was working on the hotel, she would go to all these supply houses during the day. Sometimes we would get together for lunch, but we always got together for dinner, either at some restaurant or at my house a block away. We would gossip about people and the trials and tribulations of our children. Lee wouldn't talk about past relationships unless you asked her, and I never asked. I had a house in Napa. We drove up there a few times. Looked at the grapevines. What do people do? We were happy together. And then I would go to New York. We'd go to lunches and dinner and shows. I never stayed with her. I stayed at the Carlyle Hotel. Her place was too small, and I like my privacy. And then she would come back out here. We would just bounce back and forth, and we started getting closer and closer—we never had any arguments. When you go with somebody for a while, you get used to them more than anything, I guess. Lee just got used to me.''

Once he had spent enough time in her company, Newton became the latest in a long line of those who knew Lee to notice how her fireside warmth evaporated in public. ''When we were alone, she was fine, but when she got around other people she became arrogant and snobby and bitchy, and it used to burn me up because I am not that way,'' he said. ''I like everybody. If Lee and I were standing in a room at a party and she saw somebody else approaching, she'd grab my hand and stiffen up, like she didn't want to see anybody. So I would say to her, 'Then what the hell are we doing here?'

''Once we were having dinner with friends of mine at a club I belong to, and halfway through she got up and left because my friends bored her. That gave me a little clue that we might not work out. Lee is really a very sweet gal if she wants to be. You have to know the inside of her, which is a very warm person. It's too bad she has two personalities and her warmth isn't there all the time.''

Originally, Lee was going to decorate a large number of rooms at the Huntington, but she had other commissions and her life in New York to keep going, and three years into her decorating business she was exhausted from the constant traveling. She could not get them done fast enough to meet the business requirements of the hotel, so she only did five rooms in all. ''Lee worked her head off. She's really a dedicated woman when she starts something,'' Cope noted, ''but we wanted things done in a hurry and lots of them, so finally we cooled off on her doing all those rooms.''

The Huntington Hotel had a tradition of creating a different decor for each of its rooms and suites. Lee's designs for the rooms she did were all coordinated by a vibrant color scheme: bright pink walls with a pale lime sofa and cushions in one, mauve walls in another, a melon-colored room, and then an unsuccessful chocolate one with shiny wallpaper, which guests said they found too dark and gloomy. Her color palette was showy but controlled, her designs elegant but declarative. Again, she tried to make the rooms as livable as a guest's own pied-à-terre would be, so it is not surprising that Cope had the same complaint that Mario di Genova had had: they were too well done, too expensive, and too impractical for a hotel.

Lee had an opportunity to pull out all the stops when she redecorated some of the rooms in Newton's home, a spacious apartment in a building he owned, one of San Francisco's famous old apartment houses at the top of Nob Hill. "Lee used padded fabrics," said Cope in describing her work, which she did simultaneous with the Huntington commission. "The library is salmon-colored and has faded out to where it looks quite pretty now. In the living room she used red velvet with gold trim. It was expensive but worth it because it will look good for quite a while."

Slowly but surely, Lee and Newton began to plan their futures together. When he heard that the Stanhope, a chic hotel on New York's Fifth Avenue was up for sale, he entered into elaborate negotiations to buy it. He and Lee had great plans of doing the hotel over and then living in the penthouse. "But then Sol Goldman kept changing the deal on me," Cope said. "Every time I raised the financing, he upped the price, until finally he told me it was not for sale. I got mad and quit. I didn't know he was that kind of guy."

Their engagement was announced in late April 1979, and a wedding date was set for May 3. The simple civil ceremony and a small reception were to take place at art collector Whitney Warren's showplace home on Telegraph Hill, a splendid chandeliered apartment with superb tapestries and a dizzying city view. The couple planned to live "most of the time" in Cope's apartment but were going to hang on to Lee's duplex and beach house. "We'll just bounce back and forth between New York and San Francisco until we find out what we want. We'll ask for discount tickets," Newton joked. Lee intended to continue her career as an interior decorator with an office in San Francisco. Still, lingering doubts remained in both their minds as to whether she would ever really be happy living away from the world she knew in New York.

"We didn't have very much in common," Newton conceded. "I don't know what Lee saw in me actually. Truman

Capote said to her, 'That Newton Cope out in San Francisco, that provincial little town, what's he got?' And I do not like the Kennedys. Lee thought Teddy was going to be the savior of the world, and I told her, 'That bum!' Obviously, I am a Republican.'' Lee was aware of Newton's natural limitations, but he had his net worth to make up for it, reportedly about $10 million, his half of his late wife's estate (the other half went to the children).

A week or so before the wedding was to take place, Newton was in New York. Lee and Jackie had resumed speaking at this point, and Jackie gave a dinner party for the couple at her apartment; she and Cope were meeting for the first time. They discussed their plans with Jackie, who was not going to be at the wedding, and she wished them luck. Walking back to Lee's place afterward, Newton asked her, ''Why the hell are you so afraid of your sister?'' Lee denied that she was. ''I told her I sat there all night at dinner and I saw it. Her reaction every time Jackie spoke was like her mother was about to spank her. It was as if Jackie controlled her. I could feel the tension, the vibes going between them—it was Lee, not Jackie. It was quite obvious that Jackie intimidated her. It's too bad Lee couldn't get away from that sister of hers. Being just a few blocks away, it was like an unhealthy bond she couldn't escape from—like Devil's Island or something. When she was out in California, she seemed to be happy. Back in New York, she tightened up.''

The evening in question had dire consequences. Meeting Cope that night inspired Jackie to run interference on behalf of her sister and create an unreasonable demand for money that appalled the groom-to-be. Newton recalls: ''When Lee and I got engaged, I got a lot of flak from friends, who said, 'How can you go with that woman? She and her sister are the two worst piranhas in the United States.' They told me Lee would chew me up and spit me out. Very rarely did I hear anything nice. But what no one seems to understand is that I called the wedding off, not Lee. All those articles that said I was left at the altar, and Lee called it off were wrong. I CALLED IT OFF! The press just made up the story that Lee got cold feet, because we would not talk to them. They told us that we should talk to them or else they would make up their own story. I said, 'Go ahead,' and they did.

''But here's what really happened. Before Lee and I left New York for San Francisco after the dinner with Jackie, I got a call from Jackie's lawyer, Alexander Forger. He told me that Jackie had asked him to look in on her sister because Lee did not have an attorney, and he asked me if I would sign a prenuptial agreement. I said, 'Absolutely.' But when he came over to my hotel he asked me what kind of deal I was going to make for Lee. I told him, 'I am not making any deal.' 'Well,' he said, 'how much are you going to give her each month?' I told him, 'That's none of your business.' 'Well,' he said, 'I think we should have something in writing of how much maintenance a month. What would happen if you die?' I said, 'I'll put it in my will that she gets a million bucks, how's that?' 'Well, I think we should have it in writing how much Lee gets a month.' I told him, 'I am not buying a cow or a celebrity the way Onassis did! I am in love with this woman!' And then he started apologizing, 'Now don't be upset,' he said, 'because I don't want to interfere in your love life, but why don't you just put it in writing that Lee will get $15,000 a month?' I said to him, 'Would you sign something like that?' He said, 'No.' Finally, I told him, 'Sorry, no deal,' and we parted company.

''I felt this so-much-a-month business had to have been Jackie's idea. She had just gone through that whole deal with Onassis, and she thought, 'What the hell, I'll get my little sister taken care of too.' I don't think Lee would have thought of something like that. She wasn't as money-hungry as Jackie was. Lee wanted to be taken care of, yes, but I don't think she would connive that way. And Lee would have said something to me rather than have this guy come at me out of the blue. When I talked to her about it, she just said, 'Oh, all right, if that's what you want.' That's why I felt it had to be Jackie's doing.

''So then Lee and I flew out to San Francisco, and we were a few days getting things together for the ceremony and nothing came up again. On the day of the wedding—we were supposed to be married at four o'clock—at two o' clock, I got a call from Lee, who was staying at the hotel. She was having her hair done. She said, 'I just got this call from Alexander Forger, and he said that you didn't sign anything. What's this all about?' I told her, 'Tell him to call my lawyer,' which he did. Then my attorney called me and said, 'What the hell is going on here? This is ridiculous!' I told him, 'Call Forger back and tell him that I am not signing anything,' which he did. And then Forger called Lee and said, 'He won't sign anything and something should be signed,' and all this bull. Then Lee called me and said, 'I don't know what is going on here but Forger's upset. He said you should sign something for him.'

"All of a sudden, a little light went on in my brain that something was not right here. Was it Forger or was it Lee? By that time I was confused. All along I had thought it was just Jackie and her lawyer, and then all of a sudden, it's *Lee* saying to me, 'Well, why won't you sign it?' I told her, 'Because I don't do things like that. Maybe I'll sign for ten thousand a month. How's that?' 'Why don't you sign for the fifteen?' she asked. 'What if I go broke?' I said. 'I am not going to sign my name to some damn stupid thing like that!' And then I said, 'I tell you what. Here is what we are going to do, if it's all right with you. We are going to call this wedding off until the fall. You have this guy on my back. We can't get married in a situation like this. There is something wrong here.' I could see that there was going to be some argument over this even after we got married, which might have been the shortest marriage in history. I could see something coming out of it that I didn't like—some big blowup.

"Lee said, 'But we are to be married in an hour.' I told her, 'I'll stop it.' I called up Stanley Bass, the Supreme Court justice who was going to marry us. He said, 'I just put my robe on.' I told him, 'Take it off.' Then I called the other guests and told them that Lee and I decided to wait until fall to be married so we could do it properly with both our families present. I couldn't say that we argued over money.''

Lee apparently did not let on to Newton how hesitant she herself really was about marrying him, whether the reason was money or locale or something she couldn't explain. Those who saw the pair just before the wedding said the atmosphere between them was full of static. "I just don't think Lee was certain,'' said one friend.

The couple decided to go on their two-week honeymoon in St. Martin anyway. They had a great time, and, away from the influence of her sister and all the lawyers' flak, Lee said to

Newton, "Let's get married here," so she was willing to marry him without the financial contract. But he remained leery of the situation and insisted they wait.

Newton stopped off in New York for a couple of days before heading back to San Francisco alone. He and Lee had a moment of merriment when a photographer following them fell into a garbage can as he was taking their picture. But as the weeks passed, the geographical distance between them became an emotional one. They grew more and more apart. "It's kind of hard to say exactly why Lee and I didn't get married in the end," said Newton. "I guess we just drifted off. But when Lee started in with all that Truman Capote stuff, I thought, 'There is something REALLY FISHY going on with her!' "

"All that Capote stuff," indeed. Right after Lee got back from St. Martin, she received a telephone call on behalf of Truman from Liz Smith, a gossip columnist for the New York *Daily News*. Smith asked her if she would reconsider the decision she had made earlier to not testify for Truman in his upcoming trial with Gore Vidal. Vidal was suing Capote for a million dollars for libel over an interview he had given to *Playgirl* magazine in 1975 in which he had said that Vidal was thrown out bodily from the White House for drunken and obnoxious behavior at a party the Kennedys gave for Lee in 1961. According to eyewitnesses, Vidal did have too much to drink that evening and had gotten into a nasty tiff with Bobby Kennedy, after which some of the guests politely escorted him back to his hotel, but he was never forcibly ejected. (Vidal was never invited back to the White House.)

By the time of the lawsuit, the incident was a tired anecdote of Camelot lore that had been told and retold in the press and at dinner parties—George Plimpton, who helped take Vidal back to his hotel, dined out on his version of it for years. (He said Vidal left of his own volition.) Truman claimed Lee was his source for the story as he told it in *Playgirl*. She hotly denied that she was, and she made it very clear to him right from the beginning that she wanted nothing to do with the lawsuit. Lee was furious at Truman for putting her in such a difficult position. To her, the lawsuit was just a frivolous squabble, one more example of the kind of excessive behavior that had made her so exasperated with him in the first place.

She shared Jackie's feelings about the spat, that it was "just too ridiculous." "That Truman after all these years would try to drag me into his hatred for Gore—well, it's just the most disgusting thing," Lee fumed.

Either out of loyalty to their bygone friendship or because he could not rely on her to vouch for him, Truman refrained from deposing Lee or compelling her to testify in court. She received a subpoena from Vidal's lawyer late in 1977—all the parties involved received subpoenas from one side or the other—and her attorney advised her that she had some real exposure in the suit in terms of attorneys' fees if she did not clarify her position. In response, Lee gave a sworn statement, an affidavit, to Gore's lawyer declaring that she did "not recall ever discussing with Truman Capote the incident or the evening which I understand is the subject of this lawsuit."

Truman did not find out about the affidavit until a year later, and when he did, it finished off what was left of their friendship. He was shocked and bitter and went around telling everyone how Lee had betrayed him by giving what he called a "deposition for Gore." Lee told Newton: "Oh, am I in hot water! The little worm is threatening to sue me. I've got everybody against me now." In Cope's opinion, something had happened between those two that nobody knows about. He came to this conclusion when he asked Lee at an earlier time whatever happened to her great buddy Truman Capote, and she just replied vehemently, "That little fag! That little creep!" and wouldn't talk about it.

Because Lee felt that Truman had, as usual, gone too far and needed to be reined in, she sympathized with Vidal in the dispute. But she did not give a statement for Vidal per se, as Truman claimed she had and as many people assumed. She simply gave one *for herself* so that she would not be named as a codefendant in the lawsuit. If Lee had said, "Yes, I was Truman's source," Vidal could merely amend his complaint and name her as a codefendant, rather than let either of them off the hook, as Truman assumed. Since Gore knew that he had not been cast out bodily from the White House, and that there were several witnesses at the party to contradict such a claim, if Lee backed Truman's version, well then, she was a liar too. In other words, what Truman was asking of Lee by saying she was his source was to agree voluntarily to a real possibility of being sued and to be vulnerable for a fortune in attorneys' fees and possibly a damage award, money she certainly did not have. Truman's own defense wound up costing more than $80,000. What friendship would survive such a demand?

And so, by the spring of 1979, when Truman's own calls to Lee had not been returned, he nagged Liz Smith into calling her. "No," Lee repeated to Smith, she would never testify. "I just couldn't," she told her. "The notoriety of it is too much. I am tired of Truman riding on my coattails to fame. And Liz, what difference does it make? They are just a couple of fags." Smith argued for Truman, for their long friendship, but she was stunned by Lee's unexpected scorn. She gave a weak response and hung up.

Truman, who was beside himself with anxiety over the lawsuit because of the money involved, called Smith back immediately. "What did she say?" he asked her. So that he would not go on thinking that Lee was going to come to his rescue and testify, Smith passed Lee's comments on to him. When Truman heard that Lee had called him "just a fag" he went into a tailspin. He demanded her exact words. "RODE ON *HER* COATTAILS?! IS SHE KIDDING?!" he screamed. He began ranting to Smith, yelling about all he had done for Lee over the years and how he had put his reputation on the line for her by talking David Susskind into making *Laura*, "AND YOU KNOW HOW *THAT* TURNED OUT!" he bellowed. "On and on he went," wrote Smith in her account in the *Daily News*. "I knew I had made a dreadful mistake."

If all Lee had done was just refuse to testify, Truman eventually would have come to terms with it. But to dismiss him out of hand so derisively, after all they had shared and meant to each other over the years, hurt and enraged him so much that he swore revenge. After he spoke to Liz Smith, he called Andy Warhol, who said that Truman was so mad at Lee "it was scary." Truman said he would have her "shitting razor blades" when he got finished with her. "Truman, she's so weak now, she might commit suicide," Warhol told him. "Too bad," Truman answered, and then he added: "If I told you all the things she's said about you." "I don't care. I've always known what kind of a person she was," Andy answered back.* And to another friend Warhol pondered: "If Lee was drinking *before* this feud with Truman, can you imagine now?"

To exact his revenge on "the principessa," as Truman was now sarcastically referring to Lee, he made an appearance on June 5 on *The Stanley Siegel Show,* a live local TV talk program. Playing a character he called "a Southern fag," he delivered a withering blast and revealed as much as the airtime allowed of the life and loves of the dear friend who had crossed him. Before his host interrupted him, Truman told of how Lee tried to seduce William F. Buckley on the pretext of asking him for spiritual advice and then when he didn't respond, accused him of being queer; of how Peter Beard "met this chick with less mileage on her" and dumped Lee; of how she once said that Peter Tufo "looked like a ferret and was publicity-crazy and riding on her coattails;" and of how Newton Cope was another nobody who was riding on her coattails, and was "no great catch, except maybe in a provincial town." But most of all, he told how jealous Lee was of her sister.

Truman's little performance came across as ludicrous and pathetic. Thinking he was bringing Lee down, his histrionics hurt himself as much as Lee. "It was one of the worst things I ever witnessed," said Liz Smith, who blamed herself for his behavior. "Real nut-house stuff," Vidal called it.

After the show, Truman continued his diatribe in an interview with a reporter. He condemned Lee for her "sense of the right to luxury," and told of her crush on Nureyev and of her affair with Roy Jenkins. Careful not to mention the latter's name, he said she was involved with "some old fellow in England who was going to be Prime Minister. Jackie kept urging her to marry him. Then when he didn't get to be Prime Minister, they dropped him." As for Newton Cope, well, she was just holding him in reserve.

After his fury was spent, Truman felt only sadness and regret for the loss of a friend whom he truly adored. "It's very hurtful, to put it mildly," he admitted. "Love is blind. I have been in love before with people who were just ghastly. Lee was my number-one confidante until I went through that long

---

*Once, when Warhol heard that Lee had tagged him a social climber, he retorted: "Well, she's a talent climber."

period when I was in and out of the hospital. I wasn't communicating with anybody. But of all my friends, she never wrote me once to say she hoped I was getting well or wished me luck with my problems. As far as I know, there has never been any reason for this unbelievable conduct." Either Truman was being disingenuous with that last remark, or he was completely out of touch with how his behavior had offended so many people.

Lee, needless to say, was very upset by Truman's revelations of her private life. She lay low for a few days and then refused any comment. It was Newton Cope who spoke for her. He told reporters: "What can you expect from a has-been writer who is all washed up and is fighting for any kind of publicity on the way down?"

Gore Vidal won his libel case.*

Truman may have made a fool out of himself on the airwaves, but, in a way, he did have the last word when, in a spirit of malicious fun, he made an obscene artwork titled *La Principessa en Vacances* that was supposed to be Lee.

Truman lived in an apartment at United Nations Plaza, but unknown to almost everyone, not even his roommate and lover of many years, Jack Dunphy, he also kept a smaller studio apartment in the same building and he would go there to, in effect, hide out when he was pretending to everyone that he was hard at work writing *Answered Prayers*. Between 1978 and 1980 in that studio, in between sniffs of cocaine, he created about two dozen plexiglass boxes that were inspired by the Joseph Cornell boxes of the forties.

The idea originated when he was in Georgia once on a lecture tour and someone took him to an Army camp. He came back with lots of berets and some snakebite kits, little cardboard boxes that were actual manufactured items containing paraphernalia and instructions on how to treat snakebites. Truman was delighted with the kits because of the drawing of a snake featured on the boxes. He had always been fascinated

---

*He was granted a motion for summary judgment in trial court. Capote began an appeal, but in October 1983, out of money, he asked Vidal if he would accept a letter of apology and an admission that he had lied. Vidal agreed to the settlement.

by the creatures; in fact, snake images were common in his work and in his homes.

Truman wrote to the manufacturer of the kits, who sent him first a few and then a pile of these little corrugated cardboard boxes, which could be folded to just the right size for his purposes. He would stuff the boxes with paper and then proceeded to wrap their outsides in colored paper; then he would go through magazines like *National Geographic* and *Smithsonian* looking for pictures of animals to cut out and paste on the boxes' sides. When he finished, he would place the cardboard boxes inside plexiglass containers he had custom-made with his signature on the bottom, and then he would permanently seal them.

Some of the boxes were erotic, but only mildly so in that, instead of animals, they featured magazine cutouts of naked women. *La Principessa en Vacances*, however, was blatantly pornographic and it was the only one that made a reference to a specific person. One frame of Lee's box showed a lady with a fan who had a snake cutout for a face; another frame showed a bunch of snakes with the title ''Serpentine Princess and Her Court''; the frame underneath, the dirty one, featured a picture of the Grand Canyon in the background with a snake's face hiding a woman's own while the woman copulated with a yokel.

The boxes were not made at random. Beginning with the snake on the original kits, they related in some way to themes in Truman's writing and to his Alabama childhood and to his notion of himself as a literary outlaw. To him, the snakebite kits were a kind of talisman to protect his friends, a first aid against evil forces, a magic charm. Snakes had hypnotic beauty. They were good and bad, beautiful and terrifying, charming and deadly. Like Lee Radziwill.*

*In late 1983, Truman contacted Andreas Brown of the Gotham Book Mart, a literary Manhattan bookshop with an exhibition space, and asked him if he could store all his boxes there in a hurry because he needed to give up the studio. At a later date, he told Brown of his plans for an elaborate exhibit of the boxes with dramatic lighting. Truman died in 1984 before the exhibit was arranged, but Brown exhibited them posthumously in 1985, making the snake the theme of his show. Pictorial images of Truman with snakes, accompanied by quotations from his writing about them, formed a background for the display. The boxes sold for between $800 and $2,000 each and were all

But for all the commotion, rancor, and betrayal, Truman always hoped that he and Lee would become friends again. With the passage of the years Lee mellowed too, to the point of admitting recently that she misses him: "I do. Yes, I do," she confided. "I had wonderful times with Truman. Wonderful times. There is nobody who is like him. There is nobody who even reminds me of him at all."

One would have thought that Lee had had enough turbulence in her life for a while, but only several days after her fateful conversation with Liz Smith about Truman, she was back on the telephone with the gossip columnist. This time she took potshots at Peter Tufo and Newton Cope. She and Smith had a half-hour talk, and Lee reiterated her complaint that Cope was a "San Francisco provincial." Later, she called Smith back because she wanted to add that people should really think about how men like Cope and her ex-beau Peter Tufo ride on the coattails of famous women! "Why, no one would have ever heard of them if it hadn't been for me," she announced and then went on to characterize Tufo as "a twit who buys the first, second, and third editions of the *Daily News* to see if his name has been printed."

Perhaps Lee repeatedly accused her intimates of riding on her coattails because that was exactly what she had done with her sister and brother-in-law. Or perhaps she really did think that they never loved her for herself but rather for her celebrity. But if that were true, was telephoning a gossip columnist the way to deal with it? Lee, like Truman, was out of control.

Liz Smith printed Lee's remarks in her column. A reporter contacted Newton to ask how he felt about Lee's statement, since, after all, they were still engaged to be married in the fall. "It's untrue, obviously," he initially responded, and when he phoned his fiancée, Lee denied she had ever said such a thing. Then, when Smith heard of Lee's denial, she revealed in yet another column that she had the notes to prove it—and much more that she had not printed besides. After this incident Newton no longer trusted Lee, and, not surprisingly, it was at

---

snapped up on the first day of the exhibit. *La Principessa en Vacances,* a strange memento of *Vidal vs. Capote,* was sold to a private collector.

that moment that he backed away from his intention to marry her.

In looking for an explanation for Lee's behavior one has to consider the malice-ridden milieu that bred her. She usually had nothing nice to say about her former boyfriends, and with Cope she just hastened the process. Yet to this day he still prefers to believe that Lee was in a drunken rage when she put him down. "Why would she say that against her own fiancé?" he asks now, still genuinely bewildered. "She must have been heavily involved with the bottle! She must have been! Lee wouldn't be bitchy to me then! We were going to be *married* in a few months!"

Oh, but she was. And Lee may have been drinking, but not necessarily: Truman Capote, for one, had no such rationalizations about his former confidante: "I have never known her to be loyal to anyone, or to say a generous thing about anyone that was not qualified. Lee is just a treacherous lady, and that's the truth of it. She is treacherous to absolutely everyone."

43. *Lonely*

When Lee's marriage plans to Newton Cope fell through, so did her hope of being rescued financially. She had run through all the funds from her settlement with Stas, and what she earned decorating did not cover her sizable expenditure. Now she would have to live by her wits, trying to forestall financial disaster. To raise money in 1979, she put her duplex and some of its contents up for sale and moved to a much smaller apartment two blocks away, a penthouse at 875 Park Avenue. It was the start of her moving down and making do.

Gone, along with much of her lavish furniture, were the little gold Fabergé boxes, the tortoiseshell card case collection, and the most glorious object in her whole apartment: Francis Bacon's *Man in a Cage*—"our Goya" as Lee described the modern master. The painting had hung in the foyer at 969 and, before that, in the library at Turville Grange. Actually, Lee had been trying to sell it to raise cash for about a year prior to the sale of her apartment. "When she went around trying to sell the picture, she foolishly hawked it to every dealer in town, ruining the market on it," said a source. "Then she put it up for sale at Sotheby's, where she only got $200,000. In that world you have to trust somebody and put yourself in the hands of a dealer and say, 'This is what I want. Get it for me.' Otherwise they're like vultures. They gather round you. It's a crooked, shitty world and they vultured her, because it went very cheaply, even for those days." Lee sold the painting, a superb example of the artist's work, just before the art market went crazy in the eighties, when it would have fetched millions. She was extremely sorry.*

The penthouse at 875 Park Avenue, a classic New York apartment building, had one outstanding feature: a narrow terrace wrapped around its entire perimeter. Lee played it up with blue, silver, and white plants, which created a soft aura of color when viewed from inside, and her use of a picket fence behind the plantings added to the countrylike feeling of greenery. She continued the floral motif indoors with the use of a flowery wallcovering and upholstery in the living room, which complemented the colors on the terrace. Lee's arrangement of the light-filled space was simple and fresh, the kind of artful simplicity that suggests a sophisticated way of life; and, like all her homes, it was done with painstaking originality.

After she sold the duplex, Lee stayed with Peter Tufo for a couple of weeks between apartments. The two had kept in touch with each other, and the next thing one knew, in the spring of 1980, she joined him on a skiing holiday in Zermatt, Switzerland, and their romance was on again. "You know how everybody is about these relationships. They come in and they go out. They never end up neatly just like that," said a

---

Man in a Cage has an interesting history. Back in the fifties, Stas Radziwill and a then-mistress of his, Lady Lambton, considered Francis Bacon to be a genius painter, and they subsidized him with an income until he received enough recognition to get a reputable gallery to take him over. Bacon was supposed to give a small percentage of his work to them, but he was not obligated to produce anything. When Marlborough Fine Art took over as his dealer, there was a big ruckus because they wanted all his work. A meeting took place and Radziwill and Lambton said, "What about all the money we gave him?" The end result was that they each could choose just one Bacon in settlement of the dispute in exchange for all their extraordinary generosity. "That shit Bacon never gave Stas anything!" Lee fumed for a long time afterward.

friend of Lee's. But this chapter of their relationship was an exact replay of what had gone on before, with its attendant joys and problems and with an identical ending.

Lee got herself a new dog, an all-white Westie that she hoped Peter would grow attached to, since she got the breed to please him (he told her he had had a Westie once that he was very fond of); she named the dog Whizzer, nicknamed "Wiz," after John Kennedy's only Supreme Court appointment, Justice Byron R. "Whizzer" White.

On Memorial Day weekend, the couple invited a client of Peter's, the prominent architect Jaquelin T. Robertson and his then girlfriend, Julia Bloomfield, to Southampton as guests for the holiday. At one point, Peter and Robertson were playing tennis together and Lee and Bloomfield went for a long walk down the beach. "I got the impression of a rather lonely woman," Julia recalled. "I talked openly about my relationship with Jack, which prompted her to talk about her relationship with Peter. We discovered that we both needed each other in the sense that Lee could not discuss these things in her own social context. She did not have close women friends. In a way, I was outside her group. I am a working girl. I have been in publishing and architecture all my life, and yet I fit into her group perfectly fine. But I was not part of it in a full-time way, or not born to it, let's say. Lee and I became very close friends, and I spent the next two years pretty much every weekend at her place in Southampton. I used to go there for Christmas, and once I went away with the family to Mexico for the holidays.

"Anyway, when we were walking along the beach, Lee was basically facing the impossibility of her relationship with Peter. She loved his youth and his looks and his attention—and boy was he attentive! He used to fly out from New York to see her in the middle of the week. He used to send her the most incredible plants and presents. He loved her in a really romantic way. And Lee thrived on all that, but at the same time there was always this hesitation for Lee about Peter because he wasn't, bottom-line, wealthy enough for her, and that made her feel insecure. She had big expenses, and she really needed someone who could take that financial anxiety away from her and support all that, and a lot of her life when I was closely involved with her had to do with how she should finance herself—should she sell her apartment? her house in Southampton? She wasn't doing much of anything when I met her, and we discussed several plans about what we might do together in terms of going into business. We had lots of laughs about it, but we never got serious.

"So there was this enormous amount of financial anxiety, and that was one of the reasons Lee hesitated about Peter but certainly not the only one. She felt insecure with someone younger than she was who wasn't a father figure to look after her. And the way Peter was always referred to as enjoying the limelight she got, she recognized that a bit. Now that the relationship is over, she says how awful he was and how used she felt. But at the time, I don't think she did. They were genuinely in love with each other. It was a happy time for Lee in many ways. It was just when he wasn't around her that she wasn't so happy, because she analyzed the situation and it didn't quite add up to what she needed. Peter was always there for Lee, and she just couldn't make that commitment."

Their second and final break came in August when, once again, through an act of will, they decided that they would not see each other anymore. Peter spent a weekend with Robertson and Julia soon after the split. As Julia remembers it: "Peter was incredibly upset. My God, he was miserable! He was so distraught, he said, 'There'll never be anyone else!' He was beside himself as one is after a love affair where one has been rejected. He was in a terrible state. I don't know Peter well enough to know whether he was putting on the style, as it were, but I would say there was a whole side of him that was extremely upset by the end of his relationship with Lee.

"And they went on ringing each other for quite a long time after they broke up, because after the normal period of Lee going off, she would suddenly find herself a bit lonely. I was staying with her on those weekends when she would find some excuse for me to call Peter so she could talk to him on the phone, and this and that. So they both had a hard time getting over it, and it was more difficult for Lee because she was the one who basically said, 'I can't. It's over.' "

In the politics of their relationship, Lee may have said no to Peter at that given moment, but at another time, that is, at their final defining moment, Peter once again said no to her. After Lee had endured a certain number of lonely nights in the wake of her decision—or whoever's decision it was—she told Peter that after carefully thinking it over, it was his love that meant the most to her, more than money and all her other doubts. She implored him to continue loving her. But Peter realized that although there was no doubt of her sincerity, there would come another day when her mood would be different, and she would revert back to her other sentiments and feelings. So, once again, Peter rejected Lee after she rejected him, and once again rejection was the final experience she was left with.

One could say that their relationship died of terminal vacillation. Lee's conflicted feelings toward Peter were part of that same indecision and ambivalence she had about so many things. Once again it had been made abundantly clear that going back and forth in her values and choices the way she did was her most defining personality trait, the hard outcropping of character that more than any other determined her life.

The more Lee put men off with her demands and expectations, the more she seemed to fall apart in consequence, so that by the end of her romance with Peter Tufo, she began a period in her life of total chaos. Like her father, she descended deeply into alcoholism, multiplying her woes beyond easy reckoning. The years of feeding hope with myth had exhausted her. There was no longer anything to hold off the rot and the turmoil. More than ever, her life was blurred by booze and blighted hopes and shattered ideals. Unraveled and at sea, foundering in every sort of shipwreck, career (decorating bored her now), loneliness, health, and money, she was ripe to do herself lasting harm.

Sometimes she appeared merely tranquilized or in an alert slumber, as if she were living out the end of a private dream. To others, she looked shockingly wan and wasted. An old acquaintance from the fifties ran into her one day in the supermarket in Southampton. The woman was with a companion who tried to take Lee's shopping cart by mistake, and as she described the encounter, "I told him, 'No! Let that woman have that cart,' and he said, 'Why?' And I said, 'Look. She's so sick.' Then I said something dumb like, 'That's Jackie Kennedy's little sister.' Lee was so shaken! I never saw anybody so tense! She was bone thin and literally shaking—and I mean literally. Lee just looked awful.''

To a certain extent, Lee's job as a decorator helped to hide the alcoholic stress factor. Other times, on bad days, her drinking sabotaged her business. She made errors in judgment, such as overordering fabrics and making false promises. Her alcohol-induced grandiosity caused her to raise her clients' expectations by promising that deliveries would be made by a certain date and then she could not follow through. And then, too, Lee was such a perfectionist in her work that when she could not meet the demands of her own unreasonable nature, she would become enraged and calm herself down with a drink.

To camouflage how much she drank, she hung around with people who imbibed as much as she did. Once, she got a friend to open up a bar that had already closed. Lee would be consumed with anxiety afterward as she remembered how she became argumentative with people or conversationally repeated herself to the point of embarrassment, or how she showed up way too late for appointments and engagements with her speech slurred and looking terribly sloppy—so unlike her. For hangovers, she took Valium; there was some drug dependency.

People began to talk. Apocryphal stories made the rounds: how she once fell on her face at the St. Regis Hotel and Peter Tufo just got in a cab and left her there; how she fell off chairs and stumbled over them. Sometimes the gossip was true: Lee was seen at a reception at the Metropolitan Opera one night weaving about the room.

Lee was a "periodic," the kind of alcoholic who could go for a year without a drink before she would start again. Her preferred drink was vodka, a taste she acquired from Stas and Nureyev. With the positive energy she gave off when she was sober and focused, it was hard for some people who knew Lee well to believe that she was an alcoholic at all.

Those who knew about alcoholism sniffed her out and realized she was vulnerable long before the problem got out of hand. "Lee always drank like an alcoholic, whether she drank a lot or a little," said a friend of hers who suffered from the same addiction. "It was the time she drank, how she drank, and why she drank. It was the fix that she needed."

The saddest thing about her drinking problem was the effect it had on her children. Deprived of their father, for whom they both had deep affection and love, Anthony and Tina had to take care of their mother, instead of her taking care of them, a situation which sometimes left them adrift and forlorn. "Tina and I talked about the time in her life when her mother was drunk all the time and she had to take care of her," said a friend of Tina's. "It was all part of that trauma of hers of not having love. Lee didn't have it to give, as they say. But it's great her children at least had Jackie."

That was one good thing about Jackie: she was always very protective of her family and there for them when they were in crisis. Some say, though, that her motive was just to get Lee taken care of so that she would not cause any problems for her and her children. Jackie realized that Lee needed to break through her isolation and get help, and she was instrumental in her sister's decision to do so. For too long liquor had been a detour for Lee that kept her from facing her own feelings. The time had come for her to stop the denials, the rationalizations, and the covering up, and to take an honest inventory of her life. It was time to find another way to live.

Alcoholics Anonymous is a self-help program that provides problem drinkers with the framework necessary to find the inner strength to stop drinking. By making the decision to join the program, Lee came to grips with the fact that the only way out of her crisis was through it. If the seventies were her hard-drinking years, the eighties would be her years of recovery.

Her home group in AA met at the East Hampton Episcopal church two nights a week throughout the summer season; she also went to meetings in the surrounding townships. Dressed in a turtleneck and trousers or jeans, with her hair pulled back in a ponytail and no makeup on, Lee blended into the group successfully, which was a tribute to her. In fact, according to a fellow recovering alcoholic who did the program with her, the bond that developed between Lee and the rest of the group was extraordinary: "She was exceedingly thoughtful, demure, self-effacing, and sincere," the source said, "and very popular. She had a sweetness that rang true. Lee very much wanted to become part of something that was meaningful to her, and she became part of the group based on real values, maybe for the first time in her life. She seemed to genuinely like it. AA is a great social leveler—the road to alcoholic recovery strips away a lot of the distractions. It was probably very refreshing for her not to have to be Lee Bouvier Radziwill for once.

"But Lee was very shattered. She was broken. Fifty is late in life to be making a new beginning. She knew she had big problems as a human being if she did not deal with the house on fire her life had become."

Joining in the round-robin format, with usually between thirty-five and sixty-five other people, Lee at last took a hard look at her own life. There was no grandstanding. "Lee described her life as raunchy, hard-drinking, and messy, and she confessed to how her alcoholic behavior and personality played a major role in the failure of her endeavors," said a fellow member. "She said she never felt that she was much of anything, that she always felt second in her family, and in truth, in every way. Her self-image was devastating and covered over with grandiosity. Alcohol gave her a false sense of confidence as a way to mask her painful shyness. Yet whatever she did, even if she did it to excess, it was never enough to take away the pain of her feelings of inadequacy.

"Lee also talked about the high stakes of visibility and said, 'Boy, when I screw up, I really screw up big!' She told of embarrassing her husband with her behavior, of going to pick her children up at school with alcohol on her breath, of arriving there late or not showing up at all. Above all, she told of the stigma of her alcoholic father, and she said to herself, 'I can't let that happen to me!' Her children deserved better than what she had been the recipient of, and they were one of her primary motives in seeking help—they had been through enough. One had the sense, though, that she was not there for her children but for herself. Lee didn't exude much of a maternal disposition."

The first year she did the program, Lee was in a perpetual daze. "We did the meetings in my house one summer, the summer of 'eighty-one," said Clifford Klenk, an acquaintance and neighbor in the Hamptons. "I had seen Lee at an AA meeting in Waterville, and there were a bunch of workmen there who were saying things like, 'And then I got a six-pack, and then I got sick, and then I got a bottle of . . .' It was just awful, so I decided to have meetings of my own at my house. I'd have dinner and invite people who had something in common to talk about instead of having to be with the six-packers, and Lee came along. She still continued to go to the regular AA meetings too. She'd go to two or three meetings a day; she was fanatic.

"Lee did everything you're supposed to do in AA—except stop drinking! She would always say she had to go to the bathroom, and then she'd sneak a little drink. The one thing she'd do that was awful was she would start to drink again after she stopped, and then she'd say, 'I am going to St. Martin and then I'll stop drinking,' and I'd say to her, 'Lee, you don't go to a resort to stop drinking!' "

In early sobriety alcoholics often relapse; all they can do is try to stay away from a drink one day at a time. After the setbacks of her first year, Lee achieved and maintained her sobriety. She continued going to AA regularly for several years, until late in the decade when she found Herbert Ross.

44. *Moving On*

"How would you like to join me for a vacation at Pebble Beach?" Newton Cope asked Lee in the autumn of 1981. Although their marriage plans had not worked out, they still kept in touch by talking on the telephone or corresponding every couple of months, and Lee had even visited him in San Francisco. She accepted his impromptu invitation, and, newly sober, had such a wonderful time at the popular West Coast resort that when they were driving back to San Francisco she turned to him and said: "Why don't we get married?" "I am nuts about you, but it won't work," Cope answered back. "Geographically it can't work, because you don't know anybody in San Francisco. You are not going to do any business here, and I am not going to live in New York sitting around like a toad. You wouldn't last in San Francisco six months before you'd get antsy and restless." "Why don't you give it a try?" Lee insisted. "Why do something when you see it won't work?" he told her. "It just won't work! Anybody can see that. After so many months or years—you gotta be blind!"

Lee had caught Newton by surprise with her suggestion, and his refusal had been fast and instinctive. But after he gave it some more thought, he became less pragmatic and the following summer he invited Lee to come along with him and two of his friends on a nostalgic journey on the luxurious Orient Express train to Venice, embarking in London. "In the back of my mind I thought, 'maybe we'll get married,' " he admitted. "By that time I had mellowed a bit. Maybe a good time in Venice . . . it's so romantic there. . . ."

Elaborate plans were put in place for the sentimental interlude, and at the end of July, Newton flew to New York, and then a few days later he and Lee flew to London, where they took separate suites at Claridge's. The day before their departure, an Italian client of Lee's suddenly insisted she come to Italy to discuss a decorating job. "If I want this account I have to go there right now, or else I'll have to come back here two days after I get home," she told Newton, "so I can't go on this trip." Keenly disappointed, he replied, "It's too bad we went through all the trouble of arranging this." "Of course, that could have been another phony story, I don't know," Cope says now. "Maybe Lee had a date with somebody and just wanted to get rid of me!"

Over the past several months Lee had kept her design business going in a sporadic fashion. In mid-1982 it picked up again, and she was busy for the rest of the year with projects in Los Angeles and Toronto as well as Venice. The income these commissions generated still did not pay the bills—not at the rate she spent money—so that in March 1983, she sold her penthouse to raise cash, dangerously depleting her assets. She received a handsome sum for the apartment, enough to hold her for a while anyway. The high price was due in part to its having been recently featured in *Architectural Digest;* residences usually fetch higher prices after they have been published in a prestigious magazine.

Lee moved into a transitional dwelling, a duplex apartment rental in a town house at 48 East Seventy-third Street, again a few blocks from her previous residence. She intended to acquire a more permanent nesting place in two years when her lease was up. In her anxiousness to settle in as quickly as possible, and fatigued from all her moves, she scattered artworks and other objects almost at random around the rooms. "I dropped by Lee's apartment one day and tried to help her rearrange the furniture that didn't work together," said Mario

Buatta, "and she got very angry because I couldn't put it together for her. The pieces of the puzzle didn't fit. Lee is a very high-strung woman, very rigid, and for anyone who was as unsettled in her life as she was and for whom her home was so important, it was difficult to try and put it all together when there was no reason for it, if you know what I mean. Now she has a reason—Herbert Ross."

"A woman's concept of a home and her psychological and emotional relationship to it are different from a man's," Lee declared in her own defense. "Her home is not only the place where she can function as a wife and mother, but where she can live her interior life and express her personality. A woman's home is a self-portrait."

Her new apartment was stark in comparison to her former residences, but no less engaging. From the street entrance, one climbed a winding stair to a landing that separated the living room from the dining room, two large rooms identical in size and scale. The living room came with gold cork paper on the walls, which gave off a golden glow in lamplight; by covering the ceiling in gold paper also, she succeeded in bringing the room together. "I knew full well that I wasn't going to live here forever, but I've managed to make my apartment have a feeling of permanence. That's important," she emphasized.

Lee likened the relative bareness of her new arrangement to "going on a diet to purify yourself," and she added: "I just keep paring down. I've become a little like a career diplomat, taking with me from place to place the pieces that I love and need and putting the rest in storage."

The cash she had gotten from the sale of the penthouse enabled Lee to make a momentous decision early in 1984 to wind down her decorating business. She was tired of it and did not want to do it anymore. "Lee had exquisite taste and the social contacts to have had one of the most successful businesses in the country if she wanted to," said one of her contractors. "She quit the business because she did not want to spend the time."

Decorating was a natural proclivity of hers, and until Lee got bored with it, she had run her business, for the most part, with admirable energy and discipline. She was only two years into it, however, when she started to complain about it vociferously: "Decorating is very hard work. . . . It's running from

one end of town to the other and doing endless paperwork,"
she groused in 1978. "It takes endless time and concentra-
tion. . . . The thing that holds you up the most—and it's impossible for clients to understand—is how long everything
takes to order and arrive. They think it's your fault, whereas
you can do nothing whatsoever about it. You call the uphol-
sterers, the curtain people, the carpenters, every single day,
and you just repeat the same thing the next day. Certain clients
will blame the designer for it because they don't understand
shipments, strikes, and the like.

"Little do they know. The repetitive, 'Oh, what fun it must
be to be an interior decorator!' They think you're just putting
up a lot of rose-flowered chintz curtains and strewing the room
with lovely pillows. It is incredibly detailed work. I myself
have been amazed at the minutiae it takes and how fatiguing
it can be, especially when you have a time limit and are under
pressure."

Knowing Lee's history, one could easily predict what would
eventually happen: "I don't find decorating creative any
longer," she said when she quit. "I did it until I felt boxed
in. And I've always believed that it is only when you've boxed
yourself in that you can move in a new direction. Now I can
step out." Nevertheless, there did not appear to be anything
on the horizon to fill the vacuum this dead end left in her.

"So many in Lee's set never do anything," said Mario
Buatta. "They just have lunch with their girlfriends and hang
around all day. That is why I have great admiration and respect
for everything Lee has done. At least she went out and did
them. On the other hand, I remember when I called her once
a few years ago, and I had just come out with a furniture
collection, and one of the pieces in my collection was a copy
of a cabinet, one of which belonged to her, and I told her I
had copied her piece—even though it turned out to be a fake
and there were other copies of it around. She said: 'I saw that
in the *New York Times*. You copied my furniture.' I said:
'Well, I didn't copy yours exactly. They're in the public do-
main now, and they are fakes anyway.' Then she said that
Mark Hampton copied something else of hers and a London
designer was copying another thing of hers, and then she
added: 'I could have been a furniture designer.'

"With Lee, it was always, 'I could have done this. I could

have done that.' I didn't become a success overnight. It took me twenty-five years. One has to *stick something out,* and she doesn't stick things out. She wants the success and her social life at the same time, and she can't have it both ways. Lee has to dedicate herself to something, and she never does.''

''Lee is a very nice, very attractive fraud,'' offered her old friend from Washington, Sherry Geyelin, herself a decorator. ''She is a fraud because she just isn't true to herself. I don't think she ever really knew what it was that she wanted in life, and when she got what she wanted, or what she thought she wanted, she was not content with it.''

It was only in her desire for attention and acclaim that, throughout her life, Lee never wavered. She had been playing to an audience since childhood, beginning with her trio of girl-spirits, and she never ceased to see herself through her imagined audience's eyes. It was always important to Lee, above all else, to maintain her public persona, so that whatever she was doing, she was doing at one remove, whether it was decorating, writing, acting, or any of the other things she had attempted in the past. And there were several of those personas over the years, none of which reflected the person that was inside her.

Lee's subjugation of her life to the dictates of her public image was sustained by a fickle press, which alternately fawned over and belittled her. Lee wanted to be cataloged and envied, not criticized. Yet for every compliment she received in print, there was often a corresponding barb or inaccuracy or misquotation. As she had found out, that was the danger of wanting the public to adore her.

In the early to mid-eighties, Lee lived very quietly. She still went to glamorous parties, but far fewer of them. It was her Southampton house that functioned as the gathering place of her fragmented selves. She would walk the beach over and over, she said, ''to reflect, to get things in proportion, and to refuel, to concentrate on something of value.'' She loved to read, swim endlessly, occasionally play tennis badly, and ''just breathe.'' A daily uniform of frayed jeans and bare feet were part of that same relaxation. Since often when people visited her during the season they came to swim, her social life was generally a matter of informal luncheons at the last minute around her pool.

A neighbor of Lee's, Dorothy Lichtenstein, the wife of the painter Roy Lichtenstein, often joined her on her walks along the beach: "I sensed that she was lonely, but Lee realized that regrets didn't make any sense, because one stays or leaves as one has to," Lichtenstein said. "Lee was always trying to improve herself or do something better. Really, she had a lot of motivation to want to change her life and move on. And she did succeed eventually in getting her life together. One has to give her that."

The crowd Lee spent her time with in the Hamptons often tended to be male, creative, and gay. "Lee is very simpatico with homosexuals," noted Tony Hail. "I am a homosexual, and I know why she likes me. She is automatically attracted to men who like to gossip and go dancing and talk about furniture and art and the like, and we have none of the dis-advantages of a jealous boyfriend. Nor is it uncommon for a killer like Lee not to have girlfriends. I have found in life that grown people of a certain age who are very strong and have a life of their own don't have any real friends."

Once a reporter came by Lee's house. He was doing something on the Hamptons for *W,* the fashion publication, and Lee was to appear on the cover of it. "She was very, very nervous, very shrunken into nothing," said the journalist. "When she spoke, I could scarcely hear her. Then we went walking along the beach and there was a sudden wind. Lee was only wearing a little T-shirt, and she began shivering and looked very fragile all of a sudden. I felt badly for her, so I said: 'Would you like to wear my jacket?' She crossed her arms, hands on the opposite forearm, and looked over her shoulder at me and said, 'Do you mind?' and I just melted. Truman Capote once said Lee could be incredibly seductive and geishalike. That's when I understood how it all worked."

45. *Richard Meier*

At the end of 1984, Lee was still in transition personally and professionally. By now, she no longer thought she had all the answers, "and at the moment that is exactly the way to be," she declared. "I am going into a new phase. I still haven't decided," she said of her career plans. "But I'm almost there. Whatever it is, it will involve using my eye in a new way, perhaps as an individual consultant. You see, transition is not always comfortable, but it's that discomfort that makes new things possible."

Lee settled down in her personal life, at least, when Christmas that year brought her a new romance. She met Richard Meier, the artist-architect, at a seasonal dinner party given by Tom Armstrong, the former director of the Whitney Museum.

Meier was on a roll when he met Lee. He had recently been named the recipient of an extraordinary, highly-publicized, worldwide talent search to design the J. Paul Getty Center in western Los Angeles, a sprawling six-building arts complex, one of them a museum, that was called by many the commission of a lifetime. And Meier had won the Pritzker Prize that year, architecture's closest equivalent to the Nobel, in recognition of his distinguished body of work.

Richard Meier's talent has excited comment and applause almost since he designed his first building, but it was the Smith House, a residence he built in Darien, Connecticut, in the mid-sixties, that really launched his international reputation. The white structure established a canon for what would ultimately be a subtle series of residential variations, work that reflected noncommercial values, architecture-as-art-object, put together with extraordinary precision in an elegantly composed modernist style. In the seventies and eighties he became a pre-eminent designer of museums, the High Museum of Art in Atlanta, for which he is best known, the Museum of the Decorative Arts in Frankfurt, Germany, and others. Virtually all of Meier's buildings from the sixties to the eighties were white.

During his years of apprenticeship in New York architectural firms after his graduation in 1957 from Cornell's College of Architecture, Art, and Planning, he spent his spare time honing his ability as a painter of large abstract expressionist canvases. The sensibility of the painter would remain a key ingredient of his talent.

"He cuts an impressive figure in person," *Time* wrote of him. "With his dark-rimmed glasses and conservative suits, offset by a flowing white mane, he looks as though he had designed himself."

Two such grand accomplishments in succession as the Pritzker Prize and the Getty commission earned Richard Meier a new level of fame. Suddenly he was getting attention in a way he never had before, with all the glamour, influence, and women that came with it. He had just finished being seen around town with the socialite Amanda Burden when he met Lee.

One evening soon after they had begun dating, Meier took Lee to a show on museums in Germany at Goethe House, a German cultural institution located on Fifth Avenue, where he was to receive a special award. An associate remembers seeing the couple enter the building: "It was a snowy night and they were just ahead of me, and Lee was coming through the snow in these beautiful, delicate, tiny pumps and wearing a fur dress—it was the minimal amount of clothing she could wear and still be warm—and I thought to myself, 'She probably won't get any snow on her just like Richard won't,' because one felt that way about Richard Meier—that the snow wouldn't touch him.

"Richard always had that aura of perfection about him. It came from a fastidiousness, a style of dress, a certain gallantry and courteousness and charm, and the architecture hinges on it—on the architect and the persona. Clients are buying the Richard Meier persona when they buy his architecture, and they want that same persona that he has, that aura of being able to rise above the grit and dirt of everyday life, the messiness and the disagreeable quality of it, and to be in that realm where things are neat and ordered and cerebral and beautiful."

"What is so odd is how much his sexual nature is exactly the opposite," said a former girlfriend. "There's an animal vitality that is not there in his architecture, and it comes as a surprise. One always thinks that an architect is going to act in bed the way he designs, and if the design is pristine and pure, you expect the man to be slow and very gentle and not-quite-there. But after sex with Richard, it's just back to business. His absorption is in his work and the inner self.''

Like all world-class architects, Meier at any given time has works-in-progress all over the globe, and he travels constantly to oversee them. Lee accompanied him on many of his business trips, especially to Los Angeles while he was designing the Getty project (and then, it would turn out, to his great frustration, redesigning it and redesigning it yet again). She stayed with him at the Bel Air Hotel, a romantic hideaway five minutes from his work site. Having friends there, Lee amused herself with their company and did some shopping while Richard was otherwise engaged. She also went with him to Germany, where he put finishing details on his museum in Frankfurt, and often to Paris.

On one trip Lee made to the City of Light, she worked on a story she was doing for *Architectural Digest* on Rudolf Nureyev's magnificent apartment overlooking the Seine. She had signed on as an editor-at-large for the magazine in March 1985. Her primary function and value was not to write articles but to scout the interesting homes she saw in her wide social life, and to report back to the magazine.

One house Lee arranged for the *Digest* to feature was her mother's new home on the grounds of Hammersmith Farm. Hughdie had died in 1976, nearly broke, after having poured most of his personal fortune in his last years into trying, unsuccessfully, to save his brokerage business, which was reeling from a spate of bad investments. Janet, who was remarried in 1979 to retired investment banker and widower Bingham Morris, was forced by necessity to put the main house and most of the acreage up for sale. She moved into the ''Castle,'' a twelve-room yellow farmhouse and former servants' quarters on the property which was the subject of the story. (That same March, Janet Auchincloss Rutherford, Lee's half-sister, died of cancer at thirty-nine years of age.)

On another trip to Paris, Lee and Richard joined Pierre Salinger for dinner one evening. ''Lee remained close to a lot of people she was close to when Jack Kennedy was alive,'' Meier noted, ''and I don't think that was unique to her. Everyone who was close during that period has remained so. There is a very strong bond between them."

It would have been hard for Richard Meier to guess, intrigued as he was with Lee, just how shaky her fortunes had been in the last few years. The woman he saw and enjoyed was, in his own words, "a highly concerned and focused individual with a very good intellect and knowledge and interests in a myriad of things and someone who has the unique ability to relate to both different types and different aspects of people. It comes from her own interests in a broad range of subjects."

Alluding to Lee's reputation, he went on: "When someone would imply negative things about Lee to me, I would say they did not know her. I am absolutely serious. That is not the person I lived with, and I don't know that other person." Lee had moved in with Richard at his invitation when the lease expired on her rented duplex. She put her furniture in storage, had her mail sent to his place, and settled in.

Steven Aronson happened to live right across the way from Meier's building, and one morning, as Aronson tells it, "I got out of bed and pulled the window shade up and there, opening a shade at exactly the same moment, was Lee Radziwill, naked, staring at me, naked, staring at her. Yoo-hoo!"

Meier's apartment, a spacious duplex in an elegant limestone building on East Seventy-second Street, was no ordinary home. It was a consummate modernist showcase, a cool white shell set off by an array of classic twentieth-century design objects: paintings by Frank Stella, furniture pieces by Le Corbusier, Marcel Breuer, and Mies van der Rohe, as well as his own creations, instant classics themselves.

In the architecture world there is always talk about someone as prominent as Richard Meier is, and his mania for order, shared to some extent by all architects, had long passed into the lore of the profession by the time Lee arrived on the scene. One of the things most repeated about him was how obsessively ordered and fixed and sparkling white his living space was—like his buildings. Such was his fastidiousness that his friends would tease him about whether he had glued all the objects in his apartment down in their proper places.

"Even his refrigerator was all ordered and pure too," observed a friend. "The different categories of food had their places, and they were *never* out of line." A former girlfriend of his had to learn to slice cucumbers exactly a sixteenth of an inch thick, because he wanted everything very precise for serving. So, when Lee moved in and brought her dog, Wiz, and her entourage, some in his set wondered: How is Richard going to survive?

Meier had been married not long before to fellow architect Kate Gormley and had two young children to housebreak him of his passion for domestic precision before Lee arrived. But since he and Lee were people who both had a lot invested in their surroundings and who had very different kinds of taste, living under the same roof would appear on the face of it to be fertile ground for conflict.

"We compromised," Meier said. "I replaced some pieces Lee didn't like. I felt that we were both flexible enough to be able to work that kind of thing out—it was something we would do together. She probably didn't know that much about the twentieth century. It's part of my life, so I hope I educated her. I would like to think that everyone educates those they become close to." Actually, Lee had gotten interested in contemporary things on her own. "I like the serenity," she remarked.

Although she had formally given up her decorating business, clients were still contacting her and asking her to do some work for them. She was willing to do some decorating jobs, provided she was able to do it on her own and not need the help of an assistant, and she busied herself with a few projects during this period before she gave it up altogether.

With Meier's schedule so extremely busy, Lee attended a number of social events on her own. One special occurrence was a ballooning festival in Normandy, France, in June at the invitation of Malcolm Forbes, the media tycoon. She and the other guests, a fascinating and wildly eclectic mix of Forbes's friends, enjoyed floating in balloons over the magical French countryside, and then, when they were down, watching from below the glorious color fantasy of numerous balloons in the sky simultaneously. A merry car chase followed through cow pastures and fields as they tried to keep up with the balloons as they floated away. Tents were set up on the grounds of Forbes's estate, the Château Balleroy, for dining, and there were fireworks and Norman horns in the evening.

One night Lee and Phillip Moffett, the former owner and editor-in-chief of *Esquire*, and another couple had dinner in a little restaurant in the nearby town. It was a remarkably friendly, down-home and intimate occasion, one of those times when Lee was at her best. As they all relaxed and talked late into the evening, Moffett was very taken with her: "I found her very intelligent, very lively and down-to-earth, a real human being, and full of an alert curiosity about the world," he recalled. "Lee asked me about the magazine business, and we discussed world affairs. She had opinions. It was not superficial conversation. If there was one word I would use to describe her it would be that she was so curious."

Meier missed out on the fun in France, but he and Lee shared other happy occasions: "I can remember so many pleasant times," he reminisced, "whether it was walking on the beach in the Hamptons or having dinner together, or sitting talking in an airplane. The interesting part of life is not necessarily big events but the things that make being with someone pleasant and enjoyable and meaningful day by day, and those are the times with her I remember and value."

Their shared good times together were not enough to satisfy Lee. She was disappointed with the relationship because Richard's children and his work took too much of his time to suit her. "Women usually leave him and not the other way around because Richard has this incredible force in his life, which is his work, and then there are his children, and it's difficult to make a dent in Richard Meier's life," said Julia Bloomfield, herself an old girlfriend of his.

"Lee wanted to travel with someone at a leisurely pace on her own terms, not as an accomplice on business trips, and she made remarks to me about the fact that Richard's kids stayed with him a lot, and she didn't like that. Having to be a surrogate mother didn't enter into it—Lee just doesn't like kids. She didn't want to be involved with the raising of his children.

"Scratching deeper than that, I would say they were not a very compatible couple. Backgrounds too different. One raised to be a princess, the other one raised as a nice Jewish boy with Peter Eisenman and Philip Roth in New Jersey—à la *Portnoy's Complaint*—who turns out to have an incredible talent. Richard's success has placed him in the crème de la crème of society. He's up there now because he's a famous architect, but it's not really him. He is much more at home slopping around in his slippers and looking at his books and being a teddy bear. Deep down, he really prefers to stay at home with a few old friends and not be out there, but he hasn't discovered that about himself quite yet. In the meantime, it's very seductive and fascinating to him, that glamorous life. For Lee it *is* her life. She doesn't know any other, and in the end that leads to a certain incompatibility between two people."

Meier accompanied Lee to Caroline Kennedy's wedding on Cape Cod in August 1986. It was one of their last public appearances together. "Lee told me that she wanted to leave," he confided. "I don't think this is something where there are any precise answers as to why she did it. I never discussed it with her, so I don't know why she felt it didn't work out. Life changes and people's attitudes change. Maybe she no longer loved me. Maybe she just decided she didn't want to live with me anymore or she wanted a different life. Maybe she felt I wasn't around enough, or that I was too involved with my work, or that she didn't like all the traveling, or that she didn't like my apartment—there could be fifty reasons which all added up to why she didn't want to stay. We had discussed marriage, but we had not gotten to the point of deciding whether it would or would not work out. I still think it could have worked.

"Our relationship was terrific. It worked out for as long as it could. I was disappointed when she left. These things are always a surprise to me. I was in love with her, so of course I was hurt by her decision. We never had a fight. I can also tell you that I never had a fight with my wife before she left me. Maybe that says something about me. But if someone doesn't want to be with someone, it is not a good idea to try and change her mind, because eventually her mind is going to go back to the way it was. Whatever caused Lee to leave, I wasn't going to change it by temporary behavior or effort."

46. *Armani*

"Why don't you come out and visit me at Pebble Beach?" Newton Cope asked Lee again in August of 1986. He was reciprocating for the week he had spent at Lee's beach house three years back, and this time he had a house of his own to show her. "Lee came down and talked about marriage in the same kind of way she had before," Cope revealed, "and I said to her, 'Just forget about it.'

"One night she went to bed, and I was cleaning up around the kitchen, and all of a sudden she walked in and said, 'I want to say something.' I thought to myself, 'Christ, is she going to die or something?' It sounded to me like it might be a last confession. And then she said—I'll never forget this—'I just want to tell you how terribly sorry I am for all the things I have said and done, especially to you. I am sorry for those cracks that were made in the newspapers. I am sorry for everything.' I put my arms around her and gave her a big kiss and said, 'Just forget about it.' "

A few weeks before Lee went to California, she terminated her position as a roving editor for *Architectural Digest*. She joined the staff of the Milanese fashion designer Giorgio Armani shortly after she returned from her customary August vacation in Sardinia. Her employment as his director of special events came about as a result of a relationship with him that dated back to the late seventies when she was given free clothes to wear by Gabriella Forte, the former head of U.S. operations and subsequently Armani's executive vice president and gatekeeper. "He knew my feelings about his creativeness, and I liked Armani enormously as a person," Lee acknowledged. "His clothes suit my way of life so well. They're so effortless, so easy to wear."

Armani showed his first women's collection in 1975, and Lee considered him a great talent virtually from the start. Just as she recognized it when Saint Laurent, Ungaro, and Courrèges broke with a certain chic look of their immediate pasts, which had become redundant, to produce something more lively and fresh and up-to-date, so she spotted Armani's ability to do the same for a new generation.

Giorgio Armani was the right designer for his time. He made man-tailoring feminine just at the moment when large numbers of women were entering the job market in a serious way. He blurred the distinction between sportswear and business suits for the upcoming Woodstock generation, who valued comfort above all else. His unstructured jacket, meant to have its sleeves rolled up, reshaped the way people dressed and created a new definition of style: androgynous, slouchy clothes with easy elegance—clothes of covert sensuality in a coolly understated style. The Armani faithful ranged from men coaxed out of their Ivy League tweeds and senior-level corporate women, to movie stars like Richard Gere and Anjelica Huston. ''Armani'' meant power dressing at its most elegant.

Lee was one of several customers who were given free clothes by the House of Armani in the hope that they would be photographed wearing them by the press, a common practice among fashion designers who consider it a useful form of advertising. So useful, in fact, that sometimes certain women are actually paid to wear their clothes. Any socialite or celebrity who attracts a lot of attention as a fashion plate almost never has a disinterested relationship with the designer she is wearing. Somewhere along the line there was a deal, and Lee was no exception. ''She's like all of those socialites,'' said a former Armani employee. ''Although they deny it and claim they have a lot of money, they always want to get free clothing, and Lee got a lot of things.''

When she was based in New York, Gabriella Forte cultivated a special relationship with Lee on behalf of Giorgio Armani. When Armani's business partner, Sergio Galeotti, visited New York just before collection week in March of 1980 in Milan, Forte persuaded Lee to give a dinner at her apartment just for the three of them—Lee, Forte, and Galeotti. A deal was struck that evening, and it was agreed that Lee would attend the showing of Armani's upcoming collection as the guest of honor, all expenses paid; she was to be *the* personage for that collection. In exchange, she was to be given a free wardrobe to her specifications. Lee selected simple summer outfits, mostly in her preferred colors of white and navy blue.

The arrangement the fashion house made for Lee's appearance at the showing of Armani's fall-winter collection was not unusual. Because the number of women who can afford to wear their clothes and who have the figures to do so is small and fixed, fashion designers customarily spring-load their front row with famous people to try to get an edge in the press coverage. They are all after the same fashion dollar and the competition is fierce. "They are obsessed over there—the Fendis and Gianni Versace—with who has the best people sitting in the front row," said one fashion authority. "And they all copy each other.

"Armani is no different. He loves to have big shots from the U.S. come to his shows and sit in the front row so that they can be seen by the paparazzi. He is like the rest of those big designers who, when they became famous and started raking in the dough, discovered that they could just buy these celebrities. Armani will fly one in, whether it's Tina Turner or Ali MacGraw or whoever, and everyone knows that their trips are usually paid for and that they get a fur coat or money or dresses out of it. Versace and Armani are certainly competing to get the movie stars. These guys are whores, they love stars so much. With Lee, they thought they had Jackie Kennedy there, or the queen of England, real hot stuff, not knowing that in the States, as far as the press was concerned— Lee Radziwill? Big deal."

The pecking order along the fashion front gives preference to royals and a few other celebrities as well as movie stars, who almost always arrive late so that everyone will take notice of them, or even stand up and stare. So it was with Lee: after Armani sent a makeup man and hairdresser to her hotel to make her look as perfect as possible, she was ushered into a little room near the showroom and kept there until the last possible minute. In costume and loving the game, she appeared and took her reserved seat in the front row by the runway moments before the models came shooting out.

Since Lee's behavior always depended on who was in the room with her and what the situation was, playing the role of "most distinguished personage" did not show her off at her best. She was acting the grande dame in this context and putting on airs, as Logan Bentley, a reporter for *Time* who was doing a story on the Milan collections, found out. When she saw the VIP treatment Lee got, she asked her if she were going to be working for Armani. Lee told her, no, that she had her own decorating business. Then Bentley said to her in a very friendly manner, "I remember you from Holton Arms," the Washington school they both had gone to. "Oh, that was a *long* time ago," Lee remarked in a rudely offhand way.

Apparently Lee's behavior was not much better at a dinner party Armani gave at his home that was attended by some of his staff and the publisher John Fairchild. "We on the staff all thought Lee was a lot of bullshit, because the night she came over to Giorgio's she was really playing a role," reported a source. "She was very phony. There was no real conversation going on. You know the way those socialites play it with all the designers who give them free clothes—Ungaro, Adolfo, and the rest. I mean the 'Oh, dears,' and the 'Oh, darlings.' Well, Lee was full of 'darlings' and 'dears' in that girlish, whispery voice of hers. Nothing was natural about her.

"And John Fairchild got very bitchy with her, talking about her old beau, Peter Somebody—a couple of her boyfriends actually—so that the whole evening was like a little duel between the two of them. Lee went very cool and tried to say as little as possible. We all know John Fairchild, so she was trying not to be too antagonistic. Especially in those days, he still had some power." (Fairchild was the undisputed—and unfairly advantaged—arbiter of fashion who got away with defining the "Who, What, and Wear of fashion" for decades in the pages of *Women's Wear Daily,* the fashion bible, because he owned it.)

Over the next several years, Lee was showered with more clothes and gifts by Giorgio Armani. She was on his VIP gift list, which meant that she also got costly jewelry. At one point, Sergio Galeotti selected a lovely antique pin for her. When it was pointed out to him by someone on the staff that Lee was accepting Armani's clothes but that she was frequently photographed in the pages of *WWD* and its offshoot, *W,* wearing the clothes of other designers, he was furious.*

---

*Proferring pricey baubles is common in the industry, and all that gift-giving can sometimes go too far. For example, not too long ago a trio of *New York Times* fashion writers, who were covering Karl Lagerfeld's collection for Chanel, were forced to return the booty of expensive jewelry and art given to them by him when his "generosity" was exposed to the media.

By 1985, when Galeotti died of AIDS, Lee had succumbed to being seen at big events wearing only Armani. But it was Gabriella Forte who was the driving force behind Lee's going to work for Giorgio Armani as his spokeswoman in the United States, although she says that Lee was hired in part for sentimental reasons out of respect for Galeotti, whose idea it had been originally. Upon Galeotti's death, Forte returned to Milan to step into the vacuum left by his absence in the running of the company.

"I do a little of everything," explained Lee, who went to work for Armani after he told her, "It would be great if we could join forces." It was another new beginning for her. She became a Giorgio Armani image-maker, aide, flag-waver, muse, and showpiece. She sold her name to Armani and he used it. "Designers think they have to change, otherwise there would be no fashion. But that's why Armani is so outstanding. He always keeps continuity," Lee remarked as she promoted him. "There are never violent extremes or radical changes." She also made it a point to say that the fashion business appealed to her because it wasn't far removed from the world of interior design.

Lee was hired for her social contacts, actually, to help promote Armani's fashions to her rich friends. She gave dinner parties for the designer, who always had Gabriella Forte with him translating, and she invited her monied friends to join them. The mingling process was and is how a designer establishes himself. By introducing Armani to those who decide style, Lee helped get his clothes worn by the right people. In that sense, she was a valuable marketing tool and had an important job.

Lee was hired for other, more personal reasons as well—so that the handsome, soft-spoken designer would have somebody to go around town with rather than just his own staff. "Lee was a VIP who hung around and gave Armani luster," said a Rome-based journalist who covers fashion. "On social occasions it was she who was the shining star. Armani and his executive vice president came from modest backgrounds and felt a little unsure of themselves in the big wide world. They hadn't ever mixed with high society, so they chose people like Lee to help them through the paces when they went to cocktail parties or grand occasions. She was very useful in that connection. If there were things happening in Los Angeles or New York, it was nice to go with a beautiful woman.''

Similarly, when Lee attended the shows in Milan during fashion week, she was there to mingle and to ensure that Armani was perceived as important and to give a certain kind of resonance to the house. Sometimes she made phone calls to potential guests and saw that invitations were issued, but she never actually "worked the room." Lee greeted those assembled without going out of her way. All said, she was cachet more than anything else, which is why fashion journalists would often ask: "Yes, but what does she *do?*"

One thing Lee definitely did do was to sit conspicuously in the front row during the shows, which became an embarrassment on a couple of occasions when she dozed off, probably from jet lag. "IN THE FIRST ROW AND FALLING ASLEEP!" groused one Armani employee. Another time, Armani's director of special events was shown to a second-row seat by an usher who did not recognize her. "You expect me to sit *there?*" she snapped.

Lee's title derived from organizing certain events in the States on Armani's behalf. Whenever there was a personal appearance to be made by him in the United States, especially if he came to New York, she was supposed to put a few socialites and VIPs together and set up something pressworthy. Sometimes she represented him in public when his presence wasn't possible, like the fashion show she once attended at the Neiman Marcus department store in San Francisco. Lee went there to tantalize by example and to inspire sales.

By the nineties, her contract with Armani was probably unspoken. Because she represented him, she tried to wear his clothes at all times at special occasions where she knew she was going to be photographed, and other times, presumably, she didn't. Her outfits were, of course, all given to her free. (Some of her tailored goodies, one hears, were passed on to Caroline Kennedy.) The salary Lee negotiated for herself was hefty, in the six figures, particularly when the retail value of her wardrobe and the ratio of dollars paid to time worked are factored in.

When Lee moved out on Richard Meier, she sublet an apartment on East Sixty-seventh Street briefly while she searched for a co-op. She bought one on East Seventy-second Street in a pleasant, but by no means grand building a couple of blocks down from Meier's place and right next door to Peter Tufo. It was, again, a noticeably smaller place than her last residence, and once again she sold some of her furniture to raise cash; gone were her gorgeous and valuable English Regency dining-room table and chairs, and in their place was a plain wooden table covered with fabric and ordinary chairs. Lee was really "making do" now. She was down to one small apartment with bare spots where furniture should have been and a long trail of unpaid bills, with all the animosity and ill will from creditors that state of affairs suggests. Friends speculated that Jackie had either to cosign the mortgage for her or give her some money to help pay for her apartment.

"In my many moves, I've made some costly mistakes," Lee confided of her efforts to pull her latest place together, "and it has taught me to go slowly. This time I'm making decisions with more thought."

Lee put her life on hold briefly in June 1987 when she made a special journey to Paris to visit Rudolf Nureyev, who was apparently very ill from AIDS. "He was looking so terrible," she recalled. "I knew he was sick, and I thought this would be the last time I'd see him. I think when I left the apartment he did too." Well, it wasn't. Nureyev rallied and lived another several years. But their friendship had changed considerably since those first heady days in London. They had grown very familiar to each other in the interim and quarreled often in the way that old married couples or family members do, and Rudolf's divalike exterior rendered him beguiling and temperamental by turns, causing his attitude toward others to be constantly in flux. "Nureyev, like all Slavs, can be tough to deal with. But he does have immense charm," was how Lee summed him up.

"They fought a lot because Lee was put off by Rudolf's homosexuality," a source close to him pointed out. "That was always a bone of contention. Rudolf would say to Lee he wanted 'a big cock,' and she would react with disgust. I think she realized there was no way she was going to change him. She was still in love with him, and maybe the problem was that Rudolf was much more in love with Jackie than he was with her. That probably had a lot to do with her bitterness. In a social situation, he was much more attentive to Jackie than to Lee. He thought Jackie had the more alluring personality. Lee was too common for him. Both sisters were very much attracted to his mind, his cleverness, his artistry.

"I remember once Lee telling Rudolf that Anthony was afraid of women, and Rudolf said, 'Of course. Look at you.' " (Another time, Nureyev—always outspoken—said to John F. Kennedy, Jr., who really wanted to be an actor and not the lawyer he was becoming at his mother's insistence: "Show some balls! Do what *you* want.")

When Rudolf told Lee graphically what his sexual preference was, he said so not so much because he had become exasperated with her when all else failed, but rather because he loved to shock and test others' limits. For example, he once was at a dinner party with a group of well-dressed, sedate guests and the name of a Russian public official came up. "He has a large dick," Nureyev gleefully announced across the bouillabaisse and crystal, "which he is eager to share."

That summer, shortly after Lee's return from seeing Nureyev, she sold her Southampton house to Frances Lear, the former magazine publisher and ex-wife of the television producer Norman Lear, for three and a half million dollars. Having once again dangerously depleted her finances, she had no choice. In an attempt to avoid such drastic action, Lee had gone to Jackie first for financial assistance, but to no avail. Her sister had helped her in the past, and it is said that she even set up a trust fund for Lee as well as for her children. But whatever Jackie gave her, to Lee it was not enough. To make matters worse, Jackie once told her words to the effect that all Lee had in the world was because of her. That really burned Lee up, since Onassis had been her catch, not Jackie's. "She probably felt Jackie owed her some of that $26 million she had gotten after his death," a friend remarked. "Lee should have asked for a finder's fee!"

Her sister's wealth in comparison to her own was always one of the things that plagued Lee and fed her dissatisfaction. Competing with Jackie's larger-than-life image and her bank account was very expensive, especially since Jackie was consciously determined to maintain her dominance over Lee, and she succeeded, too, because she easily had the upper hand in matters of crucial importance to both of them: status and money. Nor did it appear that Lee would ever break free of that psychological choke hold.

"Their relationship was diabolical!" said a source. "I was on the scene for more than a dozen years, and that was immediately what I picked up. Lee was always trying to be up to Jackie's level—celebrity, money, houses. She needs to have as much money as her sister did. It's that competition that would never die. Oftentimes when I was at her house, if Lee would just talk to Jackie on the telephone, she would go bananas. After speaking to her, she'd come back and say, 'She's such an airhead!' or 'She doesn't know what she's doing!' She didn't like it that Jackie was doing popular biographies at Doubleday instead of more intellectual subjects, that she was just trying to make money.

"But Lee was always being negative to me about Jackie, always having a sarcastic remark. And then one time when I saw Jackie, I asked after Lee, and she said in a very snide way, 'Oh, I haven't seen her since last summer.' It was the following January, and that's how they always seemed to be getting along. The closeness was pretty fake. And while Jackie stayed away from the press and Lee goes right after it, Jackie, on the other hand, went after the press in an underhanded way—she had other people do it. Again, it's that competition that would never die."

Late in 1987 and into the following January, Lee made several hectic trips out to the Coast, organizing a big bash for Giorgio Armani at the Museum of Contemporary Art (MoCA) in downtown Los Angeles, which took place at the end of that month. The party, a lavish black-tie dinner dance and fashion show to introduce his spring-summer collection to three hundred by-invitation-only VIPs, was intended to create awareness of the designer's new boutique, his largest in the United States, that would open some months later in Beverly Hills, and to woo the Hollywood crowd into becoming customers. "Personally, I looked at the clothes and I looked at the audience, and I saw no relation," said Gabriella Forte, speaking of the typically glitzy, overstated show biz crowd who turned out for the affair. Otherwise the evening was a smashing success.

On the last Sunday in January, two nights before the actual

event, Douglas Cramer, an avid art collector who was on MoCA's Board of Trustees, gave a dinner party at his home in Bel Air. Cramer had made his money as the immensely successful co-executive producer with Aaron Spelling of TV's *Hotel, The Love Boat,* and *Dynasty.* One of his guests was his good friend Herbert Ross, the choreographer and Hollywood director with such stylish hits to his credit as *The Seven Percent Solution, The Turning Point,* and *The Goodbye Girl.* At this time Ross was still shattered by the loss of his beloved wife, the ballerina Nora Kaye, to cancer the previous February.

"The minute Lee and Herb met at cocktails, they started talking and didn't stop," Doug Cramer has been quoted as saying. "We haven't really stopped talking since then," admitted Ross, who thought when he met her that Lee was the "most beautiful thing," with a face like Greta Garbo's. A mere forty-eight hours later Ross called his dinner host to thank him for "introducing this most enchanting woman into my life," and Cramer extended an invitation to have both of them visit him at his ranch outside Santa Barbara. The bicoastal romance had already begun.

47. *Radziwill Ross*

"I studied dancing because I had a terrible voice and I knew I'd never be an actor. I didn't know I was too tall to be a dancer or that your feet have to point or anything," Herbert Ross once said in an interview. "All I knew was I had to be in show business." A subsequent injury sustained while he was on stage dancing provided the impetus for his creation of ballets, the next rung on his career ladder, and was typical of the amazing thing about Herb Ross's long and improbable career, which ultimately spanned dance, choreography, theater, television, and film: faced with failure or mishap, he kept turning his disadvantage around.

Born in 1925 (some sources say 1927), Herbert David Ross dropped out of high school in Miami in his junior year to follow his dream of becoming a stage actor. His father was a postal clerk who had moved to Florida from Brooklyn and opened a luncheonette shortly after his first wife, Herbert's mother, died of cancer when the child was nine years old. The family had suffered in the lean years of the Depression. "I understood what it felt like to have one's nose pressed against the glass," he said. "I was very lucky, however, that we truly believed that through hard work and virtue you could achieve your goal."

A precocious child with a high I.Q., Ross quit high school over his father's strenuous objection, so strenuous, in fact, that the same day his son left home to go to New York, he dropped dead of a heart attack. But Ross has said that he felt no guilt over his father's death because he knew what he wanted to do with his life and had no choice but to leave. He supported himself in New York with odd jobs, and, after doggedly answering one fruitless casting call after another, turned in frustration to dance. Ross studied ballet, modern, and ethnic dance concurrently, practicing eight to ten hours a day, and his hard work paid off. He succeeded in landing jobs as a chorus boy in a succession of Broadway shows, fifteen in all, including *Bloomer Girl, Beggar's Holiday, Something for the Boys,* and *Look, Ma, I'm Dancin'.* In between chorus assignments he read voraciously—plays, novels, poetry—and studied drawing and classical ballet.

At twenty-three, while performing in the touring production of *Inside U.S.A.,* Ross broke his ankle on stage, and, sidelined for weeks, decided to give up dancing and devote himself to choreography. In 1950, his first ballet, *Caprichos,* inspired by the art of Goya, proved to be such a hit with the critics that he was invited to stage the work for Ballet Theatre (later American Ballet Theatre). "When I did my first ballet, I was acclaimed as the 'genius' of that season," he said. "And then I did my second ballet, and it got a devastating review in *The New York Times.* It hurt so much that I didn't do another ballet for eight years." He vowed to always have another project in the works to distract him when something did not work out, so that he would never find himself in such a vulnerable emotional position again. When Ross finally resumed choreography, he was unable to equal the impact of *Caprichos* with his other ballets, which, with the exception of an adaption of Genet's *The Maids* for Ballet Theatre, a superb work, were somber, frequently erotic, and amateurish offerings.

Ross drifted into choreography for the Broadway stage: *A*

Tree Grows in Brooklyn and *House of Flowers,* and supervised the City Center Light Opera Company's revival of *Wonderful Town.* Demonstrating great versatility at his new craft, he created supper club acts for Imogene Coca and Marlene Dietrich, staged the dance numbers for Milton Berle's and Martha Raye's television shows, and in 1954 mounted the musical production numbers for 20th Century-Fox's *Carmen Jones.* "In all, I choreographed twenty-six shows," Ross said of his Broadway experience. "But I wasn't very happy. I thought Broadway shows were frivolous. By the time I met Nora Kaye I was drifting. I was caught up in excesses. Drugs had been part of the Broadway scene since the forties, and I was smoking and drinking too much and had embraced hedonism. Nora saved my life. At the time we met, I was headed toward self-destruction."

Ross credits Nora Kaye with giving his life a new sense of purpose and stability that he apparently had failed to achieve with his roommate of thirteen years, John Ward, a dancer turned television art director with whom he lived openly in a homosexual relationship stretching from the forties into the next decade. When Ross decided to marry Nora Kaye in 1959, he chose to willfully suppress that part of himself. Ward speculated as to the reasons for Ross's crossover from gay to straight: "It may have been something he had on his mind for quite a long time. I think he thought he would be better off in the long run living that way. I couldn't blame him for doing what he wanted to do. He had that in mind before Nora. She wouldn't have influenced him that way. She liked him the way he was, absolutely. I know that she was extremely permissive about that and totally accepted the situation as it was. I believe Herbert crossed over because he thought it would be more socially acceptable in that business—the theater and Hollywood, that is. They are a very backbiting group and that had some bearing on his feeling more comfortable being 'one of the guys.'

"Herbie's sexual identity was clear but ambivalent," Ward continued. "People are not necessarily one way or the other. When he was living with me, he was still seeing women. Even today I think he'd still do the same thing. There was something deep within Herbert Ross to make that effort to be heterosexual. I was eventually able to see his point of view. I even encouraged his relationship with Nora. I thought her very ambitious and capable.'' Changing his sexual orientation when he perceived that it was not to his advantage to be gay demonstrated that Herbert Ross was, above all, a survivor, a professional animal, and that sex was not his primary interest—success was.

Nora Kaye was Ballet Theatre's reigning dramatic ballerina. She danced to fame in innovative works by Jerome Robbins and Anthony Tudor, whose protégée she became in 1939 when she joined the company. Tudor created *Pillar of Fire* for her and made her an overnight star, and together they made ballet history. Two previous failed marriages (one to the violinist Isaac Stern), a result of being on the road too much, motivated Nora Kaye to give up performing when she married Ross. But not before she and Herbert formed their own small touring company with Nora as its prima ballerina performing Ross-choreographed works of modern dance. Months on the road in Europe exhausted them, and at the end of 1960 they disbanded the ensemble. "I had had it with ballet," Ross said, and so had Nora.

At first, Ross took anything that came along, becoming in his own words, "a show doctor, a jack-of-all-trades," and then drifted back into staging the musical numbers for Broadway plays, such as *The Gay Life, Anyone Can Whistle, On a Clear Day You Can See Forever,* and *I Can Get It for You Wholesale,* which was Barbra Streisand's debut. "I discovered that you can't be a creative choreographer once you are too old to dance yourself," Herbert acknowledged. In 1965 he directed a play, *Kelly,* which opened and closed on the same day. Ross would have better luck with the theater in later years when he returned to it to direct Neil Simon's hit stage productions *Chapter Two* and *I Ought to Be in Pictures.*

Ross's work in movies began in a real way at this time when he was called on to choreograph Natalie Wood's dance numbers in *Inside Daisy Clover* and then went on to direct the musical numbers for *Dr. Dolittle,* an expensive fiasco, and for the smash hit *Funny Girl.* He came to the conclusion, however, that "coming in and helping out on other people's films was no career.

"It was when I started choreographing movies that I began to think I could direct," he explained. "I found that actors trusted me and would come to me for advice that they couldn't get from the director.'' An opportunity to direct arose in 1969 when he was called in as an eleventh-hour replacement on the remake of *Goodbye, Mr. Chips,* starring Peter O'Toole and Petula Clark. With that effort Ross had at last found his true métier. His one regret was that it had taken him so long.

Ross did *Play It Again, Sam,* a Woody Allen vehicle, and *Funny Lady,* an overproduced sequel to *Funny Girl,* and a few other features before he came into his own with *The Seven Percent Solution,* an elegant adventure story about Sherlock Holmes and Sigmund Freud. Released in 1976, the film starred Nicol Williamson, Alan Arkin, and Laurence Olivier and was Ross's coming of age as a movie director. The success of this and his other feature films, highly commercial, on-time, on-budget vehicles, gave him the confidence to embark on projects that were more of a personal statement.

In 1977 he made *The Turning Point* about his first love, the ballet. The film was a tour de force for its stars, Shirley MacLaine and Anne Bancroft. Mikhail Baryshnikov, the great dancer, and Leslie Browne, a rising young ballerina, gave touching performances in their screen debuts. All four were nominated for Academy Awards in the best acting categories, an extraordinary accomplishment for Ross. With this film, particularly, it became clear that his major strength was his "subtle, telling direction of actors." "Ross deserves to be compared to directors like George Cukor and Sidney Lumet, both of whom are known for their subtle work with actors," said film critic Stephen Farber. Ross's smooth camera moves, staged with a choreographer's rhythm, was another notable achievement. Putting his previous training to good use, he used the camera almost like a dancer, always leading the eye to where it should be in terms of detail and telling the story.

That same year Ross made another movie, an adaption of Neil Simon's stage hit *The Goodbye Girl,* with Richard Dreyfuss and Marsha Mason, which was also, along with *Turning Point,* nominated for Best Picture, a feat never accomplished before by any director. It was the apogee of Ross's career, and from then on he could write his own ticket as a director in Hollywood. By the time Lee met Herb Ross, he had made more than twenty movies in as many years and was getting $2 million per picture plus points.

Some of Ross's admirers, like Leo Janos in *The New York Times,* claim he has risen to prominence by "radiating more warmth on the screen than any director since Frank Capra." His critics dismiss him as a "feel-good director," whose films, especially his adaptations of Neil Simon's plays (*The Sunshine Boys, California Suite, I Ought to Be in Pictures*), have a quick, flashy, commercial gloss and little substance. Describing himself as a "classicist in a Hollywood way," Ross says his mission in films is to be entertaining about serious subjects, to mask them as amusement.

While most of Ross's biggest hits have been his adaptions of Simon's plays, his own favorites include *Nijinsky* and the risky *Pennies From Heaven,* an offbeat and somber musical set in the Depression, starring Steve Martin and Bernadette Peters. One big fan of *Pennies From Heaven* was Lee Radziwill, who revealed in a *Vanity Fair* interview soon after they were married how she had known about Herbert for a long while and had hoped that their paths would cross. "When I saw *The Turning Point,* Herbert's name stuck in my head for a long time," she admitted, "and then many years passed and I saw *Pennies From Heaven,* which I loved so much that I saw it three times by myself in one week. I found it the most poignant, touching, delightful story. Simply heartbreaking. . . . But I didn't meet Herbert until three years later. I think one of the most interesting things is that tremendous range he has, from the brilliant to the ridiculous to the poignant to . . ."

Soon after Herbert and Lee had met, in February 1988, they spent a weekend together at producer Ray Stark's ranch near Santa Barbara. Already an item by March, Lee kept showing up on Herbert's arm at the fashionable Hollywood eatery Spago, and she talked him into giving Nureyev's fiftieth birthday party mid-month at his home in Santa Monica. To conduct their romance, Lee checked into the Bel Air Hotel and Herbert joined her there. She would not stay at his house—too many reminders of Nora. In April, they reportedly took a holiday in Mexico together and a little later, another in St. Martin at La Samanna, Lee's favorite Caribbean resort. In May, she accompanied Herbert to Atlanta to scout locations for *Steel Magnolias.* By then, everyone knew they were going to get married. Presto, just like that.

"Lee knew Herbert still was in mourning, but she went after him at Doug Cramer's right then and there," said a longtime family friend of his. "Absolutely no question about it, she zoomed right in on him, a successful director, and he was flattered and impressed by her family, *very* impressed. Herbert likes to be with people who have made it. He's been a snob that way all his life. But Lee set her sights for him. They saw each other a lot, and then she wanted to be married, and he went for it.

"Herbert couldn't be alone. That was the reason. He and Nora were like one person. They were never separated for a moment in all those years. As far as he was concerned, his life ended with her. He was so distraught when she died, I thought he would commit suicide. It was that bad. He will never get over her death. Never! I don't care who he marries. Then when he decided to remarry so soon, it stunned everybody. It was very shocking, shocking to him, too. I guess Lee . . . her charm . . . whatever."

On location in the just-folks town of Natchitoches, Louisiana, where the filming of *Magnolias* was done over the course of the summer, Herbert took up residence in a lovely, modern, U-shaped brick home overlooking Cane River Lake, which belonged to a local couple and was rented by the movie company. Lee flew in to join him there sometimes for the weekend, and at other times she stayed for weeks at a stretch. Both of them were taken with the magic of the town, in spite of the heat and humidity. Natchitoches is an intoxicating place, lush and verdant because the water table is so high, and it still looks much as it did a hundred years ago.

Herbert and Lee spent as much time as they could manage off by themselves. They were enthralled with one another, and, better yet, shared a terrific companionship that energized and nourished both of them. This extraordinary rapport was based on the firm foundation of shared values and interests—the ballet, books, fine dining, travel, collecting, gardens (Herbert's English boxwood and topiary garden at his Santa Monica house was his pride and joy) and, of course, show business. Ross's colorful anecdotes and interesting experiences about his many years in the theater and Hollywood were in seemingly limitless supply, and Lee, of course, had much to tell of equal interest from the treasure chest of her own extraordinary history—and even broader horizons.

"Herbert is a great raconteur," said Ed Pisoni, his production designer on a few of his films and a great admirer of his. "He loves telling stories of his early days in the theater. He met a lot of people who are very influential now, and he is marvelous in any kind of social situation where the tale is all. He is more than entertaining, he is totally delightful. He has an enormous store of anecdotes, and he could go on for the rest of his life just telling stories. I would say he is exciting to be around."

A craggy-faced, intelligent man well over six feet in height, with a pronounced sense of humor, Herbert Ross is exceptionally well read and is self-taught on a wide range of subjects in addition to his other talents. His friends tell him he should have been a college professor, because he delights so much in in-depth exposition: he lectures, he teaches, he explains, and he loves an audience, wherever they are.

Though he is personally engaging, Ross's quest for perfection often renders him uptight and difficult on a movie set, and on *Magnolias* he was even more so. *Steel Magnolias* was Ray Stark's motion picture extravaganza for Tri-Star-Columbia Pictures, which was adapted by Robert Harling from his simple, poignant, off-Broadway play about the lives of six women in his home town of Natchitoches. Olympia Dukakis, Shirley MacLaine, Sally Field, Dolly Parton, Daryl Hannah, and newcomer Julia Roberts made up the all-star cast.

With his own wife's death in an intensive care unit still fresh in his mind, Ross was in tears the day he shot the scene in the intensive care unit where Julia Roberts's character dies. "No wonder Herbert is nervous and demanding," said Shirley MacLaine at the time. "He's got a picture about women and death, the two things he's coming to grips with in his own life."

To amuse herself while Herbert was working, Lee went waterskiing each morning in the Cane River, which flows through the heart of the town, choosing to ignore the alligators and creating a fuss because she refused to wear a regulation life vest. She explored her agreeable surroundings on a bicycle and wandered around, sometimes joining Herbert for lunch on the set, but always coming by to watch the dailies at the end of the day, where she wisely chose to remain very quiet and unobtrusive. She chatted a lot on the telephone and would show up at the movie company's office to take advantage of their free phones to make overseas calls, especially to her son Anthony in Korea. (He was there with NBC Sports for the Seoul Olympics. Very focused in what he wanted to do with his life, Anthony graduated from Boston University's School of Communications in 1982 and went immediately into a successful career in television production.)

One day, Rex Reed, the well-known film critic and star of the nationally syndicated television show *At the Movies*, showed up in Natchitoches on assignment from a magazine to write about the making of *Steel Magnolias*. (Reed wanted to do the article for sentimental reasons; he had gone to high school in Natchitoches and thought it would be interesting to go back after all those years.) Banned from the movie set by Herbert Ross, he hung around the town to seek out his story and spoke with the cast and crew afterhours.

"Everybody connected with that movie was more than happy to give me unflattering Lee Radziwill stories," Reed said of his experience. "She behaved like an impossible, self-centered, very temperamental bitch who made no attempt whatsoever to even try to be diplomatic with the little people of that town, and no one on the movie set would have anything to do with her, either. They all hated her there—they just hated her! She alienated so many people that they were calling me up with stories, and when *Premiere* magazine fact-checkers went to verify everything I had written, they gave them even more material than I already had.

"It was unbelievable what was going on. First off, she insisted on taking the best house for herself. Then she had some of the furniture removed because it wasn't aesthetically pleasing to her—this wasn't even her house. There was a skylight in her bedroom and she couldn't sleep with the light coming in, so she made the union carpenters shut down the set and come over to her house to cover it up with black fabric. Then *even more* fabric had to be located by the set decorator to cover the black fabric with a color the princess found aesthetically pleasing. A little tiny town in Louisiana and she had to have everything perfect for her visits.

"There were no direct flights to the area. Other people, all the stars of the film, took commercial flights. But Lee refused to change planes. They had to fly her in a private jet from New Orleans or Dallas at tremendous expense to the film company—just unbelievable nonsense from a person who was not connected with the movie in any way. She was just visiting the director.

"One of the big problems on the film was her bicycle. Lee insisted on a British Raleigh instead of the Schwinn she was given—they are identical three-speed bicycles. One had to be shipped in by Federal Express from Baton Rouge after a big effort was made to find it. She made Herbert bring home the imported caviar from the set for themselves [at $135 for a tiny jar], and then they denied that they had it. It was served at dinner when I was invited to their home on my last night there. She was really living in the grand manner in this teeny Louisiana town.

"Shirley MacLaine and I were getting together every night —she was the only one who would see me after Herbert Ross banned me from the set—and she was just devastated by the fact that this woman was truly dominating his life and already spending his money faster than he could earn it. She and I had long talks about it, and she told me: 'When Herbert was married to Nora Kaye, she used to say, "Cut out the crap, Herbie," and keep his extravagances in check. What can we do to stop this madness now?' Apparently nothing. Marrying Ross is a dream come true for Lee. She has always been determined to make some kind of name for herself, and she's always done it on the backs of other people. Now she has a toehold into show business, and Herbert Ross is the one."

Shirley MacLaine felt very protective toward Herbert because he had revived her career by making her the lead in *The Turning Point,* and they have remained friends since that time. She was obviously someone who did not care for Lee, and one of the more popular performances around the set was her send-up of Lee's mannered way of introducing herself. Lee always managed to turn a simple "How do you do" into a grand gesture. To offer a handshake, she would stick her arm straight out—it did not have a bend in it—and, as she did so, she would pronounce her name very quickly with an accent: "Lee Rad-zih-ville." When Herbert wasn't looking, MacLaine would hit her hand on her elbow, stick her arm up in the air, and say over and over: "Lee Rad-zih-ville! Lee Rad-zih-ville!"

" 'Grand' is definitely the word I would use for Lee," said Tom Whitehead, the person hired to be the liaison between the film company and the local population and who had several dealings with her. "She was a very pleasant woman one-on-one. It was just whenever anybody else was around that the grandness and pomp and circumstance got out of hand."

Mind you, Ross could be equally grandiose and demanding, but his rank in his own professional milieu, earned by dint of his talent, hard work, and success, allowed him the privilege. If Herbert was aware of Lee's unpopular behavior, he chose to ignore it. As everyone in the movie colony noticed, he was enormously happy just being around her. She was the perfect thing for him in his life right then. "We had a glorious time together," he said of his experience in Louisiana. Herbert was in love. "And whatever you can say about Lee Radziwill, she was genuinely in love with him," one of his assistants on the film made it a point to say.

In August, Lee decided to go ahead and keep the plans she had made for her annual trek to Sardinia, her favorite vacation spot in the eighties. Herbert missed her so much that he sent a private jet to bring her back to him. They set a wedding date for the week after the shooting wrapped in September; the announcement, appropriately enough, was made through the movie company's publicist.

Actually, Herbert did not want to get married so soon. He suggested to Lee that they live together for a while and see how it went. According to one of Herbert's friends, she replied that she was "not that kind of girl," which is a strange remark considering that she had cohabited with Richard Meier not long before. More than anxious to get settled now, Lee kept saying insistently to Herbert: "marriage, marriage, marriage."

At dusk on September 23, on a hot and rainy evening, the couple said their fleeting "I do's" before a judge in the red living room of Lee's apartment, attended by Rudolf Nureyev as Lee's witness, and John Taras, the associate director of the American Ballet Theatre, for Herbert. Tina was there but Anthony was still in Korea. Tearful during the brief ceremony, Lee appeared ecstatic immediately afterward and had some champagne and caviar with the rest of the small wedding party before a waiting limousine whisked them all off to Jackie's a few blocks away for the celebration dinner. The Rosses saw to it that the details of their wedding were made known to the paparazzi by means of a leak to the right gossip columnist, so that they were waiting outside Jackie's apartment when the bride and groom arrived there. As the flashbulbs popped, Lee sat momentarily in the limo holding Herbert's hand in a pose more cheesecake than bridal, as the skirt of the two-piece blue silk Armani ensemble she was wearing slid way up her leg.

Originally, the wedding dinner was going to be at Lee's apartment, but it became too small when the guest list swelled from twenty to thirty, so Jackie emptied her library for the occasion. When she was helping with the invitation list, Jackie said to someone both she and Lee knew: "I want to invite Lee's friends. Does she have any?" Apart from Jackie and her family, only a few of the people there were Lee's guests, notably her friends Catie Marron and Mark Hampton and their respective spouses, and Karen Lerner. The rest were Herbert's, mostly from his years in show business. Hollywood was represented by Steve Martin and Bernadette Peters, Daryl Hannah, Ray Stark, and the man who started it all, Doug Cramer. The dinner was a quiet, low-key, pleasant affair, with at least one guest complaining that the food wasn't very good and that there wasn't enough of it—"in other words, a typical Waspy wedding," she said.

"Isn't it wonderful that Lee's happy?" Karen Lerner asked Jackie, who had met the groom just the day before. "Isn't he homosexual?" Jackie replied. Thinking fast, Lerner retorted: "Well, I never heard he wasn't!" Jackie probably figured it would have been taken as a chop at the knees if she asked her sister the same question.

A number of Herbert's friends were against this marriage. Like Shirley MacLaine, they worried that Lee was a fortune hunter and would spend all his money and then some. A story went around Herbert's set that when one of them tried to warn him off Lee, he protested, "But I am marrying royalty!"

Commiserating among themselves, they were just as cynical about Herbert's motives as they were of Lee's, saying that he was in love with the idea of her, not the woman herself. "Little Herbie Ross from Brooklyn married to Lee Radziwill. He got the quintessential shiksa, the unattractive Jewish boy's

dream come true," said one Jewish friend of his. "And Lee
was fifty-five. Fifty-five can't be choosers. Time is passing."
"It was Ross's fag dream to have Lee Radziwill as a wife,"
said another. "Lee is white bread. Jewish people eat rye bread.
She represents that whole image, the little tea sandwiches and
flower bonnets. She is Newport rather than Long Island, which
is Jewish now, frankly."

In her Canfield–Princess Radziwill days, Lee would never
have considered marriage to someone of Herbert Ross's background. But experience had taught her to reinvent her ideals
on more practical terms, and, in her own words, life is a series
of stages one outgrows and leaves behind. Herbert Ross has
more of an intellect and maturity, a wider view of the world
and experience of real life—what one thinks of as real life—
than either of her former husbands. "He is someone who has
demonstrated considerable sensitivity and understanding of
women in a number of his films, and he obviously has insights
into people," observed an old friend of Lee's. "He may be
the first guy in her life who has that outstanding capacity for
understanding."

Marrying Herbert Ross was Lee's renaissance. It recon-
nected her to the larger world in a way she could not manage
on her own, and it fixed the hole in her heart—and in his
heart, too. Herbert and Lee were fresh and healing to one
another, their times of despair behind them. And if, like most
people on a third try, Lee was skeptical of a happy ending,
well, at least she believed in a new beginning.

48. Renaissance

Herbert got a tour by boat of the hidden beaches in Sardinia
that Lee had discovered during years of summering there,
when she went back to the island with him in tow to finish
her interrupted vacation. It was the first leg of their European
honeymoon. Mixing business with pleasure in their month-
long stay, they showed up in Milan for fashion week, where
the paparazzi made more of a fuss than usual over "*la principessa*" and her new husband from Hollywood. The Rosses
toured Verona and Mantua, ate well, and went on to Paris for

some leisurely shopping and an informal dinner party at Nureyev's with the actress Anouk Aimée. A tour of Provence concluded their trip and was so enjoyable that Lee decided to return there someday soon for a longer stay. Their favorite spot: the famous garden of the octogenarian grande dame Loulou de Waldner. "I think a garden is one of the higher forms of civilization," Herbert has said.

Back from her honeymoon, Lee did not even attempt for a month or two to open the mammoth pile of wedding gifts from the movie colony that awaited the couple. She and Herbert went straight to California to tend to the magnificent ranch property he had recently bought, four hundred acres in Foxen Canyon in the Santa Ynez Valley, not too far from Santa Barbara, and 110 miles northwest of Los Angeles. The acquisition came about when Herbert and Lee, who were houseguests of Doug Cramer a number of times during their courtship, were apprised of a property adjoining his that was for sale. Herbert had always wanted to retire to a ranch, and so he purchased it with the intention of raising imported buffalo-mozzarella cows. A number of other property owners in that area were also in the entertainment business: Fess Parker, Mike Nichols, and Ray Stark all had spreads nearby, and the Rosses' property overlooked Michael Jackson's thousands of acres in the valley below. "It's the most beautiful piece of property I've seen anywhere," said Lee of the rolling hills and indigenous oaks that graced the land.

The property came with a thriving vineyard—twenty-five acres of Chardonnay grapes, which was sold-off property from the winery next door—and a smashing homesite. The first thing the Rosses did was raze the existing house; it was built in the shape of a hexagon with long, connecting hallways that nobody liked. Herbert and Lee had a strong difference of opinion as to whether their new house, "something simple, stucco, classical," should be Tuscan farmhouse in spirit, which Herbert preferred, or Provençal farmhouse, which Lee favored. Provençal it was. Until their dream house was built, the plan was to live in a rented house on the Cramer ranch, where they were staying for a few weeks on that trip out. Herbert had meetings with his contractor and farm manager about the first necessary work: cleaning up the land and installing underground electricity and fencing. All there was on the property so far, besides the vineyard, was a trailer for the farm manager.

The newlyweds were the toast of Hollywood during their stay. Mike Ovitz, the powerful head of Creative Artists Agency, and his wife, Judy, hosted a party in the Rosses' honor one evening, with a guest list that mixed some of the new power elite with old-timers like Esther Williams and Zsa Zsa Gabor.

In New York for her birthday in March, Lee took a one-night breather from her marriage and went to dinner and a Fellini movie with Jackie and Slim Keith. Keith, like everyone else, noticed that Lee looked "better than she's ever looked in her life. She's really happy." Then it was off to Europe and another birthday celebration, this one a party for Nureyev at his Paris digs. Lee took a Danish friend of Tony Hail's along, whose life, Hail said, "was immeasurably enhanced when all of a sudden he fell into that French-speaking, international, highfalutin, artistic, bohemian crowd in one fell swoop—and Lee to boot."

Tony Hail was Lee's guest at a dinner party she gave at the end of the month at her apartment in New York. "She asked me to come early, and I did, and she showed me the architectural plans for their new house," recalled Hail, who is an architect as well as a decorator. "Herb had hired an architect, but Lee said to me, 'I can't live in that house. Can you make it okay?' So I sat myself down in front of the fire for an hour or so before her other guests arrived and together we redid the plans for her new house. It was just awful what they had drawn. The house had every kind of window—French windows, bay windows—it was a terrible house."

Actually the house was very similar in concept to the one Herbert had lived in with Nora Kaye, which had an eighty-foot-long loft-style living room floored in gray-black granite that went on forever with offices, a gym, a wine room, and guest suites, and eight bathrooms. It was custom-designed to house their vast collections of artworks, artifacts, and boisterously ornamental knickknacks, and as such was really an assemblage of Nora's personality. It reflected her attraction to the bizarre and the eccentric, the glitzy and the kitschy, exactly the opposite of Lee's taste of understated elegance and at odds with everything she liked.

"It just wasn't my thing," Lee told Tony Hail. "I am well

known for my taste. I didn't want to have those things in my house. So I told Herbert I wouldn't marry him unless he got rid of the house and everything in it.'' When Herbert told her he wanted to at least keep his bedroom clock, a favorite piece, Lee told him, no, that had to go too.

Not even his bedroom clock! It was as if Lee were trying to exorcise Nora's powerful ghost and erase her memory. Naturally, she was curious about Nora, and she once asked a former dancer some questions about her, and when the dancer offered to show her some film clips of Nora dancing, Lee replied with an emotional ''No! No! No! No!'' as if she couldn't handle it. Nora was a hard act to follow.

The Nora Kaye house was put up for sale right after Herbert and Lee married and was sold for $4 million the following year; an auction of its contents was held in December 1988 and fetched hundreds of thousands of dollars. Herbert gave Lee a large chunk of the money from both sales to spend as she pleased on their properties.

''Lee was very happy being rich,'' Tony Hail observed. ''She took me on a tour of every corner of her apartment with all that newfound money to spend. It was very pretty, with the most beautiful Easter flowers, but it was only half finished. Pieces of furniture were missing in the guest room and even the master bedroom; the dining room was half empty. Lee said to me at one point, 'I have a big hole there, you see? Can't you find me some beautiful furniture to fill it?' She described what she wanted and asked me if I would get a lot of furniture for her in Europe, because she didn't have the time to do it. She and Herb were always traveling, and she wasn't there for any length of time.

''Then the guests arrived for the dinner party, and everything was fine until Herbert fell apart in the middle of it. He had a couple of drinks and suddenly his hands were waving all over the place and he was back to his other self, the bisexual part of himself once again. It was dismaying to see because he was so obvious. I was embarrassed for Lee that here was this fellow whom she married, her bridegroom, who was so obviously a homosexual. I just think it's unfortunate to be a sissy. It seems to me I would hate that, wouldn't you?'' asked Hail, who so readily admits to being gay himself. ''I have talked to Mark Hampton about this, and he doesn't understand it either. He doesn't get it—why she would marry him. None of us do. But I have to say Lee seemed enormously happy. She was hard up for so long."

When Herbert married Lee, a mean-spirited joke made the rounds in Hollywood about "the princess who married the queen." The under-the-table conversation there for years has always been that Herbert Ross is still gay, despite his two marriages. They see the effeminate gestures—what Lee calls his "la-di-da"—and they know his history, and they ponder aloud about just what goes on behind closed doors with him. They wondered about Nora, and now they wonder about Lee. But the truth is that Herbert has never been linked with another man since he married Nora, and Nora told her closest friends that they had tried very hard to have a child and that otherwise they had completely normal conjugal relations. One has to presume from that that Herbert and Lee do also. Ironically, if that is so, Lee was married previously to two heterosexuals with whom she did not have a regular sex life, but she has found one, apparently, with her bisexual third husband.

Temporarily without a second home, the Rosses still managed to be in East Hampton for most of the summer of '89. They took over socialite Liz Fondaras's oceanfront estate on Further Lane for July, and then, in a big swap, moved across the village for the month of August to take up residence in Katherine Johnson's house on West End Road, while Johnson, in turn, took off for the villa Lee always rented in Sardinia.

Lee and Herbert had an extremely full social life in the Hamptons. There were always parties to go to and places to be seen at and people coming to see them. Caroline Kennedy came to visit from time to time with her daughter, Rose, and Anthony came every weekend. In August, Lee threw a big thirtieth birthday party for her son, and the performer Billy Joel showed up, to the delight of Anthony's guests. Lee liked to invite her favorite child's friends home and, in general, enjoyed having young, attractive people around her.

"I don't believe in luck with children," said Vincent Ropatte, who was Diane Sawyer's beauty consultant on ABC's *Prime Time Live*, where Anthony was an associate producer, and who occasionally cut his hair. "They pick up the characteristics and teachings of their parents, and Lee did something right. Anthony is a true gentleman, a worker, an athlete, a perfectly wonderful kid. Both her children are.''

At the end of July Janet died at her home at Hammersmith Farm. She suffered from Alzheimer's disease and had been ailing for a long time. Lee wept quietly at the funeral at Trinity Church and at the burial at the Auchincloss family plot in a Colonial-era cemetery north of town. Over the years Janet tried without success to lure Lee to visit her in Newport. She would drop by once in a while, but nothing more. Janet never got much time from her daughters once they became adults—their past relationships were too difficult. Jonathan Tapper, Janet's majordomo, said that in her last years Janet always spoke of Lee as her favorite child, which certainly would have been news to Lee when she was growing up. Her unexpected sentiment is an example of the way memory plays tricks on all of us.

In September, Herbert began work on *My Blue Heaven,* a comedy for Warner Brothers about a mobster informant who turns respectable, starring Steve Martin and Rick Moranis. He shot on location in central California, San Diego, and Los Angeles, finishing principal photography there in early February. When Herbert arrived on location in San Luis Obispo, where Lee was to join him for a stay of several weeks, he disliked the way his hotel suite was furnished. He rang up his set decorator on the picture, Don Remacle, early on a Sunday morning, waking him up, and requested that before Lee got there he refurnish the suite with authentic antiques rented and shipped in from Los Angeles, a great distance away. ''When you are Herbert Ross you can do that,'' said Remacle. ''You see what we do in the movie business to make these people happy?''

Lee joined Herbert on location in sporadic fashion, alternating trips out to see him with her life as usual in New York. Once in a while she joined him and his crew when they scouted locations by private jet, but she did not like to hang around the set on any of his films. Herbert was too involved to give her much attention. When she did come by, she would stay in his motor home, and he would go there to have lunch with her, and sometimes she would come by to watch the dailies later on. ''There didn't seem to be a lot of conversation going on between her and anybody else when she was on the set," said one of the crew on *Heaven*. "Lee was very retiring. It was a different world than she was used to."

When Lee was visiting and Herbert was shooting, he had his driver, John Chaney, take her around, touring the local spots of interest and doing some shopping; a couple of times they drove to the ranch to look over the property so that Lee could get some ideas about landscaping; and sometimes Chaney would join Lee for a bite to eat and a movie. This democracy extended to dinner with the boss. "I have a lot of good memories of them," Chaney said. "If Herbert and Lee weren't entertaining someone when they went out to eat, I would be included."

As Herbert's driver, Chaney had a bird's-eye view of the Rosses' relationship. "They are truly in love with each other," he said. "Herbert is not prone to paying a lot of attention to anybody, but he does to Lee. He gives her a lot of time, shows her a lot of love and affection and is very considerate. Both of them are. It is just how they handle themselves around each other. They dote on each other. They make each other happy."

"Herbert and Lee fit each other like a hand in a glove," concurred Ed Pisoni, another one who had a good opportunity to observe the Rosses. "They seem to be very good for one another, and if one perceives of it as a social arrangement, they complement each other very well. Physically they make a good couple also. Herbert knows how to present himself. He dresses well. Lee looks good on his arm. They just seem right with one another.

"Herbert has his own interests at heart more than anyone else's, except for Lee, and a lot of his life on his movies revolved around his concern for her—is she going to be well taken care of, and when is her plane arriving, and all of that; and he spent all of his free time with her when she joined him on location. When he was away from her, he was always talking on the phone to her and concerned about where she was and how she was getting on. Herbert has always been very good to his wives, gentlemanly and loving. I think he's a marvelous person and an excellent catch for an older woman. He and Lee supply needs in one another. It is a very good match."

But old habits die hard, and despite the spell of romance, there were early warning signs, like the low rumble of distant thunder, that there could be trouble ahead for Mr. and Mrs.

Ross, predictably enough, over money. When Herbert gave Lee all that cash from the sale of his home and furnishings, he got nervous when he saw how fast she ran through it. Lee purchased and shipped out to Los Angeles a ton of furniture for the ranch—some said two warehouses full—of wonderfully rustic but costly pieces that she or her agent had bought in San Francisco and back east: all this for a house that was still only a hole in the ground. Two warehouses full may have been an exaggeration, but not by much, for it was the sheer volume of her purchases that upset Herbert. Then Lee undertook to have acres of trees on the ranch property pruned and "laced out" to make them look prettier, an expensive horticultural practice that is not ordinarily done to things growing in the wild; nor did the special olive trees she had it in mind to plant come cheap.

Even the crew on the movie set noticed the problem. "On the mornings Herbert came to the set when Lee was out there, and he was in a foul mood, we knew that she had spent an exorbitant amount of money the day before," said Don Remacle. "A lot of his bad tempers were connected to her bills, because other times, when she wasn't around, he was smooth as glass."

A related story that made the rounds on the movie set and then traveled all the way to New York, where Herbert's friends gossiped about it, was that he was complaining on his car phone to his shrink that Lee was spending far too much money, and that they were quarreling. Ross had a forty-five-minute drive from the shooting location back to his hotel each day, and he would talk on the telephone in the back seat of his car, apparently oblivious that anyone with a scanner could hear them. "He had to pass the time somehow in the big limousine," said Remacle.

A colleague of Herbert's who was in on the story warned: "Don't believe the picture you have been getting about how happy Herbert and Lee are. Don't believe it for one second! Lee's whole life is about money, and Herbert's whole thing now is about making enough money to pay her bills. And I think—and so does almost everyone who knows him—that he is basically miserable. Just don't believe that they are in paradise, I am telling you!

"Now I don't know that *she's* not happy with him, I am

telling you *he's* not happy with her, which doesn't mean that the marriage won't last forever, by the way. But what no one can ever figure out is how Herbert will ever get out of it. If they ever got a divorce, she'd want money. Herbert said he had to do two pictures a year to break even, which is about $5 million a year. He doesn't have a lot of money put away. It's one of those odd little nightmares. All I know is, this is not a happy man.''

49. *Taking Control*

Herbert had other problems during the making of *My Blue Heaven* besides Lee's cash flow. He and Joan Cusack, who had a supporting role in the film, were not getting along to an extent that went far beyond the normal give-and-take of director to actress on a picture. Herbert had cast her but later decided she was wrong for the part she played (of a district attorney; it was originally written by Nora Ephron for Goldie Hawn). He did not think she was doing a good job and resorted to riding her on the set, even screaming at her at times. Cusack demanded that he treat her with the respect that was due her as a professional actress and told him he should behave like a director. They had words and Herbert got profane. He called her ''an arrogant cunt'' in front of the cast and crew, behavior that everyone felt was way out of line. And when an assistant director asked for the customary applause accorded an actress when Cusack finished her last shot, Herbert turned away and stormed off the set into his waiting limousine. He was absolutely furious at what he saw as a challenge to his authority by those on the set who applauded her.

''The man is extremely complex, and I hesitate to say why he behaved that way,'' said a crew member who was present. ''It is evidently a pattern. Herbert has been abusive to a lot of people on his pictures, but he seems to take great pleasure and make a special showing of bitchy duels with women. He takes center stage on major fights with his leading ladies. He'll also fight anyone in a random way on the set and later apologize in private—he doesn't want anyone to see him apologizing. It's happened to me and to others. All I remember is how he treated Julia Roberts on *Magnolias,* and then at the Golden Globe Awards he was the first person off his ass to step in her way to congratulate her.''

When they were shooting *Steel Magnolias,* Herbert had told Roberts that she was worthless and incompetent, and had ripped into her constantly. Julia later spoke of how she would cry in her motel room every night, and her costars would come by and comfort her. It was one of the worst experiences she had ever gone through, she said. (In fairness to Herbert, he hired Roberts for *Magnolias* over Ray Stark's and everyone else's strenuous objection. They all thought she was unremarkable. It was Herbert's ability to recognize her potential that got her the role.)

Herbert's defenders say that his behavior toward Julia Roberts was his way of bringing her into the picture; that one only has to look at the amazing performance he got out of her to see that it was justified. They say that Herbert's behavior relates to that quest for perfection he can never obtain, that he genuinely believes this is the way to get the result he wants, and that ultimately there is love there. They concede that his behavior is very easy to misinterpret and when it starts to go awry, it can really go bad. By the end of *My Blue Heaven,* he and Joan Cusack were not even saying hello to one another.

Herbert's detractors say that on every picture there is someone he uses as a whipping post—it can be anyone from a gofer to the assistant director—and that he is a martinet to work for. ''Oh, he tore into So-and-so today,'' or ''So-and-so got it today'' is typical gossip on a Herb Ross movie set. They say that over the years as he got more power, he gradually became more arrogant and impatient with those who were not on his level, and that he is far too temperamental, sarcastic, and difficult. Nor is he anecdotal, they noted. Like Lee, to talk about Herbert Ross is to complain about him.

What everybody does agree on is that since Nora died, he has gotten noticeably worse. Nora shared credits with Herbert and was a potent force on any film her husband directed. She was the glue that held him together, the strength on all his projects. She virtually cast everything and had a great eye for what was worthwhile in her choice of material, and she made his career. She was like ''Cardinal Richelieu to his Sun King,'' a colleague said. What happened with Julia Roberts and Joan

Cusack and with Imogen Stubbs on his next film, *True Colors,*
would never have happened if she were still alive. Nora, funny
and human, would have said, "Knock it off, Herbie" and kept
him in line.

"He's just angry about Nora's death—he loved her so
much," offered a friend. "He's frustrated and in some ways
miserable. He lost his partner in everything. There will never
be another one like her, and he's bitter about it. He was very
secure with her. He feels abandoned and doesn't understand
why."

Ed Pisoni made a different appraisal of Herbert's behavior:
"Herbert keeps his social and professional worlds completely
apart and functions very differently in each of them. Socially
he is very charming. Professionally, he really takes his role as
an artist seriously and struggles with each new project and
goes through a process which is arduous, and he cannot keep
it from others. Consequently, he has alienated his share of
people in the world because of his gruffness, singularity, and
aim. He thinks most people will understand what he's doing,
but they don't. Herbert has made a lot of enemies in Hollywood because he isn't the most tactful person. They don't like
the way he has treated some otherwise highly regarded crafts-
men, and when he makes a move like marrying Lee Radziwill,
he becomes vulnerable and they pick up on it."

What many associates of Herbert's criticized him for with
respect to Lee was what they saw as his pretentious behavior.
Studio executives who have had to deal with him on his last
few pictures complained that he had his nose in the air and
gave the impression that he was unconcerned with the mun-
dane, but at the same time he was overly attuned to what were
considered the best hotel suites and restaurants. "He and Lee
really tried as much as possible to take advantage of the company in terms of perks," one testified. "If there was a chauf-
feured car around, even if it wasn't theirs, they would
commandeer it without thinking twice."

One colleague of Herbert's who had a distinct feeling about
Lee's influence on his life and who spoke for many said: "I
wouldn't say Lee's influence is outright detrimental, because
Herbert does need her in his life. But Nora was a leveling
influence on him, and Lee isn't. Her background opened up a
world to him that he'd never been exposed to but probably

would have liked, and the reason he wasn't exposed to it was: 'Oh, that's a lot of bullshit, Herbert. What does it all mean?' from Nora. She used to shoot him down. Nora was one of America's greatest ballerinas, but she was still a girl from Brooklyn, and when she spoke, it was obvious.

"Lee was a very strange choice for him. It just blew me away at first. I think she was an escape from his pain. Yet Herbert is a different person since Nora died, and he'd tell you that. One would have to be blind not to see how grand he has become. When you have known him as long as I have—since the fifties—you can see the difference. For one thing, he's Armanied to death, though he has always had an interesting style about him. For another, his manner on the set seems to have become more affected. I noticed it on *Magnolias,* bits and pieces. I'd hear little things, his choice of words for example: 'Wouldn't this be amusing?' It was a carryover from her. There was no genuineness there. Only twice, maybe, when we talked about the loss of Nora and a mutual friend, did I feel he was really genuine."

"Lee Radziwill has fed Herbert's grandiose notions of himself," agreed Rex Reed, who at one time was good friends with him and Nora through Natalie Wood. "Natalie was a good friend of mine, and she just adored Herbert and Nora. Nora was the greatest thing that ever happened to Herb Ross. She completely orchestrated his career and was his best friend and right arm. She had all the talent. Herbert was dominated by Nora in a good way. She was a very healthy influence on his life. She brought out his artistry rather than his pretensions. He's changed a lot since he married Lee. He is not the old fun-loving Herb I used to know. He has become pompous and posturing. I saw it in his behavior when he was doing *Steel Magnolias.* They weren't even married yet, and I saw the change."

Ed Pisoni disagrees with Reed's assessment: "I worked with Herbert before and after Lee, and his behavior was the same. If there is a pretentious side to Herbert, it was always there. Lee opened up a new world to him—as he did to her—and I am sure his circle of friends has changed. But I think Herbert is very underrated as a director. He has worked very hard and has had a tremendous success in filmmaking. He deserves a certain amount of respect."

*   *   *

In early November of 1989, Anthony escorted Lee to the *Steel Magnolias* premiere in New York. Herbert was in California working on *Heaven* and was unable to make it, but he joined Lee for the Los Angeles benefit premiere a few days later. Lee got him to take a ten-day respite from his grueling schedule at Christmas when they rented a villa at Mexico's Hotel Costa Careyes, an isolated and low-key but luxurious resort in a spectacular natural setting situated on the coast north of Puerto Vallarta. Like two gypsies, the Rosses went straight from Mexico to Beverly Hills, where they rented a nice house for a few weeks while Herbert wound up shooting.

Lee used the California house for a hectic round of parties, including one for the financial backers of *Magnolias,* whose London premiere the Rosses would be attending after *Heaven* wrapped on February 2. The trip was a combined work-plus-vacation for Herbert; his task was to help promote *Magnolias* in the international marketplace.

The London premiere of *Steel Magnolias* was a Royal Command Performance and benefit attended by the Prince and Princess of Wales. The big ceremony at the event, which took place at the Odeon theater in Leicester Square, was not the showing of the film itself but the presentation of the stars—and the director—to the Royals before the seating.

Typically at these events, the lineup facing the Royals for presentation consists only of the people connected with the motion picture or movie studio, while their spouses, or guests, usually stand behind them in a second line. The Royals come prepared with little bits of biographical information about the movie people and they begin at one end of the line, and then after a handshake and some brief conversation—one is not allowed to speak until the Royals have spoken first—they move on to the next person. At the Odeon theater there was a first mezzanine level and lobby where almost everyone from *Steel Magnolias* was to line up, and Charles and Diana were to greet some people downstairs and then come up the big staircase and greet more people along the line there.

"Now, I was organizing this," said Steve Klain, the Columbia Pictures employee in charge of the event, "and going into this we were told that Lee was really, really difficult, and that she wanted to be known as Princess [Lee still hadn't

worked that one out!], and she was always 'Radziwill' and
never Ross. When I told Herb where he would stand—this
was months ahead—he said to me, 'I am really sorry, but I
can't stand in the reception line,' and I said, 'Why not?' and
he said, 'Because Lee is not going to be in the line,' and I
said, 'Herb, you understand this is only for people connected
with the production, and Lee will be standing right behind
you.' He said, 'I feel very strongly about this. It's not going
to happen.' So I ran to Ray [Stark] immediately and told him
about it, and, again, it was something like, 'That bitch!' Ray
had sharp words with Herb, and he eventually acquiesced.''

    The night of the premiere, Lee was present at the Odeon
theater standing right where she belonged—in the second line
behind her husband. After it disbanded, as she and Herbert
entered the hall to see the film, Klain handed each of them
numbered tickets and told them, ''You are one behind the
other.'' The seating arrangement for viewing the movie followed the same principle as the presentation: the principals sat
in the front row with their spouses and guests directly behind
them in the second row. But as Lee came down the aisle, she
spotted an empty seat in the front row and made a beeline for
it. She sat down with Herbert on her left and Prince Charles
on her right, either one or two seats away—accounts vary—
knowing full well that she had absolutely no right to be there.

    Talk about changing your placement! According to Edward
Shugrue, president of Tri-Star's Film Distribution Inc., who
was involved in the incident and under whose signature a letter
was deliberately leaked to the press afterward as a way of
adding fuel to the fire of condemnation, the seat next to Prince
Charles was reserved for Olympia Dukakis, and the one next
to her for Julia Roberts. Since Dukakis had seniority over Roberts in terms of seating, it was Roberts's seat Lee had usurped.

    When Columbia executives spotted Lee in the front row,
they went up to her as unobtrusively as possible and asked her
to move: ''She pretended she didn't hear anyone and stared
straight ahead and held firm,'' Klain recalled. Then Roberts
and Dukakis came down the aisle, apparently together. Julia
whispered to Lee that she was sitting in her seat. Lee would
not move. Julia repeated herself, and still Lee was intransigent.
In desperation, Julia sought the assistance of others. Several
people came down the aisle on her behalf and implored Lee

to give up her seat. One of those who approached her was Ray Stark, who tapped her on the shoulder and spoke to her softly. Still, Lee would not move. Never one to mince words, Stark whispered in her ear: "Lee, you are a cunt."

In the meantime, Charles and Diana kept hearing "wrong seat, wrong seat," in spite of all the whispering. As a result, Diana got up, with Charles quickly following: they thought *they* were in the wrong seats! An embarrassing flurry ensued with Charles and Diana trying to relocate but no one knowing where to go. When the Prince and Princess of Wales stood up to move about, pandemonium broke out in the theater, and every person there connected with Columbia Pictures had an anxiety attack: nothing is more nuanced and finely wrought in protocol-conscious England than who gets close to the Royals and why. Proper placement is submitted months ahead for approval by Buckingham Palace for security reasons as well. "It was really a very, very embarrassing, awkward situation," attested Klain, "and a panic for us but in a sense rather absurd to see the Prince and Princess of Wales having to stand up and change seats on account of Lee Radziwill."

Charles and Diana's movements touched off a chain reaction in the front row, with everybody moving around, and when it all settled down, Julia Roberts *and* Olympia Dukakis were displaced to the second row! That happened because no one was where he or she was supposed to be any longer, except Lee, who *still did not move* from her seat in the front row—Shugrue said that after this final shake-up Lee wound up right next to the Prince—while poor Julia Roberts, visibly shaken, with tears welling in her eyes—the real star of the show—was forced, along with Olympia Dukakis, to sit elsewhere. "It was shameful. Horrendous," said Steve Klain.

The incident cast a pall over the rest of the evening. At the party after the film at The Elephant, a restaurant on the Thames River, the atmosphere was thick with tension. When the Rosses and Ray Stark first arrived, Herbert approached Stark, who refused to have anything to do with him, although they had been friends for years. Stark just turned on his heels and walked away. During the course of the evening, Herbert kept going over to Steve Klain, saying, "It was a mistake! Ray shouldn't be angry! Explain to Ray it was a mistake!" Klain did as he was asked. "That was no mistake," Stark replied in a cold and steely voice. "That was no mistake."

"What Lee did was devastating for Herbert!" raged a source close to the situation. "It was unforgivable because it hurt him a lot with his career. Ray Stark could certainly do a number on Herbert if he wanted to—he and Columbia Pictures are one—and for a long period the two men were quiet. By not standing up to Lee, Herbert jeopardized Columbia's position, jeopardized the Prince, and jeopardized his own standing in England."

This did not die. For days afterward, Lee's behavior had the social and show business worlds talking of little else. From Los Angeles to London, she was roundly criticized and universally condemned. Guests on talk shows lacerated her. The press had a field day. Lee's friends expressed disbelief that she would ever do such a thing. Her critics called her a desperado; they said she broke every rule and what she did was what they expected from someone of her character. "Lee is very misunderstood," Herbert said lamely, convincing no one.

"He probably did not realize how many people regarded her with disdain," offered a colleague of his. "They had a very fast courtship, and he doesn't have a lot of experience with women in certain respects. He didn't understand when he married her that she was going to be a liability for him with all the people he has to suck up to."

One has to really wonder where Herbert Ross's common sense and good judgment were in all of this. "I'll tell you something about that," offered a studio executive in explanation of Herbert's apparent refusal to intervene on his stars' behalf. "I had several dealings with Mr. and Mrs. Ross, and I really got the impression that she leads him around by his you-know-what sometimes and that, for whatever glory and social elevation he gets out of it, he takes it. It's all part of a pattern of weakness. Lee just seems to take the lead, and whatever Lola wants, Lola gets." Certainly Lee was calling all the shots in her marriage to Herbert, just as she had done in her other marriages. Beard, Tufo, Cope, and Meier all stood their own ground with her, but she married men she could manipulate.

From all appearances, Lee usurped that front-row seat at the premiere of *Steel Magnolias* in indignation at not being allowed to stand in the presentation line to meet the Royals. Her behavior spoke to her driving obsession to always be out in front, and it brought out the worst in her. Lee put her own self-importance and status-seeking ahead of her husband's welfare, ahead of courtesy and decency and doing the right thing. No matter that her exclusion from the front row was an industry ranking in a business she had nothing to do with whatsoever. Being in the second row meant being publicly ranked as the second-place finisher she really was. It symbolized her lack of standing in the world and confirmed that she was just a footnote in other people's histories.

To Lee, the message delivered by the establishment that denied her the status of a front-row seat was the one that she heard in her nightmares all her life: No matter what you do or how much you try, they still don't think you belong there.

50. *Life in the '90s*

Herbert Ross had always worked steadily and relished variety. After a very brief respite in New York upon his return from London, he flew immediately to Virginia without Lee to begin *True Colors,* a political drama for Paramount that he had been preparing before *My Blue Heaven* was offered to him. Since the film was shot in Virginia and Washington for the most part, Lee could fly in and out a lot easier, and she would come down now and again for weekends or for a few days at a time. On a couple of visits she brought her children with her to Charlottesville so that they could watch the film being made.

Tina became very interested in the process and helped Herbert with the editing postproduction by arranging the film on reels for him. It made her ponder whether she wanted to pursue a career in film production. Up to then she had been working in the decorative arts doing trompe l'oeil on commission. After graduating from Brearley (she transferred there from Hewitt because she did not find it challenging enough), Tina took the Sotheby's Fine Arts Training course in London before setting herself up in New York painting illusions on floors and walls for her clients. She was very talented at it and did anything from faux marble and wood to fake bookcases. One client was Rudolf Nureyev, for whom she painted a wall at his

Dakota apartment with which he was very pleased. Another time she was asked to paint the floor of a display room for a well-attended decorators' showcase.

Tina was still extremely reticent and shy, and still very much the odd-person-out at functions with her extroverted Kennedy cousins. "She always seemed like this lost kid who was wandering around and no one knew who the hell she was," said Brian Quigley, a photographer whose specialty was the Kennedys. "I always felt bad for Tina. It seemed no one was very friendly to her, except Jackie."

"Tina still has emotional handicaps," acknowledged a friend of hers, "and Jackie's kids, too, were dominated by a tyrannical mother. I remember Rudolf Nureyev once said to Caroline: 'Why in God's name did you name your baby Rose?' and she said, 'I didn't name her. My mother did.' And what did Jackie need more money from Rose [Kennedy] for?"

Other friends claim Tina has shed her mother's concrete grip and really blossomed. Still others, like Ed Pisoni, who got to know her on the making of *True Colors,* say that she is only in the process of doing so: "It is hard to get over the problems of childhood at her age," he pointed out. "Yet I think Tina has reached a point now where she is growing up. She's coming into her own. One can see little glimmers of her making it, and eventually she will make it. Tina will be just dandy one of these days."

Of course, despite all of Lee's shortcomings as a mother, it is possible that Tina was not affected as much as one might think by having been in her mother's shadow, or even by Lee's having neglected her, but rather, her problems may have begun, in ways we do not understand, when she weighed only two and a half pounds at birth.

One Sunday afternoon in May, Lee gave an especially nice party to celebrate Herbert's birthday and invited the cast and crew of *True Colors.* She rented the Evelynton plantation outside of Richmond for the day from the family who owned it. The magnificent grounds ran down to the James River, and a tent was set up in back of the house for dining and dancing to a live band.

Another magnificent house on the water with great views came into the Rosses' lives in May of 1990 when Herbert purchased (significantly enough, in his name only) an ocean-front, twin-gabled manse in East Hampton for $4,950,500. (Many felt the $5 million he paid for the house was overpriced by at least $2 million.) Lee's dream house, located on the Highway Behind the Pond just west of the Maidstone Club of her childhood, turned into a nightmare when she and Herbert discovered shortly after moving into their traditional structure that a hideous contemporary house of reinforced concrete and steel was going up next door.

A nearly thirty-foot-high cement wall connected to the house ran down the side of the lot adjacent to their home, ruining their western view. A frustrating round of litigation followed, with the Rosses claiming the wall was a fence, not an integral part of the design of the house, and that, as such, should be torn down because it was higher than the town allowance. The wall was deemed by the authorities to be just that, an integral part of the house, not a fence, and they lost their case. "I would not have bought the house had I known those plans existed," Herbert told the local zoning board. "I have been deceived, used, and abused."

Once Lee had talked Herbert into buying a house in East Hampton, the decision to sell the California ranch followed in short order. It was a huge cash drain, and he did not have the kind of money to swing both places. Lee told Herbert the ranch was "too far out," but even if it were on the very outskirts of Los Angeles, it is doubtful that it would have made any difference. She was not really interested in living in California. Newton Cope had certainly been correct in his assessment when he said that after so many months Lee would get antsy and want to be back in New York, where, for her, all the action was. "You gotta be blind!" was how he put it. Well, Herbert was blind.

"I knew it!" said Tony Hail. "I knew Lee wasn't going to live in California, and she didn't want to live next to Doug Cramer and build that tacky house. But I don't understand how she could talk Herbert into selling his land. He didn't give it up easily, I can tell you that." Herbert wanted to keep the ranch, no doubt. He had put a lot of time, labor, and money into it. When one of his crew on *Heaven,* his production designer, Chuck Rosen, showed him some wallpaper in the French farmhouse style he thought he might like for his house,

Herbert got very nostalgic and said mournfully: "That is all a past dream now. I don't have my farmhouse in Provence anymore. I am selling it."

But Herbert did love California, and selling the ranch was just one more in the series of concessions he made to please Lee and maintain their relationship. In addition to his home and all its furnishings, right down to his favorite bedroom clock, he gave up his Portuguese cook, his housekeeper, his longtime assistant, his office in Los Angeles, and now his retirement dream ranch. Only when he was directing movies did he retain his autonomy. Otherwise, when Lee married Herbert Ross, she hauled him to New York and made him an appendage to her life there. It was what Blair Fuller had noticed of her so many years earlier: Lee the drill sergeant. "Herb is well intentioned, but he is a weak man who married two strong women," acknowledged a friend of his.

The ranch was sold in March of 1991 to the actor James Garner and his wife, Lois, for about $3 million.

True Colors wrapped in June, and after a busy summer renovating and socializing in the Hamptons, the Rosses made a trip to Venice in September to attend Giorgio Armani's spectacular Moorish soiree for 170 hand-picked guests celebrating the Venice Film Festival and its closing night film, *Made in Milan,* a documentary about the fashion master at work. The party was given in the garden of Count Giovanni Volpi's water-bound villa, where Lee and Herbert stayed as houseguests. Director Ross was one of the first to appreciate what a masterpiece of production the party was, complete with a huge silken tent, thousands of jasmine buds, half-naked Venetians dressed as Moors, and a delicious dinner from Harry's Bar.

The twenty-six-minute film about Armani's career was directed by the much-feted Martin Scorsese, but it drew critical fire because it was considered industry-insider footage that did not belong at a movie festival. "Armani was bold enough to show it at the Venice Film Festival when there was nothing artistic about it," said one of his employees. "It was a dull story, which only those in the fashion business would be interested in."

Looking stylish and cool in white, Lee acted as a hostess at the affair and sat herself down for dinner in between Giorgio and Martin Scorsese. Gore Vidal was at the same table, and not once during the course of the evening did he and Lee speak to each other or even make eye contact. The whole affair repeated itself in New York—minus the film festival, the Moors, and the canal—at the Museum of Modern Art at the end of the following month, appropriately enough, on Halloween.

Lee's duties for Armani expanded in other ways when, largely thanks to her effort, he became a major corporate funder for American public television, specifically the much acclaimed *American Masters* series of profiles on Channel 13 in New York. The series celebrated America's cultural heritage and the spirit and achievements of its national treasure of artists. It was astute of Lee to realize what a clever promotional strategy it was to identify Armani with an eclectic mix of creative geniuses and what an excellent way it was for him to enter the sponsorship arena in this country.

Eventually Lee was named to the board of Channel 13. "I always found her comfortable to be with and was amused to discover how often she was at home watching Channel 13 instead of out partying at some social function," said Dr. Bill Baker, the president of the station. "I used to tease her about it."

For her second wedding anniversary that same September, Lee asked a local artist, Barbara Siebel Thomas, to paint several views of the East Hampton property as a gift for Herbert. She wanted four watercolors done—one of the house itself, another of the patio with a view of the ocean beyond, and the other two comprised of a series of snapshotlike images, which she pointed out to the artist on a tour of the house and grounds: the corner of the library, a hat rack in the hall, the dog asleep on a chaise, the entrance gate, her garden, and the path down to the beach. Herbert was very pleased with his imaginative present and the pictures became part of the house.

The Rosses spent Christmas of 1990 on St. Barts, a speck of an island in the French West Indies. They rented the same $10,000-a-week house used at separate times by Tom Hanks, Jane Fonda, and David Letterman. Home base for the gang was a bluff-top, three-bedroom villa on the north coast. (Herbert and Lee liked it so much that they would return the following Christmas.)

Early in the new year, while Herbert edited *True Colors,* the Rosses rented for a few weeks the same Beverly Hills house that they had the previous year. Lee made daily excursions to the exercise room at the Beverly Hills Hotel where she worked out like a pro, while Herb could be found almost daily at the Beverly Hills Coffee Shop, along with the rest of Hollywood. Wendy Stark, Ray's daughter, gave a dinner on behalf of her father to welcome back the Rosses—seated, to be sure.

True Colors, a film set in Washington about the collision course of friendship and ambition, starring John Cusack and James Spader, did not do very well at the box office, nor had *My Blue Heaven.* Having two pictures in a row that sank was humbling for Herbert, and he vowed to take his time selecting his next project. Also, doing his last two pictures one right on top of the other had truly exhausted him. He decided to take a year off to rest and devote more time to his new marriage.

Herbert was slowing down both from age and from the pressure Lee put on him for attention. But there was something else. While making *True Colors,* the director felt a certain distance that had never been there before, an increased desire to spend more time alone. He said it was a consequence of changes in his personal life. "I have moved at least once every seven years," he told a reporter at the time. "I recently closed my office in California and now that I don't live in L.A., I feel more disconnected. I have no contract with a studio, and I haven't been this liberated for a long time. I wanted to bust [my life] open so I could start fresh." It was time to move on.

One of the first things the Rosses did with Herbert's newfound spare time was to spend a month in the springtime relaxing in Provence. The sojourn delighted both of them. "I spend a lot of time talking with Herbert," said Dan Melnick, the producer for whom he had directed his first Broadway show. "He and I have known each other forever, and I know he sure enjoys what he and Lee are doing with their lives. Herbert is doing things he never did before—like renting that house in Provence, and being in the Hamptons for the summer. I am jealous of how happy he is. Herbert is incredibly happy, amazingly happy."

A longtime Kennedy friend of Lee's noticed the same thing about her when he had dinner with the Rosses one night: "The dinner was nice and quiet and I thought, 'This is great. All the static is gone.' That's the best possible way I can describe it—this new relationship of Lee's had no static. This one was easy. It just looked like she was with the right guy. Ross is a good fellow, the best thing that has ever happened to her. Here Lee was, splattered around from one crisis to another, and now she's walking down the street with Herb Ross, and they're both happy.

"Lee was always nagged by some crippled ambition, and unfortunately the goading never disappeared, either because she did not have the talent to nurture or the steadfastness to carry on. That was what was so great about that dinner with Ross. It looked as though she had finally just brushed it all aside. She has come to grips with herself."

But if Jackie had remained in the public eye in her last years, Lee still would have been struggling a lot more. It was not so much that Lee had outgrown the sibling competition with her marriage to Ross as it was that with Jackie out of view the pressure to compete had lessened.

Lee has always been seen out in public a great deal more than her sister had, in any case. Added to her customary assortment of social activities these days are many movie screenings and openings and other Hollywood-related doings. "She and Ross cling to each other in public," observed the photographer Brian Quigley. "They are arm-in-arm, or else they are holding hands, and Ross is so dapper and debonair. One time Lee wore a see-through dress to an event at Lincoln Center you wouldn't believe, it was so out of character for her. It was shocking. Her breasts looked pretty good and were much larger than Jackie's—I saw those naked photos of her. And the way Ross was holding Lee, it was like he was very proud of her and it was his idea that she was wearing that dress."

"They certainly seem to be very affectionate," agreed a female friend of Herbert's. "Lee seems to be very close to him all the time, and he likes that. He is flattered that she is so needy of him. It flatters any male ego. Lee is very possessive, and if another woman looks at Herbert, she becomes very insecure. She is jealous of anybody that might make a pass at him. She is a man's woman that way."

In the Rosses' habitual round of nights out when Herbert isn't working, they are often seen at whatever packed, frenzied restaurant is the place of the moment. They have the kind of sparkle Lee likes, and the noise and the wall-to-wall crush make her feel that she is in the right place at the right time. "You always see Lee in those places," confirmed another savvy New York restaurant goer, Elaine Baxter, "and I remember one time what was so funny about it. It was a godforsaken night, absolutely pouring, a rainstorm beyond rainstorms, and to my great annoyance I had a social obligation that required that I be all the way downtown in Soho at that restaurant 150 Wooster when it was very hot, or else I wouldn't have been there for all the tea in China. Well, in walked Lee Radziwill and Herbert Ross, and I thought, 'My God, I can't believe it, that they would come all that distance in the pouring rain just for *this*,' because who would? Her son was with her. I remember how handsome he was. Ross looked fabulous and interesting and exciting and powerful."

"I'll say one thing about Herbert," said a friend. "He is in great physical shape because of Lee. He goes to trainers now. His diet and weight are much better than before he married her. She is a fitness freak and doesn't eat anything at all." Herbert said of life with his second wife: "You don't know what it's like to be married to this lady. She's up early and out jogging before she has breakfast. Boy, it's like being married to someone who is training for the gold!" Lee cracked the whip with her son, Anthony, as well. Always naturally stocky in his physique, she got him a personal trainer to knock him into shape, and now he runs marathons.

Her own regimen is equally strict. By the nineties, with the spell of Camelot broken and her own wattage dimmed appreciably, Lee's ability to stay in the limelight depends upon her appearance. Although she has always cultivated her looks in an effort to cultivate the press, obviously, with age, it takes even more of an effort to look attractive. There are the workouts, the spas, and the face-lifts, in addition to the never-ending visits to the masseuse, the manicurist, and the hairdresser. The success of all that effort in Lee's case is a matter of opinion. The majority view is that she looks fabulous for her age. To a significant dissenting few like Laura Pyzel Clark, the *Harper's Bazaar* editor who knew her in the fifties and who ran into her again in recent years, Lee is "like one of Tom Wolfe's 'social x-rays,' those thin, thin New York girls. She looked like she had just been blown away. I think she lost her real beauty to be so excruciatingly thin. That's what they like, though, the New York girls. It was a shock to see her with her skin drawn so tightly over her face."

So for all of the false career starts and the attention paid Lee Radziwill over the years, she has remained a prisoner of her generation after all. A man had to come into her life to give it some direction, and she ended up spending her time like any stereotypical fifties housewife—primping and shopping and spending her husband's money. Still, many would agree with a friend of hers who told her, "You have had an extraordinary life. If you die tomorrow, I won't be sad. I'll just sigh."

"I don't have any unfulfilled ambitions," Lee once declared. "I think I have a wonderful life. I have been very spoilt by my husband, and I couldn't really ask for more, except, perhaps, to be remembered nicely by my family when I'm gone." Lee was referring to Stas when she made those remarks, but surely her comments apply, more truthfully, to her present husband. Later she added, "Like Edith Piaf, I regret nothing in my life—absolutely nothing."

Not quite. During the summer of 1991, Robert Wilson, a major figure in avant-garde theater, received a flurry of telephone calls from Lee, who expressed a great interest in starring in one of his productions. Wilson is known for austere, dreamlike, slow-motion ventures, usually protracted, which deconstruct the conventional rules of the theater in order to allow him to begin all over again in pursuit of his own controversial and bizarre vision. Evidently Lee was trying to persuade him to arrange one of his latest productions around her (he usually has several going on at one time) and to bend him to her will by suggesting ideas on wardrobe and where she thought the show should open. Wilson complained to friends that he had never expressed any interest whatsoever in using Lee Radziwill on stage and that he was extremely annoyed at her persistence. Furthermore, he thought she had a serious reality problem.

Lee's behavior in that episode shows that despite the decades of attention, despite her recovery from alcoholism, despite her marriage to Herbert Ross, she has never given up her dream, forever unrealized, of being a star in her own right, the dream that simply will not come true for her. Not content to be "the sister of," "the friend of," or even "the wife of," her craving for adulation has never abated. Faint but persistent, like an echo that follows her wherever she goes, she can still hear that audience in Philadelphia clapping. It was lukewarm applause to be sure, but it was applause all the same.

"I wasn't so bad as an actress, was I?"

Epilogue

May 23, 1994, was bright and summerlike, reminiscent of the day Jack Bouvier had been buried. When Lee arrived at Saint Ignatius Loyola Roman Catholic Church on Park Avenue for the funeral of her sister, she was in a stretch limousine and she had plenty of room to stretch because she was all alone. Herbert Ross was nowhere to be seen, and people wondered if he were ill, and about the state of their marriage. In fact, he was shooting a film in California (*Boys on the Side*) and decided not to go to the wake or the funeral ceremony, citing the enormous cost of delaying the movie for even one day. As Lee stepped from the car dressed in a slim black suit and wearing dark glasses, she appeared to the many gawking onlookers to be poised and aloof. But inwardly she was still seething over the family's refusal to let her, Jackie's only living sister, speak at the service. Instead, Tina, beloved by Jackie, was allowed to give a reading, and Anthony was an honorary pallbearer.*

Jackie had died of lymphatic cancer a few days earlier, and Lee's lack of standing at the funeral was the family's tacit acknowledgement of the frayed connection between the two

*The following August, Anthony dedicated his marriage ceremony at Most Holy Trinity Church in East Hampton to the memory of his aunt Jackie and to the memory of his father. He had met his bride, Carole Ann DiFalco, a fellow ABC newsmagazine producer (of *Day One*), while covering the Menendez trial in California. Lee, resurrecting the family title and referring to Anthony as "Prince Radziwill," sent out invitations to the royalty of Europe for the lavish reception she gave for the couple at her home. To her chagrin, none of them came.

women. During the brief burial ceremony at Arlington National Cemetery, where Jackie was laid to rest next to John Kennedy, Lee felt she was once again pushed into the background.

Her resentment that day, however, was slight compared to the rage she felt the following week when Jackie's will was made public: Lee was cut out of it entirely. With not even so much as a trinket left to her, at least as a gesture, Lee was deeply—and publicly—mortified. And also, of course, by the time she died, Jackie, through shrewd investments, had a lot of money to give away. Her will stated clearly that she was making no provision for Lee because she had already done so in her lifetime. So what if Jackie had helped her with money in the past, Lee fumed. What are families for anyway? Jackie still should have left her something! After all, she left Anthony and Tina the income from $500,000 trust funds that she had set up for each of them, and she helped them in the past, too.

Those who were sympathetic to Lee thought that Jackie's decision was one more indication of her mean streak. Those in Jackie's camp said that Lee was so chronically jealous and resentful of her sister that Jackie's decision was understandable. By her gesture, Jackie, as expected, had the last word, once and for all.

The emotions Lee felt at her sister's death were complex. In a real sense she knew she had lost her other self, and from the moment the previous winter when she had learned that Jackie was seriously threatened by cancer she was concerned only for her sister's well-being and recovery.

Jackie's illness was brief. After the diagnosis was made in January, she underwent therapy, and at first her cancer went into remission, but by March it had spread to her brain. As late as April, however, she was still going to work at Doubleday and otherwise trying to follow her regular routine with as little interruption as possible. By May the cancer spread to her liver, and on the eighteenth, after the doctors said they could do nothing more for her, Jackie discharged herself from the hospital, where she had been undergoing her latest treatment and then, once home, she staged her own death as carefully as she had controlled her image in life.

After spending the day saying good-bye to the steady stream of friends, kin, and Kennedys she had carefully selected and summoned, she had her doctor give her medication to hasten her death. Jackie saw no point in staying alive only to suffer until her fast-approaching end. That same evening, her family gathered around her in a solemn vigil, and as she slipped into a coma, Lee remained close by. When Lee left at midnight, Jackie, who died the next night, was already unconscious and, in effect, gone from her kin forever, but not before the indissoluble bond between the two sisters had unabashedly reasserted itself. The animosity of late receded, leaving that primal essence, that indelible part of each other they both were. All they had meant to each other and shared in the past came back to Lee, and as she left Jackie's apartment building, going past the throngs of reporters, cameramen, television trucks, and mourners gathered in front, she cried freely and unashamedly for her loss.

The day after the funeral Lee went into a stationery store on Madison Avenue. There, across from the candy and cigarettes, she quickly scanned the racks of periodicals. Curious customers watched, wondering exactly which of the publications she planned to buy, for Jackie's face graced so many. They were surprised when she, like any zealous fan, suddenly began scooping up one copy each of every single magazine that paid tribute to her sister. Then she paid her bill and headed home.

Notes on Sources

Lee Radziwill declined to be interviewed for this book. Quoted material attributed to her was taken primarily from magazine and newspaper interviews she has given over the years. Other comments came from personal interviews.

Preface
As part of the research for this book, the author attended an Alcoholics Anonymous meeting at Saint Luke's Episcopal Church, Lee's home group.

Lee's remarks about her childhood are contained in Gloria Steinem's February 1968 interview with her for *McCall's* magazine, "And Starring . . . Lee Bouvier!"

Chapter One: Bouviers and Lees
The author gathered information in this chapter from many sources too numerous to mention here. Chief among the books consulted were C. David Heymann's well-researched *A Woman Named Jackie* and John H. Davis's solid family biographies *The Bouviers: Portrait of an American Family* and *The Kennedys: Dynasty and Disaster 1848–1983*, respectively.

Heymann's reporting detailed the fraudulent claims of John Vernou Bouvier, Jr.'s, family genealogy, *Our Forebears*.

I might also mention Kathleen Bouvier's *To Jack With Love*. The rest of the books consulted are listed in the bibliography and were used very selectively.

Chapter Two: Jack and Janet
Among the sources consulted by the author for this chapter other than those cited in Chapter One were "Opening Chapters," an article Lee wrote for *Ladies' Home Journal* in January 1973, and a July 14, 1967, cover story on her in *Life* by Jane Howard, "The Princess Goes on Stage."

Chapter Three: Original Sins
Previously indicated sources were helpful in this chapter. The anecdote about the piano recital was described to the author during an interview with an anonymous source.

Chapter Four: Jackie's Little Sister
Stephen Birmingham's *Jacqueline Bouvier Kennedy Onassis* was among the books consulted for this chapter.

An interview with C. David Heymann provided some details of Lee's childhood that he had uncovered in his own reporting and generously shared with me.

Details of Lee's experience with the family horse Dancestep were taken from "Opening Chapters," *Ladies' Home Journal*, January 1973.

Jenny Kuehn, the spokesperson for the subsequent owners of Hammersmith Farm, provided useful details on the estate, as did Janet Auchincloss's oral history at the Kennedy Library. A former decorator of the mansion, Elisabeth Draper, was also interviewed.

Other material in this chapter comes from interviews with Doris Francisco and some of Lee's relatives and early associates: Jamie Auchincloss, Logan Bentley, John H. Davis, Cecilia "Sherry" Parker Geyelin, and Rue Hill Hubert.

Chapter Five: Auchincloss Years
For Lee's comment "Quite a lot was expected . . ." see "Lee Radziwill In Search of Herself," Charlotte Curtis, *McCall's*, January 1975.

"It's funny, isn't it? . . ." and "I went through a period . . ." were taken from "And Starring . . . Lee Bouvier!" *McCall's* February 1968.

"I spent my whole life . . ." is from "Lee" by Andy Warhol, *Interview*, March 1975.

Personal interviews for this chapter were conducted with Florence Borda, John H. Davis, Rue Hill Hubert, Jay Mellon, Sherry Parker Geyelin, Chauncey G. Parker III, Howard Cushing, Jr., Clare Fahnestock Moorehead, Robin Corbin, Jamie Auchincloss, Daphne Sellar Thornton, Greg Strauss, Peter Reed, Jonathan Tapper, and Ross Claiborne.

Chapter Six: School Days
The material in this chapter is based primarily on interviews with Lee's early friends and her teachers and classmates at Miss Porter's School: Alice Gordon Abbett, Flora Lutz, Grace Comans, Katherine Smedley Yellig, Jane Vaughn Love, Carlin Whitney Scherer, Jill Fuller Fox, Elisavietta Artamonoff Ritchie, Howard Cushing, Jr., Florence Borda, Edith McBride Bass, Adrienne Osborne Ives, Phebe Thompson Burke, B. Bartram Cadbury, Anne Fennelly Patterson, and Joan Pierce Kernan.

Lee's remark "I believe I survived. . . ." was taken from *One Special Summer*.

Chapter Seven: Coming Out
Much of the information in this chapter is based on interviews with David Warren, Greg Strauss, Yale Toland, C. David Heymann, Rue Hill Hubert, Cass Canfield, Jr., Irma Dewey Larom, Edith McBride Bass, Tony Hail, Robin Corbin, Alice Gordon Abbett, Jane Vaughn Love, Chauncey Parker, and Talbot Adamson.

Kathleen Bouvier's *To Jack With Love* and *Maxine Cheshire, Reporter* were among the books consulted.

Newport: Pleasures and Palaces by Nancy Sirkis provided useful information about Newport.

The archives of Newport's newspapers provided the author with information about Lee's social activities.

Details of Lee's debut were obtained from the archives of Washington, New York, and Newport newspapers.

Chapter Eight: Deb of the Year

The author conducted interviews in this chapter with John P. Marquand, Jr., Rue Hill Hubert, Dick Blodget, Alice Gordon Abbett, Oleg Cassini, Blair Fuller, and Michael Tree.

Rose Kennedy's *Times to Remember* and Ralph Martin's *A Hero for Our Times* were among the books consulted.

Janet Auchincloss's comment appeared in a cover story on Lee in *People*, November 1, 1976.

The *New York Times* newspaper morgue was helpful on details of Lee's deb season.

The photograph of Lee as Deb of the Year appeared in *Life*, December 25, 1950.

The story of Lee's offer for a screen test is contained in "Lee Radziwill's Search for Herself," an article by John J. Miller in *The Column*, December 17, 1972.

Lee's comments on her European trip were taken from *One Special Summer*.

Chapter Nine: Royalty?

The material on Michael Canfield is based on interviews with his family, friends, and associates: Blair Fuller, George Plimpton, Alastair Forbes, Jill Fuller Fox, John Marquand, Chauncey Parker, Thomas Guinzburg, Jonathan Churchill, Fred Gwynne, John Appleton, Cass Canfield, Jr., Lewis Preston, Stuart Preston, William Preston, and William Douglas-Home.

The present Lord Acton (the fourth baron) and the author James Fox also gave the author helpful information.

Cass Canfield's oral history at Columbia University and his memoir, *Up and Down and Around*, were useful for details of his days in London as Harper's representative.

The author gathered information on Prince George's background from many sources. Worth mentioning here: *The Kents* by Audrey Whiting and *Edward VIII* by Frances Donaldson.

That Prince George was "a scamp" can be found in *The Windsor Story* by J. Bryan and Charles Murphy.

An account of Kiki Preston's drug habit appeared in James Fox's *White Mischief*.

Prince George's love affair with Kiki Preston has been documented in many sources. Accounts of it utilized by the author are contained in Philip Ziegler's *King Edward VIII* and Sarah Bradford's *The Reluctant King*.

A copy of Michael Canfield's adoption papers were provided to the author by Cass Canfield, Jr.

Chapter Ten: Diana Vreeland's Magazine

Personal interviews were conducted in this chapter with George Plimpton, Blair Fuller, Jill Fuller Fox, Rue Hill Hubert, Laura Pyzel Clark, Barbara Slifka, Thomas Guinzburg, Adrienne Osborne Ives, and John Appleton.

Andy Warhol's *Exposures* provided some details about Diana Vreeland's reign at *Harper's Bazaar*.

Mary deLimur Weinmann's comments appeared in *A Woman Named Jackie*. D. D. Ryan's and Polly Mellon's quotes were taken from "War of the Poses," by Michael Gross, *New York*, April 27, 1992.

"My mother taught me . . . ," "I didn't write copy . . . ," and "Sarah Lawrence wouldn't let me . . ." are from Gloria Steinem, *McCall's*, February 1968.

Chapter Eleven: Marrying Michael

Personal interviews were conducted with John Marquand, Cass Canfield, Jr., Jill Fox, Tom Guinzburg, Cleveland Amory, Blair Fuller, Mary Lumet, Rue Hill Hubert, Laura Pyzel Clark, Jonathan Churchill, Philip Geyelin, and Chauncey Parker.

Some details of the Canfields' family history were taken from Cass Canfield's *Up and Down and Around*.

The rowboat incident appeared in Pat Collier and David Horowitz's *The Kennedys: An American Drama*.

Chapter Twelve: Sister Brides

Personal interviews were conducted with Jonathan Churchill, Blair Fuller, John Marquand, Chauncey Parker, Sherry Parker Geyelin, Jill Fuller Fox, John Appleton, Alastair Forbes, Laura Pyzel Clark, Tom Guinzburg, and George Plimpton.

Mini Rhea's *I Was Jacqueline Kennedy's Dressmaker* was a useful source for this chapter.

The author gathered details of the Canfield wedding from the archives of several newspapers.

Janet Auchincloss's oral history at the Kennedy Library and the archives of the Newport *News* were helpful for details of the Bouvier-Kennedy nuptials.

Chapter Thirteen: After the Honeymoon

Personal interviews were conducted with Blair Fuller, Cass Canfield, Jr., Jonathan Churchill, Jill Fuller Fox, John Appleton, Tom Guinzburg, Carol Philips, and Cathy di Montezemolo.

"I am afraid . . ." is from Gloria Steinem, *McCall's*.

Chapter Fourteen: A Visit from Jackie
Interviews were conducted with Chauncey Parker, Tony Hail, Tom Guinzburg, Philip Geyelin, Alastair Forbes, Peter Ward, Angela O'Ferrall, Michael Tree, and William Douglas-Home.

Michael Canfield's personal diaries, made available to the author by the executor of his estate, Hugo Vickers, provided much useful information in this and subsequent chapters concerning the Canfields' social activities.

Chapter Fifteen: Le Beau Monde
Interviews were conducted with Blair Fuller, William Douglas-Home, Lord Lambton, Belinda, Lady Lambton, Philip Geyelin, Chauncey Parker, Alastair Forbes, John Marquand, John Appleton, Cass Canfield, Jr., Jill Fuller Fox, Peter Ward, and Michael Tree.

Information on the Duke of Beaufort's background came from several English newspaper and magazine sources.

Chapter Sixteen: Prince Radziwill
Interviews were conducted with Jill Fuller Fox, Alastair Forbes, Lady Lambton, Lord Lambton, William Douglas-Home, John Appleton, and David Metalfe.

"Stas was so brooding . . ." and "People I considered . . ." are from Gloria Steinem, *McCall's*.

Some facts of Stas Radziwill's background came from English newspaper sources.

A helpful account of Jack Bouvier's funeral appeared in Kathleen Bouvier's *To Jack With Love.*

"We were his life . . ." is from Charlotte Curtis, *McCall's*, January 1975.

Chapter Seventeen: The Bolting Coat
Interviews were conducted with Blair Fuller, Jill Fuller Fox, Cass Canfield, Jr., Mary Lumet, and Tom Guinzburg.

Lee's statements on fashion appeared in "There's Something About Them" by Wilhela Cushman, *Ladies' Home Journal*, December 1957.

"Everything serious in my life . . ." is from Helen Dudar, "A Natural for the Stage, Kitty Said," in the *New York Post*, June 24, 1967.

Chapter Eighteen: In VOGUE
Interviews were conducted with Cathy di Montezemolo, Mildred Morton Gilbert, Babs Simpson, Grace Mirabella, and Carol Phillips.

Print sources helpful for this chapter were *Vogue*'s tie-in issue with the Brussels World Fair, April 15, 1958, and Elsa Maxwell's *Celebrity Circus*.

"Garnering most of the attention . . ." was taken from the *New York Times*, April 18, 1958.

Chapter Nineteen: The Pauper Prince
Interviews were conducted with Gerald Smith, Sidney Morris, Leo Backer, Isabelle, Comtesse d'Ornano, Lady Ampthill, David Metcalfe, Vale Asche

Ackerman, Alastair Forbes, Andrew Ciechanowiecki, Henry Bresher, Michael Tree, Brigitte Gerney, Jo Bryce, and Greta Fenston.

Tadeusz Nowakowski's *The Radziwills* was useful on the history of the Radziwill family.

The author had the Radziwill pedigree traced and verified at The Institute of Heraldic and Genealogical Studies, Kent, England, and at a similar Polish institution.

A number of details of Stas Radziwill's background came from English newspapers.

Oliver Marriott's *The Property Boom* was a source for information on Stas's real estate business.

A version of Lee and Grace Dudley's rivalry appeared in "Princess Lee Radziwill," by Peter Evans, *Cosmopolitan*, March 1968.

Laura Marlborough's marital chart can be found in her memoir, *Laughter from a Cloud.*

Chapter Twenty: Holy Matrimony
Material in this chapter comes from a cover story on the Canfield annulment in *ABC* magazine, Milan, November 12, 1967, and supplemental newspaper coverage.

Interviews were conducted with Comtesse d'Ornano, Rue Hill Hubert, Cass Canfield, Jr., Blair Fuller, Andrew Ciechanowiecki, Lady Lambton, Alastair Forbes, and Jonathan Churchill.

Chapter Twenty-one: A Blissful Beginning
Interviews were conducted with Michael Hobson, David Metcalfe, Greta Fenston, Sherry Parker Geyelin, Nicholas Cobbold, Michael Tree, Ian Watson, Henry Bresher, Senator George Smathers, Arthur M. Schlesinger, Jr., David Powers, and Pierre Salinger.

Some details of Lee's London life appeared in a fashion personality series in *Vogue*, July 1960.

"This is really . . ." is from the London *Daily Express*, December 11, 1960.

"There are an awful lot . . ." is from the *Herald Tribune*, August 20, 1961.

Some of the facts of Lee's illness and her separation from her infant were taken from accounts in the English press.

Chapter Twenty-two: First Lady and Second Sister
Interviews were conducted with Philip Geyelin, Oleg Cassini, Leo Backer, Gerald Smith, C. L. Sulzberger, Jo Bryce, Gerald Clarke, and Eileen Slocum.

"Why do they always write about . . ." is from "In Hot Blood" by Sally Quinn, the *Washington Post*, June 6, 1979.

Some details of Lee's relationship with JFK were based on interviews with anonymous sources.

Information on Lee's activities when JFK was president was gathered from too many sources to mention here.

"We spent the rest of the night . . ." is from Kathleen Bouvier, *To Jack With Love.*

For a full description of Lee's critique of the 1961 Paris fashion collections, see "Women Who Make World Fashion," by Robin Douglas-Home and Wilhela Cushman, *Ladies' Home Journal*, October 1961.

"Had lunch with your new friend . . ." is from a note Truman Capote wrote to Cecil Beaton, February 2, 1962, courtesy of Gerald Clarke.

Chapter Twenty-three: Role Playing

The author gathered information on the State trip to India from several sources, including Letitia Baldridge's *Of Diamonds and Diplomats*, John Kenneth Galbraith's *Ambassador's Journal*, and Joan Braden's article for the *Saturday Evening Post*, "An Exclusive Chat With Jackie Kennedy," May 12, 1962.

Lee's comments about her India trip appeared in *One Special Summer*.

Sandra Paul's observations can be found in Peter Evans's *Cosmopolitan* article. "Ahh, Paris," by Lee Radziwill, appeared in *McCall's*, November 1962.

"A Conversation on Manners" by Lee Radziwill is contained in *Ladies' Home Journal*, February 1962.

"Jackie Kennedy's Perplexing Sister," Barbara Walter's account of Lee's India trip, appeared in *Good Housekeeping*, March 1963.

Interviews were conducted with John Mack Carter, Curtiss Anderson, and Cathy di Montezemolo. Benno Graziani answered questions in writing.

Chapter Twenty-four: Ari and Bobby

Interviews were conducted with Sidney Morris, David Metcalfe, Lady Lambton, David Powers, Comtesse d'Ornano, Taki Theodoracopulos, Maia Calligas, Helen Vlachos, Arthur M. Schlesinger, Jr., Alastair Forbes, Elisabeth, Lady Ampthill, Michael Tree, Charlotte Ford, and Sidney Gruson.

L. J. Davis's *Onassis, Aristotle and Christina* provided some facts on Onassis's background and behavior.

"Onassis was an outstanding man . . ." was taken from "Why My Sister Married Aristotle Onassis," an interview with Lee which appeared in *Cosmopolitan*, September 1968.

The anecdote about Stas's sleeping accommodations at the White House and some other facts about the assassination were taken from William Manchester's *Death of a President*.

Chapter Twenty-five: Restlessness

Interviews were conducted with David Metcalfe, Taki Theodoracopulos, Blair Clark, and Sidney Gruson.

Bruce Balding's remarks were made to the author personally.

Lee's play for Peter Lawford is contained in James Spada's *Peter Lawford*.

Kitty Kelley's dismissal of a Jackie-RFK affair can be found in *Jackie Oh!*

Chapter Twenty-six: Seeking the Spotlight

Interviews were conducted with Kitty Carlisle Hart, Elizabeth Wilmer, and John Sekura.

Principal sources in this chapter for quotes and details of Lee's acting experience are: *McCall's*, February 1968, Gloria Steinem; *Life*, July 14, 1967, "The Princess Goes on Stage," Jane Howard; *Look*, January 23, 1968, "The Public and Private Lee," Henry Ehrlich; *The Saturday Evening Post*, December 16, 1967, "Stay Tuned for the Princess," Terry Coleman; The *New York Post*, June 24, 1967, "You're a Natural for the Stage, Kitty Said," Helen Dudar.

Chapter Twenty-seven: The Cast and the Critics

Interviews were conducted with John Sekura, Bob Thompson, John Ericson, Erika Slezak, Zsa Zsa Gabor, and Jamie Auchincloss.

Other factual information and quotes on Lee's acting debut were obtained from too many sources to mention them all here. An exception: Chauncey Howell's review appeared in *Women's Wear Daily*, June 22, 1967.

Chapter Twenty-eight: From Stage to Screen

Interviews were conducted with Alan Shayne, Bert Stern, Dick Blodget, Farley Granger, Arlene Francis, John Moxey, Tom Moore, Jamie Auchincloss, Julie Harris, Paul Rosen, and Euan Lloyd.

Like *The Philadelphia Story*, Lee's version of *Laura* drew great press attention. Again, facts and quotes in addition to those sources already cited came from too many sources to list them all here.

Lee's fashion layout appeared in *Vogue*, September 1, 1967.

Chapter Twenty-nine: Changes of Scene

Interviews were conducted with Michael Hobson, Renzo Mongiardino, Cathy di Montezemolo, Leslie Caron, Gerald Smith, and Sidney Morris.

In addition to some of her comments, a full description of Lee's redecoration of 4 Buckingham Place and her renovation of Turville Grange appeared in *Vogue*, December 1966, and July 1971, respectively. Other remarks about renovating Turville Grange can be found in *Life*, July 14, 1967.

"I did the first comeback ..." is from Paige Rense, *Decorating for Celebrities*.

Chapter Thirty: Rudy and Truman

Interviews were conducted with Leo Backer, Gerald Clarke, David Metcalfe, Charlotte Ford, Lady Annabelle Goldsmith, and John Revson. Benno Graziani answered questions in writing.

"It wasn't easy ..." is from Bob Colacello, "The Last Days of Rudolf Nureyev," *Vanity Fair*, March 1993.

Other Nureyev comments attributed to Lee come from *Architectural Digest*, September 1985.

Lee's fashion spread wearing Courrèges appeared in *Vogue*, January 1967.

Gloria Steinem's interview with Lee can be found in *McCall's*, February 1968.

Chapter Thirty-one: Turville Grange
Interviews were conducted with Polly Devlin, Brigitte Gerney, John Moxey, Maia Calligas, Taki Theodoracopulos, Lady Ampthill, Sidney Morris, Tony Hail, Gerald Smith, Nicholas Cobbold, Julie Harris, Leo Backer, and David Metcalfe.

Information describing Turville Grange comes from "Country House In Flower" by Polly Devlin, *Vogue*, July 1971.

"It is terrible . . ." is from the London *Times*, June 6, 1968.

Facts on Roy Jenkins's background were gathered from several English periodicals.

Chapter Thirty-two: Misfortune
Interviews were conducted with William Hay, Taki Theodoracopulos, Comtesse d'Ornano, Sidney Morris, Greta Fenston, Michael Tree, Gerald Smith, and Nicholas Cobbold.

The description of the fire at Henley and Lee's car accident were taken from press reports.

"I felt this terrible . . ." was taken from Bob Colacello, *Harper's Bazaar*, November 1972.

"Picasso said . . ." appeared in "Opening Chapters," by Lee Radziwill, *Ladies' Home Journal*, January 1973.

Chapter Thirty-three: Lee and Peter
Interviews were conducted with Porter Bibb, Peter Riva, Jay Mellon, Steven Aronson, and Dotson Rader.

Much of the information in this chapter is based on interviews with anonymous sources.

"Like everyone on holiday . . ." was taken from "Lee Radziwill" by Leslie Field, London *Daily Mail*, November 16, 1971.

"I still have a chance . . ." appeared in Gloria Steinem, *McCall's*.

Chapter Thirty-four: Andy and the Movies
Interviews were conducted with Victor Bockris, Jonas Meekas, Porter Bibb, Al Maysles, Pat Hackett, Chris Makos, Paul Morrissey, and anonymous sources.

"I'm all for people . . ." and "I think the film . . ." are from Bob Colacello, *Harper's Bazaar*.

Chapter Thirty-five: Living Large
Interviews were conducted with John Revson, Paul Morrissey, Porter Bibb, Comtesse d'Ornano, David Metcalfe, Jay Mellon, Pierre Salinger, Steven Aronson, and John Mack Carter.

Victor Bockris provided the author with some helpful background information for this chapter.

"All I have to say . . ." was taken from *Newsweek*, December 18, 1972.

Some details of Lee's party for "Opening Chapters" and her comments appeared in "A Princess Writes a Story and That Makes It a Party," by Charlotte Curtis in the *New York Times*, December 20, 1972.

Chapter Thirty-six: Breaking Up
Much of this chapter comes from interviews with anonymous sources.

Interviews were conducted with Jay Mellon, Steven Aronson, Brigitte Gerney, Henry Bresher Esq., Leo Backer, Gerald Clarke, Michael Tree, Lady Ampthill, David Metcalfe, Sidney Morris, Nicholas Cobbold, Porter Bibb, Paul Morrissey, and John Revson.

Chapter Thirty-seven: A Clean Sheet
Interviews were conducted with Catherine Weinstock Rayburn, Eleanor Friede, Helen Meyer, Ross Claiborne, Al Maysles, Noreen Drexel, Isabel Cope, and Brigitte Gerney.

Lee's comments on the experience of writing her memoir appeared in an article by Paul Dacre in the London *Daily Express*, September 8, 1976.

"Sister," an article by Penelope McMillan based on an interview with Lee that appeared in the *New York News*, April 27, 1975, proved useful for this chapter.

Chapter Thirty-eight: Talk Show
Interviews were conducted with Sam Zellman, Peter Benchley, Ed Joyce, Ray Beindorf, Tom Lahey, and Tom Miller.

Lee's view of her TV career appeared in an interview she gave to Judy Klemsrud of the *New York Times*, September 1, 1974, "For Lee Radziwill, Budding Careers and a New Life in New York."

Chapter Thirty-nine: Mood Swings
Interviews were conducted with Tony Hail, Blair Fuller, and Chauncey Parker.

"I finished it . . ." was taken from *Women's Wear Daily*, March 3, 1976.

"I've painted but . . .". is from Charlotte Curtis, *McCall's*, January 1975.

"My deep regret . . ." appeared in *Interview,* March 1975.

"The rich are really scared . . ." was taken from Paige Rense, *Decorating for Celebrities.*

The story of Lee's museum visit can be found in Bob Colacello's *Holy Terror: Andy Warhol Close Up.*

"It was her breakup with Peter Beard . . ." is from Sally Quinn, the *Washington Post*, June 6, 1975.

"I don't rage . . ." was taken from Jane Howard, *Life,* July 14, 1967.

Chapter Forty: A New Career
Interviews were conducted with Jay Mellon, Jan Cushing Amory, Mario Buatta, Mario di Genova, Tony Hail, Lisa Taylor, Margaret Kennedy, Peggy Kaufman, Ron Seff, Fred Warnecke, Grace Warnecke, and Audrey Koehler.

A profile of Peter Tufo, "A Question of Power: What Makes Peter Run?" by Judy Klemsrud in the *New York Times*, March 7, 1977, proved useful for this chapter.

The author gathered information and comments from Lee about her decorating career from too many sources to list them all here. One exception: her interview with Lisa Hammel for the *New York Times*, "Lee Radziwill As Decorator: A New Step Confidently Taken," February 20, 1976.

Chapter Forty-one: Changing Partners

Interviews were conducted with Lady Ampthill, Jo Bryce, Comtesse d'Ornano, Leo Backer, Sidney Morris, Gerald Smith, Henry Bresher, Zbignie Mieczkowski, Blair Fuller, Gerald Clarke, Mark Goodson, Charles Horowitz, Peter Bradley, Mario Buatta, Patricia Hewitt, Grace Warnecke, Newton Cope, and Tony Hail.

"I think there is nothing . . ." was taken from Judy Klemsrud, *New York Times*, September 1, 1974.

"I can't think of any woman . . ." can be found in *Vogue*, June 1976.

"He was sick . . ." is from Bob Colacello, "Pas de deux," *Vanity Fair*, January 1989.

Chapter Forty-two: Newton and Gore

Much of this chapter is based on an interview with Newton Cope. Other interviews were conducted with Andreas Brown, Pat Hackett, Bob Garcia, Gerald Clarke, Leo Lerman, George Plimpton, Robert McBride, and Michael McKenzie.

The story of Lee's unwillingness to testify on Truman Capote's behalf can be found in "Truman's True Love," by Liz Smith, the New York *Daily News*, September 23, 1984.

Capote's exchange with Andy Warhol can be found in Warhol's *Diaries*.

"It's very hurtful . . ." is from "In Hot Blood," *Washington Post ibid.*

Chapter Forty-three: Lonely

Much of the information in this chapter is based on interviews with anonymous sources. Interviews were also conducted with Julia Bloomfield, Tony Hail, Elaine Baxter, Jan Amory Cushing, David Metcalfe, Michael Meehan, Tom Guinzburg, Dorothy Lichtenstein, and Cathy di Montezemolo.

A few descriptive details of Lee's apartment at 875 Park Avenue were taken from *Architectural Digest*, January 1982.

Chapter Forty-four: Moving On

Interviews were conducted with Newton Cope, Matthew Kelly, Mario Buatta, Ron Seff, Sherry Parker Geyelin, Dorothy Lichtenstein, Tony Hail, Ann McGilvry, Brigitte Gerney, Jamie Auchincloss, Stan Herman, and Vincent Ropatte.

"A woman's concept . . ." was taken from a column Lee did for *McCall's*, March 1988.

Lee's comments about her apartment at 48 East Seventy-third Street were taken from "Lee Radziwill's Interior Life," by John Duka, *Vogue*, April 1985.

For Lee's complaints about her decorating business, see her interview in *Decorating for Celebrities*.

Chapter Forty-five: Richard Meier

Much of this chapter is based on interviews with Richard Meier and anonymous sources. Personal interviews were also conducted with Steven Aronson,

Sidney Gruson, Phillip Moffett, Julia Bloomfield, Vincent Ropatte, Mario Buatta, and Audrey Koehler.

Background information on Richard Meier's accomplishments were gathered from many newspaper and magazine sources.

Chapter Forty-six: Armani

Interviews were conducted with Newton Cope, Logan Bentley, Leonora Doddsworth, Mallory Andrews, Ann Johnson, Jane Nathanson, Jackie Theis, Michael Cody, Jeff Trachtenberg, Bernadine Morris, Ann Marie Schiro, Teri Agins, Tony Hail, Richard Meier, and Clifford Klenk.

The anecdote about Nureyev's dinner-party comments are contained in Elizabeth Kaye's profile of him for *Esquire*, March 1991.

"The minute Herb and Lee . . ." was taken from "Pas de deux," *Vanity Fair*, January 1989.

Ben Brantley's *Vanity Fair* profile of Giorgio Armani, "The Armani Mystique," June 1988, and *Time*'s cover story on him, April 5, 1982, proved useful for this chapter.

Chapter Forty-seven: Radziwill Ross

The author gathered information on Herbert Ross's background and career from many sources, including *Current Biography*, August 1980; "That Hollywood Touch," Leo Janos, *New York Times*, November 12, 1978; "Herb Ross at the Turning Point," Stephen Farber, *Film Comment*, January 2, 1978; "Serious Director of Funny Hits," David Sterritt, *Christian Science Monitor*, January 30, 1978.

Lee's comments on meeting Herbert Ross were taken from "Pas de Deux," Bob Colacello's January 1989 *Vanity Fair* article on the couple which proved helpful for this and the following chapter.

Personal interviews were conducted with John Ward, Jane Bogart, Ed Pisoni, Rex Reed, Tom Whitehead, Lisa Weisenger, and Lee Pole.

Chapter Forty-eight: Renaissance

Interviews were conducted with Tony Hail, Liz Fondaras, Vincent Ropatte, Jonathan Tapper, Don Remacle, John Chaney, Ed Pisoni, Chuck Rosen, Jane Nathanson, Rex Reed, Clifford Klenk, Bob Garcia, and Lady Ampthill.

Chapter Forty-nine: Taking Control

Interviews were conducted with Ed Pisoni, Rex Reed, Steve Klain, Barry Bedig, Garrett Lewis, Bob Engelman, and Dan Melnick.

Chapter Fifty: Life in the '90s

Interviews were conducted with Charlie Baxter, Brian Quigley, Ed Pisoni, Isabel Cope, Tony Hail, Chuck Rosen, Tom Whitehead, Don Remacle, Joan Howard, Dr. William Baker, Susan Lacy, Barbara Siebel Thomas, Dan Melnick, Elaine Baxter, Cathy di Montezemolo, Laura Pyzel Clark, and Steven Aronson.

Herbert Ross's comments were taken from an interview he gave to Hillel Italie, the *Associated Press*, April 8, 1991.

"I don't have any unfulfilled ambitions . . ." was taken from Penelope McMillan, the *New York News*, April 27, 1975.

Epilogue

The statement that Jackie took medication to hasten her death is based on the reporting of C. David Heymann in *A Woman Named Jackie*, reissued in 1994.

Bibliography

Baldridge, Letitia. *Of Diamonds and Diplomats*. Boston: Houghton Mifflin, 1968.

Barrow, Andrew. *Gossip: A History of High Society From 1920 to 1970*. New York: Coward, McCann & Geoghegan, 1978.

Birmingham, Stephen. *Jacqueline Bouvier Kennedy Onassis*. New York: Grosset & Dunlap, 1978.

———. *The Right People*. Boston: Little, Brown, 1968.

Bockris, Victor. *The Life and Death of Andy Warhol*. New York: Bantam, 1989.

Bouvier, Jacqueline and Lee. *One Special Summer*. New York: Delacorte Press, 1974.

Bouvier, Kathleen. *To Jack with Love, Black Jack Bouvier: A Remembrance*. New York: Kensington, 1979.

Braden, Joan. *Just Enough Rope*. New York: Villard, 1989.

Bradford, Sarah. *The Reluctant King*. New York: St. Martin's, 1989.

Bryan, J. and Charles Murphy. *The Windsor Story*. New York: William Morrow, 1979.

Buck, Pearl S. *The Kennedy Women*. New York: Cowles, 1970.

Canfield, Cass. *Up and Down and Around*. New York: Harper's Magazine Press, 1971.

Colacello, Bob. *Holy Terror: Andy Warhol Close Up*. New York: Harper-Collins, 1990.

Capote, Truman. *A Capote Reader*. New York: Random House, 1987.

Cassini, Oleg. *In My Own Fashion, An Autobiography*. New York: Simon & Schuster, 1987.

Cheshire, Maxine. *Maxine Cheshire, Reporter*. Boston: Houghton Mifflin, 1978.

Clarke, Gerald. *Capote*. New York: Random House, 1988.

Collier, Peter and David Horowitz. *The Kennedys: An American Drama*. New York: Summit, 1984.

Curtis, Charlotte. *The Rich and Other Atrocities*. New York: Harper & Row, 1976.

Davis, John H. *The Bouviers, Portrait of an American Family.* New York: Farrar, Strauss & Giroux, 1969.

———. *The Kennedys: Dynasty and Disaster 1848–1983.* New York: Mc-Graw-Hill, 1984.

Davis, L. J. *Onassis, Aristotle and Christina.* New York: St. Martin's, 1986.

Donaldson, Frances. *Edward VIII.* Philadelphia: J. B. Lippincott, 1974.

Fox, James. *White Mischief.* London: Cape, 1982.

Fraser, Nicholas, Philip Jacobson, Mark Ottoway, and Lewis Chester. *Aristotle Onassis.* Philadelphia: Lippincott, 1977.

Galbraith, John Kenneth. *Ambassador's Journal: A Personal Account of the Kennedy Years.* Boston: Houghton Mifflin, 1969.

Gallela, Ron. *Jacqueline.* New York: Sheed and Ward, 1974.

Grobel, Lawrence. *Conversations with Capote.* New York: New American Library, 1985.

Guthrie, Lee. *Jackie, the Price of the Pedestal.* New York: Drake, 1978.

Hackett, Pat, ed. *The Andy Warhol Diaries.* New York: Warner, 1989.

Hall, Gordon Langley and Ann Pinchot. *Jacqueline Kennedy, A Biography.* New York: Frederick Fell, 1964.

Harvey, Jacques. *Mon Ami Onassis.* Paris: Editions Albin Michel, 1975.

Heymann, C. David. *A Woman Named Jackie.* New York: Lyle Stuart, 1989.

Inglis, Brian. *Abdication.* New York: Macmillan, 1966.

Kelley, Kitty. *Jackie Oh!* Secaucus, N.J.: Lyle Stuart, 1979.

Kennedy, Rose. *Times to Remember.* New York: Doubleday, 1974.

Lilly, Doris. *Those Fabulous Greeks: Onassis, Niarchos, and Livanos.* London: W. H. Allen, 1971.

Manchester, William. *The Death of a President: November 20–November 25, 1963.* New York: Harper & Row, 1967.

Marlborough, Laura. *Laughter from a Cloud.* London: Weidenfeld and Nicholson, 1980.

Marriott, Oliver. *The Property Boom.* London: Abingdon, 1967.

Martin, Ralph G. *A Hero for Our Time: An Intimate History of the Kennedy Years.* New York: Ballantine, 1983.

Maxwell, Elsa. *The Celebrity Circus.* New York: Appleton-Century, 1963.

Mitford, Nancy. *The Pursuit of Love.* London: Hamish Hamilton, 1946.

Nowakowski, Tadeusz. *The Radziwills.* New York: Delacorte, 1974.

Rense, Paige, ed. *Celebrity Homes.* Los Angeles: Knapp, 1977.

———. *Decorating for Celebrities.* New York: Doubleday, 1980.

Rhea, Mini. *I Was Jacqueline Kennedy's Dressmaker.* New York: Fleet, 1962.

Rasponi, Lanfranco. *The International Nomads.* New York: Putnam, 1966.

———. *The Golden Oases.* New York: Putnam, 1968.

Schlesinger, Arthur M., Jr. *Robert Kennedy and His Times.* Boston: Houghton Mifflin, 1978.

Sidey, Hugh. *John F. Kennedy, President.* New York: Atheneum, 1963.

Sirkis, Nancy. *Newport: Pleasures and Palaces.* New York: Viking, 1963.

Spada, James. *Peter Lawford: The Man Who Kept the Secrets.* New York: Bantam, 1991.

Thayer, Mary Van Resselaer. *Jacqueline Bouvier Kennedy*. Garden City, N.Y.: Doubleday, 1961.

————. *Jacqueline Kennedy, The White House Years*. Boston: Little, Brown, 1967.

Vickers, Hugo. *Cecil Beaton, A Biography*. Boston; Toronto: Little, Brown, 1985.

Warhol, Andy. *Andy Warhol's Exposures*. Photographs by Andy Warhol; text by Andy Warhol and Bob Colacello. New York: Andy Warhol Books/Grosset & Dunlap, 1979.

Waugh, Evelyn. *The Diaries of Evelyn Waugh*. Boston: Little, Brown, 1976.

Watney, Hedda Lyons. *Jackie O*. New York: Leisure Books, 1979.

West, J. B. with Mary Lynn Kotz. *Upstairs at the White House: My Life with the First Ladies*. New York: Coward, McCann & Geoghegan, 1973.

Whiting, Audrey. *The Kents*. London: Hutchinson, 1985.

Ziegler, Philip. *King Edward VIII*. New York: Knopf, 1991.

Acknowledgments

Over the period of time it took me to research and write this biography I enjoyed meeting and talking with hundreds of friends and associates of Lee Radziwill's who shared their memories, impressions, and opinions with me and who provided anecdotes and factual information. Without their help, *In Her Sister's Shadow* would not have been possible. I regret that I am not able to mention all of them.

My heartfelt thanks to: Alice Gordon Abbett; Vale Asche Ackerman; Talbot Adamson; Teri Agins; Cleveland Amory; Jan Cushing Amory; Elisabeth, Lady Ampthill; Kurt Anderson; Mallory Andrews; John Appleton; Jamie Auchincloss.

Leo Backer; Dr. William Baker; Bruce Balding; Edith McBride Bass; Charles Baxter; Elaine Baxter; Ray Beindorf; Peter Benchley; Logan Bentley; Porter Bibb; Dick Blodget; Julia Bloomfield; Florence Borda; Joan Braden; Peter Bradley; Henry Bresher Esq.; Andreas Brown; Mario Buatta; Phebe Thompson Burke; Jo Bryce.

B. Bartram Cadbury; Maia Calligas; Cass Canfield, Jr.; Leslie Caron; Oleg Cassini; Gwen Chabrier; John Chaney; Jonathan Churchill; Andrew Ciechanowiecki; Ross Claiborne; Blair Clark; Laura Pyzel Clark; Nicholas Cobbold; Michael Cody; Isabel Cope; Newton Cope; Robin Corbin; Howard Cushing, Jr.

John H. Davis; Baroness de Chollet; Ormande de Kaye; Helen Delmonte; Mario di Genova; Leonora Doddsworth; Isabelle, Comtesse d'Ornano; William Douglas-Home; Elizabeth Draper; Noreen Drexel.

Bob Engelman; Kathy Epper; John Ericson.

Greta Fenston; Liz Fondaras; Alastair Forbes; Charlotte Ford; Jill Fuller Fox; Arlene Francis; Doris Francisco; Eleanor Friede; Blair Fuller.

Zsa Zsa Gabor; Bob Garcia; Brigitte Gerney; Philip Geyelin; Cecilia Parker Geyelin; Mildred Morton Gilbert; Lady Annabelle Goldsmith; Mark Goodson; Farley Granger; Benno Graziani; Sidney Gruson; Thomas Guinzburg; Fred Gwynne.

Anthony Haden-Guest; Tony Hail; Yvonne Hamilton; Julie Harris; Kitty Carlisle Hart; William Hay; Stan Herman; Patricia Hewitt; William Hewitt; Michael Hobson; Claudia Porges Holland; Joan Howard; Rue Hill Hubert.

Adrienne Osborne Ives.

Ruth Jacobson; Ann Johnson; Ed Joyce.

Peggy Kaufman; Katie Keiffer; Matthew Kelly; Joan Pierce Kernan; William Kingsland; Steve Klain; Clifford Klenk.

Susan Lacy; Lady Lambton; Lord Lambton; Irma Dewey Larom; Tom Leahy; Leo Lerman; Garrett Lewis; Dorothy Lichtenstein; Euan Lloyd; Jane Vaughn Love; Mary Lumet; Flora Lutz.

Chris Makos; John Marquand, Jr.; Albert Maysles; Robert McBride; Ann McGilvry; Mike McKenzie; Michael Meehan; Sandra Meehan; Jonas Meekas; Richard Meier; Alison Melchum; Jay Mellon; Dan Melnick; David Metcalfe; Zbignie Mieczkowski; Tom Miller; Grace Mirabella; Phillip Moffett; Renzo Mongiardino; Catherine di Montezemolo; Tom Moore; Clare Fahnestock Moorehead; Sidney Morris; Paul Morrissey; John Moxey.

Jane Nathanson.

Angela O'Ferrall.

Chauncey Parker; Fess Parker; Anne Fennelly Patterson; Carol Phillips; Ed Pisoni; George Plimpton; Lucy Porges; Dave Powers; Lewis Preston; Stuart Preston; William Preston.

Brian Quigley; David Quinn.

Dotson Rader; Catherine Weinstock Rayburn; Peter Reed; Rex Reed; Don Remacle; John Revson; Elisavietta Artamonoff Ritchie; Peter Riva; Vincent Roppate; Chuck Rosen; Paul Rosen.

Pierre Salinger; Carlin Whitney Scherer; Arthur M. Schlesinger, Jr.; Ron Seff; John Sekura; Rose Tobias Shaw; Alan Shayne; Erika Slezak; Barbara Slifka; Eileen Slocum; Senator George Smathers; Gerald Smith; Lesta Stacom; Bert Stern;

Greg Strauss; Dr. Muriel Sugarman; C. L. Sulzberger.

Jonathan Tapper; Lisa Taylor; Jackie Theis; Taki Theodoracopulos; Barbara Siebel Thomas; Bob Thompson; Daphne Sellar Thornton; Yale Toland; Jeff Trachtenberg; Ulrich Trojerberg; Michael Tree; Errol Trzebinski.

Hugo Vickers; Helen Vlachos.

Rick Wahlstedt; John Ward; Peter Ward; Fred Warnecke; Grace Warnecke; David Warren; Ian Watson; Lisa Weisenger; Tom Whitehead.

Katherine Smedley Yellig.

Sam Zellman.

I would like to thank these institutions and offices for their assistance during my research: the Apostolic Nuniclature, Washington, D.C.; the Columbia University Oral History Collection; The English Speaking Union Library; The Institute of Heraldic and Genealogical Studies, Kent, England; the John F. Kennedy Library; the New York Public Library.

I am grateful for the help of my able team of researchers, Greg Annussek, Barbara C. Kaufmann, Dimitra Kessenides, and especially Cindy Milwe in New York; Sue Ramsey in London; and my transcription typist, Nancy Sparrow.

I am much obliged to Pat Hackett for her careful reading of my manuscript, to my agent, Richard Curtis, and to my editor at Little, Brown, Fredrica S. Friedman.

My special thanks to these fellow authors who provided me with helpful assistance and information: Victor Bokris, Gerald Clarke, C. David Heymann, and most of all, Steven M. L. Aronson.

And last but certainly not least, I want to thank my anonymous sources, who were key in the formation of this book. You know who you are.

Index

THE KENNEDY FAMILY SAGA

It's a story of tragedy and triumph unlike any other!

THE FITZGERALDS AND THE KENNEDYS
Doris Kearns Goodwin
_____ 90933-0 $5.95 U.S./$6.95 Can.

KENNEDYS: THE NEXT GENERATION
Jonathan Slevin and Maureen Spagnolo
_____ 92860-2 $4.50 U.S./$5.50 Can.

THE SENATOR: MY TEN YEARS WITH TED KENNEDY
Richard E. Burke with William and Marilyn Hoffer
_____ 95133-7 $5.99 U.S./$6.99 Can.

THE OTHER MRS. KENNEDY: ETHEL SKAKEL KENNEDY
Jerry Oppenheimer
_____ 95600-2 $6.99 U.S./$7.99 Can.

JACQUELINE KENNEDY ONASSIS
Lester David
_____ 95546-4 $5.99 U.S./$6.99 Can.